Colonialist Gazes and Counternarratives of Blackness

Building on the growing field of Afropean Studies, this interdisciplinary and intermedial collection of essays proposes a dialogue on Afro-Spanishness that is not exclusively tied to immigration and that understands Blackness as a non-essentialist, heterogeneous and diasporic concept. Studying a variety of twentieth- and twenty-first-century cultural products, some essays explore the resilience of the colonialist paradigms and the circulation of racial ideologies and colonial memories that promote national narratives of whitening. Others focus on Black self-representation and examine how Afro-Spanish authors, artists, and activists destabilize colonial gazes and constructions of national identity, propose decolonial views of Spain and Europe's literature and history, articulate Afro-Diasporic knowledges, and envision Afro-descendance as an empowering tool.

Ana León-Távora is Associate Professor of Spanish, Director of Modern Languages and Director of Race and Ethnicity Studies at Salem College, North Carolina. She has authored numerous peer-reviewed articles and book chapters that examine issues of social and political power relations, racial, ethnic, and linguistic discrimination in Spain, and women's, gender, and sexuality studies. She is also the co-editor and co-translator of the bilingual critical book and catalogue on contemporary Cuban art authored by Linda Howe, *Cuban Artists' Books and Prints. Libros y Grabados de Artistas Cubanos: 1998–2008* (2009).

Rosalía Cornejo-Parriego is Professor of Hispanic Studies at the University of Ottawa, Canada. She is the author of *Entre mujeres. Política de la amistad y el deseo en la narrativa española contemporánea* (2008) and the editor of two collections of essays: *Black USA and Spain. Shared Memories in the 20th Century* (2021) and *Memoria colonial e inmigración. La negritud en la España posfranquista* (2008). In addition, she has co-edited the special issue of *Romance Notes* "The Rosalía Effect. Popular Music and Culture in Contemporary Spain" (with N. M. Murray, 2023) and *Un hispanismo para el siglo XXI. Ensayos de crítica cultural* (with A. Villamandos, 2011). As part of her research project on women intellectuals in the press during Spain's Transition to democracy, she published *Ana María Moix: Semblanzas e impertinencias* (2016), an edition of Moix's journalistic writings.

Colonialist Gazes and Counternarratives of Blackness

Afro-Spanishness in 20th- and 21st-Century Spain

Edited by Ana León-Távora and
Rosalía Cornejo-Parriego

NEW YORK AND LONDON

First published 2024
by Routledge
605 Third Avenue, New York, NY 10158

and by Routledge
4 Park Square, Milton Park, Abingdon, Oxon, OX14 4RN

Routledge is an imprint of the Taylor & Francis Group, an informa business

© 2024 selection and editorial matter, Ana León-Távora and Rosalía Cornejo-Parriego; individual chapters, the contributors

The right of Ana León-Távora and Rosalía Cornejo-Parriego to be identified as the authors of the editorial material, and of the authors for their individual chapters, has been asserted in accordance with sections 77 and 78 of the Copyright, Designs and Patents Act 1988.

All rights reserved. No part of this book may be reprinted or reproduced or utilised in any form or by any electronic, mechanical, or other means, now known or hereafter invented, including photocopying and recording, or in any information storage or retrieval system, without permission in writing from the publishers.

Trademark notice: Product or corporate names may be trademarks or registered trademarks, and are used only for identification and explanation without intent to infringe.

ISBN: 9781032563497 (hbk)
ISBN: 9781032563503 (pbk)
ISBN: 9781003435051 (ebk)

DOI: 10.4324/9781003435051

Typeset in Sabon
by codeMantra

To Jahdai, Pablo, and Rosita
To Alejandro, Andrea, and Leo

Contents

List of Figures	ix
Notes on Contributors	x
Acknowledgments	xiv
Introduction: Black Spain in Afro-Europe ROSALÍA CORNEJO-PARRIEGO AND ANA LEÓN-TÁVORA	1
1 From Negrophilia to Necropolitics: Anti-Black Racism in Spanish Avant-Garde Humor Magazines ANA LEÓN-TÁVORA	21
2 The Transnational Afropessimism of Francisco Zamora Loboch BALTASAR FRA-MOLINERO	51
3 The Value of Color: Spain's Equality Stamps Fiasco JEFFREY K. COLEMAN	72
4 Using the Web to Educate Spain About Its Afro-Identity: *Afroféminas* ESTHER M. ALARCÓN ARANA	88
5 Hidden Knowledges and Diasporic Positionings: The Autobiographical and Testimonial Texts in *Metamba Miago: Relatos y saberes de mujeres afroespañolas* JULIA BORST	111
6 Un-Whitening Late Francoist Spain: Knots of Memory in Lucía Mbomío's *Las que se atrevieron* MARTIN REPINECZ	134

7 Decolonizing the History of Afro-Spaniards: *Afrofeminismo. 50 años de lucha y activismo de mujeres negras en España* (1968–2018) by Abuy Nfubea 153
DOSINDA GARCÍA-ALVITE

8 Mapping Black Women Through Art and Social Media: The Case of Montserrat Anguiano 175
STEFANIA LICATA

9 From Below and from Within: Urban Peripheries in Lucía Mbomío's *Barrionalismos* 195
ROSALÍA CORNEJO-PARRIEGO

10 An Inconclusive Conclusion: Autoethnography as a Model for Epistemic Decolonization 216
ANA LEÓN-TÁVORA

Index 237

Figures

1.1	Image in *Gutiérrez*, 11 June 1927. Courtesy of *BNE*	27
1.2	Vignette in *Buen Humor*, 23 December 1928. Courtesy of *BNE*	28
1.3	Cover of Issue 392 of *Buen Humor*, 2 June 1929. Courtesy of *BNE*	30
1.4	Cover of issue of *Buen Humor*, 2 April 1922. Courtesy of *BNE*	31
1.5	Cartoon in *Buen Humor*, 26 December 1926. Courtesy of *BNE*	36
1.6	Cartoon in *Gutiérrez*, 9 July 1927. Courtesy of *BNE*	37
1.7	Vignette from *Gutiérrez*, 14 April 1928. Courtesy of *BNE*	38
1.8	Cover of *Buen Humor*, 6 February 1927. Courtesy of *BNE*	39
1.9	Issue of *Gutiérrez* from 1927. Courtesy of *BNE*	41
1.10	Advertisements in *Buen Humor* from 1927. Courtesy of *BNE*	43
3.1	Equality Stamps. Minder, Raphael. "Spain Issued 'Equality Stamps' in Skin Tones. The Darker Ones Were Worth Less"	73
3.2	Protest Stamps. "Correos Launches 'Protest Stamps', Stamps Featuring the Voices of a Generation Against Climate Change." *Correos*, https://www.correos.com/en/sala-prensa/correos-launches-protest-stamps-stamps-featuring-the-voices-of-a-generation-against-climate-change/#	76
5.1	Examples of the brief profiles (Ekoka 55; 117). Permission granted by the author	118
5.2	Visual framework of the collection (Ekoka 15; 147). Permission granted by the author	125
8.1	1789—Sara Baartman. Permission granted by the artist	180
8.2	Floral Afrika in primary colors—red (e-Catalog). Permission granted by the artist	181
8.3	Dones de la Nasa—Triptic [Nasa's women—Triptych]: from left to right, Dorothy Vaughan, Katherine Johnson, and Mary Jackson. Permission granted by the artist	188

Notes on Contributors

Esther M. Alarcón Arana holds a PhD in Hispanic Studies from the University of Pennsylvania. Her dissertation focused on personal and national identities of displaced people in the Spanish-speaking world. She is currently Associate Professor of Spanish at Salve Regina University in Newport, Rhode Island. Since starting this position, her research focus has incorporated the study of women writers that defy patriarchy and hegemonic narratives. Her publications include the following edited volumes, *El reflejo de Medusa. Representaciones mediáticas contemporáneas de mujeres* (Advook, 2023) and *Muerte y crisis en el mundo hispano: respuestas culturales* (Peter Lang, 2020), and the essays "Re-educar para la igualdad: una nueva Caperucita contra la violencia de género en la España del siglo XXI," published in *La violencia de género en la España contemporánea* (Fundación general de la Universidad de Alcalá, 2020), and "Ni perdidos ni callados: la cultura participativa como reapropiación de la agencia en *En tierra extraña*," published in *El cine de la crisis* (UOC, 2018).

Julia Borst holds a PhD in Romance Literary Studies from the University of Hamburg and has received several academic awards, including the 2021 Heinz Maier-Leibnitz Prize, the 2019 Sibylle Kalkhof-Rose Academy Prize for the Humanities, and the 2023 Abioseh Porter Best Essay Award, granted by the African Literature Association. She is currently the principal investigator for the research project "The Spanish Black Diaspora: Afro-Spanish Literature of the 20th and 21st Century" (funded by the German Research Foundation DFG), as well as the deputy director of the Institute of Postcolonial and Transcultural Studies (INPUTS) and co-founder of the research lab "Digital Diaspora" within the interdisciplinary and collaborative research platform *Worlds of Contradiction* at the University of Bremen. In 2023, she was awarded an ERC Starting Grant for her project, "Afroeurope and Cyberspace." She is the author of a monograph on violence and trauma in contemporary Haitian novels (*Gewalt und Trauma im haitianischen Gegenwartsroman*. Narr, 2015) and other various articles in peer-reviewed journals such as *The French Review*, *French Studies*, *The Journal of Haitian Studies*, *Research in African Literatures*, *Open Cultural Studies*, and *Tydskrif vir Letterkunde*. She has also contributed several articles on Equatorial Guinean literature to the German literature encyclopedia *Kindlers Literatur Lexikon* and has co-edited special issues of the journals *Research in African Literatures*, *EnterText*, and the *Journal of Global Diaspora and Media*.

Jeffrey K. Coleman is Associate Professor of Peninsular Studies in the Department of Spanish and Portuguese at Northwestern University. He has published several articles on immigration, race, and national identity in Spanish theatre and popular culture in *Catalan Review*, *Symposium*, and *Estreno*, among other journals. His first book, *The Necropolitical Theater: Race and Immigration on the Contemporary Spanish Stage* (Northwestern University Press, 2020), explores how the intersections of race and immigration manifest in Spanish theatre from 1991 to 2016. He is also working on his next book project, tentatively titled *España Negra: The Consumption & Rejection of Blackness in Contemporary Spain*, which explores how Spanish media, popular culture, and literature have portrayed and appropriated Blackness from the early twentieth century to the present. In addition, he is the co-founder of TRECE (Taller de Raza, Etnicidad y Ciudadanía en España), a research group that actively theorizes and conceptualizes race in contemporary Spain.

Rosalía Cornejo-Parriego is Professor of Hispanic Studies at the University of Ottawa, Canada. She is the author of *Entre mujeres. Política de la amistad y el deseo en la narrativa española contemporánea* (Biblioteca Nueva, 2008) and the editor of the collections of essays, *Black USA and Spain. Shared Memories in the 20th Century* (Routledge, 2021) and *Memoria colonial e inmigración. La negritud en la España posfranquista* (Bellaterra, 2008). In addition, she has co-edited special issues of *Romance Notes* ("The Rosalía Effect. Popular Music and Culture in Contemporary Spain," with N. M. Murray, 2023) and of *Revista Canadiense de Estudios Hispánicos* ("Queer Space," with K. Sibbald, 2011) and the collection of essays *Un hispanismo para el siglo XXI. Ensayos de crítica cultural* (with A. Villamandos, Biblioteca Nueva, 2011). Her research project on women intellectuals in the press during Spain's Transition to Democracy was funded by the Social Sciences and Humanities Research Council of Canada. Part of that research resulted in the edition of Ana María Moix's journalistic writings, *Ana María Moix: Semblanzas e impertinencias* (Laetoli, 2016). Furthermore, she is the former editor-in-chief of the *Revista Canadiense de Estudios Hispánicos* and has published numerous book chapters and essays on gender and race.

Baltasar Fra-Molinero is Professor of Hispanic Studies, Latin American, and Latinx Studies and a member of the Africana Program at Bates College. His research focuses on the representation of people of African descent and the African Diaspora in Early Modern Spain and Latin America, and on Equatorial Guinea's literature. He is the author of *Black Bride of Christ: Chicaba, an African Nun in Eighteenth-Century Spain* (with Sue E. Houchins, Vanderbilt UP, 2018) and *La imagen de los negros en el teatro del Siglo de Oro* (Siglo XXI, 1995). He has co-edited with Benita Sampedro Vizcaya the unpublished poetry of Equatorial Guinean writer Raquel Ilombe del Pozo Epita, *Ceiba II (poesía inédita)* (Verbum, 2014), as well as a monographic issue dedicated to Equatorial Guinea in *Afro-Hispanic Review* (2009).

Dosinda García-Alvite is Associate Professor of Spanish at Denison University. Her teaching and research interests focus on migration, historical memory, and gender as manifested in literature, film, and music of contemporary Spain and its relations with Africa (especially Equatorial Guinea) and Latin America. She has published over twenty book chapters and articles on these topics in *Hispania*, *Revista Iberoamericana*, *Bulletin of Spanish Studies*, and *Afro-Hispanic Review*, among other journals, and in the collection of essays *Trans-afrohispanismos: Puentes culturales críticos entre África, Latinoamérica y España* (Ed. Dorothy Odartey-Wellington, Brill, 2018), *Teaching the African Novel* (Ed. Gaurav Desai, MLA, 2009), and *Memoria colonial e inmigración. La negritud en la España posfranquista* (Ed. Rosalía Cornejo-Parriego, Bellaterra, 2007).

Ana León-Távora is Associate Professor of Spanish, Director of Modern Languages, and Director of Race and Ethnicity Studies at Salem College. She holds a PhD in Philology from the Universidad de Sevilla, Spain. Her eminently comparative research focuses on global aesthetics and politics, social and political power relations, racial, ethnic, and linguistic discrimination, and gender studies. She is the co-editor and co-translator of the bilingual catalogue on contemporary Cuban art authored by Linda Howe, *Cuban Artists' Books and Prints. Libros y Grabados de Artistas Cubanos: 1998–2008*, and has published numerous articles and book chapters on literature and art as spaces for political and social debate. Her most recent publications include the book chapter "Afectos y activismo estético en *Ser mujer negra en España* de Desirée Bela-Lobedde" in *El reflejo de Medusa. Representaciones* *mediáticas contemporáneas de mujeres* (Ed. Esther Alarcón Arana, Advook, 2023), and the article on linguistic discrimination, cultural appropriation, and gender inequality in contemporary Spanish art titled "Glotofobia, apropiación cultural y privación relativa," within a special issue of the academic journal *Romance Notes* (Eds. Michelle Murray and Rosalía Cornejo-Parriego).

Stefania Licata is Assistant Professor of Spanish at Converse University. She holds a PhD in Hispanic Languages and Literature from SUNY Stony Brook University. Her research focuses on migration and cultural representations of Africa in Europe and vice versa during the twentieth and twenty-first centuries. Her interests, approached from an interdisciplinary and comparative perspective, include Afro-Hispanic Postcolonial Studies, Migration, Diaspora, and Mediterranean Studies. She has published articles about Equatorial Guinea and Migration in the Mediterranean and is part of the *Grupo de Estudios Afro-Hispánicos* based at the Universidad Nacional de Educación a Distancia (UNED) in Madrid.

Martin Repinecz is Associate Professor and Director of Spanish at the University of San Diego. He holds a PhD in Romance Studies from Duke University. His research focuses on questions of race and colonial memory in Francoist and contemporary Spain and the global Hispanophone world. His research has been published (or is forthcoming) in the *Bulletin of Hispanic Studies*, *Revista de Estudios Hispánicos*, *Hispanic Studies Review*, *Transmodernity*, *Bulletin of the Comediantes*, and *The Postcolonialist*. His book *Volatile Whiteness: Race, Cinema, and Europeanization in Spain* is forthcoming from the University of Toronto Press.

Acknowledgments

First and foremost, we would like to express our gratitude to the contributors for enthusiastically sharing their insights and expertise in this edited collection. We are also immensely grateful to the editorial team at Routledge for embracing this project. Additionally, we extend our thanks to the anonymous readers who provided essential feedback and helped shape this collection.

A special mention goes to May Morpaw and Kara Cybanski for their invaluable assistance in revising the entire manuscript. We would also like to acknowledge Salem College for granting Ana a sabbatical leave that allowed us to make significant advances in this project.

Above all, we want to express our deep appreciation to all the writers, artists, and activists who have inspired us and are the true protagonists of this book. You have challenged and compelled us to look at Spain's culture and history from new perspectives.

Lastly, we want to extend our deepest gratitude to our families on both sides of the Atlantic for their unwavering support throughout this endeavor.

Introduction
Black Spain in Afro-Europe

*Rosalía Cornejo-Parriego
and Ana León-Távora*

From April 3 to July 16, 2023, New York's Metropolitan Museum of Art (the Met) hosted the exhibition *Juan de Pareja, Afro-Hispanic Painter*. *The New York Times* greeted it with the headline, "A Familiar Face at the Met, Now in His Own Light" (Farago). Indeed, Diego Velázquez's portrait of Pareja, his enslaved assistant, is well known, but less so his own contribution to the visual arts of the Spanish Baroque. At the exhibit, Pareja's religious paintings, including *The Calling of St. Matthew*, which features his self-portrait, are accompanied by some of Bartolomé Esteban Murillo's and Velázquez's works to bear testimony to an Early Modern multiracial Spain where slavery existed. Presiding the exhibit is the quote, "History must restore what slavery took away," extracted from collector, scholar, and activist Arthur A. Schomburg's 1925 article "The Negro Digs Up His Past." In fact, Schomburg's search for Pareja frames the whole exhibit with fragments of his articles situated next to several paintings. This dialogue between Pareja and Schomburg is undoubtedly, above all, a tribute to the artist, but also to Schomburg for his lifelong political project of recovery. This Puerto Rican-born intellectual dedicated his life to "digging up" the contributions of Afro-descendant people to their societies and to highlighting their role as producers of culture.[1] Moved by a diasporic impetus, as his article "In Quest of Juan de Pareja" (1927) reveals, he had particularly African Americans in mind during his search and travels, wishing they could see and be uplifted by the paintings of the Spanish artist.

If we begin this volume by referring to the Met exhibit on Juan de Pareja, it is because it encapsulates several of the critical concepts and subjects that appear in this collection of essays. First, the focus on Schomburg asserts his desire to combat the historical amnesia that has led to the invisibility of Blackness and its erasure from national histories and discourses. To that end, he embarks on a pedagogical research journey to uncover the impact of Afro-descendants on the fabric of the nation and, consequently, use this knowledge as a source of empowerment for racialized communities and individuals. Furthermore, Schomburg's frame of reference is the African

DOI: 10.4324/9781003435051-1

Diaspora, a concept he explores across national borders and time. Equally noteworthy is his focus on Black Europe, which has traditionally occupied a marginal space within this Diaspora and has often been neglected in Diaspora Studies, as contemporary scholars and activists have observed. For Fatima El-Tayeb, "It was black Europe's heterogeneous composition, its ambiguous relation to constitutive narratives of the African diaspora as well as its complicated relation to and overlap with other communities of colour that left black Europeans at the margin of diaspora studies" (*European Others* 50). Finally, Schomburg's work adds another fundamental aspect: it carves a space for Spain within the Black European Diaspora.[2]

If we fast forward, we see a parallelism between the early twentieth-century Puerto Rican traveler and the efforts of twentieth- and twenty-first-century Black European intellectuals and artists. In *Afropeans. Notes from Black Europe*, self-proclaimed British flâneur Johny Pitts embarks on a journey through different European cities in search of Afropea. Tired of having his Europeanness questioned because of his Blackness—"My skin had disguised my Europeanness" (4)—and of always living under the assumption that he is an immigrant and not a full citizen (1), he sets out to explore Black Europe. This exploration aims to reclaim the "beauty in black banality" (6)—often eclipsed by two polar narratives that focus either on Black celebrities or Black ghettos—and his "ownership" of Europe: "As a member of Europe's black community, this Europe I speak of is all part of *my* inheritance, too, and it was time to wander and celebrate the continent like I owned it" (7; original emphasis).

In the same vein and decades earlier, German author May Ayim had already co-edited in 1986 a book on Afro-German women, *Farbe bekennen. Afro-Deutsche Frauen auf den Spuren ihrer Geschichte* [*Showing our Colors. Afro-German Women Speak Out*]. Furthermore, her poem "Afro-Deutsch" [Afro-German] explores how she is perceived as non-belonging to Germany and expected to return, at some point, to an imaginary African home (Crawley 74). More recently, the documentary *Mariannes Noires: Mosaïques Afropéennes* (Dir. Mame-Fatou Niang and Kaytie Nielsen, 2016) concentrates on Afro-French women who narrate their defense mechanisms to face everyday racism, their efforts to redefine the national narrative that has erased colonial history—while ironically, colonial stereotypes about racialized groups are alive and well—and their denunciation of the precariousness of their belonging and citizenship status. Likewise, although in the Italian context, Cristina Lombardi-Diop reflects in her preface to *The Black Mediterranean: Bodies, Borders, and Citizenship* on what it means to be a Black Italian and a Black European and poses the poignant question, "[W]hat is the place of blackness within Italy and what happens when blackness and citizenship are considered mutually exclusive?" (5). In *European Others. Queering Ethnicity in Postnational Europe*, El-Tayeb argues that the exclusion of racialized minorities from the concept of citizenship is a consequence of "the ideology of 'racelessness,'" a process that denies the existence of "race" in Europe and makes racial thinking and its effects invisible (xvii). This "colourblindness" means that "Europeans possessing the (visual) markers of Otherness thus are eternal newcomers, forever suspended in time, forever 'just arriving,' defined by a static foreignness overriding both individual experience and historical facts" (*European Others* xxv). The "foreignness" of these alleged newcomers and their erasure from Europe's past have a profound impact on present negotiations of belonging and understanding of European citizenship (*European Others* 53).

All of the above concerns are also evident in works such as Reni Eddo-Lodge's *Why I'm No Longer Talking to White People About Race*; Emejulu Akwugo and Francesca Sobande's *To Exist is to Resist: Black Feminism in Europe*; Layla-Roxanne Hill and Francesca Sobande's *Black Oot Here. Black Lives in Scotland*; *Locating African European Studies: Interventions, Intersections, Conversations* (Ed. Felipe Espinoza Garrido et al.); and El-Tayeb's *Undeutsch. Die Konstruktion des Anderen in der Postmigrantischen Gesellschaft*. These texts point to a new field of knowledge that comprises testimonial, creative, and scholarly works, but, notwithstanding Schomburg's pioneering vision of Spain as a significant location within the Black Diaspora, with few exceptions, the experience of Afro-Spaniards has been notably absent from studies about contemporary Black Europeans and Afro-Europeanness.[3] It is true, as Julia Borst and Danae Gallo González contend, that an important factor to take into account is the lack of homogeneity within the European territory and the fact that Spain and Portugal "geographically represent Europe's 'borderland' to Africa but also look back on a long history of migratory movements between the African continent and the Iberian Peninsula" (288–99), which often has not been acknowledged. Nor can we forget the geopolitical, economic, and cultural differences between the North and South of Europe and the reality that Spain is located at the crossroads of the European Union, the Mediterranean, and, due to its imperial past, the Atlantic community.[4] Despite these defining characteristics that might set the Iberian Peninsula apart, it is undeniable that racialized Spaniards share many experiences with other Black European nationals. The goal of *Colonialist Gazes and Counternarratives of Blackness: Afro-Spanishness in 20th and 21st-Century Spain* is to participate and engage in this (Afro) European dialogue about amnesia, belonging, and empowerment.

Studying Afro-Spanishness

A remarkable number of studies have addressed Blackness in Spain through a critical race studies lens. These studies have focused predominantly on immigration, that is, the arrival of migrants beginning in the late

1980s, especially after 1986, the year in which Spain joined the European Union and became a migrant destination in contrast to the 1960s when its citizens left for wealthier European nations such as Germany, Switzerland, and France (S. Bermúdez; Coleman; Cornejo-Parriego, *Memoria colonial*; Murray; Vega-Durán; Ugarte). There is also a growing area of studies that explore the insertion of Blackness in the collective imaginary and the presence of Afro-descendant people from Early Modern to twentieth-century pre-immigration Spain (Cornejo-Parriego, *Black USA*; Fracchia; Fra-Houchins and Fra-Molinero; Jones; Martin-Márquez; Molinero; Murray and Tsuchiya; Surwillo). This constitutes a direct challenge to the ideology of racelessness and colorblindness mentioned before and to the traditional belief—with critical repercussions in today's Spain—that Black existence and, therefore, the concept and problem of race, including slavery, were only relevant in the colonies, not the Peninsula. Aside from recent scholarship, initiatives such as the documentaries *Gurumbé* (2016) and *Cachita* (2020) or Juan de Pareja's Met exhibit represent steps toward remedying Spain's Afro-amnesia or what Antumi Toasijé calls "de-Africanization process" (349).

Focusing on the twentieth and twenty-first centuries, our volume builds on this budding field that acknowledges Blackness as an integral component of the material and imaginary construction of Europe in general and Spain in particular. Through an interdisciplinary and transmedial approach that encompasses film, visual art, marketing, literature, autobiography, testimony, journalism, digital communities, and social media, our collection of essays proposes a dialogue on Afro-Spanishness that is not exclusively tied to immigration and, furthermore, a dialogue that understands Blackness as a non-essentialist, heterogeneous, diverse, and diasporic notion. This will allow us to trace a transnational network that connects Afro-Spaniards to Spain's former colony of Equatorial Guinea and to critically explore the links between Afro-Spanishness and global projects such as the Black Diaspora, Pan-Africanism, and the Black Lives Matter movement.

Our essays demonstrate the resilience of colonialist paradigms and explore how racial ideologies and colonial memories circulate, promoting national narratives of whitening. However, they also examine Black self-representation in a variety of cultural texts and products. They explore how Black Spanish authors, artists, and activists destabilize colonial gazes, propose decolonial views of Spain and Europe's literature and history, articulate Afro-diasporic knowledges, and envision Afro-descendance as an affirmative and empowering tool. Furthermore, they analyze how female Black grassroots activism, urban peripheries, and online communities become diasporic spaces that seek to un-whiten and destabilize existing constructions of national identity. As a result, readers will perceive in this collection a combination of an Afro-pessimistic perspective—due to the

Introduction: Black Spain in Afro-Europe 5

resilience of colonialist paradigms and anti-Black racism—and a celebratory view of Afro-Spanishness stemming from the joy of self-representation and agency, empowering humor, and the profoundly inspiring discovery of alternative archives that expand, enrich, and question hegemonic knowledge.

Knowledge and Representation: Coloniality and Its Challenges

When we reflect on knowledge, we need to question its ontology (what do we consider knowledge and what knowledge?), its roots (where does it originate?), its motifs, and, more importantly, *its agency*: who is allowed to know and who holds the power to decide what we should know? This raises a final grammatical question: why "knowledge" in the singular form and not in the plural?[5] Indeed, as Michel Foucault argues, the relationship knowledge/power is symbiotic, a mutually feeding collaboration, which evidences that possessing a specific type of knowledge provides access to power, but, moreover, that power prescribes knowledge.

Aside from Foucault, decolonial scholars have also discussed the inextricable relationship between knowledge and power and the role of the former in the colonization process that places some nations and their epistemic systems at the geopolitical center while displacing the colonized ones to the peripheries. With the arrival of the capitalist economy and modernity in the eighteenth century, Europe imposes a concept of knowledge based on "reason" and objectivity that abandons other forms of observation. This rational knowledge dismisses "biographical locations" (Mignolo, "Epistemic" 160) and refuses tradition, creating the impression of a universal, neutral perspective, or what Santiago Castro-Gómez astutely labeled "zero-point hubris," an "impartial and sterile form of observation" emerging from a supposedly detached, abstract knower (Chapter 1).[6] This epistemic system discards other types of knowledge, claims that not all humans belong to the same intellectual category, and, consequently, validates Western colonial enterprises to gain access to new sources of wealth (Castro-Gómez, Chapter 1). The ethnic and cognitive asymmetry gives way, according to Donna J. Haraway, to a "culture of no culture" (qtd. in Mendieta 249), a knowledge that is confronted against tradition and that steals from the histories/stories that, as Eduardo Mendieta defends, make us "distinct as humans" (249). The erasure of loci of enunciations (subjects), replaced by a universal eye that transforms local history into a unifying global design, is the effect of the establishment of a center of geopolitical power:

> To the centrality of Spain, and later France, Holland, England, and the United States within the world system, there corresponds the pretension of turning their own local history into the single and universal

location for the articulation and production of knowledge. Knowledge not produced in these power centers or the circuits they control is declared irrelevant and "pre-scientific." (Castro-Gómez Chapter 1)

The devastating effects of modern colonialism are thus not only visible in the physical appropriation of territories and bodies and the inequitable distribution of wealth but also in the extermination of people's histories and the imprisonment of their minds (Fanon, *The Wretched* 49). As one of the Equatoguinean characters in Lucía Asué Mbomío Rubio's novel *Hija del camino* [Daughter of the Path] (2019) puts it, "They didn't come only to take the natural resources, cocoa or wood. They told us that what we considered religion was, in reality, superstition; that our languages were dialects; that what we found beautiful was ugly; that our artistic works were handicrafts" (303).[7] This character confirms, in fact, Frantz Fanon's theories regarding the psychological and emotional consequences resulting from the internalization of colonialist paradigms that will also lead to the belief in the inferiority of the cultural products of the colonized subject (*Black Skin*).[8]

While this Western sequestration of knowledge needs to be challenged, Devika Chawla and Ahmet Atay concur with Fanon, who acknowledged in *A Dying Colonialism* the impossibility of returning to a pure pre-colonial past (5). The choices left for a colonized person are to accept the humiliation by the self-proclaimed superior individuals or to assimilate, which ultimately implies assuming their inferiority and playing by the colonizers' rules (Mignolo, *The Politics* 333). Mignolo, however, introduces "border thinking" as an alternative that involves "changing the terms of the conversation and not just its content" (*The Politics* 332–33). Epistemic decolonization entails a "reconstitution" of knowledge that overthrows the hegemonic knowledge/power dynamics and views peripheries as valuable alternative centers of information. As Chawla and Atay propose, it also entails focusing on the experiences of non-belonging and in-betweenness and "on hybrid experiences, practices, and identities that actively question, critique, and challenge colonization" (5).

Decoloniality provides a framework to analyze not only the relationship between the metropolis and its colonies but also the current status of racialized minorities in former European colonial powers. If the knowledges of the peripheries have been rejected as non-knowledge, if their cultural production and practices have been degraded, if the history of slavery and colonialism has been forgotten, erased, or whitewashed, the construction of counternarratives and the search for alternative Black archives to remember the past critically becomes a pressing task for current transformations (El-Tayeb, *European Others* xxviii). It becomes urgent to "[u]ncover a different history of race in Europe, one in which people of color appear as insiders and agents" (xxxix). These archives are cultural and historical repositories that become a source of empowerment, as Pitts notes upon the discovery of the Black Archives in Amsterdam (135–38). Fully aware of this, Afro-Spanish activists and cultural producers have embarked on significant initiatives. For example, Tania Adam, the creator of *Radio Africa Magazine*, leads the research project "España negra" and the promotion of Black Iberian Studies. Digital communities such as *Afroféminas* (see Chapter 4), *Negrxs Magazine*, *Conciencia Afro*, and *Sevilla Negra*, as well as the social media presence and works of activists like Moha Gerehou (*Qué hace un negro como tú en un sitio como este* [2021]) and Rubén H. Bermúdez (*Y tú, ¿por qué eres negro?* [2017]), aim to change dominant narratives by "excavating," to use Mbomío's archeological terms, "the buried history" (*Hija* 62).[9] Among these initiatives, we must also include Yeison F. García López's presentation, "Madrid negro," which took place at the Prado Museum in Madrid on November 4, 2023. The poet fashioned himself after Pareja's portrait by Velázquez and imagined a poetic conversation with Pareja, all while identifying himself as *Afro-madrileño* and displaying the Pan-African flag featuring an image of the province of Madrid. Not only does he aim to establish a connection between global and local Afro-descendance, but he also seeks to "darken" an institution that symbolizes Spanish identity. Additionally, he proposes transforming "Madrid negro" into a laboratory that continues to generate memories and create archives (@yeison.f.garcia.lopez). This enterprise, while arduous, is nevertheless profoundly rewarding because, as Stuart Hall explains, the precise moment of recognizing the existence of hidden histories epitomizes the beginning of decolonization: "the speaking of a past which previously had no language" ("The Local" 35).

Hegemonic knowledge is intrinsically associated with representation, as Hall eloquently argues in *The Spectacle of the Other*. This connection is further exemplified in Chapter 1 of this collection titled, "From Negrophilia to Necropolitics: Anti-Black Racism in Spanish Avant-Garde Humor Magazines." Focusing on a selection of cartoons, vignettes, short stories, and references to the 1927 film *El negro que tenía el alma blanca*, Ana León-Távora studies several examples of anti-Black racist graphic humor in two prominent Spanish avant-garde journals, *Buen Humor* (1921–1931) and *Gutiérrez* (1927–1934). While born out of negrophilia—the obsession with Black culture prevalent in the 1920s and 1930s European artistic scene, primarily in Paris but also in other European cities—León-Távora's close examination from the perspective of Achille Mbembe's concept of necropolitics reveals the pervasive connection between Spanish modernist aesthetics and postcolonial politics. This analysis demonstrates that negrophilia ultimately constructs a necropolitical system where Black individuals are treated as peripheral commodities of modernity, never as authentic agents within it. By studying these magazines' degrading humor—with its dehumanizing tropes and colonialist stereotypes and narratives—Chapter 1 provides a point of departure to examine both the persistence and subversion of this "grammar of representation" (Hall, "The Spectacle" 251) in the following essays.

Necropolitics is also evident in Baltasar Fra-Molinero's "The Transnational Afropessimism of Francisco Zamora Loboch." Through the lens of Afropessimism, Chapter 2 studies a selection of works by Zamora Loboch, a journalist and writer born in 1948 in Equatorial Guinea but residing in Spain since the 1960s. Beginning with his first essay, *Cómo ser negro y no morir en Aravaca* (1994), Zamora Loboch depicts Blackness, according to Fra-Molinero, as a condition predestined to death in the world order of white supremacy. The writer ironically dismantles Spain's transhistorical construction of whiteness that has erased the memory of its involvement in slavery, the slave trade, and more recent colonial enterprises (e.g. Equatorial Guinea). Furthermore, *Cómo ser negro* confirms the intrinsic connection of power, knowledge, and representation by analyzing both the "invisibility" of Black characters and their depictions by canonical authors of Early Modern Spain.

Moreover, in his three novels, Fra-Molinero confirms Zamora Loboch's Afropessimism. The right to constitute a national state by Black individuals is the subject of ridicule in the author's first novel, *Conspiración en el green (El informe Abayak)* (2009), which explores the relationship between the international oil industry, African exiles, and neocolonialism. Black bodies, masculinities, and intellectual skills are trafficked transnationally in the world of sports in *El caimán de Kaduna* (2012). The colonial ontology of Blackness as non-citizenship is essential to white utopias in *La república fantástica de Annobón* (2017), a novel set during Spain's Second Republic (1931–1939), which, despite its progressive impulse, did not envision a space for Black colonial subjects. As Fra-Molinero argues, Equatorial Guinea and Africa are always at risk of falling under the coloniality of the European discourse of failure: failed states, societies, and humanity. Nevertheless, despite their pessimism, Zamora Loboch's works create a space for memory as a counternarrative to colonial discourse and white supremacy, as well as an ironic manual with survival strategies for Black people in contemporary Spain.

Their undeniable multicultural, multiracial, and multiethnic societies have led Western postcolonial nations to address issues such as racism, integration, and belonging of racialized communities. They have seen, however, numerous unsuccessful attempts. France, for example, has systematically miscarried its integration efforts, as the recurring uprisings of the *banlieues* (from 2005 to 2023) or its misguided focus on Muslim women's dress demonstrate (Cohen). Jeffrey K. Coleman's essay "The Value of Color: Spain's Equality Stamps Fiasco" (Chapter 3) explores one such attempt on Spanish soil. He captures the irony of a recent anti-Black racism initiative that backfired immensely by visually reinforcing the racial hierarchies it aimed to dismantle. In 2021, Spain's postal service, *Correos*, launched a collection of four skin-toned stamps, whose value decreased as they darkened to reflect discriminatory racial inequality. Released precisely on the first anniversary of George Floyd's murder at the hands of the police in the United States, the Equality Stamps generated widespread criticism, and *Correos* swiftly ended the campaign without an apology. For Coleman, the prompt deletion of the stamps from the official *Correos* archive connotes an unwillingness to concede wrongdoing and eliminates the need for an apology to the communities affected by this campaign. Finally, he contends that the increasing value of the stamps in the resale philatelic market lies not only in their scarcity but also in the surrounding controversy, thus demonstrating that racism sells. Consequently, this further denigrates Black Spaniards symbolically, as the funds generated in this secondary market do not benefit the anti-racism movement. While many people worldwide were appalled by this campaign, for Coleman, it constitutes "another unsuccessful attempt of the Spanish State to externalize racism as 'over there' while inflicting epistemological violence upon its racialized communities." We are faced then with one more example of the ideology of racelessness, which traditionally has asserted the nonexistence of racial conflicts in Europe, situating them in the United States, a perspective that becomes more and more difficult to defend.

As a result, current pedagogical practices adopted by different platforms and initiatives have started to denounce and confront anti-Black racism, the annihilation and dehumanization of Black subjects—materially or symbolically—and the resilience of colonialist imagery and thought examined in the previous essays. The digital magazine *Afroféminas* has played a highly significant role in this regard. In Chapter 4, "Educating Spain about Its Afro-Identity on the Web: *Afroféminas*," Esther M. Alarcón Arana examines a selection of articles in *Afroféminas*, proposing that the magazine's empowering antiracist activism and decolonial praxis challenge both national identity and dominant white feminism. Its didactic mission aims to dismantle the hegemonic concept of Spanishness and challenge the Eurocentrism of Spain's historiography and the representation of Black individuals. It also questions white feminism for failing to include racialized women on equal terms.[10] Moreover, a final section, concentrating on two discursive practices employed in these articles—dialogue and storytelling—completes the analysis of *Afroféminas*'s goal to combat Afro-amnesia and acknowledge the existence of a significant Black Spain. While the magazine includes Black academic voices like that of Antumi Toasijé, it strongly supports personal stories as a legitimate source of knowledge, asserting the role of storytelling as a compelling narrative technique that challenges the so-called "scientific" history.

In Chapter 5, "Hidden Knowledges and Diasporic Positionings: The Autobiographical and Testimonial Texts in *Metamba Miago: Relatos y saberes de mujeres afroespañolas*," Julia Borst analyzes *Metamba Miago* (2019), a collection of autobiographical and testimonial texts by Black women self-edited and coordinated by Deborah Ekoka Hernandis. Referring to approaches that conceptualize literature as a potential archive of hidden and marginalized knowledge, Borst studies how Afro-descendance is imagined not simply as political resistance to the discourse of white supremacy. For this critic, *Metamba Miago* displays specific knowledge about what it means to be a racialized individual in Spain and how to redefine Blackness from the perspective of the diasporic subject. These texts constitute empowering narratives of self-affirmation that refuse to define Blackness only in opposition to whiteness and in relation to racism. For Borst, they offer positive spaces of identification for Afro-diasporic subjects and depict the diversity of female Blackness as well as the transgenerational transfer of knowledge.[11] Echoing Minna Salami, Borst affirms that *Metamba Miago* is also invested in discovering and producing a "language of joy." Moreover, Chapter 5 addresses the relation of these Afro-descendant women to the "shifting signifier of 'home,'" which is often imagined as a metaphorical more than geographical space of Afro-diasporic belonging. The concept of Diaspora, as we will further explore in the next section, emerges as a dynamic space where diverse and multiple interpretations, affiliations, and identifications convene.

Diaspora, European Pan-Africanism, and Translocality

The previous essays demonstrate that, while Afro-Spaniards wish to assert their national belonging, they do not ignore the transnational and diasporic dimensions of their individual and collective identity. Like other Afro-Europeans, Afro-Spaniards contest both their erasure from national histories and from the European (non) memory of colonialism (El-Tayeb, *European Others* 78) and embrace their hybrid identities. This raises, for El-Tayeb, a very pertinent question: "How to theorize migrant and minority populations as integral parts of national histories and contemporary politics while at the same time recognizing their transnational components" (*European Others* 54).

The twentieth century witnessed *Négritude*, the Harlem Renaissance, Black Power, and Pan-Africanism, to name a few of the movements that inspired a transnational community. The twenty-first century has seen Black Lives Matter become a global crusade, especially after the 2020 murder of George Floyd, which mobilized Afro-descendants of different national origins, first to show their solidarity with African Americans and, second, to condemn racist practices and provide visibility to discrimination in their own countries. It is undeniable that African American history and its emblematic leaders have played a fundamental role in the Black diasporic imagination. However, many Afro-Europeans currently advocate focusing on their unique conditions and history, considering that, despite the commonalities, the US Black experience differs from the European one. Furthermore, the evolving reality of post-colonial African countries has reframed the relationship of diasporic communities with their continent of origin and, consequently, requires a revision of the concept of Pan-Africanism.

Regarding the African American community, Karo Moret acknowledges the indisputable and essential North American contribution to scholarship about the racial struggles of Black Americans and Afro-feminism. She laments, nevertheless, the lack of an equivalent intellectual reflection about Afro-diasporic subjects in other countries. Possessing only the US experience as a framework obliterates the diversity and specificity of the Black experience in other contexts (Gómez Santo Tomás). Similarly, Mbomío praises African Americans' achievements in terms of self-representation, but at the same time advises Black Spaniards to pivot to the already extensive list of Black cultural production in Spain to "find" themselves ("Narrarse"). There is a prevailing sense that the United States has occupied a dominant position within the Black Diaspora and that it is time to look toward other enclaves. In Pitt's words, "I would have to look beyond African America for answers about my situation as a black man in Europe and orientate myself more confidently along an Afropean axis" (51).[12]

In addition, considering the crucial historical changes, Omar Dieng proposes a new version of Pan-Africanism: Afro-European Pan-Africanism.[13] For Dieng, Pan-Africanism was originally invested in the liberation of Africa, which became the "symbol of success and failure for the entire black race" (340). During the post-independence period, however, it shifted its focus to the continent, and "the inclusion of Afrodiasporic subjects became irrelevant" (340). Moreover, with the departure from Europe of many African leaders, activism in Europe lost its strength (341). Ironically, this also led to the belief that France and England had been "sites of black intellectuals' collaborations rather than places of anti-black racism as clearly seen in the USA" (341). This confirms an already highlighted idea: the Black "problem" was always located in the colonies, not the metropolis, or, in more recent times, that "real" anti-Black racism is exercised in North America, not in Europe.

However, Dieng perceives an important change in Black diasporic subjects. While a continuity with the original concept of Pan-Africanism persists, there are also relevant discontinuities that lead to his definition of Afro-European Pan-Africanism as "a collective black consciousness in twenty-first-century Europe" (343). Focusing primarily on their condition as Black citizens, Afropeans are trying to define strategies of resistance (343) and demonstrate their "sense of agency and subversive practices of Europeanness" (344). Dieng cites two significant organizations: the virtual activist communities established around Pitt's *The Afropean* and the French-based Afro-feminist collective *Mwasi*, which created a "Pan-Africanist journal to articulate an Afro-feminist response to racism in Europe and the global black world" (Dieng 347). To this, we could add Germany's *Black Central Europe* (founded by the Black Central European Studies Network), whose initial statement clearly synthesizes Dieng's tenets: "We bring you over 1000 years of Black history in the German-speaking lands and show you why it matters right now." In the case of Spain, we must emphasize once more the pedagogical labor of *Afroféminas* and the research and archival work of *Radio Africa Magazine*. Their primary goal is to address coloniality from the perspective of a non-essentialist collective identity that connects with the global Black Diaspora. Through their reconstruction of Black archives, they advocate for changes in the dominant transhistorical and transcultural discourses on Blackness that directly impact the real lives of Afro-diasporic subjects in twentieth- and twenty-first-century Spain.

Nevertheless, as Hall argues in "Cultural Identity and Diaspora," the Diaspora does not respond to a unified, unfragmented, single narrative. It is rather heterogeneous since the Black experience intersects with specific historical developments, class, gender, and geographical location. As previously seen—we might recall Zamora Loboch's works and the voices in *Metamba Miago*—the Afro-diasporic experience and connection with the "homeland" are diverse. In the Spanish context, it is also important to underline a generational difference. A first wave of writers born in Equatorial Guinea who became exiles in Spain due to Francisco Macías Nguema's dictatorship (1968–1979) (Ugarte 24–25) have been heavily invested in the colonial history and post-independence challenges of their original homeland and other African nations. Donato Ndongo's *Tinieblas de tu memoria negra* (1987), *Los poderes de la tempestad* (1997), and *El metro* (2007), as well as Zamora Loboch's novels examined in Chapter 2, are significant examples. Meanwhile, the younger generation of Afro-Spaniards, who were born in Spain or arrived at a very young age, tend to explore their African roots to negotiate their own identity and belonging to Spain and Europe. Desirée Bela-Lobedde's and Moha Gerehou's autoethnographies (see Chapter 10)—*Ser mujer negra en España* and *Qué hace un negro como tú en un sitio como este*, respectively—Rubén Bermúdez's personal and historical search in his photobook *Y tú, ¿por qué eres negro?* (2017); the documentary *La puerta de no retorno* (2011), in which film director Santiago Zannou accompanies his father in his return to Benin after forty years of absence; and Mbomío's *Las que se atrevieron* (2017) and *Hija del camino*, all these works hint at the links with an African "home" but as a means of locating themselves within contemporary concepts of nationhood, Spanishness, and Afro-Spanishness.

In her first published book, *Las que se atrevieron*, Mbomío already began to search for the ties between Spanishness and Blackness, as Martin Repinecz argues in Chapter 6, "Un-Whitening Late Francoist Spain: Knots of Memory in Lucía Mombío's *Las que se atrevieron*." Her collection reflects on the intersections of race, gender, and colonial memory, recounting the stories of six interracial relationships between white Spanish women and Black Equatorial Guinean men during late Francoism and the transition to democracy. Repinecz argues that *Las que se atrevieron* not only captures the intersection of sexual and racial politics but also explores the tensions and contradictions between Francoist national narratives of whitening, the memories of colonial violence in Equatorial Guinea, the anxieties of racial mixing, and the lived experiences of interracial Spanish families. For Repinecz, Mbomío's text reflects the circulation of racial and gendered paranoias between the colony and peninsular Spain that were imagined as necessary to protect the nation's precarious whiteness during the period known as *desarrollismo*, given that "a small but visible postcolonial diaspora punctured the regime's rhetoric of national 'whitening' and presaged the nation's impending transformation into a multiethnic society." Nevertheless, Repinecz concludes that despite racism and misogyny, *Las que se atrevieron* also presents some opportunities for transracial solidarity.

Contrary to the previous essay, which establishes the inevitable diasporic ties and circulation of colonial discourses and anxieties between Spain and Equatorial Guinea, Dosinda García-Alvite's "Decolonizing the History of Afro-Spaniards: *Afrofeminismo. 50 años de lucha y activismo de mujeres negras en España (1968–2018)* by Abuy Nfubea" (Chapter 7), studies the diasporic circulation of decolonial discourses that point towards agency and empowerment. In *Afrofeminismo*, community organizer and cultural critic Abuy Nfubea traces a genealogy of Afro-descendant women who have fought for the survival of their communities in Spain, mainly in the metropolitan areas of Madrid and Barcelona, through grassroots activism and continuous political involvement. García-Alvite argues that, against the epistemic violence that erases the contributions of Afro-diasporic subjects to Spanish culture, Nfubea's *Afrofeminism* constitutes a counternarrative and an essential Black archive of female activism.[14] In his examination of this activism, Nfubea dialogues with the central tenets of Afro-centric Pan-Africanism, Womanism, and Maroonism, expanding the map of diasporic connections but, most importantly, the theoretical and philosophical apparatus to promote a decolonial approach to being an

Afro-Spaniard. For Nfubea, the recovery of these stories of resistance is essential for the empowerment of the younger generations.

In Chapter 8, "Mapping Black Women through Art and Social Media: The Case of Montserrat Anguiano," Stefania Licata analyzes the interdisciplinary work of Afro-Catalan Anguiano, who combines visual arts with poetry. Licata's analysis of Anguiano's art explains how some artists have set out to reimagine racialized images and challenge hegemonic knowledges.[15] As demonstrated by Anguiano's 2022 exhibits, *Dona, Mujer, Women* and *Referent és nom de Dona*, the Catalan artist creates within a Pan-African context that encompasses Africa, the Americas, and Spain. Her art addresses the interplay of racial and gender politics, subverting the colonial iconography of Black women and the African continent. Indeed, contrary to dominant representations of the so-called Dark Continent, Anguiano's images depict a colorful and lively continent that reframes and re-envisions Africa as a joyful place. Furthermore, she performs a pictorial reconstruction of an incomplete collective memory and genealogy of Black women leaders across the diaspora. This genealogy and archive of cultural referents and role models combine the affirmation of her identity as an Afro-Catalan woman with the desire to visually and poetically create a virtual global community of Black women.

Amid this cartography that highlights Afropeans' multiple positions, be it through the concept of Pan-Africanism, diaspora, or transnationality, El-Tayeb proposes the term "translocality." In her discussion of the intersection of urban and diasporic spaces, she observes that racialized minorities often do not find their place in national narratives and will strongly identify with concrete cities or neighborhoods (*European Others* xxxvii). In line with this observation, we can also better understand Pitt when he confesses that during his European journey, he was searching "for an energy beyond the love of the local and the aloof distance of the national and the global. A liminal, translocal energy that ultimately provided communion with a wider black European diaspora …" (16). There is an increasing feeling that the language of nationality should be replaced with the language of (multi) locality (Selasi).

This constitutes the point of departure of "From Below and from Within: Urban Peripheries in Lucía Mbomío's *Barrionalismos*" (Chapter 9), where Rosalía Cornejo-Parriego analyzes Mbomío's *Barrionalismos*, a column that appeared in Spain's leading national newspaper *El País* from 2018 to 2020. Facing constant suspicion about her citizenship status, an experience suffered by other racialized minorities in Spain and Europe, Mbomío claims a Madrid neighborhood as her own space of belonging.[16] *Barrionalismos*, as Cornejo-Parriego demonstrates, shares many features with other journalistic and creative texts by Mbomío: the preservation of collective memory, the urgency of self-representation, the blend of global and local, and the focus on diasporic communities. In her column, Mbomío confronts the traditional hegemonic gaze on the *barrio*, depicting urban peripheries as heterogeneous spaces where neighbors remember, exercise their agency, and defy stereotypes. Moreover, she explores how, in the context of the global health crisis (COVID-19), *barrios* have faced additional discursive challenges. Being fully aware of her multiple belongings, *Barrionalismos* reflects Mbomío's decision to talk about a space of local belonging from the gendered and class perspective of a Spanish woman of African descent.

***

In recent years, the Spanish book market has witnessed almost a sort of *boom* of first-person testimonies written by Afro-descendant authors. Among the most recent are the previously-mentioned ones by Bela-Lobedde and Gerehou, Asaari Bibang's *Y a pesar de todo, aquí estoy* [And Here I Am, in Spite of Everything] (2021), Adriana Boho's *Ponte en mi piel. Guía para combatir el racismo cotidiano* [Put Yourself in My Skin. A Guide to Combatting Everyday Racism] (2022), and Afropoderossa's *España no es solo blanca* [Spain Isn't Only White] (2023). Considering this proliferation, it is only fitting to conclude this volume by focusing on these narratives that center the voices of Black authors and provide an insider's perspective, rather than allow others to tell their stories and experiences. Moreover, they synthesize some of the fundamental issues addressed in *Colonialist Gazes and Counternarratives of Blackness: Afro-Spanishness in 20th and 21st-Century Spain*.

In her essay "An Inconclusive Conclusion: Autoethnography as a Model for Epistemic Decolonization" (Chapter 10), León-Távora categorizes these first-person accounts as autoethnographies and explores the pivotal role this genre plays in the decolonization of Eurocentric epistemology. Recalling the indissoluble relationship between power and knowledge as a colonial form of control, León-Távora examines them as counternarratives that include pedagogical practices and strategies of resistance and pose fundamental questions regarding the hegemonic concept of Spanish nationhood. Finally, they confront Spain's Afro-amnesia, tackling, León-Távora argues, the power of non-knowledge or ignorance as a selective choice, which is, in the end, responsible for Spain's colorblindness and inability to acknowledge and accept its own racism.

While the experiences narrated might seem to confine Blackness in Spain to an inescapable Afropessimism, these autoethnographies are also a formidable affirmation of agency and empowerment. It is an empowerment that stems from self-representation, the challenge to the Eurocentric monopoly of knowledge, and the use of humor. If we began with an essay that analyzed blatant examples of anti-Black humor, in these first-person accounts, humor becomes a survival strategy, a pedagogical tool to confront racial hegemony, an invitation to non-Black Spaniards to contemplate colonialist stereotypes from a Black person's perspective, and, ultimately, a call for shared anti-racist activism.

Notes

1 His extraordinary collection lives on at the Schomburg Center for Research in Black Culture (Harlem, New York City).
2 Although this is part of a complex ongoing debate, throughout this volume, we capitalize "Black" and use lowercase for "white" to highlight the historical discrimination of peoples of African descent. For more on this debate, see Appiah.
3 The collection *Locating African European Studies* contains one essay by Borst, "Voices from the Black Diaspora in Spain." Pitts devotes chapters to different European cities, including Lisbon, but only mentions in passing Madrid's multicultural Lavapiés neighborhood (339–40). However, he does lament in his introduction not including Spain's capital in his travel book. Spain is also missing in Michael McEachrane's "Pan-Africanism and the African Diaspora in Europe" in the *Routledge Handbook of Pan-Africanism*, edited by Reiland Rabaka.
4 It would also be appropriate to incorporate Spain to the field of Mediterranean Studies, a field that has begun to engage with race as demonstrated in *The Black Mediterranean* (Eds. Proglio, Hawthorne et al.), a collection of essays whose main focus is Italy. Lombardi-Diop proposes the use of the *Mediterraneo nero* "as a diasporic framework" (5).
5 Here we expand on Walter Mignolo's original questions: "Who and when, why and where is knowledge generated" ("Epistemic" 160).
6 For Argentinian philosopher Enrique Dussel, European modernity was initiated already by the 1492 Spanish "discovery" of America, which gave birth to a common European consciousness and the constitution of Europe as the center, while the rest of the world was regarded as its periphery, in the dichotomy of the modern, quasi-divine European "I" versus the primitive "Other" (qtd. in Ajari 26).
7 "Aquí no vinieron solo a llevarse las materias primas, el cacao o la madera. Nos dijeron que lo que considerábamos que era una religión, en realidad era superstición; que nuestras lenguas eran dialectos; que lo que encontrábamos bello era feo; que nuestras manifestaciones artísticas eran artesanía." All translations are ours unless otherwise indicated.
8 Mbomío's novel explores some of these effects and contradictions through the Equatoguinean father of the protagonist. The father tries to instill the pride of being fang, while simultaneously clarifying that he is not like the rest of his people (55) and not teaching his language to his children (259; 292).
9 "Juntos exhumaron la historia enterrada y juntos recibieron el abrazo de una realidad en la que las personas negras no eran eternas segundonas sino protagonistas, héroes y heroínas."
10 This position is very similar to the one held by the French collective *Mwasi* to whom we will refer later. See Olea.

11 *Afromayores* [Afro-seniors], a recent project sponsored by the cultural center Espacio Afro, holds great significance in this regard. The most prominent initiative thus far has been the inauguration of the photographic exhibit "Afromayores. Somos porque fueron" [Afro-seniors. We are because they were] in Alcorcón, in September 2023 ("Lesmas").
12 Pitts notes an interesting difference: "US exports its blackness. Europe does not" (48).
13 For more on revisions of Pan-Africanism, see García-Alvite's essay (Chapter 7).
14 For another effort to create a Black Female Archive as a testimony to the intellectual and activist contributions to Black Internationalism and Black Europe, see Florvil.
15 For more on location and identity of Black authors within the Spanish artistic scene, see García's *Inapropiados e inapropiables* (2018), which includes conversations with artists such as poet Yeison F. García López, singer Nakany Kanté, and actress Silvia Albert, author of the play *No es país para negras* [No Country for Black Women] (2019).
16 As El-Tayeb explains, "the majority of people of color currently living in Europe are officially and unofficially defined as being part of a 'migrant population,' even when they were born there" (*European Others* 660).

Works Cited

Ajari, Norman. *Dignidad o muerte. Ética y política de la raza*. Translated by Cristina Lizarbe Ruiz. Editorial Txalaparta, 2021.

Akwugo, Emejulu, and Francesca Sobande, editors. *To Exist Is to Resist: Black Feminism in Europe*. Pluto Press, 2019.

Appiah, Kwame Anthony. "The Case for Capitalizing the B in Black." *The Atlantic*, 18 June 2020, https://www.theatlantic.com/ideas/archive/2020/06/time-to-capitalize-blackand-white/613159/. Accessed 28 Oct. 2023.

Ayim, May, Katharina Oguntoye, and Dagmar Schultz, editors. *Farbe bekennen. Afro-Deutsche Frauen auf den Spuren ihrer Geschichte*. Orlanda, 1986.

———. *Showing Our Colors. Afro-German Women Speak Out*. Translated by Anne V. Adams. U of Massachusetts P, 1992.

Bela-Lobedde, Desirée. *Ser mujer negra en España*. Plan B, 2018.

Bermúdez, Rubén H. *Y tú, ¿por qué eres negro?* La Fábrica, 2017.

Bermúdez, Silvia. *Rocking the Boat: Migration and Race in Contemporary Spanish Music*. U of Toronto P, 2018.

Black Central Europe. https://blackcentraleurope.com/. Accessed 14 Oct. 2023.

Borst, Julia. "Voices from the Black Diaspora in Spain." *Locating African European Studies: Interventions, Intersections, Conversations*, edited by Felipe Espinoza Garrido et al. Routledge, 2020, pp. 189–208.

Borst, Julia, and Danae Gallo González. "Narrative Constructions of Online Imagined Afro-Diasporic Communities in Spain and Portugal." *Open Cultural Studies*, vol. 3, no. 1, 2019, pp. 286–307.

Cachita. La esclavitud robada. Directed by Álvaro Begines. La Mirada Oblicua Producciones and Ranna Films, 2020.

Castro-Gómez, Santiago. *Zero-Point Hubris: Science, Race, and Enlightenment in Eighteenth-Century Latin America (Reinventing Critical Theory)*. eBook, Rowman & Littlefield Publishers, 2021.

Chawla, Devika, and Ahmet Atay. "Introduction: Decolonizing Autoethnography." *Cultural Studies ↔ Critical Methodologies*, vol. 18, no. 1, 2018, pp. 3–8.
Cohen, Roger. "Muslim Students' Robes Are Latest Fault Line for French Identity." *The New York Times*, 15 Sept. 2023, https://www.nytimes.com/2023/09/15/world/europe/france-abaya-ban-attal.html. Accessed 27 Oct. 2023.
Coleman, Jeffrey. *The Necropolitical Theater. Race and Immigration on the Contemporary Spanish Stage*. Northwestern UP, 2020.
Cornejo-Parriego, Rosalía, editor. *Black USA and Spain: Shared Memories in the 20th Century*. Routledge, 2019.
———. *Memoria colonial e inmigración. La negritud en la España postfranquista*. Bellaterra, 2007.
Crawley, Erin. "Rethinking Germanness: Two Afro-German Women Journey 'Home'." *Other Germanies: Questioning Identity in Women's Literature and Art*, edited by Karen Jankowsky and Carla Love. SUNY P, 1997, pp. 74–95.
Dieng, Omar. "Afro-European Pan-Africanism: A Twenty-First Century Black Europeans' Mobilizations." *Journal of African American Studies*, vol. 26, no. 3, 2022, pp. 339–54.
Eddo-Lodge, Reni. *Why I'm No Longer Talking to White People About Race*. Bloomsbury Publishing, 2019.
El-Tayeb, Fatima. *European Others. Queering Ethnicity in Postnational Europe*. U of Minnesota P, 2011.
———. *Undeutsch. Die Konstruktion des Anderen in der Postmigrantischen Gesellschaft*. Transcript Verlag, 2016.
Espinoza Garrido, Felipe, et al., editors. *Locating African European Studies: Interventions, Intersections, Conversations*. Routledge, 2020.
Fanon, Frantz. *Black Skin, White Masks*. Translated by Richard Philcox. Grove Press, 2008.
———. *The Wretched of the Earth*. Translated by Constance Farrington. Grove Press, 1963.
Farago, Jason. "A Familiar Face at the Met, Now in His Own Light." *The New York Times*, 7 Apr. 2023, https://www.nytimes.com/2023/04/07/arts/design/juan-de-pareja-met-museum-velasquez-painter.html. Accessed 20 July 2023.
Florvil, Tiffany N. *Mobilizing Black Germany: Afro-German Women and the Making of a Transnational Movement*. U of Illinois P, 2020.
Fracchia, Carmen. *"Black but Human": Slavery and Visual Arts in Hapsburg Spain, 1480–1700*. Oxford UP, 2019.
Fra-Molinero, Baltasar. *La imagen de los negros en el teatro del Siglo de Oro*. Siglo XXI, 1995.
García, Mar. *Inapropiados e inapropiables. Conversaciones con artistas africanos y afrodescendientes*. Los libros de la catarata, 2018.
Gerehou, Moha. *Qué hace un negro como tú en un sitio como este*. Península, 2021.
Gómez Santo Tomás, Berta. "Karo Moret: 'No creo que exista un feminismo global.'" *Pikara Magazine*, 13 Mar. 2019, https://www.pikaramagazine.com/2019/03/karo-moret-no-creo-que-exista/.

Gurumbé. Canciones de tu memoria negra. Directed by Miguel Ángel Rosales. Intermedia Producciones, 2016.

Hall, Stuart. "Cultural Identity and Diaspora." *Identity: Community, Culture, Difference*, edited by Jonathan Rutherford. Lawrence and Wishart, 1990, pp. 222–37.

———. "The Local and the Global: Globalization and Ethnicity." *Culture, Globalization, and the World-System. Contemporary Conditions for the Representation of Identity*, edited by Anthony D. King. U of Minnesota P, 1991, pp. 19–39.

———. "The Spectacle of the Other." *Representation: Cultural Representations and Signifying Practices*, edited by Stuart Hall. Sage Publications, 1997, pp. 223–79.

Hill, Layla-Roxanne, and Francesca Sobande. *Black Oot Here. Black Lives in Scotland.* Bloomsbury Publishing, 2022.

Houchins, Sue E., and Baltasar Fra-Molinero, editors. *Black Bride of Christ. Chicaba, An African Nun in Eighteenth-Century Spain.* Translated by Sue E. Houchins and Baltasar Fra-Molinero. Vanderbilt UP, 2018.

Jones, Nicholas. *Staging Habla de Negros: Radical Performances of the African Diaspora in Early Modern Spain.* Penn State UP, 2019.

La puerta de no retorno. Directed by Santiago Zannou. Shankara Films and Dokia Films, 2011.

Lesmas, Rubén S. "ALCORCÓN/El proyecto Afromayores aterriza para reivindicar el legado de la 'gente negra.'" *Noticias para municipios*, 29 Sept. 2023, https://noticiasparamunicipios.com/noticias-ocio-cultura/alcorcon-el-proyecto-afromayores-aterriza-para-reivindicar-el-legado-de-la-gente-negra/. Accessed 27 Oct. 2023.

Lombardi-Diop, Cristina. "Preface: After 'the Mediterranean'." *The Black Mediterranean: Bodies, Borders and Citizenship*, edited by Gabriel Proglio et al. Palgrave MacMillan, 2021, pp. 1–4.

Mariannes Noires: Mosaïques Afropéennes. Directed by Mame-Fatou Niang and Kaytie Nielsen, 2016.

Martin-Márquez, Susan. *Disorientations: Spanish Colonialism in Africa and the Performance of Identity.* Yale UP, 2008.

Mbomío Rubio, Lucía Asué. *Hija del camino.* Grijalbo, 2019.

———. "Narrarse a sí misma." *Pikara Magazine*, 29 Apr. 2020, https://www.pikaramagazine.com/2020/04/contarse-asi-misma/. Accessed 15 Jan. 2023.

McEachrane, Michael. "Pan-Africanism and the African Diaspora in Europe." *Routledge Handbook of Pan-Africanism*, edited by Reiland Rabaka. Routledge, 2020, pp. 231–48.

Mendieta, Eduardo. "The Ethics of (Not) Knowing: Take Care of Ethics and Knowledge Will Come of Its Own Accord." *Decolonizing Epistemologies: Latino/a Theology and Philosophy*, edited by Ada María Isasi-Díaz and Eduardo Mendieta. Fordham UP, 2011, pp. 247–64.

Mignolo, Walter D. "Epistemic Disobedience, Independent Thought, and Decolonial Freedom." *Theory, Culture & Society*, vol. 26, no. 7–8, 2009, pp. 159–81.

———. *The Politics of Decolonial Investigation.* Duke UP, 2021.

Murray, N. Michelle. *Home Away from Home: Immigrant Narratives, Domesticity, and Coloniality in Contemporary Spanish Culture*. U of North Carolina P, 2018.

Murray, N. Michelle, and Akiko Tsuchiya, editors. *Unsettling Colonialism. Gender and Race in the Nineteenth-Century Global Hispanic World*. SUNY P, 2019.

Olea, Andrea. "Afrofeministas: 'Sabemos emanciparnos solas'." *Pikara Magazine*, 6 Oct. 2016, https://www.pikaramagazine.com/2016/10/afrofeministas-sabemos-emanciparnos-solas/. Accessed 27 Oct. 2023.

Pitts, Johny. *Afropean. Notes from Black Europe*. Allen Lane, 2019.

Proglio, Gabriele, et al., editors. *The Black Mediterranean: Bodies, Borders and Citizenship*. Palgrave MacMillan, 2021.

Schomburg, Arthur A. "In Quest of Juan de Pareja." *The New York Public Library Digital Collections*, July 1927, https://digitalcollections.nypl.org/items/35bba8a0-d949-013a-5087-0242ac110003.

———. "The Negro Digs Up His Past." *Survey Magazine*, 1 Mar. 1925.

Selasi, Taiye. "Don't Ask Me Where I Am from, Ask Me Where I Am a Local." *TED Talk*, Oct. 2014, https://www.ted.com/talks/taiye_selasi_don_t_ask_where_i_m_from_ask_where_i_m_a_local.

Survillo, Lisa. *Monsters by Trade: Slave Traffickers in Modern Spanish Literature and Culture*. Stanford UP, 2014.

Toasijé, Antumi. "The Africanity of Spain. Identity and Problematization." *Journal of Black Studies*, vol. 39, no. 3, 2009, pp. 348–55.

Ugarte, Michael. *Africans in Europe. The Culture of Exile and Emigration from Equatorial Guinea to Spain*. U of Illinois P, 2010.

Vega-Durán, Raquel. *Emigrant Dreams, Immigrant Borders: Migrants, Transnational Encounters, and Identity in Spain*. Bucknell UP, 2016.

@yeison.f.garcia.lopez. "Madrid Negro." *Instagram*, 4 Nov. 2023, https://www.instagram.com/p/CzQ41xcKOpU/?igshid=MzRlODBiNWFlZA==.

1 From Negrophilia to Necropolitics
Anti-Black Racism in Spanish Avant-Garde Humor Magazines

Ana León-Távora

The spread of new forms of artistic expression during the first decades of post-World War I Europe, as well as the airs of modernity and the cosmopolitan mentality from the United States at the turn of the twentieth century, were followed in Spain by a radical departure from the type of humor that had shaped its artistic scene and media in previous centuries. In new humorous publications, Spanish avant-garde authors and artists abandon the more socially and politically engaged satire to instead embrace absurdity and an aesthetic of humor akin to the new model of art that José Ortega y Gasset defended in his essay *The Dehumanization of Art* (1925). This new form of humor stemmed from the novel concept of "humorismo" formulated by Ramón Gómez de la Serna (or Ramón, as he preferred to be addressed), who defined the term not as a style or literary genre, but rather, as "an attitude towards life" (193).[1] The authors and artists that subscribed to this type of aesthetic comedy, which they designated "humor puro," or pure humor, were disciples of Ramón and formed the group later known as "The Other Generation of 1927," or simply, "the humorists."[2] Between 1921 and 1934, they would contribute prolifically to the two most prominent Spanish avant-garde humor reviews: *Buen Humor*, founded by graphic artist Pedro Antonio Villahermosa Borao (better known as Sileno) in 1921, and *Gutiérrez*, founded by graphic artist Ricardo García López (known as Ka-Hito) in 1927.

Although most of the cartoons, short stories, and vignettes found in these publications do indeed adopt a different humorous lens, reflecting the flare of absurdity characteristic of some artistic movements of the time, Dadaism for example, the reader will encounter an overabundance of racist jokes, mostly aimed at Black identities, which fall far from the socially detached, intellectually pure form of humor these artists proclaimed as their credo.[3] Fluctuating between a view of Black Africans from a colonialist perspective, on the one hand, and the portrayal of the recent presence of African American jazz performers in images suggestive of blackface, on the other, the two publications abound in cartoons, jokes, and short

DOI: 10.4324/9781003435051-2

stories that mock and stereotype Black people. In this essay, I will analyze a series of examples taken from both of these magazines, focusing principally on the issues pertaining to 1927, the year that identifies the artists' generational grouping. I claim that, despite the authors' and artists' intention to refrain from political and social commentary, the cartoons I have chosen problematize and emphasize Spain's racist mentality and its colonialist complex at the turn of the twentieth century. Indeed, as will become evident, these cartoons were clearly born out of a paradoxical mixing of Spain's past colonialist negrophobic mindset with the phenomenon of negrophilia, taken from the original French *négrophilie*, a term that conveys the obsession with Black culture that prevailed on the European artistic scene of the 1920s and 1930s (Archer-Straw).[4] My study will pay special attention to the issues that *Gutiérrez* published in 1927, which include promoting Spanish author Alberto Insúa's novel *El negro que tenía el alma blanca* [The Black Man with a White Soul]. Although first published in 1922, this novel became extraordinarily popular in the wake of Benito Perojo's 1927 silent film adaptation. A close examination of the negrophilia exposed in these publications from the perspective of necropolitics, borrowing the term from Achille Mbembe, will help corroborate the anti-Black racist tone in advertisements, cartoons, stories, and films that inundate all the social spheres of the period and reveal the conflicting reception and misrepresentation of Black culture in Spanish avant-garde artistic expressions.

The New Humor

When Pedro Antonio Villahermosa founded *Buen Humor* in 1921, Europe was already undergoing an intense process of renewal. It was the beginning of the "Roaring Twenties," a period which, both in Europe and in the United States, translates into a more optimistic outlook after the War, boosted by a rapid economic recovery, a dynamic cultural scene, and a break with tradition. In Spain, this modern mentality generates a radical renewal of the arts in general, which will be promptly followed by a much-needed reconfiguration of the type of humor that had prevailed in the works of graphic cartoonists and illustrators over the previous two centuries, where a satirical tone had dominated the genre since the publication of the first comic magazine, *El Duende de Madrid*, in 1735 (R. de la Flor 31). The new era for humor, then, begins with the publication of Henri Bergson's *Laughter* (1900) and is fueled by Sigmund Freud and James Strachey's *Jokes and Their Relation to the Unconscious* (1905). In Spain, two precursors of the new school of humor, in addition to the indisputable Ramón, were the authors Wenceslao Fernández Flórez and Julio Camba, although their use of humor was never as groundbreaking as the one set out in Ramón's theory of "humorismo," which not only implies a reconfiguration of the type of humor but also the establishment of a new social order at large: "Ramón's theory of humor centers on the collapse of the oneness of reality, which the avant-garde represents. Humor became the efficient and fast solvent to break apart all logical systems and to reinstate them into the mindless and anarchical stream of life" (R. de la Flor 31).[5] Absurdity and incongruence became the bases for this new type of humor that aspired to offer different perspectives on reality, transcending the established norm.

With *Buen Humor* having become extraordinarily successful, it was followed in 1927 by *Gutiérrez*, which called on many of the same authors as well as many other avant-garde artists who contributed to the development of this new comic vision. In addition to helping disseminate the new concept, the two became paragons of artistic experimentation. In fact, foremost avant-garde illustrators like Lluís Bagaría, Romà Bonet i Sintes (Bon), Antonio Lara (Tono), and K-Hito, to name just a few, introduced innovative artistic techniques, such as "photographic montages and techniques of inversion of reality, which even now are still being developed and perfected in humorous magazines and supplements" (R. de la Flor 36).[6] In comparison to *Buen Humor*, *Gutiérrez* was more radical and reached higher levels of absurdity, aiming to abandon the long tradition of sarcasm, mockery, and satire, which, as Ramón denounced, responded to a moralizing mission using harsh criticism (199–200).

In his condemnation of satire, Ramón was inadvertently emulating Plato and other classical philosophers and religious traditions that regarded humor and laughter through the lens of what contemporary psychologists and philosophers in Humor Studies have called the Superiority Theory. As John Morreall states, advocates of the Superiority Theory of humor "said that when something evokes laughter, it is by revealing someone's inferiority to the person laughing" (4).

Instead, a totally different approach, one more analogous to Ramón's concept of *humorismo*, is found in the Theory of Incongruity, embraced by philosophers such as James Beattie, Immanuel Kant, Søren Kierkegaard, Arthur Schopenhauer, and others. To these thinkers, laughter is caused by the perception of something "incongruous." In standard incongruity theories, as Morreall advises the reader, incongruity alone does not necessarily involve humor; to find an incongruous situation funny, it is essential to regard humor as aesthetic play (Morreall 33), taking it as a recreation and indulging in humor for humor's sake, an approach that resonates closely with Ortega y Gasset's theorizations on modern art.[7] The new absurdity of the Spanish artistic scene thus promulgates a state that Ramón—as he preferred to be known—describes as existing in between "becoming insanely crazy, versus becoming sanely mediocre" (194).[8] Moreover, the humorist, as Ramón would declare, must remain eminently antisocial and antipolitical (194). Taking the author's words as the statement of intent that represents a whole generation of humorists, thus, it would be logical to assume that modern humor would react against its precursor, as the latter fed on the ignoble feelings of ridicule and contempt.

Not only did the winds of modernity contribute to the reconfiguration of the tone in these new magazines, but it also makes sense that the authors involved, confined by the strong press censorship imposed under the dictatorship of Miguel Primo de Rivera (1923–1930), preferred to maintain a neutral political opinion. As Mathieu Gérard et al. note, Primo de Rivera's zeal in projecting a positive image of Spain after his military coup motivated him to orchestrate a system of press censorship based on a review of newspaper articles and the insertion of personal *notas oficiosas* [informal notes], by which he authorized their publication. Any publication that failed to include these notes next to a news item that might be considered controversial faced monetary sanctions and, in some cases, temporary suspensions (Gérard et al. 191).[9] And yet, despite these efforts to avoid censorship and to remain detached from the satirical tradition, the reader of *Buen Humor* and *Gutiérrez* will still be confronted by an overabundance of insidious vignettes, jokes, cartoons, and short stories targeting Black people, which is at odds with the ideal of a cosmopolitan, modern mentality and which, instead, is clearly reminiscent of the colonialist Black iconography found in the previous century.

The Colonial Gaze

The concept of *raza* [race] and its interpretations throughout Spanish history is extremely complex, so much so that authors like Joshua Goode and Eva Woods Peiró, among many others, point out that contemporary Spain's reluctance to admit its own racism—product of an unquestionable imperialistic past—is often excused through the idea of the Spanish race (interpreted as a compendium of collective, national traits) viewed as a "fusion" of different cultures, a theory that gained credibility with nineteenth-century anthropology and ethnology hypotheses about race. During the second half of the nineteenth century, the country participated in the construction of a Western capitalist epistemology based on scientific studies, mostly within the fields of anthropology and ethnology, claiming the biological superiority of Caucasians, whereas non-whites were described as semi-humans or ultimately, *"not as human as the white man"* (Sánchez Arteaga, "La racionalidad" 2; original emphasis).[10] The results of these studies promoted racism as a logical truth proven by the natural sciences, which in actuality obeyed "a *demented social order*—slavery or the nineteenth-century bourgeois imperialism" (Sánchez Arteaga, "La racionalidad" 2, original emphasis).[11] The claims of a biological white supremacy, which did not differ much from the later Nazi racial propaganda in Germany, would serve to legitimize imperialistic and colonial invasions under the premise of serving a most honorable "*civilizing mission by the superior races* over their biologically underdeveloped relatives" ("La racionalidad" 3).[12] The apparent contradiction in the avant-garde humorous magazines, therefore, can be regarded as a manifestation of what Jeffrey Herf has called "reactionary modernism" or "the accommodation of opposites" (qtd. in Goode 111), which would also explain the support of scientific advances and technical progress contrasting with the perpetuation of a nationalistic—and colonialist—Romantic mindset.

Undoubtedly, the loss of most Spanish colonies in the Americas and the Caribbean after 1898 and the feeling of defeat in Morocco after the Battle of Annual in 1921 generated a colonial complex that had already been sparked, toward the end of the nineteenth century, by the competition with neighboring nations such as France and Portugal, whose advances in the field of anthropology were far superior to Spain's conservative and outdated approach to the natural sciences (Sánchez Arteaga, "Antropología" 144–46). This yearning for the colonial past is reflected in multiple examples of cartoons, advertisements, posters, and even films during the first decades of the twentieth century that still rest on the narrative of the European savior that needs to instill civility among undeveloped peoples. Based on this premise, Black African bodies, regarded as tokens of primitiveness and wilderness, were used to construct a colonialist narrative that served to rationalize Europe's imperialist campaigns in Africa. Towards the end of the nineteenth century, for example, ethnographic museums rapidly expanded with African artifacts brought to Europe by adventurers who made private donations, while live exhibits containing Black African men and women, mostly Zulu and Ashanti, reenacted colonial battles that glorified Europeans (Archer-Straw 30). Unsurprisingly, at these fairs and expositions, European soldiers were represented fighting in an organized manner, in contrast with the African men and women who were shown half naked and in disarray (Archer-Straw 32–33). The dichotomy of chaos versus order was used to demonstrate the impeccable organization of the imperial power as opposed to a culture that was portrayed as chaotic, primitive, and, therefore, in need of being civilized by a superior one. In Spain, one of these exhibits was the human zoo put on display in 1887 at the Parque del Buen Retiro in Madrid, which presented Native Indigenous people from the Philippines, the Mariana Islands, and Malaysia, among other places.[13] Black and Indigenous bodies were used as post-colonial trophies that accentuated the myth of alterity and exoticism used to glorify the heroic expeditions of whites in foreign non-Western countries.

The media and the world of advertising quickly took advantage of the same colonial iconography of Black bodies. Certainly, the animalization of Black people has a long-standing tradition in Europe, as Baltasar Fra-Molinero recalls (64–65), not being exclusive to the imperialist mindset of the nineteenth century.[14] But, reinforced by scientific studies that affirmed the biological superiority of whiteness, comparisons of Black people to animals were frequent in the nineteenth century and the beginning of the twentieth century in Europe and America. Spanish humor magazines were not the exception: indeed, degrading photographs or pictures equating Black people to apes proliferated in both publications, as can be seen in the image below (Figure 1.1). The photograph, displaying the head of a real Black person, appears in a section titled "Cinematographic Pages," which contains fictitious and amusing news about the film industry. The caption reads: "The new cinematographic 'star' Richard Orang Ghutang, who aspires to occupy the space of Rudolf Valentino."[15]

The joke rests on the paronomasia by which the last names of the characters form the word "orangutan." Likewise, the caption uses a sarcastic tone to insinuate that the actor aspires to become the new Rudolf Valentino, a.k.a. "The Latin Lover," the internationally acclaimed Italian silent film sex symbol of the period. If being Black is seen as synonymous with wilderness and animality, it is also synonymous with ugliness and monstrosity. Although there exists a long tradition in European drama of representing the Black African as the monster or as the wild barbarian (Fra-Molinero 64), the association between beauty and whiteness was ironically institutionalized in the eighteenth century through Johann Friedrich Blumenbach's "scientific" ranking of human varieties. At the top of the ranking sat "Caucasian," which, according to Blumenbach, was the original and most aesthetically pleasant race, and at the bottom, "tawny-black," the darkest hue of black skin color (Painter 80).

Aside from being decreed an unpleasant trait, Black skin was also regarded as a symptom of impurity: of filth, in a physical interpretation, and of lust, in a moral one. The reliance on Blackness as a taint underlies a multitude of jokes in the humorous publications in Spain. For example, in the image below (Figure 1.2), a small Black boy seems disappointed to hear that he cannot play with the white girl's doll because, as she complains, his "hands are dirty."[16]

The image of a Black person to represent abjection and filth will become ubiquitous in multiple advertisements of bar soaps and other cleaning products of the time, where Black bodies are utilized as phobogenic agents to the white European mentality, to use Frantz Fanon's terminology.[17] Once again, this iconography was simply a modernized version of the old idea, established since the European Renaissance, that Black persons were dirty and impossible to clean, which can be found in many plays

Figure 1.1 Image in *Gutiérrez*, 11 June 1927. Courtesy of BNE.

of the Spanish Golden Age and in some old Spanish idioms and popular expressions (Fra-Molinero 4). In its modern adaptation, the leitmotif is extended to a view of Black bodies as a product "packed exotically for the market-place at the same time that race theories defined them as lesser

28 *Ana León-Távora*

Figure 1.2 Vignette in *Buen Humor*, 23 December 1928. Courtesy of *BNE*.

beings, and colonialism treated them as such" (Archer-Straw 38).[18] The message embedded in this type of advertising, apart from the hyperbolic efficiency of the cleaning product, is very clear: the soap alludes to the need for racial purity/cleanliness, which can only be achieved through a European agent, the European soap, a symbol of civilization. Notably, another disturbing message lies beneath the previous one: white skin is taken as the default color of humanity, and whoever does not conform to this norm is regarded as subhuman and must be civilized or *whitewashed*.

Depictions of Africans and Indigenous Americans as uncivilized heathens abound in the iconography of the two magazines, where cannibalism became a recurring trope when referring to Black cultural habits as the most grotesque form of abjection that provided colonial expeditions with a perfect excuse for legitimizing the conquests of those *salvajes* [savages].[19] In Figure 1.3, taken from the cover of an issue of *Buen Humor*, the reader may be aware of the confusing characterization of the two Black men, who are accessorized with items that are more evocative of Native American tribes than of African ones. Indeed, it is shocking to see a tipi tent in the background or the African characters wearing feather headdresses—in addition, the featherpiece on the character on the left is made of feathers and a pen, which creates a pun on the Spanish word *pluma*, both "feather" and "pen." The names by which they address each other, consisting of an animal with an attribute, "Neurasthenic Jackal," or containing a body part and a quality, "Presbyopic Eye," are also a parody of the naming tradition that is common among Native Americans. Both names are used with a clear intent to ridicule and show contempt, rather than admiration, for the two cultures simultaneously, both Native Americans and Black Africans. Whether the two ethnicities and cultures are mixed and undifferentiated is not important to the colonialist, imperialistic gaze that remains ingrained within the Spanish mentality, including the humorous publications that were considered the bastions of the new "pure humor." Neither does it go unnoticed that both men stand over a big cauldron containing the human parts of a white person. The joke under the image revolves around the polysemy of the verb "like" in the question the first character asks the second one, "What women do you like best? The American ones or the English ones?" to which the other character responds, "It's all the same to me, as long as they are served with a side of potatoes."[20]

Vignettes depicting Black characters, both male and female, engaged in cannibalistic practices or alluding to cannibalism populate *Buen Humor* and *Gutiérrez*, as can be seen in Figure 1.4, which shows a captive white explorer, trussed up like a wild pig for roasting over the fire, being carried over to a Black village where the villagers will eat him, judging from the cooking utensils the Black character is holding in one hand. Here we notice how the Black characters wear items of clothing that are assumed to belong to Western cultures, like a watch and a Western hat. Black people's immoral ways—let's not forget that their darkness is symbolic of an obscure morality—not only include murder and anthropophagy; as the drawing suggests, after killing and eating their victims, they also take possession

30 Ana León-Távora

Figure 1.3 Cover of Issue 392 of *Buen Humor*, 2 June 1929. Courtesy of BNE.

of their valuables, although making an improper use of them, like wearing the wristwatch on the leg, probably to highlight their primitivism.

Ironically, the longstanding narrative of violence, murder, cannibalism, and stealing that was bestowed on Black Africans and that inundates the humorous vignettes of the two publications, is precisely what white colonists did to Africa.

From Negrophilia to Necropolitics   31

Figure 1.4 Cover of issue of *Buen Humor*, 2 April 1922. Courtesy of *BNE*.

Comparisons that equate the dark skin of Black people to chocolate and treat Black bodies as objects of consumption, while still encountered nowadays, already proliferated across different social spheres, including the worlds of publicity, music, and the media, in the nineteenth century and at the beginning of the twentieth century (Archer-Straw 35–38).

In several oral testimonies dating from the 1800s, Black people who had been enslaved and exploited on Southern plantations in North America talked about the atrocious consumption of human flesh. Unlike the narrative that has been passed down for centuries, in these testimonies, Black people were not the consumers but the consumed, as Vincent Woodard recalls. Whether these acts of cannibalism did in fact take place is not necessarily important to the argument that, at any rate, both European and American whites developed a deeper and more insidious culture of cannibalism "wherein daily acts of violence, religious conversion, slave seasoning and breaking, and sexual brutality all fed into the master's appetite for African flesh and souls" (Woodard 31).

Cannibalistic folklore unquestionably relates to the dichotomies of self/other and subject/object, and additionally, as Harriet Goldberg points out, to the social distinction of we/they: "It says in effect: we do not indulge in this dreadful activity but others do" (114). The reason that one group denies the act of consuming human flesh but assumes other groups are perfectly capable of doing so, Goldberg argues, obeys a dehumanizing process through which "the other" is considered less than human and therefore inferior. Colonial stories about the cannibalism of Native Americans are abundant, even though there is no evidence to prove it. Spanish *conquistadores*, for example, used the narrative of the Aztecs' cannibalistic practices as a persuasive way to legitimize the Conquest (Goldberg 115), while colonizers in Africa did the same with respect to Black Africans, an accusation that was reinforced by constantly dismissing their cultures as underdeveloped in order to justify the superiority of white Europeans and their imperialistic campaigns.

In this regard, in many short stories, the magazines underline the treatment of Black cultures as primitive and uneducated by Eurocentric standards. Some of these writings introduce Black characters speaking in broken Spanish as a symptom of their inability to assimilate to European culture; other jokes make fun of African languages in an alliterative, made-up gibberish that is supposed to represent "Africanisms" to mock Black culture.[21] In the *Buen Humor* issue of November 28, 1928, for example, the section known as *Comedias Rápidas* or Quick Comedies contains a "tropical" play by Enrique Jardiel Poncela entitled "La abnegación de Domingo" [Domingo's Abnegation]. The action takes place on a colonial plantation where Domingo, a Black enslaved character, is portrayed as having a speech impediment as a result of which he cannot pronounce "Rs" and therefore pronounces words like "señor" [sir] as "señol" instead. A stage direction clarifies that the "r" sound is something that Black people, in general, cannot make, adding, "and if they can, they mustn't, because they are Black for a reason, and it is not good that they start doing the same things that whites do."[22] In addition, the plantation owner, after physically abusing Domingo, leaves the stage singing the following "tropical" (as per the original) song:

Pancha the girl
Was making *marrons glacés*
When a little Black boy arrived
And ate two or three of them.
Jamalunga tinunga, tolé,
Pinunga!
Jamalunga tinunga tolé,
Sotunga! (6)[23]

The treatment of Black people in the Spanish media as comic relief was not new and can be traced back to the theater of the Golden Age, where Black characters were depicted through a patronizing lens as both naive and dumb. The Cuban tradition of *comedia bufa* [buffa comedy], where Black people were mocked by whites wearing blackface, also seems to have had a direct influence on the Spanish blackface tradition, especially on the musical genre of *zarzuelas* [Spanish operettas] (García). Even given all the examples discussed above, however, the conflicting representation of Black identities in the Spanish media at the beginning of the twentieth century is not restricted to using these negrophobic images to counter the national humiliation of the lost colonies. To make matters worse, between the struggle caused by its attachment to its past colonial glory and its eagerness to become part of the global project of modernity, Spain witnesses in dismay how that yearned-for modernity starts materializing with the arrival of African American jazz artists who will introduce new rhythms that translate into novelty, speed, and progress. In the words of Eva Woods Peiró, "if these performers were modern, wherein lay Spanish modernity, and what did modernity mean?" (102).

The Modern Gaze

Over the first two decades of the twentieth century, many African American artists, some of whom had fought in World War I, relocated to Europe, seeking upward social mobility and leaving behind America's Jim Crow laws. Most scholarship on the influence of African American artists on the European scene at that time focuses on France, while the study of the relationships between Spain and African Americans has been scarce, as Rosalía Cornejo-Parriego reminds us (1). Yet, this Black migration also affected many major Spanish cities, where the seeds of jazz were being planted at the same time as in other European cities such as Paris, London, or Berlin

(Grooveman). The negrophobia expressed in earlier imagery gave way to a phenomenon of increasing passion for anything Black, as conveyed in the French term *négrophilie*, or negrophilia, love for Black culture, although the term had originated in the previous century with very derogatory connotations.[24] However, in the 1920s, negrophilia became synonymous with modernity, especially among the European bourgeoisie that longed to be regarded as modern and among avant-garde artists, who perceived Black culture as a paradoxical mixture of primitivism, exoticism, and novelty necessary to relieve the stress of modern life.

In Spain, avant-garde authors and artists quickly succumbed to the magnetic attraction of jazz culture, which they perceived as emblematic of "a dialectic relationship between primitivism and modernity" (Patrick 559).[25] Actually, some Black American rhythms had already become extremely popular in Spain in the nineteenth century and had been adopted in the Spanish *zarzuelas*. These African American rhythms usually traveled to Spain via Cuba, then still a colony of Spain, or via Paris and London (García 17). At the turn of the century, two other U.S. musical styles, the cakewalk and the foxtrot, gained notoriety in Spanish urban shows and celebrations.[26] In 1928, a new musical composition completely revolutionized Spain's artistic milieu: the Charleston. Between 1926 and 1928, many Spanish composers wrote songs that adopted this trendy rhythm, and they were performed by Spanish artists. This was the case, for example, for the 1928 hit "Madre, cómprame un negro" [Mother, Buy Me a Black Man]:

> So many Blacks have arrived
> To teach us how to dance the Charleston
> That all moms are in a tight spot
> To avoid frequenting the bazaar
> Where these chocolate samples
> Make the little ones cry out:
> Mother, buy me a Black man,
> Buy me a Black man at the bazaar! (Repeat)
> Who can dance the Charleston
> And play in a jazz band.[27]

Ángel Ortiz de Villalojos composed this popular song for Spanish performer Reyes Castizo, known as "La Yankee" because, although born in Seville, she joked about having been born in Cleveland, where her parents lived until they decided to move back to Spain when she was a child ("Reyes Castizo"). It premiered in 1928 at the Teatro Maravillas in Madrid; the same year, it was also part of the *Daddy-Doll* revue performed at the Olympia Theatre in Paris ("Madre, cómprame un negro"). As is evident from the lyrics by Alfonso Jofre and Mariano Bolaños, Black individuals are still seen as possessions at the service of the rest of the population and are destined to teach them how to dance the Charleston, while the comparison of their skin color to chocolate helps reinforce the objectification of Black bodies for cannibalistic consumption.

When examining *Buen Humor* or *Gutiérrez*, it is nearly impossible from 1920 onwards to find a single issue of either that does not contain a reference to jazz, while it is likewise hard not to notice three constant characteristics in most images. The first one is the perpetuation of the colonial portrayal of Black identities with animal features. Some of these examples are as conspicuous as the one presented in the image below (Figure 1.5), which shows Adam and Eve in Eden, both white and perfectly human, versus the jazz performers seen as monkeys in the background, and therefore, less evolved—to the point of being dehumanized—than the white characters. There is no doubt that the cartoon refers to African American jazz musicians since the image is embedded in a story about the origins of "EL CHARLESTON."

The second feature is the persistence of the narrative of Black people as savages and of their cultures as uncivilized. Even though jazz was an essential component of the new modern life, it was stigmatized as a wild and primitive type of music. In the following cartoon by Francisco López Rubio—brother of José López Rubio, the humorist writer—(Figure 1.6), the joke is based on the idea that dancing the Charleston is simply an exercise of manic jumping without any coordination. The caption that accompanies the vignette reads: "Very new and efficient procedure used by a professor in New York to teach 'the Charleston' and similar rhythms," while the image shows a platform built over a furnace, on which some people jump frantically, presumably because their feet are being burned by the flames rising from below.[28] Their agonizing jumps are equated to the dancing typical of the Charleston, thus creating a comparison between the new dance and torture and between its moves and those born out of a primal instinct.

As Petrine Archer-Straw argues, in Paris, jazz had garnered several nicknames which associated the musical genre with diseases, such as "l'epidémie," [the epidemic] "le virus noir," [the Black virus], or "la rage" [rage]. Some music critics, like André Levinson, complained that jazz contained "a pathological trait originating from more primitive societies, and as such, it was 'contagious'" (qtd. in Archer-Straw 113–14). The influence of African American artists and their proliferation in European cities, therefore, was observed with ambivalent feelings of both admiration and fear, as well as eliciting a dichotomy between primitivism and progress, which is evident in the vignette below that appeared in *Gutiérrez* (Figure 1.7). The scene shows a village crowded with disparate Black characters, some of whom are depicted as possessing traits typical of a colonialist view of

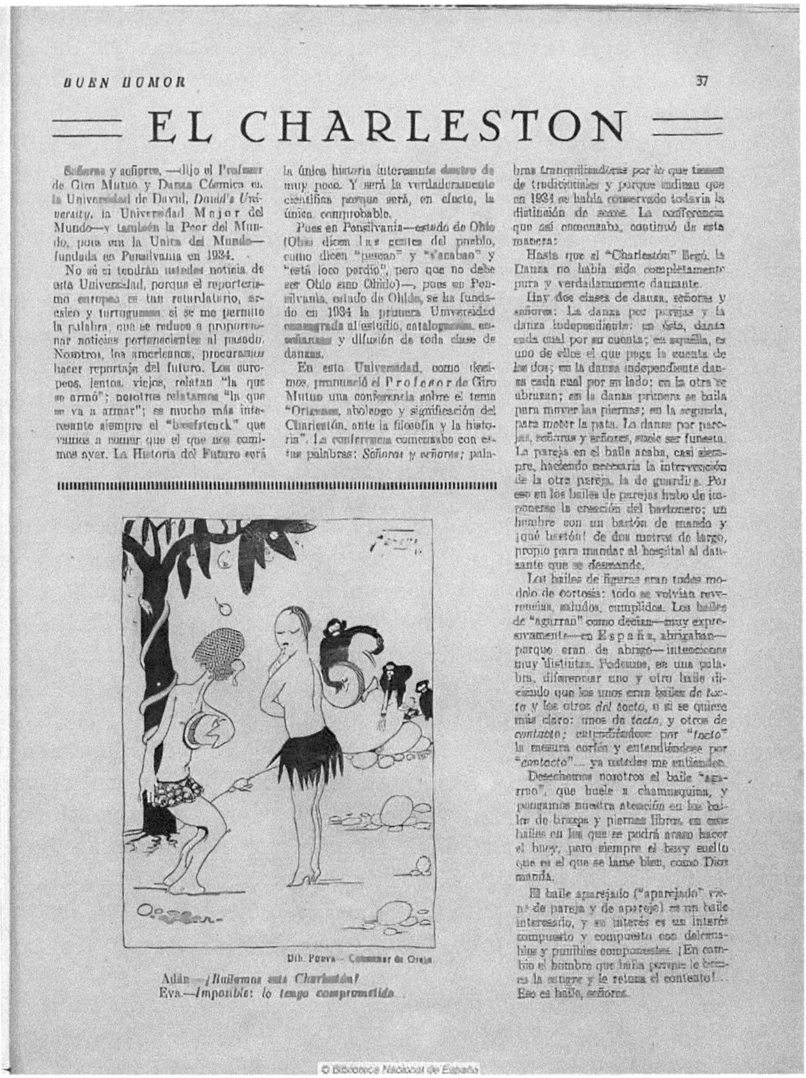

BUEN HUMOR 37

EL CHARLESTON

Adán.—*¡Bailemos ese Charlestón!*
Eva.—*Imposible: lo tengo comprometido*...

Figure 1.5 Cartoon in *Buen Humor*, 26 December 1926. Courtesy of *BNE*.

the Black African, while others are engaged in activities that better align with the modernized version of the new Black American, such as boxing or playing in a jazz band. The caption reads, "The looks of a brutish village after the success of Black people all over the world."[29] In the middle of the right side, under a palm tree, a poster signals: "Calle de Josefina Baker" [Josephine Baker Street].

From Negrophilia to Necropolitics 37

Novísimo y eficaz procedimiento que un profesor de Nueva York utiliza para enseñar a bailar el "charleston" y otros similares.

Figure 1.6 Cartoon in *Gutiérrez*, 9 July 1927. Courtesy of *BNE*.

Although Baker did not perform in Spain until her debut in Madrid in 1930 (Prescott and Cornejo-Parriego 73), when she arrived in Paris in 1925, her international fame had preceded her, as is obvious in this cartoon from 1928.

38 *Ana León-Távora*

Figure 1.7 Vignette from *Gutiérrez*, 14 April 1928. Courtesy of *BNE*.

Finally, the last feature the reader can clearly perceive in these images is the use of blackface, the practice of white people applying black paint and exaggerated red lipstick to mock Black people, a custom that is still prevalent in contemporary Spanish culture and which is visible in the lower left

From Negrophilia to Necropolitics 39

corner of the image above, showing a Black character covering a white character in black paint. But blackface also involves a type of caricature known as "darky" iconography, in which Black people are depicted with exaggerated googly eyes, prominent white or red lips, and ink-like black skin, as seen in the members of the jazz band in Figure 1.8.[30]

Figure 1.8 Cover of *Buen Humor*, 6 February 1927. Courtesy of *BNE*.

The "darky" iconography arose as part of the American Reconstruction towards the last decades of the nineteenth century, when the inferiority of Black people was accepted as an established fact. This was reflected both in commercial products and in the media, such as in the popular cartoon series by Thomas Worth known as *Darktown Comics*, produced between 1880 and 1890. They often depicted Black characters as ignorant victims of their own stupidity, according to J. Michael Martinez (197). One of the most popular of these characters was Little Black Sambo, originally designed by Scottish author Helen Bannerman, who named the character, a little boy of mixed race, after the Spanish and Portuguese word *zambo*, a person of mixed Native American and African heritage (Martinez 199). William Marriner reinvented this character between 1904 and 1914 in a version that would settle the characteristic features of the pickaninny child, rendered with "bulbous eyes, protruding lips, [a] tortured dialect, and [a] seeming inability to reason his way out of the simplest, and most inane situations" (Martinez 200). The same "darky" iconography became ubiquitous all over Europe in the 1920s and 1930s. Strongly associated with Art Deco, it was used profusely by many avant-garde artists.

In fact, on 26 January 1929, at the second cultural gathering of *Cineclub Español*, founded by author Ernesto Giménez Caballero in 1928 and headed initially by film director Luis Buñuel, Ramón, who was invited to deliver the opening remarks before the showing of an American film, showed up in blackface to read a fragment of his piece titled "Jazzbandismo." As Evelyn Scaramella reflects, "This image highlights the problematic nature of avant-garde experimentation with jazz, and the way in which, for many writers, an interest in black culture soon bordered on racist misappropriations" (24). Certainly, the problematic nature of this supposedly benevolent negrophilia resides in the fact that the love and appreciation of Black culture are rooted in its misappropriation and the distortion of Black bodies through stereotypical narratives inherited from traditions, fueled by the influence of American media. Ramón's use of blackface on this occasion, therefore, grew out of a long tradition of mocking Black bodies that was further emphasized here by the film he was introducing, *The Jazz Singer* (1927). In the film directed by Alan Crosland, a young white Jewish man played by actor Al Jolson decides to confront his family with his wish to pursue his dream. This dream is no other than to become a famous jazz singer, which he achieves by performing in blackface, as the film poster already suggests to its audience. Not surprisingly, the adaptation to silent film of Alberto Insúa's novel, *El negro que tenía el alma blanca* [The Black Man with a White Soul], takes place the same year. Directed by Benito Perojo, the film was a collaboration between Spain and France, originally titled *Le Danseur de Jazz* [The Jazz Dancer]. The role of the protagonist, a Black Cuban character, was played by a white

Argentinian actor in blackface, in imitation of the American film. Though Insúa's novel was originally published in 1922, its 1927 film adaptation made it popular, which is probably the reason why almost every single issue of *Gutiérrez* from that year advertises the book (Figure 1.9).[31]

Figure 1.9 Issue of *Gutiérrez* from 1927. Courtesy of *BNE*.

In the film version, the protagonist, born Pedro Valdés in Cuba but having adopted the more cosmopolitan stage name of Peter Wald, is an internationally acclaimed dancer known as "le Roi du Charleston" [the King of the Charleston]. His name surfaces often in the news, sometimes with descriptions of him as "a virtuoso of this form of rhythmic epilepsy called the Charleston."[32] The description underlines the idea of jazz as a type of music closer to a spastic disease, as previously discussed. The film relies on a flashback through which the audience discovers Peter (Pedro)'s hardships in Cuba, where he was the servant of a white family that he had to escape after a racist confrontation with the family's young son. After his talents as a dancer are discovered in Europe and he performs in big cities like Paris and New York, the plot gains momentum when, hired to dance in Madrid, Peter meets and falls in love with Emma, his white dance partner. Emma, however, cannot see past Peter's skin color, which both repulses and frightens her in equal measure. No matter how famous Peter becomes, he still suffers from the anxiety of Blackness caused by the white woman's rejection because, in line with the thoughts of Fanon, being loved by a white woman opens the door to becoming part of white culture. Emma's rejection leads to Peter's moment of "sociogenesis," when he faces his positioning as a Black person in a world of white people: "From the moment the black man accepts the split imposed by the Europeans, there is no longer any respite" (Fanon 63).

One of the most emblematic scenes in the movie is the one when Emma falls asleep and has a nightmare about Peter. From the opening of the film, the audience sees several shots of Emma's bedroom, including a poster mounted above her bed advertising a popular brand of tobacco rolling paper, Bambú, marketed since the beginning of the century. In fact, a similar advertising image was carried in multiple issues of *Buen Humor* (Figure 1.10). In Emma's nightmare, where she is overwhelmed by revulsion for Peter, the image metamorphoses into an eerie laughing visage evocative of blackface. The man on the poster seems to be laughing at Emma through a broad smile featuring extraordinarily white teeth that contrast with his exaggerated dark skin.

Suddenly, still in Emma's nightmare, a Black African man in tribal attire materializes in her bedroom, kidnaps her, and carries her off to the jungle, where she is placed in front of an African tribe led by Peter. The irony rests on the fact that the leader of the Black Africans in this scene is precisely the only role that is not performed by a real Black actor. In addition, the scene when Emma is kidnapped and faints in the arms of her kidnapper bears an extraordinary resemblance to a print published in the Paris humor magazine *Le Rire* of April 18, 1896. Titled *Comme un succube, l'Afrique pèse sur le repos de l'Europe* [Like a Succubus, Africa Weighs on the Repose of Europe], it parodies an original painting by Henri Fuseli titled

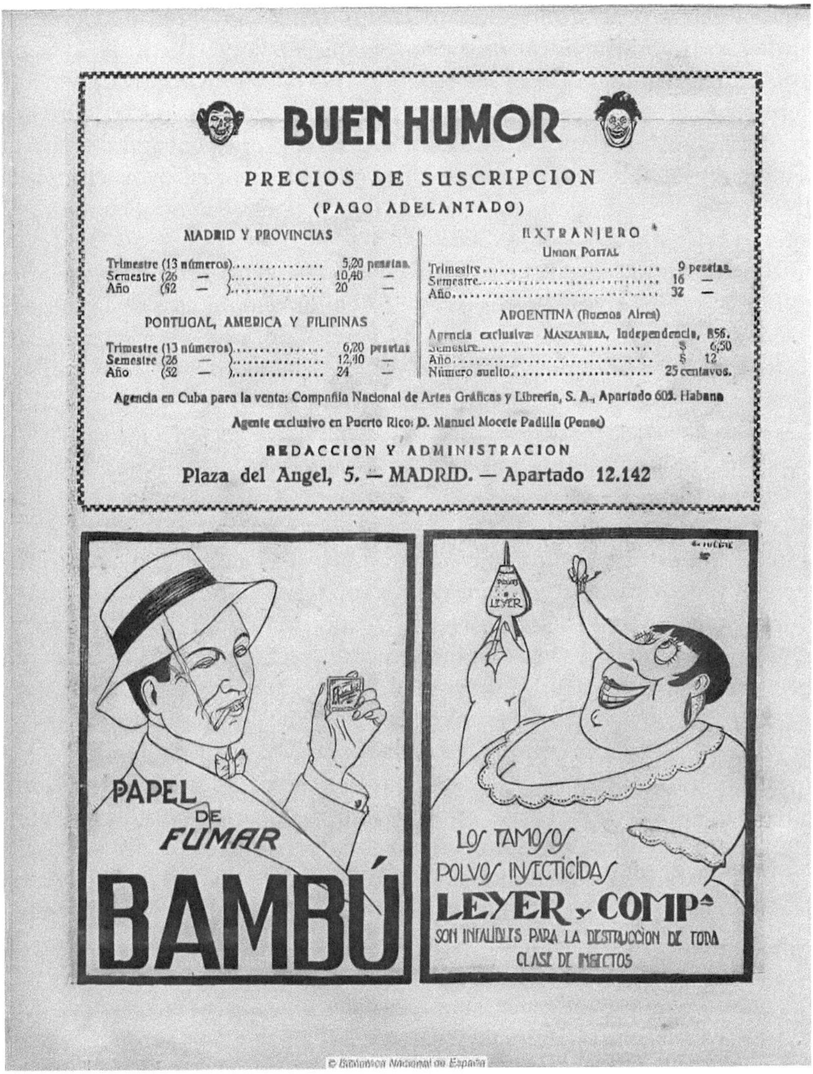

Figure 1.10 Advertisements in *Buen Humor* from 1927. Courtesy of BNE.

Le Cauchemar [The Nightmare], which depicts an incubus or male demon lying on top of a dreaming woman. In the Paris parody, Africa is represented by a succubus instead of an incubus that threatens Europe's sleep. Although Europe is still personified as a damsel, the succubus is a female demon, probably a colonialist interpretation of the colonized territories as feminine and, therefore, weak by comparison to the masculinity of the imperialistic power, in addition to constituting a financial and political burden to the independent European young woman lying in bed. In the film, Emma embodies the crude reality of European negrophilia, which is merely a form of negrophobia in disguise: negrophilia is not genuine love for anything Black but rather love for the misappropriated and dissociated Black cultural elements as filtered through and narrated by a white lens. This, in the film, translates into loving Peter's talents, but not Peter himself, because he is still inexorably Black.

To mark the success of both the book and the film, *Gutiérrez* published a short story by Miguel Santos titled "La conmovedora vida de los negros. Peter Wal" [The Moving Life of Blacks. Peter Wal], which appeared on August 11, 1928. The supposedly funny story, which does not even spell the name of the protagonist correctly, abounds in racist, colonial descriptions that blur African Americans with primitive stereotypes of Black Africans, including the notion of the need to cleanse the race, the cannibalistic accusations, the mockery of gibberish mimicking African languages, and the use of blackface.

In all the stories about Peter Wald, be it Insúa's novel, the film, or this parody, the protagonists endure the necropolitics of a system that refuses to accept them, according to Mbembe's concept. In both the novel and the film, Peter's death is twofold: a literal death, because he falls lovesick and dies in the end, but also a social one. As Mbembe explains, not belonging to a system that, while seeming to uplift him, still makes it clear that he possesses a liminal identity, he must remain at the margins, or simply must die. In the version disseminated in *Gutiérrez*, the story ends with a letter in which Peter's friend informs him that he has murdered Peter's parents. After this news, according to the narrator, "Peter Wal se quedó blanco" (9), a pun on the idiomatic expression meaning that "he became livid," but also the literal idea of turning white. As absurd as the ending sounds, it seems to solve all the character's problems; even as a joke, the pun on whiteness perfectly captures Fanon's pessimistic axiom, "there is but one destiny for the black man. And it is white" (xiv). Although Peter was raised by whites and achieved success, he remains perceived as the Other. Only by transmuting to whiteness will he be integrated into the system, either by dying and thus leaving behind his dark complexion and exposing his soul—which is white, according to the title—or, as the magazine version suggests, by becoming white in a literal, albeit surreal, manner.

As seen in the examples above, although *Buen Humor* and *Gutiérrez* were originally founded with the aim of propagating an intellectual type of humor that nurtured a modern vision of reality from a subversive, absurd angle, in accordance with the form of humor prevalent in modern Europe at the time, it is evident from these types of cartoons and jokes that Spanish humor still suffered from the vestiges of a satirical view based on the mockery and dehumanization of the subject. As Archer-Straw points out when examining this European tradition of mocking Black bodies, "It was only by presenting them as different and exotic, by showing them as slaves, servants, entertainers and humorous characters related to animals, that their racial inferiority could be communicated" (38). Clearly, by laughing at the stereotyped Black bodies, the Black identities are ridiculed and projected as inferior. The "absurd humor" that promised to become a revolution rooted in the principle of incongruence, in that sense, still suffers from the vestiges of a sense of humor based on the Superiority gaze, which mocks and laughs at those whom it intends to humiliate. The humorous avant-garde publications, in effect, still exhibit signs of a residual colonialist complex: by emphasizing the inferiority of previously colonized people, Spain seeks to diminish the importance of having lost its territorial possessions. At the same time, the idealization of an abstract concept of aesthetics completely detached from political debate, first proposed by Ortega y Gasset and supported in the form of the new "humorismo" by Ramón and his disciples, seems, in this case, far from attainable. It is clear through these examples that, in modern Spain, just as in other modern European countries, the reception of Black culture is impaired by the twofold misrepresentation of Black people from a colonial perspective, on one hand, and from the construct of negrophilia, on the other. While the negrophilia of the 1920s and 1930s in Europe creates the illusion of an appreciation for Black culture, the cartoons, short stories, advertisements, and films discussed here prove that negrophilia ultimately gives rise to the construction of a necropolitical system where Black identities are treated as peripheral commodities of modernity but never as authentic agents within it.

Notes

1 "Una actitud frente a la vida." All translations are my own unless otherwise indicated.
2 For a comprehensive list of all the authors and artists who were included in this generation and contributed to the humorous journals, see José Luis R. de la Flor (44).
3 Tristan Tzara's "Dada Manifesto" is a perfect illustration of pure absurdity and reconciliation of opposites: "I am neither for nor against and I do not explain because I hate common sense" (4).
4 This essay will rely on Frantz Fanon's interpretation of "negrophobia." Defined as a socio diagnostic phenomenon, it describes the hatred and fear of Black people and culture by whites, as well as the internalized racism or "neurosis" that leads to a "Black negrophobia," by which Black people end up hating other Black people and Black culture as a reflection of the trauma caused by the constant identification of Blackness with everything evil in society (Fanon 42–43; 51–61).
5 "La teoría del humor ramoniano se centra en el desplome de la unicidad de lo real representado por las vanguardias. El humor era el disolvente eficaz y

rápido para descomponer los sistemas lógicos y reintegrarlos a la corriente descerebrada y anárquica de la vida."
6 "montajes fotográficos y las técnicas de inversión de lo real, todavía hoy desarrolladas y perfeccionadas en las revistas y suplementos actuales humorísticos."
7 As R. de la Flor argues, the experimental spirit of the new humorist journals found strong intellectual support in the aesthetic theories on the new artistic trends developed by Ortega y Gasset in *The Dehumanization of Art* (34).
8 "el enloquecer de locura o el mediocrizarse de cordura."
9 In fact, although both journals made a conscientious effort to steer clear of political controversy, *Gutiérrez* was sanctioned and suspended for a month in the summer of 1927 due to the publication of a poem that alluded to the Dictator, written by a spontaneous contributor to the magazine (Gérard et al. 191).
10 "*no tan humanos como el hombre blanco.*" By 1775, German anthropologist Johann Friedrich Blumenbach had already promulgated his *norma verticalis*, by which he assigned physical differentiations to different races, and had started using the term "Caucasian" to refer to white people (Painter 72–74).
11 "un *orden social demencial*—el esclavismo o el imperialismo burgués decimonónico."
12 "*misión civilizadora de las razas superiores* sobre sus parientes biológicamente subdesarrollados."
13 A photographic exhibition at the Museo Nacional de Antropología in Madrid in 2017 offered images of the celebration of the 1887 human zoo. In an interview for *La Vanguardia* with journalist María Sanz, Fernando Godoy, curator of the show, explains that these human exhibitions helped Spain, which had already lost most of its colonies, maintain a balance with other European imperialist powers, such as Great Britain, which initiated the practice of human exhibits during the celebration of the 1851 Great Exhibition (Sanz).
14 In his analysis of the play The Prodigy of Ethiopia [*El prodigio de Etiopía*], Fra-Molinero mentions several works written between the sixteenth and the seventeenth centuries in Spain, France, and England, in which Black people are equated to animals, specifically to apes, emphasizing lust as their most outstanding animal feature.
15 "El nuevo 'as' cinematográfico, Richard Orang Ghutang, que aspira a ocupar el puesto de Rodolfo Valentino."
16 "[tiene] las manos sucias."
17 Fanon uses the concept of phobogenesis, derived from psychiatry and psychoanalysis, by which a thing or a person, the "phobic object," generates an exaggerated feeling of threat in a subject. To Fanon, the Black person is regarded as a catalyst of anxiety and fear by white people.
18 Many of these old anti-Black racist ads can be found on multiple online websites, including the blog of Xavier Sierra i Valentí.
19 The accusations of anthropophagy among Black people had started to spread widely after 1883, when the *Sociedad Española de Africanistas y Colonialistas* [Spanish Association of Africanists and Colonialists] sponsored a series of expeditions to the African colonies of Equatorial Guinea and the Spanish Sahara territories with the intention of competing with the anthropological advances of other European nations. In 1886, Spanish doctor Amado Ossorio, who participated in these expeditions, published some notes, presumably of strong "scientific rigor" in the naturalist journal *Anales de la SEHN* (Spanish Society of Natural History), in which he described the Guinean Bubi ethnic group as tremendously evil and cannibalistic, arguing that their anthropophagy obeyed "the satisfaction of the thirst for revenge that is so customary amongst Blacks"

[una satisfacción de la venganza a que son tan aficionados los negros] (Sánchez Arteaga, "Antropología" 152).
20 –"¿Qué mujeres te gustan más? ¿Las americanas o las inglesas?" –"… lo mismo me da con tal de que me las sirvan con patatas." Even though not overtly sexual, the joke around the attractiveness of the women and their literal consumption stands out as an exception in the journals. Although there exists a long tradition within Spanish culture to hypersexualize Black people, especially Black women, who are eroticized and described as voluptuous and sensual (Romero-Díaz 96), the humorous journals are for the most part free of any sexual innuendos, probably due to censorship during the dictatorship of Primo de Rivera.
21 Once again, this is not a very original way to mock Black Africans since it was common in the theater of the Golden Age to use this type of nonsensical language, known as "Black speech" or also "Afro-Hispanic speech" as comic relief (Otele 63; Fra-Molinero 22–23). As Olivette Otele points out, apart from the comical intention, this reminded the audience "that these characters were outsiders who could not speak the [Spanish] language fluently" (63).
22 "y si pueden no deben hacerlo, porque para algo son negros y no es cosa que hagan las mismas cosas que los blancos." Nicholas R. Jones, on the other hand, successfully demonstrates that in many Golden Age texts, the misappropriation of Black African speech by white authors could be read instead as an instrument to provide Black characters with agency to use their voices as "viable discourses" that serve to consolidate the presence and resistance of the African diaspora in Spain (4–6). The same perspective, however, does not apply to Jardiel Poncela's short story, given the different historical context and the author's evident ridiculing objective.
23 "Estaba la niña Pancha / haciendo *marrón glacé* / y entonces llegó un negrito / y se comió dos o tres. Jamalunga tinunga, tolé / ¡pinunga! / Jamalunga tinunga, tolé / ¡sotunga!"
24 The term was used pejoratively in the nineteenth century. To be called a negrophiliac, or "n***** lover," was an insult that denoted being a supporter of the abolition of slavery and, in certain cases, having a sexual appetite for Black people (Archer-Straw 9).
25 "una relación dialéctica entre primitivismo y modernidad."
26 The cakewalk became so popular that numerous commercial brands adopted the name of the music style to sell their products; for example, it became the name of a perfume and the name of a brand of rolling paper. Its popularity went even further: Spanish *matador* Gallito allegedly adopted some cakewalk dancing moves during one of his bullfighting routines, and the dance also appeared in the first act of playwright Jacinto Benavente's comedy *Al natural* (1904) (García 20).
27 "Son tantos negros los que han venido / para enseñarnos el charlestón / que las mamás se ven morás / para evitar ir al bazar / donde esas muestras de chocolate / a los pequeños hacen exclamar: / ¡Madre, cómprame un negro, / cómprame un negro en el bazar! (bis) / Que baile el charlestón / y que toque el jazz-band" (qtd. in Grooveman)."
28 "Novísimo y eficiente procedimiento que un profesor en Nueva York utiliza para enseñar a bailar el 'charlestón' y otros similares."
29 "Aspecto de una aldea cafre después del éxito de los negros en todo el mundo."
30 Numerous Spanish activists and online platforms, such as the online journal *Afroféminas*, authors like Desirée Bela-Lobedde, Lucía Asué Mbomío Rubio, and Moha Gerehou, social media accounts like *SOS Racismo Madrid*,

and artists and public figures like Silvia Albert Sopale, Asaari Bibang Ngui, and Lamine Thior, among many others, have repeatedly condemned Spanish traditions that continue to make use of blackface, like the *Reyes Magos* (the three Magi), the "Negra Tomasa" figure in the Canary Islands, the "Negro de Baynoles" in Catalonia, and more recently, the characterization of white celebrities as Black artists to participate in the TV show *Tu cara me suena*.
31 There was a second film adaptation, this time with sound, in 1934.
32 "un grand virtuose de cette forme d'épilepsie rhytmée appelée le Charleston."

Works Cited

Archer-Straw, Petrine. *Negrophilia. Avant-Garde Paris and Black Culture in the 1920s*. Thames & Hudson, 2000.
Bergson, Henri. *Laughter. An Essay on the Meaning of the Comic*. Manor, 2008.
"Comme un succube, l'Afrique pèse sur le repos de l'Europe." *Le Rire*, 18 Apr. 1896, no. 76.
Cornejo-Parriego, Rosalía. "African Americans and Spaniards. 'Caught in an Inescapable Network of Mutuality.'" *Black USA and Spain: Shared Memories in the 20th Century*, edited by Rosalía Cornejo-Parriego. Routledge, 2020, pp. 1–20.
"El negro que tenía el alma blanca/Le Danseur de Jazz. (1927). B. Perojo." *YouTube*, uploaded by PELICULAS MUDAS/Silent Cinema, 22 Oct. 2017, www.youtube.com/watch?v=zTVZykFE5bw.
Fanon, Frantz. *Black Skin, White Masks*. Grove Press, 2008.
Fra-Molinero, Baltasar. *La imagen de los negros en el teatro del Siglo de Oro*. Siglo XXI, 1995.
Freud, Sigmund, and James Strachey. *Jokes and Their Relation to the Unconscious*. Norton, 1989.
Fuseli, Henri. *The Nightmare (Le Cauchemar), 1781*. Detroit Institute of Arts, https://dia.org/collection/nightmare-45573.
García, Jorge. "El trazo del jazz en España." *El ruido alegre: Jazz en la BNE*. Biblioteca Nacional de España, 2012, pp. 17–71, https://www.bne.es/export/sites/BNWEB1/es/Micrositios/Exposiciones/Jazz/resources/img/estudio1.pdf. Accessed 24 July 2023.
García López, Ricardo (K-Hito), ed. *Gutiérrez*. Hemeroteca Digital. Biblioteca Nacional de España. hemerotecadigital.bne.es/hd/es/card?sid=5308186. Accessed 16 Apr. 2023.
Gérard, Mathieu, et al. "Prensa y censura en España durante la dictadura de Primo de Rivera (1923–1930). El ejemplo de la reacción del periódico *El Sol* al golpe de estado." *Ab Initio*, vol. 7, no. 13, 2019, pp. 181–98.
Goldberg, Harriett. "Cannibalism in Iberian Narrative: The Dark Side of Gastronomy." *Bulletin of Hispanic Studies*, vol. 74, no. 1, 1997, pp. 107–22.
Gómez de la Serna, Ramón. *Ismos*. Poseidón, 1943.
Goode, Joshua. *Impurity of Blood. Defining Race in Spain, 1870–1930*. Louisiana State UP, 2009.
Grooveman, Manu. *La música es mi amante*. http://lamusicaesmiamante.blogspot.com/?m=1. Accessed 21 July 2023.
Insúa, Alberto. *El negro que tenía el alma blanca*. Castalia, 1998.

Jardiel Poncela, Enrique. "La abnegación de Domingo." *Buen humor*, Hemeroteca Digital. Biblioteca Nacional de España, no. 261, 1926, pp. 6–7. https://hemerotecadigital.bne.es/hd/es/viewer?id=1c566859-445f-45e2-9352-c2eb86209b97&page=6. Accessed 16 Apr. 2023.

Jones, Nicholas R. *Staging* Habla de Negros: *Radical Performances of the African Diaspora in Early Modern Spain*. Pennsylvania State UP, 2019.

"Madre, cómprame un negro." *El quicio de la Mancebía [EQM]*, 18 Aug. 2010, https://elquiciodelamancebia.wordpress.com/2010/08/18/madre-comprame-negro-1929/. Accessed 16 Apr. 2023.

Martinez, J. Michael. *A Long Dark Night. Race in America from Jim Crow to World War II*. Rowman & Littlefield, 2016.

Mbembe, Achille. *Necropolitics*. Duke UP, 2019.

Morreall, John. *Comic Relief. A Comprehensive Philosophy of Humor*. Wiley-Blackwell, 2009.

Ortega y Gasset, José. *The Dehumanization of Art and Other Essays on Art, Culture, and Literature*. Princeton UP, 1968.

Otele, Olivette. *African Europeans. An Untold History*. Basic Books, 2021.

Painter, Neil Irving. *The History of White People*. W.W. Norton & Company, 2010.

Patrick, Brian D. "Presencia y función del jazz en la narrativa de vanguardia." *Hispania*, vol. 91, no. 3, 2008, pp. 558–68.

Prescott, Laurence E., and Rosalía Cornejo-Parriego. "Josephine Baker in Spain: The Ambivalent Reception of an African American Female Superstar." *Black USA and Spain: Shared Memories in the 20th Century*, edited by Rosalía Cornejo-Parriego. Routledge, 2020, pp. 73–94.

R. de la Flor, José Luis. *El negociado de incobrables: la vanguardia del humor español en los años veinte*. Ediciones de la Torre, 1990.

"Reyes Castizo." *Real Academia de la Historia*, https://dbe.rah.es/biografias/114717/reyes-castizo. Accessed 23 July 2023.

Romero-Díaz, Nieves. "La sexualidad masculina y negra a debate en la España de la temprana modernidad." *Romance Notes*, vol. 58, no. 1, 2018, pp. 95–104.

Sánchez Arteaga, Juan Manuel. "La antropología física y los 'zoológicos humanos': exhibiciones de indígenas como práctica de popularización científica en el umbral del siglo XX." *Asclepio*, vol. 62, no. 1, 2010, pp. 269–92.

———. "La racionalidad delirante: el racismo científico en la segunda mitad del siglo XXI." *Revista de la Asociación Española de Neuropsiquiatría*, vol. 27, no. 2, 2007, pp. 1–11.

Santos, Miguel. "La conmovedora historia de los negros. Peter Wal." *Gutiérrez*, Hemeroteca Digital. Biblioteca Nacional de España, 1928, pp. 8–9. https://hemerotecadigital.bne.es/hd/es/viewer?id=b07f7cdf-1434-4975-ade1-e29c2e29c8b7. Accessed 16 Apr. 2023.

Sanz, María. "Macabro testimonio en fotos de los 'zoos humanos' de Madrid llega a Paraguay." *La Vanguardia*, 3 May 2015, www.lavanguardia.com/cultura/20150503/54430373371/macabro-testimonio-en-fotos-de-los-zoos-humanos-de-madrid-llega-a-paraguay.html. Accessed 16 Apr. 2023.

Scaramella, Evelyn. "Reading the Harlem Renaissance in Spanish: Translation, African American Culture, and the Spanish Avant-Garde." *Black USA and Spain:*

Shared Memories in the 20th Century, edited by Rosalía Cornejo-Parriego. Routledge, 2020, pp. 23–51.

Sierra i Valentí, Xavier. "Anuncios de jabón racistas." *Un dermatólogo en el museo*, 16 Feb. 2021, http://xsierrav.blogspot.com/2021/02/anuncios-de-jabon-racistas.html. Accessed 16 Apr. 2023.

The Jazz Singer. Directed by Alan Cosland. Warner Bros Pictures, 1927.

Tzara, Tristan. "Dada Manifesto." *Seven Dada Manifestos and Lampisteries*. Translated by Barbara Wright. Alma Books, 2018.

Villahermosa y Borao, Pedro Antonio (Sileno), ed. *Buen humor*. Hemeroteca Digital. Biblioteca Nacional de España. https://hemerotecadigital.bne.es/hd/es/card?sid=4729514. Accessed 16 Apr. 2023.

Woodard, Vincent. *The Delectable Negro. Human Consumption and Homoeroticism within US Slave Culture*. NYU Press, 2014.

Woods Peiró, Eva. *White Gypsies. Race and Stardom in Spanish Musicals*. U of Minnesota P, 2012.

2 The Transnational Afropessimism of Francisco Zamora Loboch

Baltasar Fra-Molinero

We need to begin with a tautology. The ontology of the transnational is central to the discussion of being Black. The Spanish term *negro* started to be used transnationally in relation to the forcible movement of African people away from the continent through the slave trade since the fifteenth century. The physical ties to Africa were severed but not the symbolic ones. Music, religion, language, and social structures survived and were transformed. However, this is not the model of transnational experience we focus on in this essay, although the two are interrelated. Transnational refers to migration, a form of human population movement across (regional and/or national) geographic borders that includes the preservation of deep ties to the place of origin. Communication and transportation systems in the twenty-first century have created dual and transnational identities, in which place of residence and place of origin challenge the concept of the self (Pries 9–10). The transnational individual produces symbolic systems such as literature, music, religious expression, political activism, and material culture that can be shared in a globalized world. The problem for Black transnationals, however, is that their existence as humans is perceived as dangerous by non-Blacks. The assumption is that being Black means being from somewhere else. That "somewhere else" is (understood as) the former territories of conquest and colonization. This is an imaginary of death.

Like the other members who comprised the first generation of Equatorial Guinean writers, Francisco Zamora Loboch (b. 1948) is a transnational figure. In his texts location, place of enunciation, and subject matter are defined by movement across national borders. This essay is an attempt to examine his works through the lens of Afropessimism, the philosophical practice that posits that, based on the experience gained over at least the last five hundred years, "Blacks are not Human subjects, but are instead structural inert props, implements for the execution of White and non-Black fantasies and sadomasochistic pleasures" (Wilderson, *Afropessimism* 15).[1] Afropessimism, as Frank B. Wilderson III

DOI: 10.4324/9781003435051-3

explains, is not a religion or an ideology, but rather, a lens through which to analyze the historical violence perpetrated against Black people, a practice that non-Blacks need to undertake (*Afropessimism* 40). Zamora Loboch explores the perilous survival of the Black subject and the concept of Afropessimism in his essays, poetry, and fictional narrative. While his two volumes of poetry—*Memoria de laberintos* (1999) and *Desde el Viyil y otras crónicas* (2008)—constitute an exercise in Black counter-gaze, in his three novels—*Conspiración en el green (El informe Abayak)* (2009), *El caimán de Kaduna* (2012), and *La república fantástica de Annobón* (2017)—the Black subject's humanity is negated systematically. Zamora Loboch's Black characters are the embodiment of ironic situations that serve as his sardonic allegations against racism, which he had already initiated in his book-length essay *Cómo ser negro y no morir en Aravaca. Manual de recetas contra el racismo* (1994). This paper explores the transnational Afropessimism of Zamora Loboch's narrative works and seeks to discern how they present survival strategies, a way to name slavery and colonialism, as well as a space for memory.

A Manual of Cultural Survival

Equatorial Guinean writers of the first postcolonial period had to wrestle with colonial subjectivity and the trauma of the Francisco Macías Nguema dictatorship (1969–1979) that had either expelled them from their own homeland or not allowed them to return (Brancato, "Afro-European Literature(s)" 10).[2] Paradoxically, Equatorial Guinean writing arose in the transnational experience of exile and migration. This writing emerged in Spain, the former metropolis, amid an unequal cultural exchange (Sampedro Vizcaya 202).

Zamora Loboch's biography reflects the instability of being Black in the world. He was studying in Spain when Equatorial Guinea obtained its independence in 1968. Over the course of a few months, he transitioned from being a Spanish citizen to an Equatorial Guinean national with dual citizenship to having to choose between being a Spanish national or becoming a stateless person.[3] The 1969 failed coup against President Francisco Macías Nguema had dramatic consequences for Equatorial Guineans living abroad. They had to either beat a hasty return to a country now ruled by a dictator or become exiles in a nation ruled by another dictator, General Francisco Franco. In fact, prominent figures in Franco's government bore responsibility for the political crisis in Equatorial Guinea long before its independence (Mba Ncony 206). In addition, the isolation of exiled Equatorial Guineans in Spain was so extreme that one of the few means they had to keep informed about their relatives at home was through the regular lists of the deceased compiled by the Red Cross (Aixelà Cabré 14; 26).

Zamora Loboch recalls these events in his essay "En septiembre de 1969 Madrid no era ninguna fiesta:"

> "Stateless." The word jumped off the pages of María Moliner's *Dictionary* on a hot summer morning in 1971. It spread like wildfire through boarding houses, cheap residence hotels, university college dorms, flats, and wherever those Equatorial Guineans at one time called to rule over the future of their country resided ... "Exiled and stateless." With one hand in front of them and one behind. Without papers, without a fucking cent, without a country. To be an Equatorial Guinean student in Spain in the seventies became an odyssey, an adventure only suitable for strong stomachs. Nothing but pure natural selection. (453–54)[4]

After graduating with a degree in journalism, Zamora Loboch embarked on his career in the midst of a double contradiction. In 1971, the Franco regime had declared all news related to Equatorial Guinea *materia reservada*, a forbidden subject ("Guinea Ecuatorial"). As an exile, Zamora Loboch could only write within the limits that Franco's censorship permitted. Furthermore, he could not publish anything related to current events in his country of birth. This lasted until 1977, when the Spanish government, by then a democracy, lifted the news embargo almost as an afterthought.

Together with Donato Ndongo Bidyogo, Zamora Loboch became one of the creators of the Equatorial Guinean literary canon. Their efforts to publish in 1977 a volume of four short stories, *Nueva narrativa guineana*, was a harbinger of Equatorial Guinean literature as a postcolonial phenomenon, still marked by its transnationality to this day. Three of the short stories develop a transnational theme (slavery and postcolonial migration), and all four attest to what Jared Sexton refers to as that "Black life [which] is not lived in the world that the world lives in, but it is lived underground, in outer space" ("The Social Life" 28). In his first published essay, *Cómo ser negro y no morir en Aravaca* (1994), Zamora Loboch dissected the problem: to be Black in Spain is to be slated for death. Blacks in Spain are permanent aliens in the dominant white imaginary. *Cómo ser negro* becomes then a counter-textbook, a tool to analyze how Spain sees itself as white.

Aravaca, a town on the outskirts of Madrid, made the news at the end of 1992, the iconic year of the Olympic Games in Barcelona, the World Expo in Seville, and above all, the celebration of the Quincentennial of Columbus's "discovery" of the American continent. But the news in Aravaca was far from the celebratory cultural effervescence of the moment. There, on November 13, a civil guard and three male minors murdered Lucrecia Pérez Matos, a Black woman born in 1959 in Barahona, in the Dominican Republic. While Madrid is the capital of Spain, Zamora Loboch sees

Aravaca, a nearby bedroom community, as a synecdoche that represents the country's anti-Blackness.

Cómo ser negro conveys from its very title the negative equation of Blackness with a condition predestined for death in the world order of white supremacy: *ser negro y no morir*, to be Black and not die. The title plays ironically with Blackness as a mode of operation, while the book offers suggestions on how a Black person needs to conduct themself to avoid the fate of Lucrecia Pérez Matos. Being a transnational Black person requires awareness for sheer survival, because Blackness signifies foreignness, non-Spanishness. A Black person living in Spain inhabits a "problem space," one in which "person" indicates humanity, yet "Black" is a signifier of fungibility (Warren 392).[5] The humanity of a Black person in Spain is undoubtedly in question.

Cómo ser negro is a vade mecum. The book is divided into different sections that touch on Spanish and white supremacist obsessions regarding Blacks and Blackness, such as the alleged Black (male) superiority in sports and sexual prowess. At the same time, the author explores the underside of these alleged areas of Black superiority. Furthermore, he presents European colonialism in Africa as unidirectional *mestizaje* [race mixing] (*Cómo ser negro* 125) and as a practice that produces and reproduces the phantom of a world of illegitimate humans.

One of the two implied readers of *Cómo ser negro* is a Black male immigrant who represents Africa in the new Spain that now belongs to the European Union, a club for the rich—read: white. This reader is new to a country that has erased not only the memory of its historical ties to slavery and the trans-Atlantic slave trade but also its most recent history of colonialism in Equatorial Guinea, Western Sahara, and Morocco. This reader must "learn" strategies of survival through a rapid course on the racial history and anthropology of Spain. The aim of the book is, therefore, the ironic deconstruction of the (white) Spaniard as a transhistorical category. The Spaniards in *Cómo ser negro* are a distillation of an eternal Spaniard, from the Middle Ages to the present day. This Spaniard acquires whiteness through a process of expulsions, exclusions, and enslavement of impure populations. Central to the book is how Black people appear within the Spanish national imaginary as a counter-narrative.

Through the Brechtian technique of defamiliarization, Zamora Loboch invites the second, white implied reader to confront a racialized view of Spain through a series of well-known phenomena: colonial history, classical literature, soccer, and racist jokes. *Cómo ser negro* connects Spain's past exclusions and present racism that together constitute the identity of the (white) Spaniard in the late twentieth century: "The first Moor to whom Spain applied the Statute of Foreignness was Boabdil."[6] Emir Muhammad XII (Boabdil)'s expulsion is as much an act of racial politics as the deportation of any modern "Moor" (read: Moroccan, Maghrebi) through the application of current immigration laws. Shifting to the implied Black reader, one who is imagined as ignorant of Spanish history, Zamora Loboch "others" (white) Spaniards as a third person subject responsible for actively turning a blind eye to Spain as a cradle of racism and anti-Blackness:

> Spaniards have succeeded in keeping their hydra lying dormant between mint and camphor, wrapped in linen sheets, tucked among hisses of domestic comfort so that several generations ended up believing that racism did not exists in a country whose patron saint is Saint James (aka the Moor Slayer), and which is the motherland of Cardinal Cisneros, Torquemada, the Catholic Monarchs, Quevedo, Pedro Blanco, or the Duke of Santoña. (21)[7]

As a reader of the Spanish classics, Zamora Loboch interprets them from a Black perspective. Writing in 1994, he is the first intellectual to tackle the representation of Black people in Spanish letters in a systematic manner. Through quotations from writers such as Lope de Rueda (1510–1565), Francisco Gómez de Quevedo (1580–1645), Miguel de Cervantes (1547–1616), and Félix Lope de Vega (1562–1635), he demonstrates how Black characters appear in direct relation to Early Modern slavery. This exercise in looking at canonical authors in a defamiliarized way invites an Equatorial Guinean reader of his generation, educated in the Spanish colonial curriculum, to reconsider their relationship to *Hispanidad*. Yet it also forces white Spanish readers to accept what they did not know about themselves.

As the author questions the concept of *Hispanidad*, exile and migration are conflated in his literary production as two contingent forms of diaspora, which constitute a loss not only for the person expelled but also for the community left behind (Hendel 3). However, his view of diaspora also includes the experience of slavery and colonialism (Repinecz, "Raza or Race" 28). In fact, the murder of a diasporic Black woman in Aravaca is coupled with pleasure. The four male killers were performing a colonial slavery fantasy in the violation of a Black female body, the afterlife of slavery, in the words of Saidiya Hartman ("Belly" 82). Personal history is obliterated by slavery and colonialism, and the transnational subject—whether from Equatorial Guinea or the Dominican Republic—carries the burden of non-personhood, of non-humanity in their Blackness.

Whether exiled for political reasons and/or seeking economic opportunity/relief, the Black protagonist of Zamora Loboch's Spanish literary universe is an *emiexile*, to use the term coined by Michael Ugarte (2). A majority of the native (white) population and the political authorities representing them locate all Black Africans in an imaginary non-place, where political persecution and crushing poverty do not amount to a legal or legitimate claim that justifies their presence in Spain (Brancato, "Voices Lost" 4). Diasporic Africans are unsovereign or always at risk of having their sovereignty challenged: "documentación, por favor" [papers, please]. Asking a Black person for their official papers recalls the practice of requiring "passes" and other legal documents from enslaved people in the Americas. The Black slave, the Black colonized subject, and the Black transnational share this lack of sovereignty, consisting of "the natal, the nation and the notion" (Sexton, "The *Vel*" 168). All three categories are present and discussed in *Cómo ser negro*, in which a figure of the stature of Amílcar Cabral (1924–1973)—the Bissau-Guinean intellectual and political leader—represents the real purpose of anti-colonialism. According to Zamora Loboch:

> Cabral was anything but a poor and ignorant illegal immigrant looking for a Western hamburger to alleviate African famine ... "National liberation—he wrote—the fight against colonialism and for independence will make no sense to the people unless their living conditions improve." (*Cómo ser* 55–56)[8]

Ironically, as a counterexample, post-colonial tyrants such as Idi Amin of Uganda, Jean-Bédel Bokassa of Central Africa, or Macías Nguema ("Macías de España") are sandwiched between the paragraphs dedicated to Amílcar Cabral and Nat Turner, two Black figures of liberation who met a tragic end at the hands of white supremacism:

> Looking at things in a dispassionate way, one could easily infer that there has been and still exists a conspiracy, an enormous and flagrant collusion in the West to strip the African continent of ideas, deactivate it culturally, and discredit it economically in order to turn it into a wasteland. Then, this vast domain will turn into a warehouse for toxic waste, a laughingstock, a universal venue for charity events, an ideal setting for photo of the year, a source of clandestine immigrants, a permanent missionary territory, as well as a land of infectious diseases. (61)[9]

Black transnationality has its origin in modern slavery, the institution Spain and Portugal started developing in the fifteenth century. As Selamawit D. Terrefe argues, slavery not only maintained a system of racial hierarchy that regulated how Black and non-Black people negotiated physical space but also organized the conceptual and psychic spaces determining the classification of the Human and the Black, the living and the dead, individuals who can be victims—whose suffering registers—and objects that have no capacity to suffer. In Zamora Loboch's universe, living in Spain is a practice in which the non-Black is identified as human, and the

Black is not. *Cómo ser negro* ends with a colonial practice: the glossary. Much like the one that El Inca Garcilaso de la Vega placed at the end of his *Comentarios reales* (1609), this glossary accompanies works of history and fiction of racialized difference as a supplement of otherness. Twisting this tradition of the colonial glossary, Zamora Loboch again defamiliarizes Spanish household terms with surprising new definitions, such as the one for *Africa*: "African. From there. Detritus. Nothing" (154); for *ballet dancing*: "Ballet. Western tribal dance" (155); for *future*: "Future. Credit Africa lacks" (162); or for *skin*: "Skin. A commodity always valued in financial markets" (169).[10]

Memory as Counter-Narrative

Memory is what sustains the transnational exile. Memory allows exiles to reconstruct the past and build an imagined future. Having been expelled and excluded from their country, for exiles the present is a void and they are condemned to oblivion. Exiles have learned the customs, they may even know their new country better than its native inhabitants, but they also know that their Blackness is a permanent barrier to ever be part of it.

Equatorial Guinea and Africa are always in need of an explanation at the risk of falling under the coloniality of the European discourse of failed states, failed societies, and failed humanity. *Conspiración en el green (El informe Abayak)*, Zamora Loboch's first novel, explores the relationship between the international oil industry, African exiles, and neocolonialism through an Annobonese private detective. His second novel, *El caimán de Kaduna*, is a Bildungsroman in which a nameless teenage soccer player from Cameroon is transplanted to Spain in a modern version of the slave trade, including imprisonment. Finally, in *La república fantástica de Annobón*, the island of Annobón and its denizens are subjected to the utopian plans of a Spanish civil guard whose dreams of human social progress do not include decolonization. All three novels present an account of African reality and history that acts as a counter-narrative to the colonial discourse.

Conspiración en el green's transnationality is ironically established by the fact that not a single episode takes place within the territorial boundaries of Equatorial Guinea, yet the nation's history since independence in 1968 is the leitmotiv of the novel. It is a literary exercise that rewrites the tone of disdain and the neocolonial perspective present in other non-fictional accounts of the 2004 failed coup against Teodoro Obiang Nguema such as Adam Roberts' *The Wonga Coup* (2006). The chapters are divided into two sections, the second one bearing the name of a green in an unnamed South African golf course, the site of the conspiracy against the sovereignty of a Black African nation.

Ton D'Awal is the transnational hero par excellence. He is the fictional protagonist in charge of writing an *informe* [report] for the Spanish Intelligence Services about the impending 2004 (non-fictional) failed coup against President Teodoro Obiang Nguema Mbasogo. His condition as a doubly marginalized Black person—Equatorial Guinean and Annobonese—makes him a cipher to others. His knowledge of colonial history leads him to equate European non-government organizations with the colonial Catholic missionary efforts of the past (Zamora Loboch, *Conspiración* 159). As a transnational African, he has become an expert in European cultural signs of identity. Within the ironic atmosphere of the novel, this detective is an Afropolitan who knows where to find the best *tapas* [appetizers] in Madrid. Food and drink are another leitmotiv in this urban novel, as part of a literary homage to Pepe Carvalho, Spanish writer Manuel Vázquez Montalbán's famous detective. Ton D'Awal shares the same eating habits as the police officers in charge of expelling undocumented foreigners, and all frequent the same bars. His job as an informant for the Spanish secret services takes him not only to Nigeria and Cameroon but also to New York and New Jersey, and back to Spain. Time collapses between his participation in a botched coup attempt against Macías in the seventies and the historical events that unfold in front of him around the 2004 conspiracy against Obiang led by an assortment of white South Africans and Rhodesians, British neocolonialists, and other international merchants of oil, weapons, and death.

In the style of investigative journalism (Marmonti 297), the stories in this novel summarize years of newspaper reports on Equatorial Guinea, some of which Zamora Loboch himself wrote. They contain the actual names of people accused of murder, torture, embezzlement, drug dealing, and corruption. The Equatorial Guinean characters in the novel, mostly male, have long memories and tell a narrative of neo-slavery. As exiles, they forge an identity as Equatorial Guineans in part because they are united against the dictatorships of Macías and Obiang (Cusack 30). In Chapter 12, a religious leader of the Santa Madre Iglesia Panafricanista de Lavapiés called Abu Dodó tells Ton D'Awal what the latter already knows about the relationship between the Spanish banking industry and slavery. This relationship includes the game of golf itself, which explains the deep meaning of the novel's title:

> If with this information you don't want to accept the clear connection between slave trafficking and the current state of affairs, then you must be blind. It's evident that rich whites from Texas or Virginia have kept the same model of exploitation used in the days of slavery. [Equatorial] Guinea is a plantation held by slave owners with Obiang acting as their

foreman, and the Raymonds of this world amass huge fortunes while they play that absurd sport consisting of hitting a ball until it falls into a hole. –Golf, it's called golf. (276)[11]

Abu Dodó's position as a priest of Pan-Africanism in the multicultural neighborhood of Lavapiés in downtown Madrid belies the fact that he is telling the truth in terms of accurate information and that he represents the archive of anticolonial memory. He tells D'Awal a story connecting Kwame Nkrumah, the leader of Ghana's independence, to a plan to turn his country into a nuclear power (Zamora Loboch, *Conspiración* 279).[12] Abu Dodó's is the discourse of the lone prophet, and so are the long tirades delivered by other African exiles. Their words contrast with the cynical information about Equatorial Guinea and Africa that the Lebanese character provides Lord Mark.[13] The conversation between these two is a summary of essentialist notions, propounded by the academic world, about African post-independence states that cannot rise to political stability due to their cultural limitations (Bryceson 426). The South African golf course operates as an enclave of white exclusivism with "wide green alleys" that keep away the "difficulties" in the form of trees, bushes, or bunkers present in other golf courses (Zamora Loboch, *Conspiración* 79; 124; 243). This white enclave is designed to reproduce the white enclaves of the international oil industry in Punta Fernanda on the island of Bioko and keep Equatorial Guineans off their own land (Appel 78–88).

The Afropessimism of the novel is not without poetic justice and dramatic irony. In the last chapter, an Equatorial Guinean exile in New Jersey, Thompson Bohó, writes a long letter to Tom D'Awal revealing his plans to participate in the coup. He even includes his planned address to the Equatorial Guinean people upon being installed in the presidency. In the second part of the chapter, the white participants in the coup are happy, toasting with champagne the imminent success of the invasion of Equatorial Guinea. The educated reader knows better: the historical coup was put down within hours (Roberts 192). A group of Black and non-Black people ultimately failed in their plan to bring anti-Black violence to an African nation.

Anti-Black violence as a historical global ontological crisis is what Afropessimism attempts to theorize. The Black human is the object of gratuitous violence, the Black past is one devoid of heritage, and post-colonial Black Africa is a plan for complete disorder. The Black human has become a phobogenic object, one who generates fear and hatred (Wilderson, "The Prison-Slave" 78). As this essay is being written, the news is dominated by the anti-Black verbal assault against soccer player Vinícius José Paixão de Oliveira Júnior (Vinícius Júnior). After his celebration of the goals he scored, multitudes in stadiums began to sing chants in which, due to his African descent, he was equated with a monkey.[14] In a replay of the historical U.S. lynching of Black men, in January 2023, four individuals hung a black mannequin wearing Vinícius Jr.'s Real Madrid team shirt, his name, and his number from a bridge in Madrid (Peiró).

The anti-Black violence that permeates the world of soccer, which Zamora Loboch has denounced during his long career as a sports journalist, is distilled in his second novel, *El caimán de Kaduna*. Structured as a Bildungsroman, a genre also cultivated by other writers who have narrated the migrant experience in Spain and questioned the country's white Europeanness (Bernechea Navarro 224–26), *El caimán de Kaduna* is a novel of incarceration. When the protagonist's soccer skills are spotted in his Cameroonian homeland, he is quickly taken away from his mother, town, and community through a religious ceremony—much like the one referred to by Hartman (*Lose* 117)—to cut all ties with the past (Zamora Loboch, *El caimán* 127–28). He is transplanted to Spain and to the Real Madrid team, nicknamed *el club blanco* [the white club]. He will be fed well (51), assigned a white woman—called Alba of all names, which is a synonym for white in Spanish—as a sexual partner (141), and finally discarded through a drug smuggling operation in which he will become the unwitting carrier. Everyone abandons him: his team, his sports agency, and Alba, the white woman (165). Once in jail, the protagonist learns the other rules of soccer and life as a goalkeeper through the violent manhood practiced there and by honing a very personal research method to become a writer: orality. He will write an unauthorized biography of Spanish soccer star Iker Casillas, nicknamed at one point *El caimán de Kaduna* [the Alligator of Kaduna]. Zamora Loboch builds on adynaton, the rhetorical figure of things being turned upside down, to make a Black writer adopt an African cultural practice in which the source of information is a white fellow prisoner. In a postcolonial ironic turn, the Spanish star goalkeeper—a world champion—takes his nickname from the city of Kaduna, in Nigeria, where he first staked his claim to fame. Black Africans, therefore, were the first to discover a white future star.

The novel is a reflection on the prison system as slavery. Its unnamed protagonist becomes involved in a racket that employs inmates to write master's theses and doctoral dissertations for white people who pay to enhance their professional curricula. The protagonist, thus, embodies the demetaphorization of the Spanish meaning of the term *negro* as "ghost writer" while also recalling racialized slavery, as the word was synonymous with *enslaved* in the past.[15] This incarcerated anonymous Black protagonist upholds the white supremacist social structure through his unpaid work. His transnationality is a signifier of lack of citizenship, much like the slave is a permanent non-citizen. His Blackness makes his claim to citizenship invisible, a direct result of neocolonialism, a practice that continues slavery and the slave trade through the denial of African political institutions. As a postcolonial text, *El caimán de Kaduna* is a reminder that the mark of slavery does not disappear. Slavery is the condition of social death, and by extension, being Black is being relegated to a non-presence state where the Black African protagonist is already nameless before his incarceration in a Spanish prison after being used as an unwitting drug carrier.

The protagonist is called on to reproduce the relationship between Black enslavement and the writerly world of the Spanish empire. He must negotiate his Black masculinity and gain respect through calculated displays of violence and his soccer skills. His prison nickname of *Caimán* [alligator] is taken from Iker, the Alligator of Kaduna. With this name, he embodies the product of his written work, just as enslaved Africans were forced to adopt the names of their enslavers for whom they produced wealth. His Black body produces a white canon, the biography of a white soccer player, perpetuating what Aníbal Quijano calls the coloniality of power, the unequal relations of production based on race that European colonialism created centuries ago (qtd. in Repinecz, "Don Quijote" 609). The protagonist's work is just labor. He belongs to the caste of people who do not have the right to earn wages. His work and his namelessness are extensions of the will of his jailer. Prison, like slavery, provides him with a new name, Caimán, while his own name is absent in the text. Whether as a colonial subject or as a slave, his incarcerated body and mind (his intellectual work) have suffered an annexation (Hartman, *Lose* 40).

The Afropessimism of this novel is articulated in its ambiguously hopeful ending. After his release from prison, still a non-citizen because of his foreign status, with his Africanity converted into a criminal record, and seeing his book published under someone else's name—a white person's name—he rejects a possible career of humiliation by staying in Spain. Traveling light, carrying only a small suitcase that symbolizes the asymmetric exchange between Europe and Africa, the protagonist makes his way back to the African continent, to South Africa. The location of Spain's 2010 soccer glory—the first time it won the FIFA men's World Cup—represents the end of his transnational travels. There he will teach soccer to South African boys of Indian descent, children of another colonial diaspora. The final chapter of the novel is written in the future tense. Hoping to reverse the equation of Blackness with non-humanness, he will convey through soccer that these children have the right to be human:

> And I shall teach them to dream. Because they will be able to dream. They have the right to dream of a country like theirs. Real dreams that can be achieved without having to abandon family or childhood friends. Dreams they can and must realize without risking either life or dignity.

South African dreams. Dreams of their own, not bastardized ones like mine, which can be snatched away by a police raid, a gang of ruthless criminals, or the abyssal waters of the Strait of Gibraltar. (259)[16]

The African protagonist of *El caimán de Kaduna* is a European version of the slave as prisoner, or the prison-slave-in-waiting that Wilderson describes for the United States ("The Prison-Slave" 68). Although he works while in jail, he is not a worker. He is a *negro*, a slave. Wilderson sees the difference between work and production. While the worker strikes to demand changes in the conditions of production, calling into question the legitimacy of exploitation, the slave exists only as a purveyor of production without a say in the improvement of working conditions. The slave demands an end to the working conditions themselves, through the abolition of the slavery system (Wilderson, "The Prison-Slave" 73). Slavery can only end with its destruction or through self-liberation, but this comes at the price of exile. Like so many slaves before him, the protagonist of *El caimán de Kaduna* chooses freedom in exile and embarks on a transnational journey in the opposite direction, from Europe to Africa. In this case, to an African country that defeated the white supremacist system of Apartheid. South Africa becomes a land of promise.

The study of white supremacy as a transnational phenomenon takes place in the context of Spanish colonialism during the Second Republic (1931–1939) in *La república fantástica de Annobón*, where Sergeant Restituto Castilla weaponizes his whiteness to forge an ideal society of progress on the island of Annobón. The Afropessimism of this historical fiction resides in its very thesis. The Spanish Second Republic did not include Black people in its democratic impulse. The novel thrusts a fierce jab at a discourse that legitimized colonialism. The colonial discourse is a fiction that defends its commitment to human progress, justice, and the civilizing mission on the premise that the Black colonized is insufficiently human. Castilla's absolute rule is the expression of colonial reason as exposed by Achille Mbembe: colonial reason is a series of erudite fabulations with the goal of domination (70). The Annobonese are the subjects of an experiment on how to create a civil society without democracy.

Castilla knows he is a white alien in a land of Blackness. He intends to demonstrate that the Republic's ideals of social progress—free non-religious education for both boys and girls, public hygiene, economic opportunity—can become a reality even among the Black inhabitants of the island of Annobón, the most distant territory in the most distant colonial enclave of a derelict Spanish empire, the Spanish Territories of the Gulf of Guinea. Distance is a construct that elevates the metropolis as a mental center and historical point of departure. Sergeant Castilla will explore the island in an act of possession as "the monarch of all [he] survey[s]" that characterizes imperialist gestures (Campoy-Cubillo and Sampedro Vizcaya 4).

The protagonist is based on the historical Restituto Castilla who ruled as *subgobernador* [deputy governor] of Annobón in 1931–1932, where he was one of four white male Spaniards residing on the island, including two Claretian missionaries and a nurse practitioner. Like the fictional Castilla, the historical figure managed to alienate everyone, both the local population and his fellow white colonials (Nerín Abad 320).[17] His rule ended abruptly and tragically in November 1932 when he killed Gustavo Sostoa, the governor of the colony, who had arrived on the island to remove Castilla from his position as deputy governor. In the novel, Castilla uses a barber's blade, the civilized tool of his morning toilette.

Castilla will enforce the Constitution of the Spanish Republic but maintain the island in a state of exception, that is, not extending constitutional rights to anybody. Like other utopian colonialists, the fictional Castilla is infatuated with Annobón and begins a love relationship with Mapudul, a young Annobonese woman. His relationship with Mapudul resembles Pygmalion's with his carved statue. Castilla teaches Mapudul to read and write, trying to make her into the image that he has of a civilized woman. But when Mapudul imagines herself walking the streets of Madrid, Castilla dismisses the idea as absurd. His civilized creature only has meaning in a colonial setting. It is not transferable. Black female agency is unthinkable for Sergeant Castilla's colonial mind and erotic desire.

The death of their unborn child highlights the contradiction of colonialism and its patriarchal order. Mapudul and her mother insist on attending the three-day account of the heroic deeds of Lodán, the hero who liberated Annobón from a foreign invasion that includes a fatal love affair with a foreign princess (Zamora Loboch, *La república* 194–98). The history of the island as told by the Annobonese collides directly with the Spanish colonial discourse that cancels Black history. On their way back, a pregnant Mapudul goes into labor on the boat transporting them, and despite her mother's efforts, the child does not survive. Castilla reacts by ordering the public flogging of Menfoy, Mapudul's mother (198). The love between a colonizer and a colonized person has no future, as the colonized body, like the enslaved body, can be reduced by the colonizer/enslaver to tortured flesh (Spillers 67; 79).

Sergeant Castilla's utopian republic with Black citizens is undermined by his understanding of the Annobonese as subalterns. His utopian vision mirrors the assumption of the Claretian missionaries he has banished from the school they used to run before his arrival. The civilizing mission does not come with a sunset date. The presumably future civilized people of Annobón will never be able to decide when they will become autonomous and sovereign because, for the colonizer, their Blackness is a condition outside of history that precludes full citizenship.

La república fantástica de Annobón uses Sergeant Castilla's story to tell the history of the island's efforts to remain independent (Manera 245). The history of Annobón is narrated from below. Old women, like Tatan D'Awal, deliver centuries-old oral accounts to the young born after the 1968 independence of Equatorial Guinea. This includes, for example, how the Dutch tried to steal water, cotton, and foodstuffs from the island, but could not capture slaves (220–23). Conversely, Castilla and the missionaries seek to end the political autonomy of Annobón by destroying its historical memory, represented by institutions like Opa, the traditional calendar, and the Viyil, the meeting place where men debate the interests of the community. In this fictional republic, its leader Castilla cannot see the autonomous forms of republican government the Annobonese have established since their days as a Portuguese slave enclave (Caldeira 296).

Colonialism is a transnational project, and as such, Sergeant Castilla's educational plan is a continuation of it. He simply seeks to replace the Catholic missionaries, whose educational program identified the Church with Spanish national culture (Castro and Calle 277), with the ideas of progress and modernity championed by the Second Republic. If the missionaries upheld a hierarchical social system in which civilization was white and barbarism was Black, Castilla shares this belief, despite his love for a Black woman. In addition, he embodies a white savior. His regime of order and justice from above leaves no room for debate or possible opposition. After a scene describing the capture of a whale and her calf by courageous and experienced fishermen, Restituto Castilla imposes his utopian order of equal distribution *manu militari*. The Annobonese are left with no say in this reversal of traditional sharing of whale meat that privileged the young and male over the older and female (Zamora Loboch, *La república* 172).

In an ironic take on *Moby Dick*'s Captain Ahab, the white whale of injustice Sergeant Castilla wishes to slay proves to be the monster of colonialism that ends up swallowing him when he kills the governor, who has traveled to the island to replace him. He fails to recognize the real republic of Annobón that lives on in the oral memory of the Ambo, as the Annobonese call themselves. The island's history and institutions are anticolonial and republican, something a young man named Nanandji is trying to record from the oral memories related by Tatan D'Awal, the old woman, whose sense of tradition tells her it is time to commit ancestral memory to paper and ink. Her first lesson to the young recorder of history is to decolonize his epistemology:

> Since what happened is not written in books, and what one reads there was written by the Spaniards, you, the young educated by white priests,

believe only what is told in them. You always accept as a settled matter the white man's version. What a *name faculim* may say makes you laugh, but what a bearded charlatan dressed in a white robe says always deserves your agreement. (226; original emphasis)[18]

Tatan D'Awal draws attention to the relationship between affect and time, or how the past influences the present in material ways (Slaby 174). The white historian who writes in books is untrustworthy. The true history that lives in the memory of the Annobonese is about to be lost and only committing it to the written page—that untrustworthy medium—can help bring awareness of the past. For Zamora Loboch, this woman's efforts represent an attempt to preserve history from its erasure by utopians like Restituto Castilla and other white colonial saviors from the left (Nerín Abad 328).

In this novel, Francisco Zamora Loboch continues the project he initiated with *Cómo ser negro y no morir en Aravaca*, which is to tell the history of Africa and colonialism from the perspective of the colonized, and to rewrite the history of Spain and Europe from a Black decolonial perspective. The novel also illustrates the need for a critique of Spanish colonialism from within, as the conversations between Castilla and the nurse practitioner Lorenzo Sanjuán—what the latter tells the former—demonstrate. Once again, Zamora Loboch must explain Spain to the Spanish. This novel also ends with a glossary of Annobonese terms, the attempt of the colonized to create meaning.

In the literary universe of Zamora Loboch, there is no redemption or restoration. His writings document the concept of Blackness, in Wilderson's words, as a paradigm of absence (*Afropessimism* 16). His Black characters become aware of their absence in the imaginary of the world. The main tenet of white supremacy holds that Blacks—all over the world—are not human. The transnational Afropessimism of Zamora Loboch is a call to reflect on the (in)human condition of Blackness today, with the awareness that Black life itself is a global enterprise that transcends national boundaries. Zamora Loboch makes Sylvia Wynter's view of the human condition his own: "*humanness* is no longer a noun. *Being human is a praxis*" (qtd. in Wynter and McKittrick 23, original emphasis).

Notes

1 This essay does not subscribe to an earlier meaning of the term "Afropessimism" used by other scholars and the media to mean that "something is wrong with Africans," as the continent does not "live up to a set of criteria" of development, in the eyes of former Western empires (de B'béri and Louw 337). The news media portrayal of Africa in almost exclusively negative terms—with the underlying idea that Africans cannot rule themselves—requires theoretical

analysis and critique (Beer 599). The current conception of Afropessimism has also faced critics who accuse its proponents of erasing the history of Black resistance to slavery and colonialism and of privileging "Americanism" in its view of Black history (Thomas 294).

2 After the failed coup in March 1969, President Macías Nguema ordered a generalized repression of his political opponents and declared himself President for Life (Sundiata 604; Siale Djangany 95).

3 The people of Spanish Guinea acquired legal equality with the rest of the Spanish population after the colony was divided into two provinces, Fernando Poo and Río Muni, in 1959. The decree of provincialization stated that legal changes in the status of the Black population would "respect the natural and customary peculiarities of that overseas region" which in practice meant that the new provincial governing institutions would inherit much of the old colonial regime (Ndongo Bidyogo 198–99). With the creation of the two provinces and two secondary schools, new cohorts of Black Spanish Guineans obtained scholarships to study in the metropolis. The newly independent Equatorial Guinea, and Spain, as the former colonial power, recognized dual citizenship for all Equatorial Guineans. Spain unilaterally rescinded this dual citizenship after the 1969 failed coup against President Macías Nguema.

4 "'Apátridas'. La palabreja salió a galope de las páginas del diccionario María Moliner una cálida mañana de verano de 1971 y recorrió como el fuego las fondas, pensiones, Colegios Mayores, pisos y donde fuera que se albergaran los estudiantes guineanos antes destinados a regir el futuro de su país … 'Exiliados y apátridas'. Con una mano delante y otra detrás. Sin papeles, sin un puto duro, sin país. Ser estudiante guineano en la década de los setenta en España se convirtió en una odisea, una aventura sólo apta para estómagos fuertes. Selección natural pura y dura." All translations are mine.

5 Calvin Warren uses the term "problem space" in his analysis of the murder of Steen Keith Fenrich, a gay Black man, at the hands of his white stepfather, who dismembered the body and carved "Gay Nigger #1" on his stepson's skull.

6 "El primer moro a quien España aplicó la Ley de Extranjería se llamaba Boabdil." This is in reference to the last emir of Granada, who was expelled to Morocco after his surrender in 1492.

7 "Los españoles han sabido guardar su hidra adormecida entre hierbabuena y alcanfor, envuelta en sábanas de Holanda y arropada en siseos de mesa camilla, hasta hacer creer a varias generaciones que no era racista un país cuyo santo patrón es Santiago (alias Matamoros), que es patria del Cardenal Cisneros, Torquemada, los Reyes Católicos, Quevedo, Pedro Blanco o el duque de Santoña."

8 "Cabral era todo menos un pobre e ignorante inmigrante ilegal en busca de una hamburguesa occidental con la que calmar la hambruna africana … 'La liberación nacional—dejó escrito—la lucha contra el colonialismo y por la independencia no tendrán ningún significado para el pueblo a menos que se mejoren sus condiciones de existencia.'"

9 "Vistas las cosas sin pasión alguna, cabría deducir fácilmente que aquí ha existido y existe una conjura, un enorme y flagrante contubernio occidental para desideologizar el continente africano, deasctivarlo culturalmente y desacreditarlo económicamente hasta transformarlo en puro barbecho y, a continuación, dedicar tan vasto latifundio a almacén de residuos tóxicos, caja

de risas, salón universal para guateques de caridad, marco ideal para fotos del año, bolsa de inmigrantes clandestinos, tierra permanente de misión y área de enfermedades infectocontagiosas."
10 "Africano. De ahí. Detritus. Nada," "Ballet. Baile tribal occidental," "Futuro. Crédito del que carece África," and "Piel. Valor que siempre ha cotizado en Bolsa."
11 "Pues si con esos datos no quieres reconocer la clara conexión entre la trata de negros y el estado actual de las cosas es que eres ciego. Es evidente que los ricos blancos de Texas o Virginia mantienen el modelo de explotación de la época de la esclavitud. Guinea es una plantación, un ingenio negrero. Obiang ejerce de capataz y los Raymond de toda la vida amasan fortunas ingentes mientras juegan a ese absurdo deporte que consiste en asestarle golpes a una pelota hasta que se cuela por un pequeño hoyo. – Golf, se llama golf."
12 Kwame Nkrumah was one of the earliest proponents of nuclear disarmament, as were most Pan-Africanists and Black anticolonialists in the 1940s and 1950s, who protested France's use of the Sahara to test nuclear bombs (Allman 94). Once in power, Nkrumah advocated for energy independence through the building of a nuclear reactor to help the electrification of Ghana. This would make Africans producers of scientific knowledge, rather than colonial consumers of it. His plan never took effect once he lost power (Osseo-Asare 171).
13 Lord Mark is based on Mark Thatcher, the son of former British Prime Minister Margaret Thatcher and a principal actor in the conspiracy to organize the 2004 failed coup, a crime in South African law for which he pleaded guilty ("Analysis").
14 The incidents occurred before, during, and after a soccer match between the Valencia and Real Madrid teams. An international outcry ensued. On his Twitter account, Vinicius Jr. responded to the President of the Spanish soccer league: "It was neither the first, nor the second, nor the third time. Racism is normal in La Liga" [Não foi a primeira vez, nem a segunda e nem a terceira. O racismo é o normal na La Liga] (@vinijr).
15 The comparison between a Black person and enslavement is used, as a joke, to explain the rhetorical figure of synecdoche in the first grammar of the Spanish language: "I bought a Black man, his hair curly, his teeth white, his lips swollen" [Io compre un negro, crespo los cabellos, blanco los dientes, hinchado los beços] (Nebrija 122).
16 "Y les enseñaré a soñar. Porque ellos sí pueden soñar. Tienen derecho a soñar con un país como el suyo. Sueños reales que se pueden materializar sin tener que abandonar a la familia ni a los amigos de la infancia. Sueños que pueden y deben lograr sin arriesgar la vida ni la estima. Sueños sudafricanos. Propios, no bastardos como los míos, que te los puede arrebatar una redada, una banda de desaprensivos o las fosas abisales del Estrecho."
17 Luis Leante's novel *Annobón* (2017) also tells Sergeant Castilla's story of utopian politics and murder, but with an emphasis on the aftermath of his trial, sentence, release, and persecution at the end of the Spanish Civil War.
18 "Como lo que sucedió no consta en los libros y lo que sí viene lo escribieron los españoles, vosotros, los jóvenes educados por los sacerdotes blancos, creéis solo lo que en ellos cuentan. Dais siempre por sentada la versión del hombre blanco. Lo que diga una *name faculim* produce risa y lo que dice un charlatán barbudo vestido con bata blanca merece siempre vuestro amén."

Works Cited

Aixelà Cabré, Yolanda. *Guinea Ecuatorial: Ciudadanías y migraciones transnacionales en un contexto dictatorial africano*. Ediciones Ceiba, 2010.

Allman, J. "Nuclear Imperialism and the Pan-African Struggle for Peace and Freedom. Ghana. 1959–1962." *Souls*, vol. 10, no. 2, 2008, pp. 83–102.

"Analysis: Mark Thatcher Pleads Guilty to Criminal Charges in Alleged Coup Attempt in Equatorial Guinea." *Morning Edition*, National Public Radio, 13 Jan. 2005, https://link.gale.com/apps/doc/A161907977/OVIC?u=bates_main&sid=summon&xid=f4603f6c.

Appel, Hannah. *The Licit Life of Capitalism. US Oil in Equatorial Guinea*. Duke UP, 2019.

B'béri, Boulou Ebanda de, and P. Eric Louw. "Afropessimism: A Genealogy of Discourse." *Critical Arts*, vol. 25, no. 3, 2011, pp. 335–34.

Beer, Arnold S. de, "News from and in the 'Dark Continent': Afro-Pessimism, News Flows, Global Journalism and Media Regimes." *Journalism Studies*, vol. 11, no. 4, 2010, pp. 596–609, https://doi.org/10.1080/14616701003638509.

Bernechea Navarro, Sara. *Literatura de la migración en España (2001–2008): Negociación de las expectativas a través del Bildungsroman*. 2021. Universidade de Santiago de Compostela, PhD dissertation, http://hdl.handle.net/10347/26016.

Brancato, Sabrina. "Afro-European Literature(s): A New Discursive Category?" *Research in African Literatures*, vol. 39, no. 3, 2008, pp. 1–13.

———. "Voices Lost in a Non-Place: African Writing in Spain." *Matatu*, vol. 36, 2009, pp. 3–17, https://doi.org/10.1163/9789042028166_002.

Bryceson, Deborah Fahy. "Of Criminals and Clients: African Culture and Afro-Pessimism in a Globalized World." *Canadian Journal of African Studies/Revue canadienne des études africaines*, vol. 34, no. 2, 2000, pp. 417–42, https://doi.org/10.2307/486424.

Caldeira, Arlindo M. "Organizing Freedom: De Facto Independence on the Island of Ano Bom (Annobón) During the Eighteenth and Nineteenth Centuries." *Afro-Hispanic Review*, vol. 28, no. 2, 2009, pp. 293–310. http://www.jstor.org/stable/41349290.

Campoy-Cubillo, Adolfo, and Benita Sampedro Vizcaya. "Entering the Global Hispanophone: An Introduction." *Journal of Spanish Cultural Studies*, vol. 20, no. 1–2, 2019, pp. 1–16. https://doi.org/10.1080/14636204.2019.1609212.

Castro, Mariano de, and María Luisa de la Calle. *La colonización española en Guinea Ecuatorial (1858–1900)*. Ceiba Ediciones, 2007.

Cusack, Igor. "Being Away from 'Home': The Equatorial Guinean Diaspora." *Journal of Contemporary African Studies*, vol. 17, no. 1, 1999, pp. 29–48.

Garcilaso de la Vega, El Inca. *Comentarios reales de los Incas*, edited by Carlos Araníbar, Fondo de Cultura Económica, 1991.

"Guinea Ecuatorial seguirá siendo 'materia reservada' para la información." *Informaciones*, Madrid, 13 Aug. 1976, https://digital.march.es/fedora/objects/linz:R-73469/datastreams/OBJ/content.

Hartman, Saidiya V. *Lose Your Mother: A Journey Along the Atlantic Slave Route*. Farrar, Straus and Giroux, 2007.

———. "The Belly of the World: A Note on Black Women's Labors." *Souls. A Critical Journal of Black Politics, Culture, and Society*, vol. 18, no. 1, 2016, pp. 80–90.

Hendel, Mischa G. "Francisco 'Paco' Zamora Loboch. Periodista y escritor de Guinea Ecuatorial (Madrid, España)." *Iberoromania*, vol. 73–74, no. 1, 2012, pp. 116–22, https://doi.org/10.1515/ibero-2012-0001.
Leante, Luis. *Annobón*. HarperCollins Ibérica, 2017.
Manera, Danilo. Review of *La República fantástica de Annobón*, by Francisco Zamora Loboch. *Tintas. Quaderni Di Letterature Iberiche e Iberoamericane*, vol. 9, 2020, pp. 245–46, https://doi.org/10.13130/2240-5437/14644.
Marmonti, Alessa. Review of *Conspiración en el green (El informe Abayak)*, by Francisco Zamora Loboch. *Tintas. Quaderni Di Letterature Iberiche e Iberoamericane*, vol. 1, 2011, pp. 295–98, https://doi.org/10.13130/2240-5437/1820.
Mba Ncony, Diosdado. "Muchos actores para una independencia: Guinea Ecuatorial." *Afro-Hispanic Review*, vol. 28, no. 2, 2009, pp. 203–08.
Mbembe, Achille. *Crítica de la razón negra*. Translated by Enrique Schmukler. Futuro Anterior Ediciones, 2016.
Nebrija, Antonio de. *Gramática de la lengua castellana. Muestra de la istoria de las antiguedades de España. Reglas de la ortographia en la lengua castellana*, edited by Ignacio. González-Llubera. Oxford UP, 1926.
Nerín Abad, Gustau. "Socialismo utópico y tiranía: La isla de Annobón bajo el cabo Restituto Castilla (1931–1932)." *Afro-Hispanic Review*, vol. 28, no. 2, 2009, pp. 311–30, http://www.jstor.org/stable/41349291. Accessed 2 Oct. 2023.
Osseo-Asare, Abena Dove. *Atomic Junction: Nuclear Power in Africa after Independence*. Cambridge UP, 2019.
Peiró, Patricia. "Una muñeca hinchable, una foto y unas cervezas en un bar: Así fue la investigación del muñeco de Vinicius ahorcado." *El País*, 23 May 2023, https://elpais.com/deportes/2023-05-24/una-muneca-hinchable-una-foto-y-unas-cervezas-en-un-bar-asi-fue-la-investigacion-del-vinicius-ahorcado.html.
Pries, Ludger. "Transnational Migration: New Challenges for Nation States and New Opportunities for Regional and Global Development." *Reports & Analyses*, vol. 1, no. 6, pp. 1–21, http://pdc.ceu.hu/archive/00004803/01/rap_i_an_0106a.pdf.
Repinecz, Martín. "Don Quijote in Africa: Fictionality as an Antidote to Racism." *Bulletin of Hispanic Studies*, vol. 94, no. 6, 2017, pp. 607–23, http://dx.doi.org/10.3828/bhs.2017.39.
———. "Raza or Race? Remembering Slavery in Equatorial Guinean Literature." *Hispanic Studies Review*, vol. 4, no. 1, 2019, pp. 121–35.
Roberts, Adam. *The Wonga Coup*. Profile Books, 2006.
Sampedro Vizcaya, Benita. "African Poetry in Spanish Exile: Seeking Refuge in the Metropolis." *Bulletin of Hispanic Studies*, vol. 81, no. 2, 2004, pp. 201–14, https://doi.org/10.3828/bhs.81.2.4.
Sexton, Jared. "The Social Life of Social Death: On Afro-Pessimism and Black Optimism." *InTensions Journal*, vol. 5, 2011, pp. 1–41, https://intensions.journals.yorku.ca/index.php/intensions/article/view/37359/1816.
———. "The *Vel* of Slavery: Tracking the Figure of the Unsovereign." *Afro-Pessimism. An Introduction*, edited by Wilderson III et al. Racked and Dispatched, 2017, pp. 148–69.
Siale Djangany, José Fernando. "Partido único y colonialismo endógeno. Reflexiones sobre los fundamentos históricos y psicológicos del Partido Único." *Guinea Ecuatorial (des)conocida. (Lo que sabemos, ignoramos, inventamos y*

deformamos acerca de su pasado y su presente), edited by Juan Aranzadi and Gonzalo Álvarez Chillida. Universidad Nacional de Educación a Distancia, vol. 2, 2020, pp. 85–104.

Slaby, Jan. "The Weight of History: From Heidegger to Afro-Pessimism." *Phenomenology as Performative Exercise,* edited by Lucilla Guidi and Thomas Rentsch. Brill, 2020, pp. 173–95, https://doi.org/10.1163/9789004420991_012.

Spillers, Hortense. "Mama's Baby, Papa's Maybe: An American Grammar Book." *Diacritics,* vol. 17, no. 2, 1987, pp. 65–81, https://doi-org.lprx.bates.edu/10.2307/3177494.

Sundiata, Ibrahim K. "La Diáspora y un pequeño rincón de África." *Guinea Ecuatorial (des)conocida. (Lo que sabemos, ignoramos, inventamos y deformamos acerca de su pasado y su presente),* edited by Juan Aranzadi and Gonzalo Álvarez Chillida. UNED, 2020, pp. 597–610.

Terrefe, Selamawit D. "Phantasmagoria; or, the World Is a Haunted Plantation." *The Feminist Wire,* 10 Oct. 2012, https://www.thefeministwire.com/2012/10/phantasmagoria/. Accessed 1 Oct. 2023.

Thomas, Greg. "Afro-Blue Notes: The Death of Afro-Pessimism (2.0)?" *Theory & Event,* vol. 21, no. 1, 2018, pp. 282–317, https://muse.jhu.edu/article/685979.

Ugarte, Michael. *Africans in Europe: The Culture of Exile and Emigration from Equatorial Guinea to Spain.* U of Illinois P, 2010.

@vinijr. "Não foi a primeira vez, nem a segunda e nem a terceira. O racismo é o normal na La Liga. A competição acha normal, a Federação também e os adversários incentivam. Lamento muito. O campeonato que já foi de Ronaldinho, Ronaldo, Cristiano e Messi hoje é dos racistas. Uma nação linda, que me acolheu e que amo, mas que aceitou exportar a imagem para o mundo de um país racista. Lamento pelos espanhois que não concordam, mas hoje, no Brasil, a Espanha é conhecida como um país de racistas. E, infelizmente, por tudo o que acontece a cada semana, não tenho como defender. Eu concordo. Mas eu sou forte e vou até o fim contra os racistas. Mesmo que longe daqui." *Twitter,* 21 May 2023, 4:18 p.m., https://twitter.com/vinijr/status/1660379570149683200?lang=en.

Warren, Calvin. "Onticide: Afro-Pessimism, Gay Nigger# 1, and Surplus Violence." *GLQ: A Journal of Lesbian and Gay Studies,* vol. 23, no. 3, 2017, pp. 391–418, https://doi.org/10.1215/10642684-3818465.

Wilderson, Frank B. III. *Afropessimism.* Liveright Publishing Corporation, 2020.

———. "The Prison-Slave as Hegemony's (Silent) Scandal." *Afro-Pessimism. An Introduction,* edited by Wilderson III et al. Racked and Dispatched, 2017, pp. 148–69.

Wynter, Sylvia, and Katherine McKittrick. "Unparalleled Catastrophe for Our Species?: Or, to Give Humanness a Different Future: Conversations." *Sylvia Wynter: On Being Human as Praxis,* edited by Katherine McKittrick. Duke UP, 2015, pp. 9–89.

Zamora Loboch, Francisco. "Annobón no es un estercolero." *Guinea-Ecuatorial,* 13 July 2012, http://ecuatorial-guinea.net/inicio.asp?cd=ni8446.

———. *Cómo ser negro y no morir en Aravaca. Manual de recetas contra el racismo.* Ediciones B, 1994.

———. *Conspiración en el green (El informe Abayak).* SIAL Ediciones, 2009.

———. *Desde el Viyil y otras crónicas*. SIAL Ediciones, 2008.
———. *El Caimán de Kaduna*. Paréntesis, 2012.
———. "En septiembre de 1969 Madrid no era ninguna fiesta." *Afro-Hispanic Review*, vol. 28, no. 2, 2009, pp. 449–57, http://www.jstor.org/stable/41349309.
———. "Es hora de que el hombre negro escriba su historia." *20 minutos*, 10 Nov. 2009, https://www.20minutos.es/noticia/562356/0/paco/zamora/negro/.
———. *La república fantástica de Annobón*. Sial Ediciones, 2017.
———. *Memoria de laberintos*. Editorial Morandi, 1999.

3 The Value of Color
Spain's Equality Stamps Fiasco

Jeffrey K. Coleman

On May 25, 2021, Correos (the Spanish postal service) launched a set of four skin-toned postage stamps known as Equality Stamps that sparked an international controversy over how they attempted to reflect and counter racial discrimination. The agency collaborated on this campaign with El Chojín (Domingo Edjang Moreno, 1977–), an Afro-Spanish rapper known for his commitment to fighting racism, and the Federación SOS Racismo, one of the leading anti-racism organizations in Spain. The controversy arose in part from the decision to link the value of the stamps to different skin tones, with the palest stamp priced at 1.60€ and the darkest at 0.70€ (Figure 3.1). Despite the campaign's intention to "reflect an unjust and painful reality, which should never exist," anti-racism organizations, mainstream media outlets, and the general public both in Spain and abroad immediately deemed the stamp series racist (Medina; Minder; Noack). In response to this widespread criticism, Correos ended the campaign after only three days.

The campaign was part of European Diversity Month, an annual European Union (EU) initiative that promotes diversity in different forms (gender, sexuality, race, age, disability, etc.), whose 2021 theme was workplace inclusion.[1] The launch of the series also aligned with the first anniversary of the murder of George Floyd in the United States, a foundational event that triggered anti-racism protests. Floyd's death elevated global discussions of anti-Blackness and anti-racist movements to an international and transnational scale. Yet, the emerging racial justice movements also centered the United States as a false universal for anti-Black violence—a message that Correos exploited as justification for a new set of stamps.

This chapter critiques this failed postal initiative through the analysis of the stamps and their marketing, as well as El Chojín and SOS Racismo's responses to the backlash and, finally, the philatelic afterlife of these stamps. Although it was short-lived, the Equality Stamps campaign reveals another unsuccessful attempt by the Spanish State to externalize racism as "over there" (i.e. foreign), while inflicting epistemological violence on its own

Figure 3.1 Equality Stamps. Minder, Raphael. "Spain Issued 'Equality Stamps' in Skin Tones. The Darker Ones Were Worth Less."

racialized communities. The anti-Blackness embedded in the collection's value system simultaneously exemplifies Spain's problematic history with Blackness domestically and its desire to demonstrate its purported whiteness internationally. The campaign's deliberate use of the English language positions the US as the false universal site of anti-Black violence, which is misleading given Spain's contemporary history and hinders the development of the anti-racism movement in Spain. El Chojín and Federación SOS Racismo are, therefore, co-opted as tools by the State to ultimately send a message that harms the communities they serve, diminishing their legitimacy in the fight for racial justice. The swift deletion of the Equality Stamps from the official Correos archive connotes an unwillingness to admit wrongdoing and eliminates the need for an apology to the communities affected by this campaign. Finally, the increasing value of the stamps in the resale philatelic market lies not only in their scarcity but also in the surrounding controversy, thus demonstrating that racism sells. Consequently, on a symbolic level, this further denigrates Black Spaniards as the funds generated in this secondary market do not benefit the anti-racism movement.

What Brought Us to This?

To understand how such a campaign could have been approved in the first place, a historiographical account of Spain's contemporary relationship with its communities of color is needed. Spain's transformation into a multiracial, multicultural nation did not truly begin until the 1990s. After the end of the Franco regime in 1975, Spain desperately wanted to be seen as part of the European community, which it achieved by entering the EU in 1986. This political initiative was a way for Spain to disavow the oft-cited notion that "Africa begins at the Pyrenees," a reference to the historical fact that Spain was part of an Islamic empire for nearly eight centuries (711–1492). Until the 1980s, Spain was perceived as a second-tier European nation. After joining the EU, the country began to flourish economically, which in turn led to immigration, primarily from Africa and Latin America. This influx of immigrants coincided with the emergence of neo-Nazi groups that wanted to preserve racial homogeneity in Spain. In addition to the spread of racist violence, there was also the pervasive presence of casual or "everyday racism," to borrow the words of Philomena Essed. Spain has remained conflicted with regard to race, often seen as the "racial other" of Europe at the same time it practices racial discrimination on a national level.[2] As Helen Graham and Antonio Sánchez note in their pivotal chapter about the impact of the year 1992:

> So Spain, in spite of its own long and painful history of underdevelopment, economic emigration, and otherness, far from recognizing a commonality and attempting to integrate the experience of the marginalized into its self-proclaimed pluralistic culture, has instead assumed the stance of "First World" Europe. It is almost as if constructing and adopting the same "others" or outgroups as the rest were considered the hallmark of Spain's membership of the "club." (415)

One widely reported example of this stance is the murder of Lucrecia Pérez Matos on November 13, 1992. Pérez Matos was killed by four white supremacists (three teenagers and a member of the *Guardia Civil*) at the abandoned Four Roses nightclub in Aravaca. Her death was designated the first hate crime in Spain and marks a watershed moment for the anti-racist movement. Many anti-racist organizations, including the Federación SOS Racismo, were founded in the 1990s in response to the increasing discrimination and violence. However, that did not stop the flow of immigrants. By 2004, Spain had the second highest immigration rate in the world, behind only the US (Moffette 3–4). Today, racialized communities constitute nearly 15% of the population, a significant demographic shift in just over a generation. This stamp controversy, therefore, takes place when many members of the second and third generation of citizens of color have never been seen as Spanish because of their skin tone.

Stamps as Signifiers

In the age of social media, postage stamps may not seem to be of much importance. However, as Vida Zei notes in "Stamps and the Politics of

National Representation," they are "state symbols that participate in the cultural production of (among other cultural discourses) the sovereign nation-state" (65). Stamps act as an extension of the nation-state as they travel domestically and internationally, communicating a sociopolitical view of the nation that is assumed to represent a national consensus. On the other hand, the Equality Stamps series and its subsequent deletion from the official Correos archive evince a lack of consensus because, as Guillermo Navarro Oltra asserts, "Like any image, postage stamps transmit all their information simultaneously. Therefore, an inadequately designed postage stamp can produce the opposite effect to that desired, especially if it is directed to a certain segment of the population" (25).[3] The rapid criticism and withdrawal of the campaign signal a disconnect between the intended goal of Correos and the way the public interpreted the campaign.

The name of the stamp collection provides valuable insight into the message that Correos, and by extension, the Spanish State, intended to transmit to its citizens. The choice of the English language for the campaign is odd, given that Correos is a Spanish governmental institution. However, the language choice continues along the lines of a previous series, "Protest Stamps," released in November 2019 in conjunction with the Madrid Climate Summit, which took place across the street from the Palacio de Correos, Spain's Central Post Office ("Correos Launches"). That series of ten stamps is "a collection of stamps to fight against climate change," inspired by signs seen at climate change protests (Figure 3.2).[4] Seven of the ten stamps feature slogans in English, which could be read as an invocation of the English language as one of universality in the field of climate change. Equality Stamps, as "a collection of stamps to fight against racism," attempts to follow the same path as Protest Stamps through its use of English.[5] However, given the release date, the name Equality Stamps linguistically marks issues of racial inequality as belonging to the English-speaking world (to be read largely as the US). As Mónica G. Moreno Figueroa and Emiko Saldívar Tanaka assert in their article on the 2005 Memín Pinguín stamp controversy in Mexico:

> This belief and common stereotype has been made possible partly through the silencing of public discourse on the existence of black people in comparison to the well-known history of slavery, segregation, racism and criminalization of African Americans in the United States. (519)[6]

In Spain (and, until recently, in Mexico), there is no category for race on the national census, thereby making it impossible to quantify a Black citizenry. This, in turn, allows for Black people to be constantly discussed in public discourse in terms of immigration, regarded as perpetual migrants who invade the nation and are graciously allowed to stay. Racism and the corresponding physical violence are therefore externalized as foreign,

Figure 3.2 Protest Stamps. "Correos Launches 'Protest Stamps', Stamps Featuring the Voices of a Generation Against Climate Change." *Correos*, https://www.correos.com/en/sala-prensa/correos-launches-protest-stamps-stamps-featuring-the-voices-of-a-generation-against-climate-change/#.

allowing Spain to take the moral high ground as a benevolent nation that treats its racialized subjects *con cariño*. This posture connotes the State's anxiety about race in the face of its rapidly changing demographics, which are widely discussed in various studies (Coleman, "Autochthonous Anxieties"; *The Necropolitical Theater*; Donovan; Folkart).

The face value of the stamps, increasing from the darkest to the lightest skin tone, corresponds to postal rates A (domestic letters and cards up to 20g), A2 (domestic letters and cards 20g–50g), B (international letters and cards within Europe), and C (international letters and cards posted to nations outside of Europe, with some exceptions) (Figure 3.1) (Correos, "Tarifas 2021: Península y Baleares" 4–5). In contrast to the Protest Stamps, which were all postal rate A, the Equality Stamps bear different postal rates and functions, signaling that Correos not only wanted these stamps to have more of a global impact but also that matching skin tones to postal rates was deliberate. This raises a central question: what are the international and domestic messages this stamp collection transmits based on the values and postal rates assigned to each skin tone? The lightest skin tone is the stamp with postal rate C, which already implies a projection of Spain's putative whiteness to the rest of the world. In addition, keeping in mind that mail bearing this stamp would likely be destined for nations of the Global South since postal rate C is not sufficient and thus not valid for correspondence intended for the US, Canada, Japan, Australia, or

The Value of Color: Spain's Equality Stamps Fiasco 77

New Zealand, it connotes a posture of racial superiority as it obliges the senders of mail and/or remittances to people in the Global South to use the white stamp on their envelopes. In short, Black and Brown Spaniards sending mail to distant family and friends would be forced to purchase the stamps with the lightest skin tone for their correspondence. At the other end of the spectrum, the Black stamp with postal rate A would only circulate within Spain unless multiples were used. If a person wanted to buy this stamp for international mail, they would need three stamps totaling 2.10€, surpassing the 1.60€ rate for postal rate C on the white stamp, which places an additional financial burden on anyone wishing to correspond with those abroad. While the 50-cent difference may be negligible to some, it is significant enough to prevent many from choosing this option. The relationship between the stamps' skin tones and their respective postal functions aligns symbolically with Spain's history with race. By limiting the Black stamp to domestic use, metaphorically, Spain is hiding its blackness and its Black history from the rest of the world in order to project and invest in hegemonic whiteness internationally.

Due to their limited three-day run, these stamps were sold exclusively as a set. The consumer's understanding of the campaign could vary widely when seeing the stamps together as a series on the striped poster of skin tones rather than as individual stamps on a letter or parcel. Indeed, viewing these stamps in isolation reminds us of Pantone, the company known worldwide for color matching and mixing. Isolated colors, displayed through Pantone swatches, become globalized signifiers, such as in the marketing of the Color of the Year (a Pantone initiative since 2000). Each year's color is chosen in accordance with trends and global events.[7] The four swatches selected for this Spanish stamp campaign present a similar approach. Considering that a marketing and design firm was hired for this campaign, some level of discussion, perhaps via the comparison to Pantone swatches, likely took place to decide on each skin tone. This then presents a quandary in that the fourth stamp is pitch black. Rather than being a two-dimensional representation of Black skin, this stamp seems to represent Blackness by means of Blackface, which is often achieved in Spain using black shoe polish. Simply put, the black stamp is the perverse perspective of what Black people look like.

El Chojín's Role in the Campaign and Its Fallout

The Correos stamp campaign's voice and/or face was El Chojín, who narrated both the Spanish and English trailers. The choice of El Chojín was an apt one given that he has produced music about racism and discrimination in Spain, such as the song "Mami, el negro está rabioso" on his 1999 debut album, *Mi Turno*.[8] By placing him at the forefront of this collection,

Correos attempts to legitimize the goals of the campaign as working in support of the anti-racism cause. However, in the days following the release of the stamps, fans and members of the Afro-Spanish community excoriated El Chojín for his role in the campaign. A close reading of the trailer and El Chojín's May 30th response to the criticisms provide insights and raise further questions worth exploring.[9]

The one-minute trailer is packed with imagery and is symbolic of what Kirstie Dorr notes: "postal images are often produced at moments of ideological or economic crisis, designed to promote and naturalize specific national mythologies, nationalist 'values,' and modes of citizenship and belonging" (20). In this case, the trailer in particular and the campaign in general are linked to global conversations about racial discrimination, specifically anti-Black violence. The English version of the text that El Chojín narrates is as follows:

> The world has had enough. It is time to draw a line in the sand. Thousands have taken to the streets to condemn racial discrimination, and Correos, the Spanish postal service, wants to play its part too. That's why we created a new series of stamps. Correos presents: EQUALITY STAMPS, a collection of stamps that reflect an unjust and painful reality, which should never exist. There are people who think the value of a person depends on the color of their skin. That's why these stamps have a different value depending on the color of the skin they represent. The darker the stamp, the lower its value. That means you need more black stamps than white ones for your deliveries. That way every letter and every parcel will be a reflection of the inequality generated by racism. A protest, EQUALITY STAMPS, a collection of stamps demanding that color should not determine the value we place on a person's life.[10]

From this, it is apparent that the point of the campaign was to highlight the injustice of racial discrimination to incite us all to reflect more on how we should be contributing to making the world more equal. This is achieved in several ways in the video. First, it is shot almost entirely in black and white, adopting a journalistic aesthetic that connotes a level of sociocultural significance. Color appears only on the stamps themselves or the Correos logo. The grayscale serves not only to equalize skin color (except in the case of the actual stamps) but also to interpolate images from anti-racism protests at the beginning of the video. Second, the protest images are a mix of contemporary examples taken from Sweden, the US, and Spain as well as images from the American Civil Rights Era. These images are designed to establish the long narrative arc of the fight for racial justice. However, the vast majority of the signs in the crowds are in English, with a few in Swedish. The only hint of Spanish in the protest segment is a poster that says, "Todos somos iguales" [We are all equal]. Finally, throughout the video, El Chojín speaks in the first-person plural, linguistically linking himself not only to Correos but also to potential buyers of the stamps and the Spanish community at large. I believe it is this use of the first-person plural that led many to believe that El Chojín was intimately involved in the design of this campaign.

One of the main arguments raised in opposition to the Equality Stamps collection is that the stamps decrease in value as they darken, implying that darker-skinned people have less value than lighter-skinned people. However, according to the trailer, the purpose of the differing values is to reflect the injustice and inequality of the world rather than to project an image of what the world *should* look like. This hermeneutical incongruence between the Arena Media marketing team that designed the collection and the general public lies at the crux of the polemic. This difference of interpretation exemplifies what Harlan J. Strauss asserts in his 1975 article on stamps as tools of propaganda "If visual stimuli, i.e., postage stamps, simultaneously compete with audio stimuli, then the visual stimuli – ceteris paribus – will be the more powerful" (178). The Spanish State's messaging in the trailer ultimately could not compete with the visual messaging of the stamps themselves.

Caught in this controversy, El Chojín, a Black Spaniard, on May 30, 2021, posted a 16-minute video on his YouTube channel, *Pero de buen rollo*, explaining his perspective on the campaign and his role in it. One key argument he puts forth is that there is not "a clear definition of what racism is. A lot of people seized onto this explanation because, of course, if there's no clear definition, it seems evident that any act that one person considers racist, someone else could consider not to be racist."[11] This argument aligns with Susannah Heschel's description of the tenacity of racism. She argues that:

> racism is slippery, hard to define, constantly changing, and often disavowed and not recognized. Denials of racism cannot be taken at face value but require constant questioning. Racism's tenacity is deeply troubling, and the roots of this tenacity need to be sought not simply through their outward manifestations but also in our deepest, most hidden, and even unconscious motivations. Even as we repudiate racism, we may be unwittingly—or deliberately—perpetuating it.
> (23)

In other words, she defends that what is racist to some may not be to others. Furthermore, even those fighting against racism are capable of perpetuating it unintentionally, as in the case of this stamp campaign. El Chojín, though recognizing that racism is polysemic in nature, asserts that those who have interpreted the campaign to be a racist representation of a person's value have misunderstood it because "[c]learly, [he sees] it as an erroneous and simple interpretation because what in fact the campaign purports to do (according to what they told [him]) is strictly the opposite."[12] If the interpretation is indeed wrong, then El Chojín is able to absolve himself of any responsibility for the ensuing fiasco. As he states later, "The only thing I do in the campaign is read a text. A text that I agree with intellectually. Is it up for debate? Of course! But I agree with it."[13] His body language in this part of the video makes it clear that, rather than being apologetic, he is quite firm in his stance, not seeing anything fundamentally wrong with his participation in the campaign.

One particularly striking aspect of this video is that El Chojín explicitly spells out that his apology "is solely and exclusively for members of the Afro-descendent community in Spain that may have felt that the campaign wasn't morally acceptable."[14] This is stressed twice at the beginning when he outlines the two-part structure of the video, both as an explanation and an apology, then reiterated at the end just before he apologizes. Other viewers of the video are only to receive the explanation of what happened and his role in the campaign because, as he states, "I don't think I have to explain myself to them."[15] By racially segregating his apology, on the one hand, El Chojín is making clear that his loyalties as an artist and activist lie with the Black community, while on the other, he dismisses any others who may have been offended. This distinction may serve as a way for the artist to shield himself from further criticism, as he believes that only those within his own community are in a position to criticize him. However, his approach is myopic given the globalization of his music, the stamp campaign, and Blackness more generally. As Dorr notes, "global economic restructuring has consistently required the (re)imagination of geographies of racial capitalist exchange and of how the linkages between these different places are relatively and relationally articulated" (21), because, ultimately, Correos was selling a product whose message on race and racism traveled much further than perhaps was anticipated. Given the nature of the internet, particularly social media, it is irresponsible not to recognize or consider the international reception and impact of this campaign. It is within this context that El Chojín offers his apology:

> I know that Correos's intention at the time of launching this campaign was the best. I know this because, even though I wasn't in the kitchen, so to speak, I spoke with them, and I saw what they wanted to do. It seemed to me that they were getting themselves into a mess, as I said before, and even so, they did it anyway. And in that moment, it seemed great. But I also know that there have been people that it has bothered. And well, even knowing that, as I said before, the intention was

good, if it has bothered them, if it has hurt, if it didn't sit well, it's my responsibility, the least I can do given that I put my voice on this video, to apologize. I apologize, calmly.[16]

The apology is predicated on those who feel offended while not having understood the true intent of the campaign. Semantically, this apology absolves El Chojín of guilt as *he* understood Correos' underlying intention, even if others were oblivious to or misinterpreted it. As of the time of writing, less than one-tenth of his 77,000 YouTube subscribers had viewed the video, which was not shared on his Instagram account with its 366,000 followers nor on his Twitter account with 188,200 followers. This omission from his larger social media platforms implies an attempt to leave this controversy behind, following Correos's path of erasure.

El Chojín was hired for the Correos campaign due to his decades-long thread of anti-racist stances in his music and public activism. Although the campaign was intended to spark conversation and awareness about the presence of racism in Spanish society, the message received was instead that Correos was promoting racism. The hire/purchase of El Chojín is yet another manifestation of the Spanish consumption of Blackness for the benefit of hegemonic whiteness. Furthermore, the choice of El Chojín as the face of the campaign erodes trust in his commitment to anti-racism.

SOS Racismo: Communication Breakdown

The other participant in the Correos campaign was the Federación SOS Racismo, one of the leading anti-racism organizations in Spain. The federation is the umbrella organization that brings together the eight autonomous SOS Racismo associations in Spain: Aragón, Asturias, Bizkaia, Catalunya, Galicia, Gipuzkoa, Madrid, and Navarra. The collaboration with the Federación SOS Racismo adds legitimacy to the Correos campaign as it suggests that Spain has done or is currently doing the hard work needed to be anti-racist in ways in which the US has not. In addition, as spelled out on the back of the set of stamps, "part of the proceeds from the sale of these stamps will go to SOS RACISMO."[17] Even if the exact share of proceeds that would have benefited the federation is unknowable, the gesture is another reflection of the good intentions of Correos. This campaign was not simply paying lip service to the existence of racism but rather evidence that Correos wanted to use its national platform to help eradicate it.

In the now-deleted tweet published on the day the stamps were issued, the federation's account stated, "Are our lives not worth the same? @Correos launches the #EqualityStamps campaign together with @ElChojin_net to denounce the #racism that thousands of racialized people in

Spain face."[18] SOS Racismo's tweet was the only explicit reference to the presence of racism in Spain throughout the whole campaign, as it does not appear in the Correos trailer or its marketing materials. Given that the federation's mission "is to fight the distinct manifestations of racism in Spain," its participation in the Equality Stamps campaign confused many and caused an uproar among the autonomous branches of the organization.[19] Upon the release of these stamps, branches of SOS Racismo denounced the campaign and denied having been consulted on this project. For example, SOS Racismo Madrid published a seven-part thread on its Instagram and Twitter accounts on May 27, stating: "The unfortunate Correos campaign highlights the need to create greater anti-racist awareness in Spain. Racism is not only because of the color of one's skin, it is a systemic and historical issue constructed to privilege some sectors of society and demean others."[20] From their perspective, the campaign reduces racism to phenotypic differences instead of acknowledging the structural factors that allow racism to persist in Spain today.

That same day, SOS Racismo Galicia issued a press release written in Galician on its Instagram and Twitter accounts. Entitled "We do not support the #EqualityStamps campaign," it expresses their discontent with the campaign, reiterates their autonomy from the federation, and offers possible solutions to Correos and all those involved in the development of the campaign.[21] They assert that, while the intention of the campaign is valid, its message is unclear, resulting in the reification of racist structures that affect racialized people, particularly those of dark skin.[22] Two paragraphs later, they continue:

> We urge those responsible to reflect on what happened and, in this case, we strongly encourage them to develop positive and enriching practices that will truly make a difference in the fight against the racism and racial discrimination that is deeply rooted in this country: for example BY HIRING RACIALIZED PEOPLE IN CORREOS.[23]

This sentence emphasizes a common thread highlighted in many of the social media comments related to this campaign: Correos is complicit in perpetuating racism in Spain. Thus, even those not necessarily opposed to the campaign itself found it to be entirely tone-deaf, given the lack of racial representation among the organization's employees. The press release ends with two poignant reflections:

> We believe that if the opinions and perspectives of racialized people had been taken into account, the campaign would have had a sound approach to fighting racial discrimination and today we would not be lamenting that a public institution like Correos spent money on an unfortunate campaign.[24]

The lack of input from racialized people resulted in a campaign that was condemned globally and did not last even half a week. Additionally, because Correos is a public institution, the very people harmed by this campaign helped pay for it, as all Spaniards supported this campaign financially with their taxes. The Galician response offers a path forward for Correos, one that the organization ultimately chose not to pursue.

The responses of the various SOS Racismo branches harken back to El Chojín's reflections on the lack of a clear definition of racism. The federation thought it was promoting anti-racism by joining the Equality Stamps campaign, while the branches saw the collaboration as perpetuating racism. With no unified voice raised in response to the campaign, it appeared as though SOS Racismo was at odds with itself, which ultimately hurts the anti-racist advocacy work it is doing all over the country. Furthermore, the speed at which the branches had to respond to the controversy also demonstrates that the average Spaniard is unaware of the autonomy of the branches within the federation, which calls into question the effectiveness of its structure and its communication protocols.

The Afterlife of the Equality Stamps

At this point, there remains no official trace of the Equality Stamps campaign. According to the Correos website, no new stamps were released in May 2021. Unlike El Chojín and SOS RACISMO, Correos never offered an apology or an explanation for the campaign. Given the 24-hour news cycle, the three-day controversy faded away as news of Eurocopa 2021, the possible need for COVID-19 booster shots, and the new COVID-19 Delta variant soon consumed the nation's attention. By erasing the campaign altogether, Correos was able to act as if the fiasco had never happened and thus absolved itself from having to take steps toward improving its relationship with racialized communities. Since then, Correos has not released any stamps that directly address questions related to race and racism in Spain nor issued any media releases on the topic.

Even so, the memory of the Equality Stamps campaign lives on through social media and the philatelic market. Since only 600 sets were produced, and it is unknown how many were sold before the campaign was halted, the collectors' value for these sets is quite high. While the retail price for each set was 4.60€, in 2022, I paid 235€ for one on eBay. However, I have seen some collectors offering the sets for sale online for prices as high as 620€. The secondary life of the Equality Stamps collection indicates that not only does scarcity dictate its desirability, but that controversy does as well. What is clear is that the value lies in the entire set rather than in any individual stamp, implying that a multiracial society does indeed have value. However, that value seems to flow entirely from the controversy, not from the educational point, which was never properly disseminated, never

84 Jeffrey K. Coleman

appreciated by El Chojín nor by Correos, and never ultimately resolved, as the campaign was just ended without correction or explanation.

The short-lived Equality Stamps campaign highlights how the Spanish State continues to demonstrate its racial anxieties in the face of a growing multiracial citizenry. By teaming up with El Chojín and SOS Racismo, Correos attempted to ground its campaign in an anti-racist approach. Unfortunately, the result was exactly the opposite. The backlash and subsequent erasure of the campaign demonstrate that in the 30 years since the death of Lucrecia Pérez Matos, the Spanish State still has not figured out how to confront issues of race and racism on a national level. Instead, it resorts to externalization (i.e. blames the US) as a discursive practice through which to address the matter or simply carries on as if racism does not exist at all in Spain. What remains to be seen is whether Correos and, by extension, the Spanish State have learned from this debacle to recognize the intrinsic value of all people, no matter the color of their skin.

Notes

1 According to the now-deleted product page for Equality Stamps, "En Correos no nos mantenemos al margen frente a la discriminación racial, por eso, en el mes Europeo de la Diversidad y coincidiendo con el primer aniversario del asesinato de George Floyd, lanzamos una colección de sellos que refleja una injusta y dolorosa realidad a la que se enfrentan millones de personas cada día. Cuanto más oscuro es el color del sello, menor valor tendrá. Convertimos así cada carta y cada envió en un reflejo de la desigualdad que crea el racismo, y en un paso más hacia su desaparición definitiva." [We at Correos don't want to remain on the margins with regard to racial discrimination. Therefore, during European Diversity Month and coinciding with the first anniversary of the murder of George Floyd, we are launching a collection of stamps that reflects an unjust and painful reality that millions of people face every day. The darker the stamp, the less value it will have. That way we turn every letter and every package into a reflection of the inequality that racism creates, and into one more step towards its outright erradication.]
2 In his book ¿Qué hace un negro como tú en un sitio como este?, Moha Gerehou lists several examples of everyday racism including: the innocuous use of racist phrases such as "merienda de negros" [Black mischief] (146), the ban on Blacks and Arabs in dance clubs (119), the hurling of racist slurs at Black players on the soccer pitch (122–23), the inability to rent housing as a Black person or family (157–58), and the racial profiling of Black and Brown people by the police who constantly ask them for their national identity card to prove their nationality (162–66).
3 "Como cualquier imagen, los sellos postales transmiten toda su información simultáneamente. Por eso un sello postal diseñado inadecuadamente puede producir el efecto contrario al deseado, especialmente si está dirigido a un determinado grupo de población."
4 "una colección de sellos para luchar contra el cambio climático."
5 "una colección de sellos para luchar contra el racismo."
6 In 2005, the Mexican Postal Service released a series of stamps commemorating Memín Pinguín, a beloved comic book character. The release of these

stamps was condemned by U.S. officials and civil rights leaders as racist. This came during an already tense time in U.S.-Mexico relations as a result of a racially charged statement made by Mexican President Vicente Fox just a few weeks prior stating that Mexican immigrants in the US "are doing jobs that not even blacks want to do."

7 "Pantone's team around the world typically spends the year studying trends in fashion, consumer products, social media and technology. It looks for influences that best describe the current mood of society and picks a color to reflect those elements" (Kavilanz).
8 For an analysis of this song, see Silvia Bermúdez, *Rocking the Boat*.
9 Both trailers contain the same imagery; I cite the Spanish version.
10 "Es suficiente. El mundo ha dicho 'Basta.' Miles de personas se han levantado en contra de la discriminación racial. En Correos no hemos querido mantenernos al margen. Por eso, hemos creado una nueva serie de sellos. Correos presenta: EQUALITY STAMPS. Una colección de sellos que refleja una injusta realidad que nunca debería existir. Hay gente que piensa que el valor de una persona depende de su color de piel. Por eso los sellos tienen un valor distinto según el color de la piel que representan. Cuanto más oscuro sea el sello, menor valor tendrá. Así que para enviar algo lejos necesitarás más negros que blancos. Convertimos así cada carta y cada envío en un reflejo de la desigualdad que crea el racismo, en una protesta. EQUALITY STAMPS: una colección de sellos que reivindica que el valor de una vida no debería tener color."
11 "una definición clara de lo que es el racismo. A eso se agarró un montón de gente porque, claro, si no hay una definición clara, parece evidente que cualquier acto que uno considera racista, otro puede considerar que no lo es."
12 "Claro, yo lo veo una interpretación errónea y simple. Porque lo que, de hecho, se pretende, según se me contó a mí, es estrictamente lo contrario."
13 "yo lo único que hago en la campaña es leer un texto. Un texto con el que, intelectualmente, estoy de acuerdo. ¿Que es susceptible de ser discutido? Por supuesto. Pero con el que estoy de acuerdo."
14 "es única y exclusivamente para las personas de la comunidad afrodescendiente en España que hayan podido sentir que la campaña moralmente no estaba bien."
15 "no creo que tenga que disculparme entre ellos."
16 "Sé que la intención por parte de Correos a la hora de hacer la campaña ha sido la mejor. Y lo sé porque, aunque yo no he estado ahí en la cocina, digamos, he hablado con la gente y he visto que es lo que querían hacer. Me parecía que se estaban metiendo y como he dicho antes, en un marrón y aun así lo han hecho. Y en su momento, a mí me pareció, bien. Pero también sé que ha habido gente a la que le ha molestado. Y bueno, aun sabiendo que, como he dicho antes, la intención era buena, si se ha molestado, si ha dolido, si ha sentado mal, en lo que me toca, qué es lo poquito de haber puesto la voz en el vídeo éste, pues yo me disculpo. Me disculpo, tranquilamente."
17 "parte de los beneficios obtenidos por la venta de los sellos irán destinados a SOS RACISMO."
18 "¿Nuestras vidas no valen igual? @Correos lanza la campaña #EqualityStamps junto a @ElChojin_net para denunciar el #racismo que viven miles de personas racializadas en España."
19 "es luchar contra las distintas manifestaciones del racismo en España."
20 "La desafortunada campaña de @Correos pone de relieve que es necesario crear mayor conciencia antirracista en España. El #Racismo no es solo por el color de la piel, es una cuestión sistémica e histórica construida para privilegiar a sectores de la sociedad e inferiorizar a otros."

21 "Non apoiamos a campaña #EqualityStamps."
22 "Comprendemos que o obxectivo da campaña era intentar visibilizar e denunciar unha xerarquía racial existente relativa ás diferentes tonalidades da pele, coñecida por colorismo, que privilexia e promove os resgos e aparencias cercanas á branquitude, pero nin a mensaxe nin a perspectiva usada deixa clara esta mensaxe. Todo o contrario, acentúase máis a discriminación e submisión que sufrimos as persoas con tons de pele escuras."
23 "Instamos a que as persoas responsables podan reflexionar sobre o acontecido e, neste caso animámolas, encarecidamente, a desenvolver prácticas positivas e enriquecedoras que, verdadeiramente, marquen unha diferenza na loita contra o racismo e a discriminación racial fortemente arraigados neste país: como pode ser a CONTRATACIÓN DE PERSOAS RACIALIZADAS EN CORREOS."
24 "Consideramos que si se tiveran en conta as opinións e perspectivas das persoas racializadas a campaña tería un enfoque acertado para loitar contra a discriminación racial e hoxe non estaríamos lamentando que unha institución pública como Correos gastase os cartos en realizar unha desafortunada campaña."

Works Cited

Bermúdez, Silvia. *Rocking the Boat: Migration and Race in Contemporary Spanish Music*. U of Toronto P, 2018.

Chojín, El. "Campaña de Correos." *YouTube*, uploaded by *Pero de BUEN ROLLO*, 30 May 2021, https://youtu.be/gqOnRtnhsM0.

Coleman, Jeffrey K. "Autochthonous Anxieties, Immigration, and the Dangers of Demagoguery in Juan Diego Botto's 'Arquímedes'." *Estreno*, vol. 44, no. 1, 2018, pp. 71–89.

———. *The Necropolitical Theater: Race and Immigration on the Contemporary Spanish Stage*. Northwestern UP, 2020.

Correos. "Tarifas 2021: Península y Baleares." 2021, http://www.sovafil.es/Tarifas-2021-Peninsula-y-Baleares.pdf.

"Correos Launches 'Protest Stamps', Stamps Featuring the Voices of a Generation Against Climate Change." *Correos*, https://www.correos.com/en/sala-prensa/correos-launches-protest-stamps-stamps-featuring-the-voices-of-a-generation-against-climate-change/#.

Donovan, Mary Kate. "'Se ríen de la crisis': Chinese Immigration as Economic Invasion in Spanish Film and Media." *Revista de Estudios Hispánicos*, vol. 51, no. 2, 2017, pp. 369–93.

Dorr, Kirstie. "'Putting a Stamp on Racism': Political Geographies of Race and Nation in the Memín Pinguín Polemic." *Aztlán*, vol. 39, no. 1, 2014, pp. 13–40.

Equality Stamps: La colección de sellos que refleja la injusta realidad del racismo [The Stamp Collection That Reflects the Unjust Reality of Racism]. 2021.

Essed, Philomena. *Everyday Racism: Reports from Women of Two Cultures*. Translated by Cynthia Jaffe. Hunter House, 1990.

Folkart, Jessica A. *Liminal Fiction at the Edge of the Millennium: The Ends of Spanish Identity*. Bucknell UP, 2014.

Gerehou, Moha. *¿Qué hace un negro como tú en un sitio como este?* Península, 2021.

Graham, Helen, and Antonio Sánchez. "The Politics of 1992." *Spanish Cultural Studies: An Introduction*, edited by Jo Labanyi and Helen Graham. Oxford UP, 1995, pp. 406–18.

Heschel, Susannah. "The Slippery Yet Tenacious Nature of Racism: New Developments in Critical Race Theory and Their Implications for the Study of Religion and Ethics." *Journal of the Society of Christian Ethics*, vol. 35, no. 1, 2015, pp. 3–27.

Kavilanz, Parija. "The Color of 2017 Is …" *CNN Money*, 9 Dec. 2016, https://money.cnn.com/2016/12/08/news/color-of-the-year-2017-greenery-pantone/.

Medina, Miguel Ángel. "La campaña de sellos antirracistas que se ha vuelto contra Correos." *El País*, 28 May 2021, https://elpais.com/sociedad/2021-05-28/la-campana-de-sellos-antirracistas-que-se-ha-vuelto-contra-correos.html.

Minder, Raphael. "Spain Issued 'Equality Stamps' in Skin Tones. The Darker Ones Were Worth Less." *The New York Times*, 29 May 2021, p. 8A.

Moffette, David. *Governing Irregular Migration: Bordering Culture, Labour, and Security in Spain*. U of British Columbia P, 2018.

Moreno Figueroa, Mónica G., and Emiko Saldívar Tanaka. "'We Are Not Racists, We Are Mexicans': Privilege, Nationalism and Post-Race Ideology in Mexico." *Critical Sociology*, vol. 42, no. 4–5, 2016, pp. 515–33.

Navarro Oltra, Guillermo. *Autorretratos del Estado: Una aproximación al sello postal del franquismo como medio de emisión de mensajes ideológicos (1936–1975)*. 2009. Universidad de Castilla-La Mancha, PhD dissertation.

Noack, Rick. "Spain's Postal Service Introduces Skin-Tone Stamps to Fight Racism—And Makes the Whitest One the Most Valuable." *The Washington Post*, 27 May 2021, https://www.washingtonpost.com/world/europe/spain-stamps-racism/2021/05/27/d1885c80-beef-11eb-922a-c40c9774bc48_story.html.

"¿QUIÉNES SOMOS?" *Federación SOS Racismo*, 24 May 2016, https://sosracismo.eu/quienes-somos/.

SOS Racismo Galicia. "Compartimos comunicado onde explicamos a posición de non apoio de Sos Racismo Galicia a campaña #EqualityStamps de @correos." *Instagram*, 27 May 2021. https://www.instagram.com/p/CPYrYJJjFYK/.

SOS Racismo Madrid. "La desafortunada campaña de @Correos pone de relieve que es necesario crear mayor conciencia antirracista en España. El #Racismo no es solo por el color de la piel, es una cuestión sistémica e histórica construida para privilegiar a sectores de la sociedad e inferiorizar a otros." *Instagram*, 27 May 2021, https://www.instagram.com/p/CPXjTcGD5zV/.

Strauss, Harlan J. "Politics, Psychology and the Postage Stamp." *The Congress Book 1975: Forty-First American Philatelic Congress*. The American Philatelic Congress, 1975, pp. 157–80.

Zei, Vida. "Stamps and the Politics of National Representation." *Javnost*, vol. 4, no. 1, 1997, pp. 65–84.

4 Using the Web to Educate Spain About Its Afro-Identity
Afroféminas

Esther M. Alarcón Arana

While Spain's colonialist connections to the African continent are neither new nor relegated to the past, for a very long time, they have not been accurately recorded in historical texts, if recorded at all (Toasijé 19).[1] The nation's mainstream cultural scene has also failed to offer a complete representation of this influence (Blanco 15–26).[2] In fact, the most prevalent depictions of these relationships elicit both fear and pity, thus falling into the trap of what Nigerian author Chimamanda Ngozi Adichie called in her famous TED Talk the "single story," which reduces people's identities and perspectives to one dimension.[3] The Eurocentric education imparted in Spanish classrooms and the social Afro-amnesia that stems from the nation's artistic production promote, on the one hand, the perpetual aspiration of Spain to be considered part of the modern Northern European continent and, on the other, the rejection and even a sense of having been offended if related to the African continent.[4] In addition, the refusal to acknowledge Spain's African connections hampers the understanding and acceptance of Afro-descendant people in Spain. This fosters the criminalization of racialized people and the constant questioning of their belonging to Spain, thus harming them and creating, as Ana León-Távora has affirmed while recalling W.E.B. Du Bois concept of *double consciousness*, a sense of alienation and indignity (206).[5]

In contrast to this imperialistic view of national identity, groups of Afro-descendant citizens and immigrants have started to claim their space in the Spanish cultural terrain by legitimately occupying the public sphere. While not yet widely represented in mainstream media, racialized people are using online spaces to combat their invisibilization and other forms of discrimination. They do so through websites, blogs, magazines, social networks, and other audiovisual media. Some of these online communities are *NGXMGZ, Coop. Periferia Cimarronas, Conciencia Afro*, and *Afroféminas*, the magazine that is the subject of this essay. *Afroféminas* is an online collective that Antoinette Torres Soler founded in 2014.[6] In the *Proyecto* section of the site, the collective introduces itself as an online

Using the Web to Educate Spain About Its Afro-Identity: Afroféminas   89

community that invites Spanish-speaking Black/Afro-descendant and racialized women to share their experiences and life lessons. In the introduction to her book, *Viviendo en modo Afroféminas*, Torres Soler envisions the online magazine as a

> form of personal empowerment, as a meeting place with other Black women, in order to turn the magazine into a space of empowerment, of visibility for many female voices, of entrepreneurship and construction of Spanish Afrofeminism. The fact that it is written in Spanish is very important because *Afroféminas* maintains a very special connection with Latin American racialized women. This project intends to establish a dialogue in Spanish because of the lack of this kind of information in our language and its predominance in English and in French … The nation with the most Afroféminas' readers is Spain. (13)[7]

The emphasis on dialogue and the desire to overcome the lack of information underscore the group's didactic focus, illustrated by its magazine articles, bookstore, and consulting services (such as workshops and talks). In addition to giving voice to Black and other racialized women, the numerous Afro-activist writings that deal with Spain speak to white people, too, offering a decentralized historical perspective and challenging the racism that has characterized Spanish society. The strong didacticism of these texts aims not only to empower the marginalized individual but also to create a conscious culture that will bring about social change.

This chapter explores the Eurocentrism that dominates Spanish culture and analyzes how *Afroféminas*'s antiracist activism challenges the hegemonic concept of Spain's national identity.[8] It does not propose an exhaustive analysis of the online site—for example, the connections with Latin America that feature prominently will not be discussed here—focusing instead on a selection of articles that deal with two main subjects: the representation of people of African descent in the history of Spain and contemporary white feminism's failure to take racialized women's issues seriously. Moreover, a final section, concentrating on two discursive practices employed in these articles—dialogue and storytelling—completes the analysis of the collective's attempts to overturn the country's Afro-amnesia and acknowledge the existence of a significant Black Spain.

Decolonizing Spanish History: #EstadoEspañolNoTanBlanco

In his book *Qué hace un negro como tú en un sitio como este* [What's a Black dude like you doing in a place like this?] (2021), journalist and activist Moha Gerehou draws attention to his readers about Spanish institutional anti-Black racism by connecting his life experiences—in the form of a Bildungsroman—with histories, news, and academic studies that demonstrate the structural nature of this ideology. Gerehou recalls the time when he popularized the hashtag #EstadoEspañolNoTanBlanco [#NotSoWhiteSpanishState] on Twitter—inviting racialized Spanish people to post a picture of themselves on this social media with the hashtag—and received countless threats in response, showing he had touched a raw nerve with white Spain. Recalling U.S. antiracist activist and author Ibram X. Kendi's words, Gerehou argues that "[t]he opposite of antiracist knowledge is not ignorance. It is racist knowledge" (229).[9] The articles in *Afroféminas*, like Gerehou's work, constitute examples of a decolonial praxis, which challenges colonial knowledge and power. The collective seeks to distance itself from the traditional Eurocentrism that suppresses the contributions of non-Western people who have endured the consequences of white imperialism. Importantly, as Yuderkys Espinosa Miñoso explains, a decolonial perspective:

> produces a genealogy of thought from the margins by feminists, women, lesbians, and racialized people in general; and it dialogues with the knowledge produced by intellectuals and activists committed to dismantling the matrix of multiple oppressions assuming a non-Eurocentric perspective. (152)

Afroféminas is committed to this non-Eurocentric perspective and aims to revise the racist teachings and learnings that characterize Spanish education to ultimately offer an antiracist alternative.[10] It attempts to correct the history delivered in the classroom, challenging the connections schools, and culture in general create between race and belonging to a geographic location. Based on their belief in education as a tool to combat racism, their *Proyecto* echoes the Enlightenment motto—based on Cicero—of *docere-delectare-movere* [teach, delight, move], affirming that, through journalism, literature, and poetry, *Afroféminas* "aspires to educate, inspire, and entertain." The *Revista*, particularly in subsections such as "Afro-Reflexión" and "Historia," vindicates the Black presence in and belonging to Spain in articles such as "Afroreferentes [sic] para una afrodescendiente" [Afro Role Models for an Afro Descendant Woman] (Banora), "La visibilidad es poder" [Visibility Is Power] (*Afroféminas*), "El racismo también está en el periodismo" [Racism Is Also Present in Journalism] (Zuri), "Identidades" ["Identities"] (Mballo), or "Y tú por qué eres negro?" [And Why Are You Black?] (Mbomío).[11] These articles focus on the need to emphasize role models of African descent in Spain (and elsewhere) in order to *un-whiten* hegemonic—racist—thinking regarding national identity and foster a new concept of nationhood.

In this regard, the feature that stands out the most in *Afroféminas*—just as in the works of fiction and non-fiction that racialized Spanish people

Using the Web to Educate Spain About Its Afro-Identity: Afroféminas

write—is the recurrent allusion to how frequently they are questioned about their right to be part of the country given their phenotype. In fact, Black and Brown people, in particular, are generally assumed to be immigrants, often undocumented, which leads to being criminalized. For instance, in a 2020 *Afroféminas* article promoting his newly published novel *El aroma de los mangos*, Paulo Akam (1982) wrote:

> Being an Afro-descendant in Spain ... and to recognize oneself as such. I have read sentences such as: *"There are now second and third generation Afro-descendants in Spain..."* or *"The new diverse Spain...,"* as if we had just arrived. And every time I read things like this my mind travels back to the past and I see myself, as a seven- or eight-year-old child, sitting next to my grandfather, who was born in Galicia.[12]

Besides revealing deep-seated grief, his comment also exposes the willful ignorance and hypocrisy of a state that insists on maintaining its constructed whiteness. The idea of a "new diverse Spain" implies a nation that claims to accept the foreign, "the Other," as a newcomer but that cannot accept their offspring, born and raised in Spain, as belonging to the country. By assuming this perspective, the State denies Akam and others their very existence, their belonging, and their history. Far from being simply a mistake, this ignorance is a clear manifestation of systemic racism, as institutions actively bury the nation's colonial connections to the African continent. In fact, in another interview for *Afroféminas*, Antumi Toasijé denounces this invisibilization, stating that there are documents that prove the presence of Afro-descendants in Spain dating back to the Middle Ages. While in this interview Toasijé does not provide specific examples of this presence, in a series of teaching modules about racism in Spain, he explained how the focus on religious differences in medieval historical texts simplified the racial diversity of the Iberian Peninsula. Moreover, in an online session about race in Spain, he insists on the "Catholic leuco-Europeanization of the Iberian Peninsula and Abya Yala" (Koli), citing as a pragmatic example the progressive whitening of Ibn-Humayyah, the leader of the Morisco Revolt during King Phillip II's reign, in artistic representations.[13] The omission of this part of Spanish history and Ibn-Humayyah's whitening over time demonstrate, according to Toasijé, the institutional efforts to erase anything African from the national narrative (Koli).

The idea of nation has traditionally been defined as an artificial construct based on a number of shared characteristics, such as religion and ethnicity. Ernest Gellner's definition maintains that "[t]wo men are of the same nation if and only if they recognize each other as belonging to the same nation" (7). This definition, which describes how nations have been theorized, becomes problematic when considered prescriptively. First comes the question of what the shared characteristics of a culture or a people are. For instance, among many other questions, must one be born in Spain in order to be Spanish, must one's ancestors also be born in Spain, and if so, how many generations back must one look? Moreover, the suggestion that two people need to recognize each other as part of the same nation demonstrates the supremacy of a dominant identity over others, which validates a specific set of characteristics over others, thus not permitting the mutual recognition required to share a national identity. This leads those belonging to the dominant culture to question, and even insult, marginalized people when they speak for themselves. For instance, in a 2016 article promoting a talk by Spanish activist Desirée Bela-Lobedde, then known for her blog and YouTube channel "Negra Flor," *Afroféminas* denounced the verbal abuse by white supremacists that she had to endure and the lack of repercussions for this abuse in the public space. YouTube's inaction regarding the racial slurs directed at Bela-Lobedde and its statement that they "did not see any comments that violated the platform's norms" demonstrate the bigotry of the space as well as the lack of norms in Spain to protect marginalized people.

It is generally difficult for mainstream Spain to picture racialized people as part of themselves since, as Baltasar Fra-Molinero has claimed, "Spaniards have seen themselves as white since early modernity" (147). In fact, ever since the fifteenth century, this idea of Spain, conceived in the eleventh century to refer to the population of the Peninsular Christian kingdoms (Fusi 56) and disseminated by epic poetry, the *romancero castellano*, and the chronicles and annals of the time, created legends that generated the myth of a lengthy white Spanish past. This imaginary was based on the politics of exclusion, such as the expulsion of the Jews (1492) and of the *Moriscos* (1609), the statutes of blood purity (starting in 1449), and the vigilance of the Inquisition, which the Catholic Monarchs established in 1478 and which lasted until well into the nineteenth century. As Antonio Feros has argued:

> Spanishness was the combination of features and characteristics that distinguished the Spanish from other nations—other Europeans but especially other nations (Jews, Arabs, Americans, and Africans) who lived in territories controlled by Spain.
>
> The transition in the eighteenth century toward the definition of Spaniards as members of the "white race," and the exaltation of this race as morally and physically superior, was the prerequisite to the categorical representation of the rest of humanity as members of naturally inferior other races—no longer just nations. (9)

Since the nineteenth century, the connection between Spanish national identity and racism has become more deeply embedded, originating in the belief that "some races are superior to others and that these inferior races could endanger the purity and cultural identity of the superior races if allowed to live among them" (Feros 8). There is abundant evidence today that skin color is a determining factor when considering whether a person does or does not belong to Spain, influencing the way racialized people are treated. Some examples that illustrate this approach are the police profiling and abuse of people based on their skin tone (Neild et al.) or rental discrimination (Agencias Girona). These complaints have reached the National Police, the Constitutional Court of Spain, and even the United Nations' High Commissioner for Human Rights.

Afroféminas has also tackled the drastic consequences of foreignizing and criminalizing racialized people. In an open letter to "Querido policía" [Dear Policeman], Torres Soler conveys her fear as a Black person at the sight of the police, even before the whole world witnessed the murder of George Floyd in the United States in 2020 at the hands of those whose job it was to protect him:

> Do you know what happened to me not so long ago? I was leaving a fantastic workshop with my female colleagues and we saw some African brothers celebrating. They were being watched by the National Police. And among all the partying, the rejoicing, and our surprise, one of these National policemen approached me. I swear to you that I felt terror at that moment. I was not doing anything wrong, but just by being a Black woman in Spain, I have an 80% probability of being arrested by one of your colleagues, of being publicly humiliated and there would be zero consequences ... My terror was such that I did not realize that the policeman in front of me was the father of one of my daughter's school friends, and he had come over to greet me.[14]

Although the murder of George Floyd became—rightly—a viral affair that exposed this kind of violence, his death was neither an isolated incident nor an event that only happens in the US For example, a 2017 report by the Spanish State's Federation of Associations of SOS Racism (Federación de Asociaciones de SOS Racismo del Estado Español 111) denounces the reality of racial profiling by the police as well as racist verbal and physical aggressions in various regions of Spain (112–18). In Torres Soler's letter, the joy and celebratory mood of the Black brotherhood contrast with her paralyzing fear when she realized that a policeman was approaching her, as her words—"terror," "detenida," "humillada," and "pavor"—demonstrate. Torres Soler's description of her personal experience underlines the fractures in the society that she inhabits, revealing that this fear originates in the pattern of police brutality against racialized people. It also demands institutional changes that recognize that non-white individuals belong to Spain: "Dear policeman. I am a migrant and a Spaniard, too."[15]

Furthermore, toward the end of the article/letter, Torres Soler offers her services to help change the systemic racism within the police: "I offer my free services to train you if needed. And note that I do not like to do anything for free, but I consider this problem so serious that I am willing to make an exception."[16]

If It's Not Afro-Centered, It's Not Feminism

Mainstream feminism has traditionally failed to recognize the heterogeneous groups of people the word "woman" embraces and, therefore, neglected to place issues from outside the white mainstream at the core of its agenda. It has been criticized for its Eurocentrism (Suárez Navaz and Hernández 32), that is, for its lack of representation and absence of space for the feminist struggles experienced and theorized by women from the Global South and racialized women in general. In the United States, Black women have condemned white feminists' analyses of patriarchy for being, as Kimberlé Crenshaw wrote in her seminal 1989 article, "rooted in white experiences" (157). In addition, bell hooks stated on numerous occasions that Betty Friedan's *The Feminine Mystique* (1963), considered a foundational feminist reading, did not resonate with her. Indeed, in her 1984 book, *Feminist Theory: From Margin to Center*, hooks claims that Friedan presumed all women's experiences and desires resembled her white middle-class married life without contemplating "who would be called in to take care of the children and maintain the home if more women like herself were freed from their house labor and given equal access with white men to the professions … She ignored the existence of all non-white women and poor white women" (1–2). But even before these two cultural icons, abolitionist activist Sojourner Truth and women's rights activist Anna Julia Cooper had exposed these same paradoxes in the nineteenth-century United States.

In Spain, the situation has not been different. That is why Elvira Swartch Lorenzo begins her article "Ayuda para feministas blancas" by speaking to white women in the following manner:

> I know you are all very proud of your recent and past feminist milestones (so am I of my own). But ladies, we must deal collectively with both issues of race and the feminist movement. I want to help you as much as possible so that we can all become more empathetic and look at women different from ourselves with much less ignorance. I know we can do this and there is one thing you do not know: I want you alongside me.[17]

This fragment is a call for white feminists to become true allies by connecting patriarchy and racism. This is crucial because, even though feminists from the center—as opposed to the margins, as seen in hook's book cited above—may recognize their personal and political advantage in a society that is systematically racist, if they/we do not highlight the voices of racialized women, they/we end up perpetuating white privilege (Heuchan). Swartch Lorenzo's call was preceded by many others. For instance, Abuy Nfubea affirms in *Afrofeminismo: 50 años de lucha y activismo de mujeres negras en España (1968–2918)* that today's Afro-feminist movement is not new but rather a resurgence of a type of activism that dates back to the 1960s. He condemns the marginalization of race in institutional feminist discourse and denounces the damaging effects of these dominant views on Black women, whose subjectivity "is built over the experience of white women, because they [white women] do not take into consideration that other women who are not exactly like them exist, the result of an inherited supremacist gaze" (23).[18] In the academic world, Esther (Mayoko) Ortega Arjonilla, too, has accused mainstream Spanish feminism of the invisibilization of African women and those of African descent and has highlighted the importance of decentering hegemonic feminist discourses to include the whole of current Spanish society (52).

Over the last few years, *Afroféminas* has published numerous articles that have created multiple opportunities to tackle the debate regarding racism within feminism (Johnson; Swartch Lorenzo; Torres). Especially significant are the statements published annually since the first large-scale *Huelga Feminista* [Feminist Strike] in Spain on International Women's Day in 2018, also known as 8M Strike. With these texts, the collective has addressed their absence from this large yearly event. These articles call out the insincerity of white Spanish feminism, as well as its complicity with patriarchy and neoliberalism—the same systems white Spanish feminism criticizes in its manifesto—as it does not acknowledge or provide space for racialized women. The lack of recognition of this axis of oppression virtually erases these racialized women's contributions to the feminist movement and their very existence in the national territory. *Afroféminas*'s goal with this act of dissidence—as they see their non-participation in the Strike—is to encourage white feminists to reflect on their tokenism and to listen to other perspectives. At the same time, their statements also shed light on Black women's empowerment as they fight for their right to be recognized. In their praxis of intersectional feminism, *Afroféminas* criticizes the movement's inaction regarding equality for all as a result of the fear of losing their white privilege.

In the subsection "International 2018," embedded in the "*Huelga feminista*" tab, the website www.hacialahuelgafeminista.org describes the origins of the 2018 Feminist Strike and its connections with feminist movements worldwide, maintaining that their objective was "networking with women from as many countries as possible to simultaneously struggle together against the patriarchal oppression." The manifesto condemns violence against women as well as the discrimination they experience in both the private and public spheres, and it demands radical social changes to end oppression, such as LGBT-phobia, salary discrimination, and the precarization of care, emphasizing the feminization of poverty. While the 8M Manifesto claims the movement is intersectional, adopting phrases such as "Juntas somos más" [Together We Are More], "La sororidad es nuestra arma" [Sisterhood Is Our Weapon], and "somos diversas" [we are diverse], *Afroféminas* has challenged this alleged inclusivity, precisely by opposing the idea of "common objectives" in the fight against patriarchy. In "Por qué *Afroféminas* no se suma a la Huelga Feminista" [Why Does *Afroféminas* Not Join the Feminist Strike?], they acknowledge the "manifesto's timid attempts at being inclusive."[19] Nevertheless, they unequivocally deem these efforts insufficient: "facts are stronger than words, and actually, the invisibilization of racialized women in this movement is practically absolute."[20] Essentially, the 2018 and 2019 statements—as well as previous articles, such as the 2017 "Cuando solo somos una foto. Invisibilización de los otros feminismos en los actos del 8 de marzo" [When We Are Just a Photo. Invisibilization of Other Feminisms in the Events of March 8th]—draw attention to the problems that Black women have historically criticized: that white feminism replicates many of the same discriminatory patterns and dynamics they condemn in their struggle against patriarchy. Two significant ways in which the hegemonic movement does this are first, the non-representation/inclusion of the voices of racialized people, and second, their foreignization.

First of all, the way the concept of "woman" is universalized erases the specific oppression of Black women in Spain (and elsewhere). *Afroféminas* accuses the Strike Manifesto of not going beyond the reiteration of phrases that proclaim the diversity of the 8M Feminist demonstration. Therefore, including statements such as "No woman is illegal. We say ENOUGH! to racism and exclusion," without putting these oppressions at the center of their demands, demonstrates how white feminists still tokenize marginalized women and continue to appropriate the language of intersectionality.[21] The 8M Manifesto highlights the roles of patriarchy and neoliberalism in oppressing women and claims this feminist approach throughout the text: "TOGETHER WE ARE MORE," "Sisterhood is our weapon," and "Our identity is multiple, we are diverse" are some of the mottoes at the start of each paragraph, thus putting emphasis on the diversity of the movement.[22] However, for *Afroféminas*, in spite of these words, by not giving voice to marginalized women themselves, they fail to recognize the intimate relationship between patriarchy, neoliberalism, and racism. The 8M manifesto reveals the emptiness of its words when the hegemonic group's actions repeat the same discriminatory patterns as patriarchy, as *Afroféminas* declares in the 2018 statement: "[u]nfortunately, intersectionality is still a word whose meaning hegemonic feminism empties out when it has to put it into practice."[23] The collective is aware that white feminists acknowledge and recognize the importance of this concept in calling on marginalized women to fight by their side. However, the following year, they wrote another article to explain their continuing absence, owing once again to the same reasons:

> [W]e are still treated as second-class citizens, in conference panels and feminist spaces we find affirmations that still perpetuate racism and invisibilize the oppressions that come with it. Understanding that NOT "all of us are the same" and that in this diversity there exist different demands and forms of struggle is fundamental to eliminating social patterns of structural racism.[24]

It was not until 2021 that *Afroféminas*, despite not yet having taken part in the demonstration, started noticing some change within the main movement. For this reason, they dedicate their text to their "hermanas y aliadas" [sisters and allies] but still justify their absence since "changes within hegemonic feminism are too slow" and racism is still present within the movement.[25]

In addition to the erasure of Black voices, the language of the manifesto confirms this white bias as it foreignizes racialized people. By juxtaposing "illegal" and "exclusion" to "racism" in that phrase, the statement is, in fact, assuming that not being white makes a person an immigrant, nefariously characterizing racialized people as illegal. This is probably the most repeated form of discrimination that Blacks and other people of color must face in Spain, as *Afroféminas*' 2019 statement highlights: "Being a Black or racialized woman puts you in a constant position of foreignization and of not belonging."[26] In fact, Torres Soler remembers the time when she approached Zaragoza's "Casa de la Mujer" to propose an exhibit on Black women and was directed instead to the "Casa de las Culturas" (*Viviendo* 27–28). Torres Soler's complaint is not new in Spain, nor is it in other places populated predominantly by white people. In the United States, for instance, bell hooks recalls that the first time she taught a course on Black women writers from a feminist perspective, it was not included in the Women's Studies program but only in the Black Studies program (*Teaching*).

In this context, the intersectionality of the 2018 8M Feminist Manifesto appears as both tokenizing and duplicitous because it does not practice the theory it claims as the basis of the movement. Just as bell hooks wrote in *Teaching to Transgress*, theory means nothing if we do not live it, unless it engages with practice. Intersectionality is, thus, a tool to explain the complex and various situations of discrimination, but most importantly, to end the structural discrimination that affects different people.[27] In her book, Torres Soler states:

> I understand Black Feminism basically as a praxis, in opposition to this cold theory, from which, in my perspective, anyone can write, appropriate and even obtain relevance without any impact on Black women's empowerment ... Black Feminism is not an "ornament theory," that is, a theory to become prominent while lacking all action.[28]

Torres Soler's idea of Black Feminism evokes the ones African American feminists such as Kimberlé Crenshaw, Audre Lorde, bell hooks, and Patricia Hill Collins have been defending and disseminating for decades. To them, Black feminist and intersectional theory cannot be separated from undertaking the actual work to advance Black women's equality. According to the articles *Afroféminas* has published from 2018 to 2023 in relation to the 8M Feminist Strike, Spain's mainstream feminist movement is not serious about change. Instead, it continues homogenizing feminism, thus ignoring the needs of non-white women. *Afroféminas* sees the 8M appeal to fight together in the same manner as bell hooks did in the past: "as yet another expression of white female denial of the reality of racist domination, of their complicity in the exploitation and oppression of black women and black people" (*Teaching*).

The Magazine's Discursive Strategies

Although *Afroféminas* clearly seeks to empower women of African descent, the articles analyzed here are concerned with the collective's didacticism aimed at Spain's white population. While previous sections have discussed the articles' content regarding *Afroféminas*' teachings, this section engages with their online discursive strategies designed to instill the activism and teachings they strive to convey to their white audience. In this regard, the Internet has provided *Afroféminas* with a valuable tool to fulfill its didactic mission and remedy the institutional bias regarding issues of nationality and race. Its strategies are dialogical form and storytelling.

In spite of the criticism directed at digital media—for example, the rise of dis/misinformation due to the consumption of pseudo-informative content (Romero-Rodríguez and Aguaded) and the fact that these tools are managed through a neoliberal type of logic—they also provide the opportunity to create meaningful communities (Villegas Simón and Navarro Bosch 234–35), to increase the visibility of social movements, and even to transform people's lives (Mendes et al. 4). For example, the role of the Internet in the success of the 8M Feminist Strike in Spain was undeniable, as confirmed by the headlines in its aftermath, which called it a "historic mobilization for the rights of women" (Gómez and Marcos).[29] The Web 2.0, and particularly the proliferation of social networks, have indeed had a strong impact on contemporary activism, changing the way people communicate (Casero-Ripollés 536; Candón Mena and Benítez Eyzaguirre 7; Pecourt Gracia 77). Andreu Casero-Ripollés identifies three main factors that contribute to the success of online activism: first, the direct production and dissemination of content by activists themselves; second, the monitoring of political and social action, denouncing corruption and other forms of abuse; and third, the way regular citizens can distribute content in a more open and accessible manner (537).

The Internet also reflects the fractures within feminism. For example, Nuria Varela claims that it "is allowing feminism to build a strong, popular, reactive *online* movement" (106), which unites all women in their struggle against patriarchy. However, the *Afroféminas* articles examined in this chapter problematize the idea that social networks "are provoking a new kind of action, led by anonymous, rapidly, and precisely organized multitudes, with clear and *common objectives*" (Varela 106; my emphasis).[30] In fact, just as the *Afroféminas* articles examined in the previous section illustrate, researchers have also determined that digital feminism reproduces the same bias as hegemonic feminism (Villegas Simón and Navarro Bosch 243), challenging the gap between white and racialized feminists' perception of their "common objectives."

Aimed at white readers, the articles are often written in a dialogical form, as if part of a conversation with the intended audience. While not an actual dialogue, these statements clearly speak to the readers—"you"—they are seeking to engage. However, although this "you" is called upon more frequently in the later articles, the 2018 statement displays a strong opposition between the use of "we" and "them." The repetition of the pronoun dyad highlights the chasm between racialized and white people. In contrast to the 8M call for solidarity, the repetitive opposition between the collective *nosotras*, "we," and "them," referring to white feminist, puts the focus on the differences between the two groups of women and the fact that white feminism erases these differences. In the first half of that statement, *Afroféminas*'s predominant use of the direct and indirect object pronoun "nos" underscores the calls to uniting forces they received from the active "they"—white feminists. It is not until the breach between white and racialized women is asserted that the active use of "we," transmitted through the verb form, starts. Most paragraphs begin with the first-person plural ("we know," "we think," "we applaud"), stressing their presence and activism. The statement concludes with an ironic rhetorical question—Why criticize them for not wanting to unite forces?—and these final words: "we leave it for you to reflect on." In this manner, "they" becomes "you," the ones addressed by the article, proof that, while trying to engage with the audience, there is no recognition of belonging to the same group.[31] Ultimately, this ending suggests the possibility, or wish, that white feminists take a step back and let marginalized people move to the center and take the lead.

The engagement with white feminists—"you"—becomes more explicit in the 2020 statement about the planned 8M Strike, which was canceled due to the COVID-19 pandemic. This letter begins with: "Dear sisters, allies and comrades."[32] While maintaining their position due to the persistence of white feminist discrimination, *Afroféminas*'s direct discourse serves the collective's mission of educating its audience about intersectionality. This strategy is especially evident in articles directed to the magazine's white audience, such as Viviana Santiago's query, "Are you a white person and sometimes bothered by some of the things regarding anti-racism? This message is for you!" where both the message and the intended recipient are made explicit in the title, or in Marián Cortes Owusu's article, "Para el recién llegado al antirracismo" [For the Newly Arrived at Anti-racism].[33] The directness of the language is accompanied by a conversational and ironic tone to ensure the audience stands in the speaker's shoes and understands the changes they must make to become a real ally. Each short paragraph in Cortes Owusu's article offers specific guidance to the white ally, such as "get ready for the conversations you'll need to have with people who are incapable of listening or understanding," "this task won't only become harder the more committed you become," and "I know you think you have lots of good ideas for the fight," but then: "Please, don't tell us about the hard road that brought you here."[34] In reality, while *Afroféminas* might hope that white feminists become allies to racialized women, the irony displayed in many of these articles exhibits a degree of skepticism that is derived from experiences like the ones portrayed in their 8M statements.

Storytelling supports the dialogic form of these articles. This narrative technique constitutes a conscious choice to root the presence of a significant Black history in Spain as a way to ultimately rewrite the colonialist and racist official history. In his book *The Writing of History*, Michel de Certeau examines the practice of making history (in the Eurocentric world) as a "science" that uses writing as a way of producing meaning.[35] In it, he draws attention to the creative part of the writing of history, where facts, which de Certeau calls "choices" (59), are selected and presented under a particular light depending on the power it serves—a king, a prince, or an institution, for example. By underlining this process, de Certeau argues that making history is tantamount to erasing it, challenging its supposed "scientific" neutrality.

In contrast to the production of official history, *Afroféminas*'s reflections—including those of Paulo Akam and Antoinette Torres Soler's, as well as the 8M statements—present a part of Spanish history that is institutionally denied when they assert the existence of Black Spaniards. For example, when Akam reminisces about how his life contradicts the hegemonic narrative, he questions the storyline that racialized people represent the immigrants that make up a new twenty-first century Spain. To oppose this historical lie, he compares being an Afro-writer to "expecting that in History class the teacher would say that in Spain there were Afro kings, and not only *godos* or *Borbons*, even while knowing that the Moors were in the peninsula for over eight hundred years (longer in fact than those who came later)" (Akram).[36] In other words, a Black Spanish writer in Spain is seen as a simple curiosity in the ocean of white Spanish writers. Ironically, Akam reflects in this fragment on the invisibilization of a lineage of Afro-descendant people in Spain, which parallels the historic erasure of the North African dynasties that reigned there for centuries.

Journalist and novelist Lucía Mbomío reflects on the same topic in an article she wrote for *Afroféminas* in 2017 to promote Rubén H. Bermúdez's photograph book *Y tú, ¿por qué eres negro?* [And Why Are You Black?] Both her writing and the book she is reviewing use the personal storytelling technique. Speaking to Bermúdez, Mbomío asserts:

> Your work starts with that unrelenting question, the one they have asked since you started to be able to respond, because you are a Spaniard and this seems strange to them; because your parents are white and that seems impossible to them and because they have believed they had the right to get inside you, without even asking. Your life is black, I repeat, and therefore your experiences have been different from those of the majority and that has changed everything.
>
> You know what? I also used to support Holland and France in soccer because they didn't only have white players on their teams, and I used to get excited when African Americans won in track. Even more, I've cried watching films about slavery or South African Apartheid. I will confess to you that when Lucrecia was killed, I clenched my teeth because I thought I had no tears left, but they flowed when fifteen people were assassinated at Tarajal Beach.
>
> And I'm telling you this because you, generously, have told your story to demonstrate to us that it's not yours, but ours, the story of all of us who also had to answer why we were Black women.[37]

In contrast to the "you" that addressed white people in the other articles, the "you" in this fragment is the author's "brother," and the message becomes very emotional. This promotional article becomes a confession—"You know what?"—of the shared experience of foreignization Black people feel in their own country. The stories in Bermúdez's photographs, like Mbomío Rubio's words, strive to touch people's feelings, to make them, in her words, "feel, blush, smile, and get mad."[38]

By sharing the authors' personal experiences, not only do these articles contradict the official history, but they also carve out a space for empathy, with the hope that readers might educate themselves further and rally to the antiracist cause. While the magazine includes Black academic voices like that of Antumi Toasijé, it strongly supports personal stories as a legitimate source of knowledge, asserting the role of storytelling as an effective narrative technique that challenges the so-called "scientific" history.

"To Historians for Having Left Us Out"[39]

This chapter has analyzed how *Afroféminas* has set out a series of problems related to systemic racism in Spain. For example, the collective shows that a Eurocentric education promotes unfounded ideas regarding what it means to be a Spaniard and fails to take into account the demographic diversity that has always been part of the nation. Quoting its long-term contributor Yolanda Arroyo Pizarro's neo-slave narrative collection *Las negras*, the title of this conclusion alludes to the main issue *Afroféminas* strives to elucidate, that is, the erasure of Spanish and African connections, the whitening of the country.[40] The collective, thus, demonstrates how Spanish history, as generally taught, still obviates the country's ties to Africa, not in relation to recent migrations but through its long history of imperialism. The online magazine highlights that the erasure of Afro identity is part of a pattern of systemic racism, which habitually criminalizes and foreignizes racialized people.

Since the online magazine approaches these issues from an Afro-feminist perspective, this article is also concerned with the collective's relationship between nationalism/nationhood and the fourth feminist wave, whose supposed intersectionality is called out for being insincere. In their criticism of the 8M Feminist Strikes since 2018, *Afroféminas* demonstrates that, once again, white hegemonic power narrates the evolution of its own supremacy. White feminism, like history, tends to intrinsically ignore all the marginalized stories that make white Spaniards uncomfortable. As a result, *Afroféminas*' discursive strategies—the dialogic and directness of their language and storytelling—create a space for individual stories to write history by underscoring experiences and breaking with the myth of universalizing theories that attempt to blend everybody into a homogenous "all."

Notes

1 For example, Spain conquered the Canary Islands in the fourteenth century; was an active participant in the slave trade for centuries; and possessed, until recently, African territories such as the Republic of Equatorial Guinea—which

did not achieve independence until 1968. In addition, Ceuta and Melilla, port cities in Northern Africa, are still part of Spain.
2 In fact, the United Nations has established 2015–2024 as the International Decade for People of African Descent as a strategy to implement policies that recognize and promote the rights and contributions of African people and people of African descent (Mamadou 12).
3 Ngozi Adichie illustrated this idea very well when she recalled her college experience in the United States:
My roommate had a single story of Africa: a single story of catastrophe. In this single story, there was no possibility of Africans being similar to her in any way, no possibility of feelings more complex than pity, no possibility of a connection as human equals.
While lately television programs and films have included racialized characters—*Mar de plástico* and Élite, among others—they, particularly women, are still exoticized, vilified, or represented in vulnerable situations. In fact, in her book *Viviendo en modo Afroféminas*, Antoinette Torres Soler complained that these representations foster the perception of racialized people as "despojados de inteligencia, capacidad de empoderamiento, autonomía, etc" [deprived of intelligence, capacity for empowerment, autonomy, etc.] (23).
4 This aspiration dates to the nineteenth century when, after losing its last colonies overseas, Spain launched a new imperial campaign in Africa, considering colonialism as a "precondition of modernity" (Murray and Tsuchiya 3).
5 Recent literary works by Spanish authors of African descent have explored this idea. Some of the most prominent examples are *Hija del camino* (2018) by Lucía Mbomío Rubio, *Ser mujer negra en España* (2018) by Desirée Bela-Lobedde,*¿Qué hace un negro como tú en un sitio como este?* (2021) by Moha Gerehou, and *Siete martes* (2022) by El Chojín. They all share moments in their lives of both microaggressions and structural anti-Black racism in Spain.
6 *Afroféminas* dissolved briefly. The last article before the official dissolution was published on April 17, 2022 (although articles were published for three more days). After a hiatus, albeit not a consistent one, new articles appeared at the end of the summer of 2022. However, many of the sections mentioned in this chapter—such as *Proyecto*, which explains the mission and purposes of the online magazine—no longer exist. While I had originally been told that *Afroféminas* would disappear, according to an email exchange with Torres Soler in the summer of 2022, this decision was reversed and *Afroféminas* continues its mission with a new structure as of September 2022 (email, August 10, 2022). The website has slightly modified its logo and structure with specific tabs on Anti-racism, Feminism, Activism (*Denuncia*), and Mental Health, and it has added Premium Content. This article focuses on earlier content. Additionally, a new community named *Afrocolectiva* started on Instagram (as Afrocolectivx, or Afrocolectiva) on April 18, 2022, created by a few former *Afroféminas* collaborators. They have an online presence on social networks, such as Instagram, TikTok, LinkedIn, Twitter, and a WordPress blog (*Afrocolectiva*), which reiterates the *Afroféminas* motto almost verbatim: "Nuestra existencia es resistencia" [Our existence is resistance].
7 "forma de empoderamiento personal, como punto de encuentro con otras mujeres negras, para luego convertir la revista en un espacio de empoderamiento, de visibilización de muchas voces femeninas, de emprendimiento y de construcción de afrofeminismo español. Que sea en castellano es muy importante porque Afroféminas mantienen una conexión muy especial con las

mujeres racializadas latinoamericanas. Es un proyecto para dialogar en castellano por la falta de información de este tipo en nuestro idioma y el predominio de ella en inglés y francés … El primer país que lee Afroféminas es España" (13). All translations are mine.
 8 I acknowledge that, as a white heterosexual cis woman, it is in fact my *privilege* to study literature and other cultural forms from an antiracist perspective. I recognize that I have benefitted from white supremacy and only hope that, with this work, I can be part of the current antiracist conversations and praxis that contribute to the empowerment of those marginalized by structural racism.
 9 "Lo contrario del conocimiento antirracista no es la ignorancia. Es el conocimiento racista."
10 In a 2015 interview for *Afroféminas*, the magazine's founder asserted that despite the belief that Black women would constitute most of the magazine's readers, "El público es mucho más amplio. Está llena de lectoras blancas y de hombres que leen con seriedad los artículos y dan su opinión" [The audience is much broader. It's full of white female readers as well as men who read the articles seriously and offer their opinion] (Sánchez Salcedo).
11 It is worthwhile noting that what was named "Revista" [Magazine] is now labeled "+Categorías" and that is where "AfroReflexión" and "Historia" are embedded.
12 "Ser afrodescendiente en España … y reconocerse como tal. He leído frases como: '*Ya hay en España afrodescendientes de segunda y tercera generación…*' o '*La nueva España diversa…,*' como si acabásemos de llegar. Y siempre que leo cosas así mi mente viaja al pasado y me veo siendo un niño de siete u ocho años, sentado junto a mi abuelo, nacido en Galicia" (original emphasis).
13 By leuco-Europeanization, Toasijé is referring to the fact that people in the Iberian Peninsula, as well as in the American continent, were being depicted as white Europeans even though they were often of African or Indigenous origin.
14 "¿Sabes qué me ha pasado hace poco?: Salía de un fantástico taller con mis compañeras y encontramos a unos hermanos africanos de celebración. Estaban siendo custodiados por policías nacionales. Y entre la fiesta, la algarabía y la sorpresa nuestra, se me acerca un policía Nacional. Te juro que en ese momento sentí terror. No estaba haciendo nada malo pero sólo con ser una mujer negra en España tengo el 80% de probabilidad de ser detenida por uno de tus compañeros o compañeras, de ser humillada en público y que no ocurra nada … Tanto era mi pavor, que no me di cuenta de que el policía que tenía delante era el padre de un amiguito de mi hija del cole y que venía a saludarme."
15 "Querido policía. Soy migrante y también española."
16 "Yo me ofrezco gratuitamente a daros formación si es necesario. Y fíjese que no me gusta hacer nada gratis, pero este problema me parece tan serio, que estoy dispuesta a hacer una excepción."
17 "Sé que todas vosotras estáis muy orgullosas de vuestros hitos feministas de hoy y de ayer (yo también de los míos). Pero chicas, tenemos que tratar los asuntos de la raza y el movimiento feminista colectivamente. Quiero ayudaros lo mejor que pueda para que todas podamos ser mucho más empáticas y mirar con mucha menos ignorancia a otras mujeres. Sé que podemos hacerlo y hay una cosa que no sabes, yo te quiero a mi lado."
18 "está construido sobre las experiencias de las [mujeres] blancas, ya que no tienen en cuenta que existen otras mujeres que no sean exactamente como ellas, fruto de una mirada supremacista heredada." For more on Nfubea's *Afrofeminismo*, see Chapter 7.

19 "los tímidos intentos del manifiesto por ser inclusivo."
20 "los hechos son más fuertes que las palabras, y en realidad la invisibilización de las mujeres racializadas es absoluta."
21 "Ninguna mujer es ilegal. Decimos ¡BASTA! al racismo y la exclusión."
22 "JUNTAS SOMOS MÁS," "La sororidad es nuestra arma," and "Nuestra identidad es múltiple, somos diversas."
23 "Desgraciadamente la interseccionalidad sigue siendo una palabra que el feminismo hegemónico vacía de contenido cuando la tiene que poner en práctica."
24 "Seguimos siendo tratadas como ciudadanas de segunda, en los paneles de ponencia y espacios feministas encontramos afirmaciones que continúan perpetuando el racismo e invisibilizando las opresiones producto de este. Entender que no 'todas somos iguales' y que en esa diversidad existen distintas demandas y formas de luchas, es fundamental para eliminar los patrones de racismo social estructural."
25 "Los cambios dentro del feminismo hegemónico son demasiado lentos."
26 "Ser mujer negra o racializada te coloca en una posición de constante extranjerización y no pertenencia."
27 Patricia Hill Collins defines intersectionality as a "recognized form of critical inquiry and praxis" (1) and "critical analysis and social action" (3).
28 "Entiendo el Feminismo Negro sobre todo como una praxis, a diferencia de esa teoría fría, de la que desde mi punto de vista, cualquiera puede escribir, apropiarse, obtener incluso relevancia sin que repercuta en lo más mínimo en el empoderamiento de la mujer negra … El Feminismo Negro no es una 'teoría florero,' una teoría para figurar careciendo de toda acción."
29 "Movilización histórica por la igualdad de las mujeres" [Historic mobilization for women's equality] (*El País*). Other headlines include "International Women's Day 2018: Beyond #MeToo, With Pride, Protests and Pressure" (*New York Times*), "International Women's Day: 'Millions' join Spain strike" (*BBC*), "En Espagne, les femmes font grève pour 'arrêter le monde'" [In Spain, Women Strike to "Stop The World"] (*Le Monde*).
30 "Internet está permitiendo al feminismo construir un movimiento *online* fuerte, popular, reactivo. Las redes sociales provocan a su vez un nuevo tipo de acción, la de las multitudes anónimas organizadas de forma rápida y precisa, con objetivos claros y comunes, con una estrategia que puede discutirse y planificarse."
31 "Lo dejamos para vuestra reflexión."
32 "Queridas hermanas, aliadas y compañeras."
33 "¿Eres una persona blanca y a veces te molestan algunas cosas de la lucha contra el racismo? ¡Este mensaje es para ti!"
34 "vete preparando para las conversaciones que tendrás que tener con gente incapaz de escuchar y entender," "esta tarea no solo se hará cada vez más difícil cuanto más te impliques," "se [sic] que crees tener muy buenas ideas para la lucha …," pero "[p]or favor, no nos cuentes la difícil travesía que te ha traído hasta aquí."
35 De Certeau uses quotation marks as he himself questions the use of the word in relation to history.
36 "Esperar a que en clase de historia digan que en España hubo reyes afro, y no solo *godos* y *borbones*, aún sabiendo que los moros estuvieron en la península más de ochocientos años (Más años, de hecho, que los que vinieron después)."
37 "Tu obra parte de esa pregunta que no cesa, la que te han hecho desde que puedes replicar, porque eres español y eso les resulta raro; porque tienes padres blancos y eso les parece imposible y porque se han visto con el derecho a

meterse dentro de ti, sin ni siquiera llamar. Tu vida es negra, repito, así que tus experiencias han sido diferentes a las de la mayoría y eso lo ha cambiado todo. ¿Sabes? Yo también iba con Holanda y con Francia en el fútbol debido a que no sólo había blancos en sus plantillas y me emocionaba que los afroamericanos ganaran en velocidad. Te digo más, he llorado con películas de esclavitud o sobre la Sudáfrica del Apartheid. Te confesaré que cuando mataron a Lucrecia apreté los dientes porque pensé que ya no me quedaban lágrimas, pero brotaron todas cuando asesinaron a quince personas en la playa de Tarajal.

Y te lo cuento a ti porque tú, de manera generosa, nos has trasladado tu historia para demostrarnos que no es la tuya, sino la nuestra, la de aquellas que también tuvimos que responder por qué somos negras."

38 "Para sentir, ruborizaros, para sonreír y enfadaros."
39 "A los historiadores/por habernos dejado fuera" (Arroyo Pizarro 7).
40 A neo-slave narrative is a contemporary narrative genre that writers from the Black Atlantic have made popular. This type of story follows the antebellum slave narrative genre in order to relate the histories that were erased or minimized in the predominantly white literature that has formed the canon (Babb; Anim-Addo and Lima).

Works Cited

Afrocolectiva, https://afrocolectiva.wordpress.com. Accessed 20 Aug. 2022.

Agencias Girona. "SOS Racisme señala a varios negocios de Girona por racismo inmobiliario." *La Vanguardia*, 28 July 2022, https://www.lavanguardia.com/local/girona/20220728/8436799/sos-racisme-senala-negocios-girona-racismo-inmobiliario.html. Accessed 1 Aug. 2022.

Akam, Paulo. "Ser escritor afro en España es ser una rareza." *Afroféminas*, 27 Feb. 2020, https://afrofeminas.com/2020/02/27/ser-escritor-afro-en-espana-es-ser-una-rareza/. Accessed 7 July 2022.

Anim-Addo, Joan, and Maria Helena Lima. "The Power of the Neo-Slave Narrative Genre." *Callaloo*, vol. 41, no. 1, 2018, pp. 1–8, https://muse.jhu.edu/article/736806. Accessed 23 Feb. 2023.

Arroyo Pizarro, Yolanda. *Las negras*. Boreales, 2016.

Babb, Valerie Melissa. *A History of the African American Novel*. Cambridge UP, 2017.

Banora, Manuela. "Afroreferentes [sic] para una afrodescendiente." *Afroféminas*, 27 Mar. 2022.

Blanco, Alda. *Cultura y conciencia imperial en la España del siglo XIX*. Publicaciones de la Universitat de València, 2012.

Candón Mena, José, and Lucía Benítez Eyzaguirre. "Introducción: Movimientos sociales, tecnología y democracia. Una relación conflictiva." *Activismo digital y nuevos modos de ciudadanía: Una mirada global*, edited by José Candón Mena and Lucía Benítez Eyzaguirre. Universitat Autònoma de Barcelona, 2016, pp. 7–12.

Casero-Ripollés, Andreu. "Estrategias y prácticas comunicativas del activismo político en las redes sociales en España." *Historia y Comunicación Social*, vol. 20, no. 2, 2015, pp. 535–50.

Certeau, Michel de. *The Writing of History*. Translated by Tom Conley. Columbia UP, 1992.

Chojín, El. *Siete martes*. eBook, Grijalbo, 2022.
"Comunicado Afroféminas 8M 2021. A nuestra [sic] hermanas y aliadas." *Afroféminas*, 8 Mar. 2021. https://afrofeminas.com/2021/03/08/comunicado-afrofeminas-8m-2021-a-nuestra-hermanas-y-aliadas/. Accessed 15 July 2022.
"Comunicado de Afroféminas por el 8 de marzo 2020." *Afroféminas*, 4 Mar. 2020, https://afrofeminas.com/2020/03/04/comunicado-de-afrofeminas-por-el-8-de-marzo-2020/. Accessed 15 July 2022.
"Cuando sólo somos una foto. Invisibilización de los otros feminismos en los actos del 8 de marzo." *Afroféminas*, 2 Mar. 2017, https://afrofeminas.com/2017/03/02/cuando-solo-somos-una-foto-invisibilizacion-de-los-otros-feminismos-en-los-actos-del-8-de-marzo/. Accessed 17 July 2022.
Cortes Owusu, Marián. "Para el recién llegado al antirracismo." *Afroféminas*, 29 July 2019, https://afrofeminas.com/2019/07/29/para-el-recien-llegado-al-antirracismo-2/. Accessed 17 July 2022.
Crenshaw, Kimberlé. "Demarginalizing the Intersection of Race and Sex: A Black Feminist Critique of Antidiscrimination Doctrine, Feminist Theory and Antiracist Politics." *University of Chicago Legal Forum*, vol. 1989, no. 1, art. 8, 1989, pp. 139–67.
Espinosa Miñoso, Yuderkys. *De por qué es necesario un feminismo descolonial*. Icaria, 2022.
Federación de Asociaciones de SOS Racismo del Estado Español. *Informe anual 17 sobre el racismo en el estado español*, Tercera Prensa-Hirugarren Prentsa S.L., 2017, https://sosracismo.eu/wp-content/uploads/2017/09/Informe-Anual-2017-SOSweb.pdf.
Feros, Antonio. *Speaking of Spain. The Evolution of Race and Nation in the Hispanic World*. Harvard UP, 2017.
Fra-Molinero, Baltasar. "The Suspect Whiteness of Spain." *At Home and Abroad: Historizing Twentieth-Century Whiteness in Literature and Performance*, edited by La Vinia Delois Jennings. U of Tennessee P, 2009, pp. 147–69.
Fusi, Juan Pablo. *Historia mínima de España*. Turner Publicaciones, 2012.
Gellner, Ernest. *Nations and Nationalism. New Perspectives on the Past*. Cornell UP, 1983.
Gerehou, Moha. *Qué hace un negro como tú en un sitio como este*. Península, 2021.
Gómez, Manuel V., and José Marcos. "Movilización histórica por la igualdad de las mujeres." *El País*, 9 Mar. 2018, https://elpais.com/economia/2018/03/08/actualidad/1520545956_654616.html. Accessed 25 Sept. 2022.
Heuchan, Claire. "Las blancas que critican el 'feminismo blanco' perpetúan el privilegio blanco." *Afroféminas*, 9 Feb. 2020, https://afrofeminas.com/2020/02/09/las-blancas-que-critican-el-feminismo-blanco-perpetuan-el-privilegio-blanco/. Accessed 23 Apr. 2023.
Hill Collins, Patricia. *Intersectionality as Critical Social Theory*. Duke UP, 2019.
hooks, bell. *Feminist Theory from Margin to Center*. South End Press, 1984.
———. *Teaching to Transgress*. eBook. Routledge, 1994.
"International Women's Day: 'Millions' Join Spain strike." *BBC*, 8 Mar. 2018, https://www.bbc.com/news/world-europe-43324406#. Accessed 7 July 2022.

Johnson, Maisha Z. "Guía afrofeminista de frases racistas que muchas feministas blancas dicen." *Afroféminas*, 14 Oct. 2022, https://afrofeminas.com/2022/10/14/guia-afrofeminista-de-frases-racistas-que-muchas-feministas-blancas-dicen/. Accessed 3 Jan. 2023.

Koli, Marta. "Antumi Toasijé: 'Hay una invisibilización total de los aportes de las personas africanas y afrodescendientes en la historia de España.'" *Afroféminas*, 2 Jan. 2018, https://afrofeminas.com/2018/01/02/antumi-toasije-hay-una-invisibilizacion-total-de-los-aportes-de-las-personas-africanas-y-afrodescendientes-en-la-historia-de-espana/. Accessed 25 June 2022.

"La visibilidad es poder." *Afroféminas*, 19 Sept. 2022, https://afrofeminas.com/2022/09/19/la-visibilidad-es-poder/. Accessed 20 Apr. 2023.

León-Távora, Ana. "Afectos y activismo estético en *Ser mujer negra en España*, de Desirée Bela-Lobedde." *El reflejo de Medusa. Representaciones de la mujer en la España contemporánea*, edited by Esther M. Alarcón Arana. Advook, 2023, pp. 203–17.

Mamadou, Isabelle. "Decenio internacional de las personas afrodescendientes, 2015–2024." *Seminario sobre el legado de las personas africanas y afrodescendientes a España*, edited by Observatorio Español del Racismo y la Xenofobia, 2020, pp. 11–16, https://www.inclusion.gob.es/oberaxe/ficheros/documentos/PDF-17-Seminario-sobre-el-legado-de-las-personas-africanas-a-Espaa__ARN_-OK-y-ACC-12.11.20.pdf.

"Manifiesto 8M Afroféminas." *Afroféminas*, 4 Mar. 2019, https://afrofeminas.com/2019/03/04/manifiesto-8m-afrofeminas/. Accessed 17 July 2022.

Mballo, Maoude. "Identidades." *Afroféminas*, 6 Feb. 2019, https://afrofeminas.com/2019/02/06/identidades/. Accessed 20 Apr. 2023.

Mbomío, Lucía. "Y tú por qué eres negro." *Afroféminas*, 12 Sept. 2017, https://afrofeminas.com/2017/09/12/y-tu-por-que-eres-negro/. Accessed 20 Apr. 2023.

Mendes, Kaitlynn, et al. *Digital Feminist Activism. Girls and Women Fight Back Against Rape Culture*. Oxford UP, 2019.

Morel, Sandrine. "En Espagne, les femmes font grève pour 'arrêter le monde.'" *Le Monde*, 8 Mar. 2018. https://www.lemonde.fr/europe/article/2018/03/08/en-espagne-les-femmes-font-greve-pour-arreter-le-monde_5267305_3214.html. Accessed 7 July 2022.

Murray, Michelle, and Akiko Tsuchiya. Introduction. *Unsettling Colonialism: Gender and Race in the Nineteenth Century Global Hispanic World*, edited by Michelle Murray and Akiko Tsuchiya. SUNY P, 2019, pp. 1–16.

Neild, Rachel, et al. *Bajo sospecha. Impacto de las prácticas policiales discriminatorias en España*. Open Society Foundations, 2019. https://www.justiceinitiative.org/uploads/9136fbe2-514d-4955-97dd-ba4a5d6b24f6/bajo-sospecha-impacto-de-las-practicas-policiales-discriminatorias-en-espana-20190924.pdf.

Nfubea, Abuy. *Afrofeminismo: 50 años de lucha y activismo de mujeres negras en España (1968–2018)*. eBook, Ménades Editorial, 2021.

Ngozi Adichie, Chimamanda. *The Danger of a Single Story*. TEDGlobal, 2009. https://www.ted.com/talks/chimamanda_ngozi_adichie_the_danger_of_a_single_story?language=en.

Ortega Arjonilla, Esther (Mayoko). "Intersecciones múltiples en torno a la raza y al género." *Seminario sobre el legado de las personas africanas y afrodescendientes a España*, Ministerio de Inclusión, Seguridad Social y Migraciones, edited by Observatorio Español del Racismo y la Xenofobia, 2020, pp. 49–54, https://www.inclusion.gob.es/oberaxe/ficheros/documentos/PDF-17-Seminario-sobre-el-legado-de-las-personas-africanas-a-Espaa__ARN__-OK-y-ACC-12.11.20.pdf.

Pecourt Gracia, Juan. "La esfera pública digital y el activismo político." *Política y Sociedad*, vol. 52, no. 1, 2015, pp. 75–98, https://revistas.ucm.es/index.php/POSO/article/view/45423. Accessed 20 Sept. 2022.

"¿Por qué Afroféminas no se suma a la Huelga Feminista?" *Afroféminas*, 5 Mar. 2018, https://afrofeminas.com/2018/03/05/porque-afrofeminas-no-se-suma-a-la-huelga-feminista/. Accessed 17 July 2022.

Romero-Rodríguez, Luis M., and Ignacio Aguaded. "Consumo informativo y competencias digitales de estudiantes de periodismo de Colombia, Perú y Venezuela." *Convergencia*, vol. 3, no. 70, 2016, pp. 35–57. https://www.scielo.org.mx/scielo.php?pid=S1405-14352016000100035&script=sci_abstract. Accessed 25 Sept. 2022.

Sánchez Salcedo, Javier. "Entrevista a Antoinette Torres Soler, creadora de Afroféminas." *Afroféminas*, 25 June 2015. https://afrofeminas.com/2015/06/25/entrevista-a-antoinette- torres-creadora-de-afrofeminas/. Accessed 10 Feb. 2020.

Santiago, Viviana. "¿Eres una persona blanca y a veces te molestan algunas cosas de la lucha contra el racismo? ¡Este mensaje es para ti!" *Afroféminas*, 30 July 2017. https://afrofeminas.com/2017/07/30/eres-una-persona-blanca-a-veces-te-molestan-algunas-cosas-de-la-lucha-contra-el-racismo-este-mensaje-es-para-ti/. Accessed 17 July 2022.

Spain: End Racial Profiling and Invisibility of People of African Descent, UN Experts Urge. United Nations Office of the High Commissioner of Human Rights, 26 Feb. 2018, https://www.ohchr.org/en/press-releases/2018/02/spain-end-racial-profiling-and-invisibility-people-african-descent-un. Accessed 25 Aug. 2022.

Suárez Navaz, Liliana, and Rosalva Aída Hernández, editors. *Descolonizando el feminismo. Teorías y prácticas desde los márgenes*. Cátedra, 2008.

Swartch Lorenzo, Elvira. "Ayuda para feministas blancas." *Afroféminas*, 8 Jan. 2018, https://afrofeminas.com/2018/01/08/ayuda-para-feministas-blancas/. Accessed 21 Apr. 2023.

Toasijé, Antumi. "La historicidad de las comunidades africanas y afrodescenentes designadas como negras en España." *Seminario sobre el legado de las personas africanas y afrodescendientes a España*, edited by Observatorio Español del Racismo y la Xenofobia, 2020, pp. 17–24, https://www.inclusion.gob.es/oberaxe/ficheros/documentos/PDF-17-Seminario-sobre-el-legado-de-las-personas-africanas-a-Espaa__ARN__-OK-y-ACC-12.11.20.pdf.

Torres, Silvia Elena. "Aquí, entre feministas." *Afroféminas*, 3 Oct. 2017, https://afrofeminas.com/2017/10/03/aqui-entre-feministas/. Accessed 3 Jan. 2023.

Torres Soler, Antoinette. Módulo de Historia y Legislación, ¿Qué es el racismo? Perspectivas Afro desde la Historia, la Psicología y la Sociología. Laboratorio de Construcción. 8 Aug. 2022. https://desireebela.mykajabi.com. Accessed 15 Aug. 2022.

———. "Querido policía." *Afroféminas*, 24 June 2019, https://afrofeminas.com/2019/06/24/querido- policia/. Accessed 2 Sept. 2022.

———. *Viviendo en modo Afroféminas*. La Tija Edicions, 2018.

Varela, Nuria. "El tsunami feminista." *Nueva Sociedad*, vol. 286, 2020, pp. 93–106, https://nuso.org/articulo/el-tsunami-feminista/. Accessed 27 July 2022.

Villegas Simón, Isabel, and Celina Navarro Bosch. "Retos, utopías y adversidades del feminismo digital: un territorio en disputa." *Aquelarre. La emancipación de las mujeres en la cultura de masas*. Advook Editorial, 2020.

Zuri, Ayodemi. "El racismo también está en el periodismo." *Afroféminas*, 15 Sept. 2019, https://afrofeminas.com/2019/09/15/el-racismo-tambien-esta-en-el-periodismo-%EF%BB%BF/. Accessed 20 Apr. 2023.

5 Hidden Knowledges and Diasporic Positionings

The Autobiographical and Testimonial Texts in *Metamba Miago: Relatos y saberes de mujeres afroespañolas*

Julia Borst

Lately, the debate on the African diaspora in Europe and on emerging Afrodiasporic subjectivities has snowballed, in which fluid identities are negotiated within a context of notions such as "Afroeurope" or "Afropean(ness)." Unlike countries such as the United Kingdom or France, Spain has dealt with its African/Afrodescendant population cautiously and comparatively recently. Nevertheless, the Iberian Peninsula has also witnessed a notable boost in *activismo afro*. Terms such as *afrodescendencia* and *afroespañolidad* have surfaced to describe diasporic positionings and multiple frames of reference to which Afrodescendant Spaniards might relate.

This boom in Black[1] activism in Spain, specifically since the 1990s (Antumi Toasijé, "Challenges" 51; 54), and the escalating debate on a diasporic *in-between* include theoretical and activist writing while also extending to literary texts and other artistic artifacts that explore these issues. Vivid examples from the last few years encompass fictional and autobiographical writing by Lucía Asué Mbomío Rubio, Desirée Bela-Lobedde, and Moha Gerehou; Silvia Albert Sopale's theatrical performances; activist writing in collections of non-fictional texts, such as *Metamba Miago: Relatos y saberes de mujeres afroespañolas* (2019) [Metamba Miago: Stories and Knowledges of Afrospanish Women], *Cuando somos el enemigo: Activismo negro en España* (2019) [When We Are the Enemy: Black Activism in Spain], and *Las españolas afrodescendientes hablan sobre identidad y empoderamiento* (2018) [Spanish Afrodescendant Women Speak About Identity and Empowerment]; online magazines such as *Afroféminas* and *Negrxs Magazine*; and cinematographic works and (audio)visual art by Rubén H. Bermúdez, Agnes Essonti Luque, or Santiago Zannou, to name a few.

These examples not only highlight the diversity of genres, but many of them also reflect the importance of female voices in this field. They

DOI: 10.4324/9781003435051-6

articulate knowledge produced by people who have been racialized as Black and have been confronted by shared experiences of racism and daily microaggressions in Spanish society. This knowledge of what it means to be the racialized Other, how to cope with this experience, and how to reevaluate Blackness from a diasporic perspective exceeds a mere objective representation of facts. It includes a subjective-emotional dimension that echoes Afrodiasporic subjects' traumatic burden of being othered. It also shows how they deal with these realities and how they imagine a space of belonging and commonality by forging diasporic identity constructions that allow for plural affiliations.

In this article, I analyze *Metamba Miago: Relatos y saberes de mujeres afroespañolas* (2019), a crowdfunded collection of autobiographical and testimonial texts self-edited and coordinated by Deborah Ekoka Hernandis and United Minds, a bookstore founded in 2014 and specializing in African and Afrodiasporic literature.[2] From this example and referring to approaches that conceptualize literature as a potential archive of hidden and marginalized knowledge—or, more precisely, knowledges to conceptually reflect the diversity and plurality of forms of knowledge—I study how Afrodescendance is imagined as not just political resistance to a discursive regime of white supremacy. I show that it is also imagined as an empowering narrative that transcends defining Blackness in opposition to whiteness and in relation to racism. Notable is how the texts also offer positively connotated spaces of identification for Afrodiasporic subjects.

Afrodiasporic Texts as Archives of Knowledge(s)

Unlike former generations of African exiles and migrants, which tend to look back to the *lost home*, a new generation of Afrodescendant writers and activists represents an explicitly diasporic perspective, for many of them were born in Spain (Antumi Toasijé, "Challenges" 50; 52). This perspective is characterized by an experience of exclusion in the receiving society and an idea of a common connection to a "homeland" or, according to more recent approaches, a collective vision of "home-making" (Cohen and Fischer, "Diaspora" 6) as a framework of belonging that increasingly transcends territorial references, extending to shared histories and narratives with which people in the diaspora can identify (Faist 12–13). This condition, consequently, gives rise to a group solidarity and diasporic subjectivities of being "bi- or multi-local" (Tölölyan 28). Paul Tiyambe Zeleza fittingly sums up this specific in-betweenness as "multiple belongings" (32) that oscillate between "a 'here' that is often characterized by a regime of marginalization and a 'there' that is invoked as a rhetoric of self-affirmation, of belonging to 'here' differently" (32).

This condition has indisputably shaped Afrodiasporic communities in many European countries; it places them in a position of specific vulnerability, and their condition can be defined as one of contingent belonging (Butt et al. 21–22; Espinoza Garrido et al. 2). According to Felipe Espinoza Garrido et al., however, this contingent belonging of "African Europeans" is not to be understood solely "as symptomatic of white hegemony" (3) but as a "contingency *from below* as part of a deliberately chosen identity politics, foregrounding ... a scope for agency and self-determination by rejecting the need to 'properly' belong in a white hegemonic society" (3–4; original emphasis) or, as Zeleza's quote affirms, to belong here "differently" (32). This belonging creates "frictions that have the potential to loosen the grip of racism, and open[s] up spaces for pluralism and fluctuating identity narratives that challenge whiteness and nativism" (Espinoza Garrido et al. 4).

In this regard, texts written by this new generation of Afrodescendant writers in Spain frequently echo the experience of being racialized as Black in a European society where whiteness is considered the norm. This experience creates "an ambivalent situation of belonging and exclusion, for Spanish society tends to relegate people 'who look different' to the margins and the status of being 'a foreigner' or a migrant who has never truly arrived" (Borst 171). According to Antumi Toasijé, this "hypertrophy of the European identity known as white" ("Challenges" 48) can be traced back to Spanish modernity and beyond. The historian argues that racism has constituted a key element of Spain's "instrumental ideology for world domination" (48). However, he adds, the situation is particularly paradoxical for the more recent generations: "[t]his group had to face growing racism with great perplexity and confusion because of the fact that they were, by official papers, Spaniards" ("Africanity" 352). At the same time, Antumi Toasijé underlines Spain's tenacious denial of the country's "colonial and enslaving past in Africa" (349) and the invisibilization of African influences on its history, identity, and culture (350; 354). The literary and activist texts written by this new generation write back to this denial, claiming a space for a self-determined debate on racism and Afrodiasporic identities in Europe. They articulate the frictions related to contingent belonging, bear witness to a continuity of experiences of racism, and, by offering new frames of references and identification, narrate how the subject might cope with those experiences.

In psychology, coping is defined as "the ongoing behavioral, cognitive, and emotional processes people use to manage those life circumstances that threaten feelings of stability" (Blum et al. 596). It describes a reaction to stressful and/or traumatic events that aims at dealing with and avoiding the negative effects of those events (Lazarus 237). As for the discriminatory experiences related in *Metamba Miago*, the circumstances that give rise to individuals of African descent living through episodes of (structural) racism are often beyond their control, and this explains why the coping strategies evident in the texts tend to entail emotion-focused elements in the sense that they try to proactively "reduce the impact of distressing feelings" (Blum et al. 598) by conveying positive reinterpretations of Afrodescendance as a way of encouraging belonging. These coping mechanisms empower both the writing and the reading subject, strengthening internal coping resources by providing specific knowledge. Furthermore, they create a community based on solidarity and support, one that includes others who can relate to the writing subject's individual experiences and that, thus, enables them all to "pool[.] resources" (599).

From a psychological perspective, one can consider the writings in *Metamba Miago* as a way of confronting the traumatic experience of racism and, thus, of "reframing it" (Soper and Von Bergen 151) through writing. Studies argue that confronting stressful events can help "reconstruct[.] them as being more meaningful and more controllable" (151; Park and Blumberg 598–600). Yet I do not want to read *Metamba Miago* merely as the personal coping strategies of the individual authors. Psychology's insights into coping also offer us a fascinating framework of interpretation if we read the testimonial and autobiographical texts as narratively staged archives of an Afrodiasporic community's shared knowledges. Such a framework allows us to consider the texts as aesthetic spaces collectively exploring experiences of racism, how to cope with them, and how to create meaningful narratives for a marginalized group.

Hispanic studies scholar Joanna Boampong has shown both the scope of racism female Afrospaniards endure on a daily basis and the importance of coping strategies to deal with this "sense of unbelonging, illegitimacy, and instability" (289) that others impose on them. Of particular interest is Boampong's observation of the dynamic shift in coping strategies between the individual and the collective sphere. While, on a personal level, these women might decide to avoid a confrontation with the aggressor and/or the system, as activists and members of a community, they might commit to counter-acting and "fighting ... as a collective" (296). Consequently, I read *Metamba Miago* not as mere personal testimonies relating individual experiences. Instead, I emphasize the texts' collective dimension as narratively staged knowledge about racism and coping strategies that goes beyond the individual case to produce a shared, collective knowledge, a knowledge that feeds a common archive of what it means to be Black and/or "live and survive" as a racialized subject in Spain (cf. the German wordplay *über-leben*; Ha 378–82). Hence, the texts translate the personal experience into a collective knowledge. But how can texts turn into archives of knowledge?

The Autobiographical and Testimonial Texts in Metamba Miago 115

Indeed, as the Romance studies scholar Ottmar Ette emphasizes, literature can be considered an archive that both conceptualizes and intensifies modes of conduct of life, "while referring back to the most diverse segments of knowledge and academic discourses" ("Literaturwissenschaft" 18).[3] Literature, however, does not simply reflect reality but experiments with and generates new/other knowledges as well. Furthermore, Ette argues that, due to their intended ambiguity and openness (37), literary texts not only make diverse and complex knowledges available but "enable readers to experience them aesthetically" ("Literature" 987). Elaborating on Ette's notion, Ansgar Nünning highlights this potential of literature to not just reflect a political, historical, and cultural context but to configure worldviews and knowledge(s) that might affect our perception of literature and reality (52–53). He argues that literature is not just an archive. It is also "a narrative-fictional space of exploring new and suppressed forms of knowledge as well as an active and eminent medium of generating knowledge for living" (57).[4] However, this reasoning is not limited to fictional texts. Ette also refers to (auto)biographical and testimonial writing as a medium to translate one's own experiences into knowledge to which others can relate ("Literature" 990–91). Likewise, *Metamba Miago* is conceived as a collection of texts that—uniting short essays, reflective statements, and interviews inspired by the authors' own lives—explicitly aim at sharing "with all of us their feelings, their emotions, their experiences, and their modes of being a racialized woman in today's Spain" (Ekoka 11).[5]

Yet, literature not only generates "new" knowledges, as Ette says, but also constitutes a space to unveil what social critic and founder of the award-winning blog, *MsAfropolitain*, Minna Salami would call "hidden knowledges." Salami complains that using terms such as "new" or "alternative" when discussing the perspectives of Afrodescendant people fosters normative whiteness as "the axis around which everything else must turn" (2). Instead, the notion of hidden perspectives decenters a Eurocentric and patriarchal worldview. By making visible the perspectives previously hidden from the Spanish public sphere, *Metamba Miago*'s texts display a specific knowledge, a knowledge of what it means to be the racialized Other in Spain, how to cope with this experience, and how to explore and re-define Blackness and Afrodescendance from the perspective of the diasporic subject.[6] If we follow Salami's reasoning, the texts constitute spaces that enable the authors to *safely* voice their own experiences as racialized subjects, address the community, and put the racialized subject itself at the center. As such, the texts picture knowledge, or more precisely, knowledges that empower persons being othered, since "it is important to develop language and knowledge that works for and not against those excluded from the privileges of the status quo" (Salami 4). This also explains why *Metamba*

Miago has been crowdfunded on the platform Verkami as an "exercise in collective responsibility" (Abé Pans, "Deborah" 58) from within the Afrospanish community.[7] The book's back cover similarly states that

> Metamba Miago tells our stories, through the communal, *it is a dialogue between us* that we want to share with everyone, such as we do in symposiums or safe places where we give ourselves those spaces *to express openly how we have felt* during our processes, in search of an identity that has been and, sometimes, still is questioned and denied because of our skin color. (Ekoka, back cover; emphasis added)[8]

Salami also advocates a new approach to knowledge in general, one that foregrounds its multiple layers, englobing the rationale and measurable as well as the emotional and imaginative (14). She states that this "sensuous knowledge" gives rise to other narratives that challenge how we interpret the reality in which we live. Likewise, the texts in *Metamba Miago* do not simply fall back on objectifiable facts or statistics on racism in Spain. They explicitly allow for subjective experiences and exhibit affective-emotional aspects that symbolically speak to others. And all these aspects converge in an archive of Afrodiasporic knowledges others can relate to, a multifaceted one that challenges established Eurocentric narratives of African migration to and presence in Spain. This conceptualization matches Salami's argument that knowledge is based on more than rationality and logic. It extends to "emotions, senses, and embodied experience" (12), which is why "[a]rt is a way to understand and change reality just as much as quantifiable information is" (13). Therefore, knowledge about the situation of Afrodescendant people in Spain is conveyed not only through official reports with statistics and figures but also through autobiographical and testimonial literary statements.

Furthermore, we will see that *Metamba Miago* unveils previously "hidden" narratives that shift the focus from feeling one is a victim to being self-confident and empowered (Salami 19). The texts, thus, offer a vision of Blackness that responds to Salami's critique of a general politicization of identity as resistance to oppression (Salami 77–78; 89):

> we emphasize political blackness to the detriment of what blackness also should conjure—the history, the knowledge, the stories, the epics, the civilizations—basically, the collective memory—of black people themselves and not only their painful encounters with whiteness. (93)

Accordingly, Blackness is not only about conceiving Black identity as "a source of resistance" (79) and "performance of dissent" (78) in a political struggle, one that "helps achieve representation in public discourse and popular culture" (77) and stages an empowering counter-discourse that deconstructs the dominant "Europatriarchal" perspective (89). Instead, as Salami highlights, Blackness is also:

> a transmitter of shared history, ancestry, lineage, and belonging. Blackness is a repository of a people's philosophy and of folklore and of epics that convey collective attitudes to fundamental matters of life such as birth, death, love, work, and pleasure. *We need to free blackness from the semantic burden to continually producing a language of dissent while not concurrently producing one of joy.* (96; my emphasis)

Salami's insistence on the versatility of Blackness draws attention to the knowledges articulated in *Metamba Miago* as indeed having many different facets. Of course, the texts frequently touch knowledges related to racism in its diverse forms ranging from microaggressions in daily life to the lack of (political) participation and structural discrimination. However, in a self-determined discourse, they also deal with the question of belonging and the subject's search for identity, creating positive role models and offering inspiration for the subject to relate to their African heritage. The texts represent the diasporic condition as a "kind of voyage that encompasses the possibility of never arriving or returning, a navigation of multiple belongings, of networks of affiliation" (Zeleza 32), and that can be explored and (re-)defined through writing. I elaborate on how this experience is voiced in *Metamba Miago* in the next section, which analyzes the representations of knowledge(s) and self-positionings articulated in the texts as well as their narrative and argumentative structures.[9]

"We Have to Celebrate Who We Are"—Afrospanish Women's Knowledges and Diasporic Positionings in *Metamba Miago*

Metamba Miago comprises thirteen texts (and a prologue) written by African and Afrodescendant women "that narrate their vision of Afrodescendance in Spain" (Abé Pans, "Deborah" 57).[10] Among these women, the reader will find well-known contributors to the community, such as Lucía Asué Mbomío Rubio, Desirée Bela-Lobedde, and Rita Bosaho Gori.[11] These texts, which explore "blackness from diverse positions and intersections" (Ekoka 107), consider a wide range of topics such as migration, (Black) feminism, the arts, the Spanish media landscape, intersectional discrimination of disabled or sexually *dissident* women, the importance of role models, digital activism, interracial adoption, and structural racism in politics.[12] As a result, they delve not only into issues of anti-Black racism but also intersectional forms of discrimination, and they deal with

118　*Julia Borst*

Figure 5.1 Examples of the brief profiles (Ekoka 55; 117). Permission granted by the author.

the specific oppression and inferiorization of racialized and/or migrant women, single parenting, functional diversity, and non-heteronormativity.

The book's configuration is striking: each text is introduced by a brief author profile (Figure 5.1). We could say that each one of them "is given a face," as this profile consists not only of a short self-description but of a photograph as well, one that frequently shows the woman who has written the specific text and visually disrupts the invisibilization of Afro descendant women in Spanish society.

These profiles identify *Metamba Miago* not just as a collection of short texts but as one that links individuals and their self-positionings as well. The brief profiles describe who the women are and their respective fields of competence and engagement in activism. Yet, the first thing we learn after the authors' names is their birthplaces. At first glance, this does not appear to be unusual. Profiles of all kinds commonly include this information. However, in this case, it is not as trivial as it might appear: indicating the city of birth—in all but three cases, Spanish cities—can be read as a political statement, a claim of belonging to Spain. Although readers might still

The Autobiographical and Testimonial Texts in Metamba Miago

qualify the single testimonies as subjective accounts, the place of birth is an objective fact framing these women's stories and lurking between the lines whenever they report on how their belonging has been challenged.

As the majoritized Spanish society continues to challenge Afrodescendant Spaniards' Spanish citizenship and they need to deal with this experience of constantly being othered, they are faced with a diasporic identity that, according to the editor of Metamba Miago, "forces you to position yourself" (Ekoka and Mbomío Rubio).[13] In their statements, the collection's authors do this within the diverse spectrum of diasporic labels using terms such as "Afromadrilenian" (Ekoka 33), "Andalusian and Bayangue" (55), "Afrodescendant adolescent" (95), "antiracist feminist activist" (105), "black woman" (117; 129), or "Afrodescendant member of parliament" (139).[14] We can see that they employ a variety of self-designations that highlight various aspects of their lives and of how they see themselves. What they have in common is that they underline their condition of being a woman (which is more evident in the Spanish originals since they often include a gender suffix) and intersectional discrimination. Moreover, they open up a multipolar net of belonging that locates the subject in Spain as someone from Madrid, from Andalusia, or (as a political function) as a member of parliament in the Spanish political system.

Yet, these terms simultaneously insist on an ambivalent moment of difference for being Black and of African descent (Afro, Bayangue, Black, and Afrodescendant), a difference that evidently shapes these women's identities: it is both the basis of their being othered and a source of empowerment as it endows them with other ways of belonging. What is obvious is that some authors do not opt for generalizing notions but take what Lucía Asué Mbomío Rubio would call a position *de barrionalista* [of a "neighborhoodite"] ("Volver al telefonillo"). Rather than being related to Europe or Africa as a whole, they see themselves as belonging to a local context such as Madrid or Andalusia, or, in the case of Agnes Essonti Luque, to a specific African community (Bayangue). Mbomío Rubio writes elsewhere that, "[f]or many children of migrants …, the neighborhood is the only space of recognition, the place where we feel as and, this is important, where they feel us as their equals, it is the place we call home, in which we have a name, a face and a history" ("Volver al telefonillo").[15] These diverse and heterogeneous affiliations indicate that Afrodescendance cannot be demarcated as a particular space of belonging or to a fixed identity construction. Instead, it is described as a fluid positioning and, even, a particular mindset or knowledge of being that emerges from an awareness of "blackness, and I don't speak of being a black woman, I speak of knowing and feeling where you're from and what you, as a person, mean for the dominant culture in the place where you live" (Ekoka 17).[16]

The variety of self-designations that appear in the actual texts is as rich as that found in the profiles: the authors refer to themselves as Black, Afrodescendant, Afrospanish, etc. Yet, regardless of the exact term chosen, they all articulate an experience of Otherness in a Spanish society in which, despite a past and current presence of people of African descent, whiteness is considered the norm. This experience of being othered is closely connected to the authors consciously having become aware of their own Blackness, frequently in an encounter with normative whiteness and/or through the white gaze. This white gaze, as Frantz Fanon (95) concluded, dissects the Black woman and racializes her body. It is a gaze that entails that "suddenly, I felt different" (Ekoka 20; 57; 82–83).[17] This experience challenges women's identities and sense of belonging, forcing them to the margins of Spanish society or beyond. In this regard, texts such as Noemí Ondo Mesa's candidly re-claim Spanishness by using the term "afroespañola," that is, not only in terms of "making ourselves visible in the environment we live in" (Ekoka 35) but also in terms of a conceptual terminology that translates knowledge into language.[18]

Simultaneously, the women wrest the meaning of Blackness from a majoritized position of whiteness that usually shapes the discourse in Spanish society, redefine it and, in the process, create a new narrative — or, to use Salami's words (2), visibilize a hidden narrative. They reorganize knowledge(s) about Blackness and disclose its hidden meanings, echoing a continuity of Black resistance to Othering and imaginings of Afrodiasporic subjectivities (Salami 2; 4).[19] Hence, adscriptions that originally cause discrimination are converted into a source of identification and empowerment, as Johanna Province López confirms:

> being a black woman and with functional diversity ... are three aspects that define me and a source of empowerment ... it is up to us to give them [the people who discriminate] the cold shoulder and to laugh at ourselves with humor and optimism and to move (or in my case roll) forward with head held high, loving ourselves and proud to be part of this half of the world that has put up with more things, of the stronger and feistier one. (Ekoka 85)[20]

The quote shows that the feeling of belonging to a supportive and vibrant community serves as a source of self-affirmation for the subject, fostering a positive self-image. This is why, although the use of terms such as "africanidad" or "africana" by some of the authors conceptually links the subject to the African continent as both a geographical and cultural space, Africa, in fact, turns into a shifting signifier of "home" in an abstract sense. It is detached from a precise geographical location and imagined as a metaphorical space of Afrodiasporic belonging. As Stuart Hall argues, it is an

Africa that arises from a diasporic imagination, one re-imagined and retold from an Afrodiasporic perspective (17–18). It turns into a fluid and dynamic space of belonging in which different affiliations clash and overlap, one that shifts according to the subject's points of identification. Therefore, the knowledge about diasporic belonging presented in *Metamba Miago* is not absolute and one-dimensional. It is always relative, diverse, and, at times, even contradictory. The deferral Hall discusses is reiterated by Essonti Luque when she describes that, traveling to Cameroon, she felt that people she met and places she saw "*somehow* already belonged to me" (Ekoka 59; my emphasis).[21] This *somehow* (*de alguna forma*) emblematizes the ambivalent relationship of the diasporic subject to the land of origin as an imagined "home," yet not quite, a place that, in fact, is not "home" but still offers a symbolic matrix of belonging.

This fluidity also translates into the self-designations, as some of the authors forgo consistent terminology. Instead, they resort to different notions synonymously or bring into play "slashed" terms such as "black/mixed-race woman" (Ekoka 118) or "black/afro/afrodescendant women" (114) to affirm the openness and dynamic of belonging.[22] Moreover, this openness also manifests in self-positionings that refuse any fixed affiliations and turn the feeling "to live in the limbo of identity" (20) into a positively-connoted floating identity.[23] For instance, in Ekoka Hernandis's own account, "I'm neither white nor black, but I'm at the same time white and black. I'm what I want, when I want, and no one will tell me what I am, or what I ain't, I assert my right to self-designation" (20).[24] Another example comes from Essonti Luque, who explains that "I'm not able to choose, I cannot say that I'm white or black or that I'm Spanish or Cameroonian. I'm both things" (Ekoka 60; 119; 121).[25] Striking in both cases is that none of the authors try to create a synthesis of the binary concepts they enumerate but appropriate both poles: they are not just "half" anything (60).[26] Finally, Lydia Cortés Damian goes one step further by consciously dismissing any categorization in terms of cultural, ethnic, or social origin, "I don't need a narrative to explain me to myself, and, at the same time, I have given up any need to belong to any group. My tribe is the people who love me ... I simply am" (Ekoka 92).[27]

Now, if we return to the profiles, we can observe that they offer further valuable information. The authors' self-positionings emphasize their commitment to feminist and antiracist activism and/or the arts, a commitment that goes hand in hand with their search for identity and their place in a society that keeps marginalizing them. They accentuate their activism (Ekoka 105; 129), their rebellion against the status quo, "a fighter and nonconformist" (33), "with a pile of energy" (43), and consider artistic engagement as a "weapon of combat, expression and liberation. A tool for a search for identity and personal harmony with which to find answers and healing" (117; 120).[28] The last quote is revealing in this context: it stresses the importance of developing one's own perspective—or, as photographer Essonti Luque states, "the radical act to speak about oneself" (Ekoka 55).[29] At the same time, it also points to the need to heal from the traumatic experience of not being sure who you are and where you belong, of constantly being confronted by marginalization, and of not being represented in Spanish society (16–17). The introductory chapter also draws on this aspect of healing and the need to "liberate all this pain" (17), which is described as characterizing the experience of people of African descent around the world and throughout history.[30] Both examples clearly point to the potential of literary and artistic expression to face these issues on a symbolic level, to convey a knowledge of how to cope with these experiences within a "process of self-awareness" (63)—for both the authors or artists themselves as well as for others inspired through writing or art.[31]

Moreover, the profile pages contradict an existing prejudice that Black women underperform and miss out on social or professional advancement, a bias that the collection's texts also critique. Probably not by coincidence, some authors include their educational and professional background in their self-descriptions, picturing themselves, for example, as a "black woman who has graduated in Sociology" (Ekoka 117), "the first Afrodescendant member of parliament in the history of Spanish democracy" (139), "researcher and lecturer" (105), "psychologist" (81), "graduate in sociology and political sciences" (87), author of a book (71), or a cyberentrepreneur (132).[32] These positionings echo Salami's argument that Blackness is not to be reduced to political struggle. It includes many more elements, such as cultural aspects that produce this *language of joy* Salami (96) has described. For instance, the authors refer to their artistic endeavors (Ekoka 55), expressing their urge "to create content in which I see myself represented ... and with which others can identify" (58; 61), to their commitment to promoting Afrodescendant literature and culture (19), to their status as writers (43; 71), or simply to their leisure activities such as the Afrobrazilian martial art of capoeira (63).[33] Angela Nzambi agrees that it is crucial to reconceptualize Afrodescendance as a multifacetedness that reaches beyond the merely political. This reconceptualization requires creating positive spaces of encounter and cultural self-affirmation in addition to perceiving art and culture as an alternative way "de luchar" or "to fight" (Ekoka 61):

> Culture and the arts can serve us as tools [to share those values that we carry, forms of being and doing things that may contribute to the common good] .... It is not about returning to old battles ... but about

The Autobiographical and Testimonial Texts in Metamba Miago

initiating others that have as a perspective what we want to be, on an individual and collective level, and what we can contribute to constructing a society we are a part of. For this purpose, it is important to acknowledge our capacities, and attitude. (53)[34]

The authors in *Metamba Miago* emphasize that, in addition to fostering the visibilization of the Afrodescendant community in Spain, their testimonies also seek a positive reappropriation of Blackness in all its facets, and they demand equal rights: "most importantly, we are full-fledged citizens" (12).[35] In effect, it is not only a political struggle but "a form of cultural resistance [that] must be promoted," as Antumi Toasijé ("Challenges" 56) claims. Gabriella (Nuru) Bita Rankovic makes the same argument:

We have to start to revalue ourselves and to be conscious of our abilities and not feel shame. Care for our body and our mind. Break free from the shell where we have always been put and where we keep being put until today. We are more than this.... We have to celebrate who we are. (Ekoka 126)[36]

Crucial aspects emerge from these lines: the need for self-empowerment by insisting on agency, a re-conceptualization of Blackness as self-esteem and one that goes beyond experiences of racism by highlighting the diverse achievements and capacities of Afrodescendant women, the need to liberate oneself from being categorized by others and to think beyond a narrative of victimization (140). Bita Rankovic adds that it is crucial to "take our features (skin, hair) as a sign of identity and a weapon to fight, not as a hindrance. Not as something that needs to be softened or tamed" (Ekoka 126).[37] Instead, as Nzambi affirms, the narrative of Blackness needs to be changed—"the form in which we tell our stories, the perception of our presence and position" (Ekoka 45)—to create spaces of mutual appreciation and respect that not only show how people of African descent contribute to fundamental matters of humankind but also produce the *language of joy* (Salami 96) that allows subjects of African descent to decolonize and value their bodies, cultures, and knowledges (Ekoka 130).[38]

Another essential aspect of the conceptual design of *Metamba Miago* is the entanglement of the individual and the collective dimensions. By having the profile pages focus on the authors, the texts are identified as explicitly personal. Nonetheless, the testimonies also represent a collective fact, as Remei Sipi Mayo writes in the prologue:

These women are united by a collective fact, the fact of being Afrodescendant Spanish women in Spain, who make their stories heard and where every story isn't reduced to a personal anecdote, instead they go beyond this, they are much broader, they transcend the individual to turn into collective experiences.[39] (Ekoka 11–12)

Sipi Mayo highlights the intersubjective relatedness of the texts that do not hide their subjectivity while still asserting their validity on a collective level. Bita Rankovic agrees with Sipi Mayo when she says, "I write to heal and in some way to heal the people who can identify with what I write" (Ekoka 61; 120).[40] Cortés Damian addresses this issue in a similar way, underscoring that her text "is nothing more than my own experience" (Ekoka 88) but that she hopes, nevertheless, to inspire and help by putting it in writing.[41]

As subjective statements, the texts in Metamba Miago do not merely list facts about discrimination and exclusion. They bear witness to the emotions that flow from these experiences, turning the subjective into something indisputable, for "[n]o one can debate with you how you feel" (Ekoka 16; 22).[42] Thus, the texts do not conceal that they are personal. Yet, many of them oscillate between the singular and plural of the first person, relating the personal experience to the reality of others. They join in a shared chorus that denounces structural racism in modern-day Spain and tries to guide Black women to lead self-confident and meaningful lives, to not give in to being othered. The collection's diversity of voices and stories merges into a collective goal of denouncing racism and reappropriating the discourse on Blackness. To reach this objective, the collective dimension is essential, as Nzambi confirms: "It is the way to make ourselves seen, be heard and make our rights count, to fight against the invisibility we are submitted to, to encourage our recognition" (Ekoka 52).[43]

Ondo Mesa imagines this collectivity as a subversive space of mutual support and learning, an "hogar Afro" [Afro home] (Ekoka 39) that encourages Afrodescendant women to join forces and unite in rebellion to self-determinedly "cultivate our IDENTITY… Our sense of belonging… Proud to be WOMEN AND AFRO. Whatever person is at your side will love what you project" (39; original emphasis).[44] Her notion of belonging is clearly conceived as a collective and collaborative safe space to generate Afrodiasporic knowledge. Of particular interest in this respect is Rita Bosaho Gori's text, which denounces the non-representation of Black people in Spanish society and highlights the need to visibilize the heterogeneity of modern-day society, "the diverse Spains" (Ekoka 143).[45] Her statement actually projects beyond the Afrospanish community and points to the potential of joining forces and establishing a bond of solidarity with other marginalized groups that share the experience of being racialized and othered. Bosaho Gori does this in terms of content while also using the

The Autobiographical and Testimonial Texts in Metamba Miago   125

Figure 5.2 Visual framework of the collection (Ekoka 15; 147). Permission granted by the author.

integrative first-person plural that conceptually creates a collective of the marginalized in Spanish society: "we are Afrodescendant, Latinamerican, black, Romani, Indigenous, Muslim persons" (Ekoka 145).[46]

This link between the individual and the collective is also presented in two pages with a text and a photograph that frame the collection (Figure 5.2). The very first photograph and the final one in *Metamba Miago* show a group rather than an individual woman. Both pages frame the collection at once visually and in terms of its content. First, from a visual perspective, the two photographs stage the authors as part of a collective on both a synchronic and a diachronic level, thus creating a genealogy of female resistance comprising past, present, and future generations that have all contributed and will keep contributing to the knowledge of what it means to be a woman of African descent in Spain (Ekoka 13; 17; 115). This transgenerational transfer of knowledge is also mentioned by Ondo Mesa, who projects her own self-recognition and consciousness as an Afrospanish woman onto future generations: "We relate experiences we have experienced ourselves. ... Our children will continue to live in the same hostile territory we already know" (39).[47]

Second, in terms of content, the texts on the two pages (Figure 5.2) underscore the project's goal of being an activist encounter of different voices that emerged from the "necessity that our stories, our words, will be read, that our bodies will be felt and to claim our recognition in the territory in which we live" (Ekoka 16).[48] It is an intellectual encounter giving rise to a polyphony of voices that draw their strength from their particular subjectivities: "My intention is not to tell an absolute and immovable truth ... I only want to tell my story, and it has been my intention to select those of other female authors, so that they tell theirs" (16).[49] The page that completes the collection revisits these goals and projects them onto a future that is yet to come, "to give to those who will follow what we have lacked" (147).[50] Namely, it refers to role models with whom future generations can identify, visibility from which they can benefit, and coping strategies and "strategies of surviving" (90) to which they can refer.[51]

All these references extend the "dialogue between us" (back cover) and, thus, the passing on of knowledge(s), both beyond the book and the present, and point to a dynamic process of reciprocity that Essonti Luque tackles in her account: "It is magical when some brother or sister approaches me to tell me how much they like my work, I can feel their energy, see in their eyes that they see what I intend to transmit in my photos, I see that, like myself, they have found something familiar" (Ekoka 61).[52] Other texts express this desire to feel proud and to pass on this pride to others as well. The writers consider it to be a crucial competence "to survive, share and transmit knowledges" (115) that emerge from self-representation, with the goal being to "educate [themselves]" (26).[53] To this end, some accounts even articulate distinct instructions to handle specific issues and directly address an implicit reader to offer guidance: "Black, Afrospanish woman, recognize yourself, accept yourself, create links with other black women, incite your consciousness and your afro consciousness" (40). The directions are followed by this encouraging advice: "Empower yourself, sister!" (41).[54] This quote echoes Essonti Luque's remark that she has been longing for guidance in her search for identity—"that someone tells me that," "that someone explains to me how" (57)[55]—until she was able to immerse herself in African and Afrodescendant knowledge systems (e.g. watching African cinema, reading Black writers and artists, participating in talks and workshops). Likewise, she points out the value of education: "I educated myself, I've achieved what I've been longing for so much in other moments: my first weapons to fight against white supremacy, in my way" (59).[56] Producing, unveiling, and passing on this knowledge to others is identified as the basis for conceiving of Afro diasporic identity no longer as a "deficiency" but as "a vessel of joy" (Salami 78) that frees the subject "from predefined notions of identity" (78) and the role of the victim. Instead, the women in *Metamba Miago* determinedly self-define themselves, for, as Salami confirms: "the biggest 'fuck you' a black woman can give to Europatriarchy is to take genuine pleasure in being alive" (79).

* * *

Using the example of *Metamba Miago*, a collection of autobiographical and testimonial texts written by women of African descent, I have shown how they voice a shared knowledge of what it means for women racialized as Black to belong to Spain "differently," a knowledge that emanates from personal experience but extends to a collective level. Their texts articulate a genuine Afrodiasporic knowledge of how to deal and cope with both racism and a feeling of non-belonging by empowering the Afrodiasporic subject and offering previously hidden or unseen spaces of identification and affiliation. The authors self-confidently claim multilocal belongings that blur the homeland/hostland dichotomy as their fluid self-positionings do not refrain from exhibiting cultural difference within a Spanish context. These positionings not only refer to the political sphere but also articulate the value of African and Afrodiasporic cultures for the subject's search for identity. Thus, the knowledges enunciated in the text are not just about racism and how to cope with it. Instead, they also embrace further spheres of identification that inspire the subject and provide her with agency. The Verkami crowdfunding website captures this vision succinctly by affirming that "it is a collective project for and by us, in search of our roots, of our two parts, the African one and the Spanish one, their recognition. Those who follow shall not have to live like us, and they shall have the right to self-identify and to belong to this territory" ("Metamba").[57]

Research funded by the Deutsche Forschungsgemeinschaft (DFG, German Research Foundation)—project number 353492083.

Notes

1 Black/Blackness and white/whiteness are not to be understood as mere color terms but as inherently political terms that refer to racialized identities and lived realities that are often related to an absence or presence of privilege. See also the introduction of this book.
2 According to the book's prologue, "metamba miago" means "our roots" in the Ndowé language (Ekoka 12). Ndowé is one of the languages spoken in Equatorial Guinea, the ancestral country of many of the authors or their families.
3 "und dabei auf die unterschiedlichsten Wissenssegmente und wissenschaftlichen Diskurse zurückgreift." All translations of quotes into English are mine.
4 "ein narrativ-fiktionaler Explorationsraum von neuen oder verdrängten Wissensformen sowie als aktives und eminent eigenständiges Medium zur Generierung von Lebenswissen."
5 "con todas y todos nosotros sus sentires, sus emociones, sus experiencias y su modo de ser mujer racializada en la España de hoy."
6 This line of argument does not aim at essentializing the knowledge of African/Afrodescendant people. The knowledge Salami and this article refer to is to

be understood as a knowledge stemming from an individual and/or collective experience that is linked to racialization and an absence of privilege. This knowledge (or this multiplicity of knowledges) tends to be ignored and/or silenced by a white-dominated majoritized society that masquerades its own archive of knowledge as being universal. Texts such as *Metamba Miago* challenge this alleged universality and unveil the silenced/hidden knowledge(s) of Afrodescendant individuals and communities.

7 "ejercicio de responsabilidad colectiva."
8 "Metamba Miago cuenta nuestras historias, atravesando lo comunitario, *es un diálogo entre nosotras* que queremos compartir con todas y todos, tal y como hacemos en coloquios o lugares seguros donde nos damos esos espacios *para expresar abiertamente cómo nos hemos sentido* durante nuestros procesos, en busca de una identidad que ha sido y sigue siendo, aún en ocasiones, cuestionada y negada por nuestro color de piel."
9 The narrative strategy to articulate Afrodiasporic knowledges through autobiographical and testimonial texts that will be elaborated for *Metamba Miago* can be found in other texts as well: see for instance, Odome Angone's collection *Las españolas afrodescendientes hablan sobre identidad y empoderamiento* (2018) and Moha Gerehou's autobiography *Qué hace un negro como tú en un sitio como este* (2021) or the video interview series *Nadie nos ha dado vela en este entierro* (on YouTube since 2017), examples that would also merit future investigation.
10 "que narran su visión de la afrodescendencia en España."
11 In the following, *Metamba Miago* will be quoted under the name of its editor as Ekoka. Besides Remei Sipi Mayo (Prologue) and Deborah Ekoka Hernandis (Introduction), the following women have contributed a text to the collection: Noemí Ondo Mesa, Angela Nzambi, Agnes Essonti Luque, Jadisha Sow Paíno, Lucía Asué Mbomío Rubio, Johana Province López, Lydia Cortés Damian, Lídia Mont Ferragud, Esther (Mayoko) Ortega Arjonilla, Gabriella (Nuru) Bita Rankovic, Desirée Bela-Lobedde, and Rita Bosaho Gori.
12 "negritud desde diversas posiciones e intersecciones."
13 "te obliga a posicionarte."
14 "[a]fromadrileña"; "andaluza y bayangue"; "adolescente afrodescendiente"; "[a]ctivista feminista antirracista"; "mujer negra"; "diputada afrodescendiente."
15 "[p]ara muchos hijos de migrantes ..., el barrio es el único espacio de reconocimiento, el sitio en el que sí nos sentimos e, importante, nos sienten como propios, al que denominamos casa, en el que tenemos nombre, rostro e historia." See Cornejo-Parriego's essay on Mbomío's column *Barrionalismos* in this volume. See also a debate on Afrospanishness in *Afroféminas* from 5 March 2015 (Mbomío Rubio, "¿Afroespañolas?").
16 "negritud, y no hablo de ser negra, hablo de saber y sentir de dónde vienes y qué simboliza tu persona para la cultura dominante en el lugar donde habites."
17 "[d]e repente me sentí distinta."
18 "visibilizarnos en el entorno en que vivimos."
19 In this context, Esther Mayoko identifies the need to constantly (re-)think Blackness in its heterogeneity to embrace *dissident* positionings as well (Ekoka 106).
20 "el ser mujer negra y con diversidad funcional ... son tres aspectos que me definen y una fuente de empoderamiento ... en nosotras está el vivir dándoles [a la gente que discrimina] la espalda y con humor y optimismo reírnos de nosotras mismas y andar (o en mi caso rodar) hacia delante con la cabeza bien alta, queriéndonos y orgullosas de pertenecer a esa mitad del mundo que más cosas ha aguantado, a la más fuerte y luchadora."

The Autobiographical and Testimonial Texts in Metamba Miago 129

21 "*de alguna forma* ya me pertenecían."
22 "mujer negra/mestiza"; "mujeres negras/afro/afrodescendientes."
23 "a vivir en el limbo de la identidad."
24 "No soy blanca ni negra, pero a su vez soy blanca y negra. Soy lo que quiera, cuando quiera, y nadie me va a decir lo que soy, o lo que no soy, yo tomo mi derecho de auto designación."
25 "no soy capaz de escoger, no puedo decir que soy blanca o negra o que soy española o camerunesa. Soy las dos cosas."
26 These polarities also echo Essonti Luque's personal experience as having been categorized both as white (in Cameroon) and as Black (in Spain) (Ekoka 60).
27 "no necesito de una narrativa para explicarme a mí misma, y al mismo tiempo he abandonado cualquier necesidad de pertenencia a ningún grupo. Mi tribu es la gente que me ama …. Simplemente soy."
28 "luchadora e inconformista"; "con un montón de energía"; "arma de lucha, expresión y liberación. Una herramienta de búsqueda de identidad y armonía personal con la cual encontrar respuestas y sanación."
29 "el acto radical de hablar sobre sí mismo."
30 "liberar todo ese dolor."
31 "proceso de autoconciencia."
32 "mujer negra graduada en Sociología"; "la primera diputada afrodescendiente en la historia de la democracia española"; "investigadora y docente"; "psicóloga"; "licenciada en sociología y ciencias políticas."
33 "de crear contenidos en los que me viese representada … y con los que otros se sientan identificados."
34 "La cultura y las artes nos pueden servir como herramientas [para compartir aquellos valores que traemos, formas de ser y de hacer que pueden servir al bien común]. No se trata ya de retomar viejas luchas, … sino de iniciar otras que tengan como perspectiva aquello que queremos ser, individual y colectivamente, y aquello con lo que podemos contribuir a la construcción de la sociedad de la que formamos parte. Para eso es importante el reconocimiento de nuestras capacidades, y la actitud."
35 "sobre todo y por encima de todo, somos ciudadanas de pleno derecho."
36 "Hemos de empezar a revalorizarnos nosotras mismas y ser conscientes de nuestras aptitudes y no sentir vergüenza. Cuidar de nuestro cuerpo y nuestra mente. Salir del cascarón donde siempre y hasta el día de hoy se nos ha metido. Somos más que eso…. Tenemos que celebrar lo que somos."
37 "[t]omar nuestros atributos (piel, pelo) como señal de identidad y arma de lucha no como un estorbo. No como algo que se ha de suavizar o domar." See Essonti Luque's realization when travelling to London that "for the first time in many years …, being black, being African, stopped being something bad" [por primera vez en muchos años …, ser negra, ser africana, dejó de ser malo] (Ekoka 59). See also Bela-Lobedde's account on aesthetic activism and her fight against Eurocentric beauty standards (Ekoka 129–38) as well as the analysis of aesthetic activism in Borst and Neu-Wendel.
38 "la forma en la que contamos nuestras historias, la percepción de nuestra presencia y posición."
39 "A estas mujeres les une un hecho colectivo, el de ser mujeres afrodescendientes españolas en España, que ponen voz a sus historias y donde cada historia no está reducida a la anécdota personal, sino que van más allá, son mucho más amplias, trascienden lo individual para convertirse en vivencias colectivas."
40 "escribo para sanar y de alguna forma sanar a las personas que se pueden identificar con lo que escribo."

41 "no es más que mi propia experiencia."
42 "[n]adie puede debatirte sobre cómo te sientes." Other examples are the following statements: "We black women are exhausted" [Las mujeres negras estamos exhaustas] (Ekoka 126); "being mixed race ... for me has always been very painful. I have suffered rejection from both sides and this has affected me in every sense" [ser mestiza ... para mí siempre ha sido muy doloroso. He sufrido rechazo de ambas partes y me ha afectado en todos los sentidos] (56); "Us, the black women, we are unprotected. It has been instilled in us to be tough but sometimes the solitude hurts" [Nosotras, las mujeres negras, estamos desprotegidas. Se nos ha inculcado ser duras pero, a veces, la soledad duele] (122); "Today, ... I will return to reading, embracing, loving that text ... . This text of the past, now ... seems valuable to me although for many years it didn't seem like it to me. It wasn't a text of which I felt proud, it made me feel uncomfortable" [Hoy, ... vuelvo a leer, abrazar, amar ese texto ... . Este texto de antaño, ahora ... me parece valioso aunque durante muchos años no me lo pareció. No era un texto del que me sintiese orgullosa, me producía incomodidad] (107).
43 "Es la forma de hacernos ver, escuchar y hacer valer nuestros derechos, de luchar contra la invisibilidad a la que se nos somete, de favorecer nuestro reconocimiento."
44 "cultivar nuestra IDENTIDAD... Nuestro sentido de pertenencia... De orgullo de ser MUJERES Y AFRO. Cualquier persona que esté a tu lado amará lo que tú proyectes."
45 "las diversas Españas."
46 "somos personas afrodescendientes, latinoamericanas, negras, gitanas, indígenas, musulmanas."
47 "Contamos con la experiencia en carnes propias. ... Nuestros hijos siguen viviendo en ese mismo territorio hostil que nosotras conocemos."
48 "necesidad de que se lean nuestras historias, nuestras palabras, que se sientan nuestros cuerpos y de reivindicar nuestro reconocimiento en el territorio en el que habitamos."
49 "Mi intención no es contar una verdad absoluta e inamovible. Yo solo quiero contar mi historia, y esa ha sido mi intención al seleccionar a las otras autoras, que cuenten las suyas."
50 "para darles a lxs que vienen lo que a nosotras nos ha faltado."
51 "estrategias de supervivencia."
52 "Resulta mágico cuando algún hermano o hermana se acerca a mí para decirme lo mucho que le gusta mi trabajo, puedo sentir su energía, ver en sus ojos que saben lo que intento transmitir en mis fotos, veo que como yo, ellos han encontrado algo familiar."
53 "para sobrevivir, compartir y transmitir los saberes"; "educarnos a nosotras mismas."
54 "Mujer negra, afroespañola, conócete, acéptate, crea lazos con otras mujeres negras, azuza tu conciencia y tu conciencia afro. No tengas miedo a ser diferente"; "¡Empodérate, hermana!."
55 "que alguién me dijese que," "que alguien me explicase cómo."
56 "Me eduqué, conseguí lo que tanto había anhelado en otro momento: mis primeras armas para luchar contra la supremacía blanca, a mi manera." Other texts, such as Bela-Lobedde's and Cortés Damian's, for instance, are rhetorically evocative of manuals in terms of providing advice for future adopting parents (of racialized children) or persons interesados en getting involved in digital activism and entrepreneurship.

57 "es un proyecto colectivo de nosotras para nosotras en busca de nuestras raíces, nuestras dos partes, la africana y la española, su reconocimiento. Que las y los que vienen no tengan que vivir como nosotras, y tengan el derecho de autoidentificarse y pertenecer a este territorio."

Works Cited

Abé Pans, Jeffrey. "Deborah Ekoka, el triunfo del colectivo." *Cuando somos el enemigo: Activismo negro en España*, edited by Jeffrey Abé Pans. Mey, 2019, pp. 57–61.

Angone, Odome, editor. *Las españolas afrodescendientes hablan sobre identidad y empoderamiento*. Sial, 2018.

Antumi Toasijé. "The Africanity of Spain: Identity and Problematization." *Journal of Black Studies*, vol. 39, no. 3, 2009, pp. 348–55.

———. "The Challenges Facing African and Afro-Descendant Communities in Spain." *Africa Report*, edited by Itxaso Domínguez de Olazábal and Elsa Aimé González. Fundación Alternativas, 2020, pp. 47–58.

Blum, S., et al. "Coping." *Encyclopedia of Human Behavior*, edited by Vilayanur S. Ramachandran. Elsevier, 2012, pp. 596–601.

Boampong, Joanna. "Coping to Survive? A Study of Female 'Afro-Diasporic' Actors of Spain." *Women's Perspectives on (Post)Migration: Between Literature, Arts and Activism—Between Africa and Europe*, edited by Julia Borst et al. Olms, 2023, pp. 279–301.

Borst, Julia. "Imagining Afrodescendance and the African Diaspora in Spain: Re-/De-Centering Belonging in Literature, Photography, and Film." *Research in African Literatures*, vol. 52, no. 2, 2021, pp. 168–97.

Borst, Julia, and Stephanie Neu-Wendel. "Decolonized Bodies: Aesthetic Activism in Afrofeminist Blogs from France, Spain and Italy." *Women's Perspectives on (Post)Migration: Between Literature, Arts and Activism—Between Africa and Europe*, edited by Julia Borst et al. Olms, 2023, pp. 205–51.

Butt, Nadia, et al. "Rethinking Postcolonial Europe: Moving Identities, Changing Subjectivities. Introduction." *Postcolonial Interventions*, vol. 7, no. 1, 2022, pp. 14–49.

Cohen, Robin, and Carolin Fischer. "Diaspora Studies: An Introduction." *Routledge Handbook of Diaspora Studies*, edited by Robin Cohen and Carolin Fischer. Routledge, 2018, pp. 1–10.

Ekoka, Deborah, editor. *Metamba Miago: Relatos y saberes de mujeres afroespañolas*. United Minds, 2019.

Ekoka, Deborah, and Lucía Asué Mbomío Rubio. "'Metamba Miago,' la doble lucha de ser mujer negra en España." *Radio Exterior*, Artesfera, 11 Apr. 2019, www.rtve.es/alacarta/audios/artesfera/artesfera-metamba-miago-doble-lucha-ser-mujer-negra-espana/5135031/. Accessed 11 May 2022.

Espinoza Garrido, Felipe, et al. "Introduction: African European Studies as a Critique of Contingent Belonging." *Locating African European Studies: Interventions, Intersections, Conversations*, edited by Felipe Espinoza Garrido et al. Routledge, 2020, pp. 1–28.

Ette, Ottmar. "Literature as Knowledge for Living, Literary Studies as Science for Living." Translated by Vera M. Kutzinski, *PMLA*, vol. 125, no. 4, 2010, pp. 983–93.

———. "Literaturwissenschaft als Lebenswissenschaft: Eine Programmschrift im Jahr der Geisteswissenschaften." *Literaturwissenschaft als Lebenswissenschaft. Programm—Projekte—Perspektiven*, edited by Wolfgang Asholt and Ottmar Ette. Narr, 2010, pp. 11–38.

Faist, Thomas. "Diaspora and Transnationalism: What Kind of Dance Partners?" *Diaspora and Transnationalism: Concepts, Theories and Methods*, edited by Rainer Bauböck and Thomas Faist. Amsterdam UP, 2010, pp. 9–34.

Fanon, Frantz. *Black Skin, White Masks*. Grove Press, 2008.

Gerehou, Moha. *Qué hace un negro como tú en un sitio como este*. Península, 2021.

Ha, Kien Nghi. "Ethnizität, Differenz und Hybridität in der Migration: Eine postkoloniale Perspektive." *PROKLA: Zeitschrift für kritische Sozialwissenschaft*, vol. 30, no. 3, 2000, pp. 377–97.

Hall, Stuart. "Cultural Identity and Cinematic Representation." *Black British Cultural Studies: A Reader*, edited by Houston R. Baker Jr. et al. U of Chicago P, 1996, pp. 210–22.

Lazarus, Richard S. "Coping Theory and Research: Past, Present, and Future." *Psychosomatic Medicine*, vol. 55, 1993, pp. 234–47.

Mbomío Rubio, Lucía Asué. "¿Afroespañolas o negras?" *Afroféminas*, 5 Mar. 2015, www.afrofeminas.com/2015/03/05/afroespanolas-o-negras/. Accessed 17 May 2022.

———. "Volver al telefonillo." *El País*, 10 Sept. 2018, elpais.com/ccaa/2018/09/09/madrid/1536527913_267225.html. Accessed 17 May 2022.

"Metamba Miago: Relatos y saberes de mujeres afroespañolas." *Verkami*, www.verkami.com/projects/22206-metamba-miago-relatos-y-saberes-de-mujeres-afr. Accessed 11 May 2022.

Nadie nos ha dado vela en este entierro. YouTube, uploaded by Nadie nos ha dado vela en este entierro (video channel created on 16 Oct. 2017). www.youtube.com/channel/UClEeFFcfEga8NzYIdG4XfZw/featured. Accessed 11 May 2022.

Nünning, Ansgar. "Lebensexperimente und Weisen literarischer Welterzeugung: Thesen zu den Aufgaben und Perspektiven einer lebenswissenschaftlich orientierten Literaturwissenschaft." *Literaturwissenschaft als Lebenswissenschaft. Programm—Projekte—Perspektiven*, edited by Wolfgang Asholt and Ottmar Ette. Narr, 2010, pp. 45–63.

Park, Crystal L., and Carol Joyce Blumberg. "Disclosing Trauma Through Writing: Testing the Meaning-Making Hypothesis." *Cognitive Therapy and Research*, vol. 26, no. 5, 2002, pp. 597–616.

Salami, Minna. *Sensuous Knowledge: A Black Feminist Approach for Everyone*. Zed Books, 2020.

Soper, Barlow, and C. W. Von Bergen. "Employment Counseling and Life Stressors. Coping Through Expressive Writing." *Journal of Employment Counseling*, vol. 38, 2001, pp. 150–60.

Tölölyan, Khachig. "Diaspora Studies: Past, Present and Promise." *Routledge Handbook of Diaspora Studies*, edited by Robin Cohen and Carolin Fischer. Routledge, 2018, pp. 22–30.

Zeleza, Paul Tiyambe. "Diaspora Dialogues. Engagement Between Africa and Its Diasporas." *The New African Diaspora*, edited by Isidore Okpewho and Nkiru Nzegwu. Indiana UP, 2009, pp. 31–58.

6 Un-Whitening Late Francoist Spain
Knots of Memory in Lucía Mbomío's *Las que se atrevieron*

Martin Repinecz

Although the contemporary Afro-Spanish writer and journalist Lucía Asué Mbomío Rubio is best known for her novel *Hija del camino* [Daughter of the Path] (2019), her first published book, *Las que se atrevieron* [The Women Who Dared] (2017), offers a powerful meditation on the intersections of race, gender, and colonial memory.[1] This earlier text is a creative memoir that recounts the stories of six interracial relationships between white Spanish women and Black Equatorial Guinean men during late Francoism and the Transition, a period that has received limited attention from scholars of race in Spain.[2] In this article, I argue that *Las que se atrevieron* highlights the formation of "knots of memory," to borrow Michael Rothberg's term, around unsettled memories of colonialism and its aftermath, on one hand, and the enduring legacies of a national narrative of whitening that accompanied the *desarrollismo* era of the 1960s and 1970s, on the other.[3] Although, as Rothberg argues, these knots of memory can be symptomatic of unresolved traumas, they also underscore opportunities to create "new imaginations of relation across difference" (11). In *Las que se atrevieron*, the knotted memories of dictatorship and colonialism pave the way for motherhood, in particular, to emerge as a source of transracial empathy.

The six chapters of *Las que se atrevieron* are all narrated in the first person singular from different women's points of view. Some are recounted from the vantage point of a participant in an interracial romance; others are narrated by a family member, such as a daughter or mother. The first chapter, titled *Mis padres [My Parents]*, tells the story of the author's own parents, who are also depicted on the book's front and back covers. Mbomío Rubio explains that she was inspired by women like her mother, who, "one fine day, decided to stand up to their time and their society for love" (27).[4] She views her white women protagonists as trailblazers of their time because: "They spoke in first person plural when they spoke about Equatorial Guineans… and whether they were separated, widowed or single, they passed on to their children a Black and/or African identity" (27).[5]

DOI: 10.4324/9781003435051-7

The author collected her stories by interviewing women who lived in Equatorial Guinean enclaves in suburban Madrid, while adding that: "I changed their names; I altered several aspects of their story so that no one would know who I'm talking about; I incorporated real anecdotes, from them and others; and I created characters based on the descriptions they gave me" (27).[6] Through this complex layering of autobiography, fiction, and investigative journalism, Mbomío Rubio draws a parallel between the generic hybridity of her text and the instability of various socially constructed binaries, especially those surrounding the Black/white and Europe/Africa dichotomies. For just as Mbomío Rubio and other characters might be said to live in a "Third Space"—that is, a "contradictory and ambivalent space of enunciation" between these various identities—so, too, does the text itself dwell in a "Third Space" between fiction and nonfiction, past and present, personal narrative and oral history (Bhabha 37).

The interracial love stories of *Las que se atrevieron* offer a necessary revision to contemporary memories of late Francoism and the Transition by showing how Spain's national narratives during this period were entangled with rhetorics of racial whiteness and with unsettled memories about Spain's colonial ties to Equatorial Guinea. In doing so, *Las que se atrevieron* calls attention to the emergence of "knots of memory," to use Rothberg's formulation, around the tensions and contradictions between Francoist national narratives, spectral memories of colonial violence, and the lived experiences of interracial families in Spain. Rothberg's concept of the *noeuds de mémoire*, or knots of memory, was conceived as an alternative to Pierre Nora's formulation of the *lieux de mémoire*, or sites of memory. While Nora's influential concept imagined history and memory as discrete forces with roots in a specific community, such as a nation, Rothberg proposes the idea of "knotted" memory to challenge Nora's binary opposition between memory and history, as well as his vision of memory as bound to a particular community or identity. Rather, as Rothberg argues, "acts of memory are rhizomatic networks of temporality and cultural reference that exceed attempts at territorialization… and identitarian reduction" (7). Similarly, Rothberg contends that the idea of memory as knots allows us to see its "dynamism," that is, how it "emerges from unexpected, multidirectional encounters … between diverse pasts and a conflictual present [and] between different agents or catalysts of memory" (9). For Rothberg, the multidirectional encounters that emerge from rhizomatic memories are especially powerful because they can create new, unexpected forms of solidarity across differences, including those forms of difference that structure Black/white, Europe/Africa, or gender binaries.

Rothberg's vision of knotted memories as rhizomatic, deterritorialized, and anti-identitarian is helpful for analyzing *Las que se atrevieron*, which underlines the rhizomatic movement of colonial memories between past and present and between Spain and its former empire. These knotted memories puncture hegemonic national narratives of late Francoism and the Transition, notably those that established a linkage between Spain's economic development, its Europeanization, and its ascent into racial whiteness. As I have argued elsewhere, the late Franco regime's promises of development, peace, and prosperity were inseparable from a narrative of racial whitening (Repinecz, "Spain Is [Not So] Different"). According to this logic, the Spain of the 1960s and 1970s, which was newly integrated into global capitalism, imagined itself as leaving behind the "blackness" associated with the backwardness, poverty, and repression of the Black Legend and consequently as ascending into the "whiteness" of Northern Europe and the United States. This narrative, which was widely trumpeted in hegemonic cultural forms such as popular cinema, obfuscated the eclipse of Spain's imperial dominion in Africa, whose bloody aftermath was masked by *materia reservada* [classified information] laws and other censorship strategies.[7] Mbomío Rubio's text both recalls and deflates late Francoism's myths of national whitening in a number of ways. For one, it illustrates how Spanish society's desire to belong in global whiteness during this period was underpinned by anxieties about the looming blackening of Spanish society by immigration, even before immigration had begun on a large scale.[8] Similarly, despite the regime's efforts to hide colonial and postcolonial violence, Mbomío Rubio's text reveals that colonial violence was, in fact, being openly enacted in peninsular Spain through the ostracism and punishment of interracial relationships, especially those that formed between white Spanish women and Equatorial Guinean men. Consequently, her text shatters one of Francoism's most enduring false claims, namely, the idea that racism was a foreign problem that had never taken root either in Spain or anywhere in its empire. This argument enabled Spanish intellectuals to distance Francoism from Nazi Germany in the wake of World War II (Goode 3–4) and to justify Francoism's efforts to resist a global trend toward decolonization from the 1950s onward (Nerín 12; Stucki 129–36).

As *Las que se atrevieron* demonstrates, late Francoist anxieties around interracial relationships bore an uncanny resemblance to older racialized and gendered imaginaries that proliferated in the faraway Guinean territory under Spanish colonial rule. After all, it is no coincidence that in colonial Guinea, too, relationships between Black men and white women were heavily stigmatized and severely punished, as they were framed by an economy of stereotypes in which Black men were seen as hypersexual predators and white women as the gatekeepers of racial whiteness. As Gustau Nerín has argued, Spanish colonial discourse constructed Black Guinean men as violent, hypersexual, and jealous beings who were prone to kidnapping women, including white women, whom they were thought to desire more intensely than Black women (84–91). Nerín compellingly notes that the construction of the Black man as hypersexual and aggressive was, in part, a strategy that enabled white men to control the sexuality of white women, whose potential desire for Black men was considered a threat to the purity of the white race (90–91). Since relations between Guinean men and Spanish women were seen as indistinguishable from rape, accusations of sexual relations between them frequently resulted in the lynching or execution of Black Guinean men (92–93). By contrast, as Alberto Elena has observed, although relations between white men and Black women were also somewhat stigmatized and officially forbidden in the Guinean colony, they were nonetheless widespread and tacitly tolerated, especially in the forms of cohabitation and prostitution (177–78). This double standard, in which interracial sex was more permissible for white men than for white women, was reflected in colonial legislation, which regulated the rights of children of white men and Black women, but was utterly silent on the subject of children born to Black fathers and white mothers (Nerín 92).

Mbomío Rubio's text highlights how these colonial-era anxieties about gender roles and interracial mixing outlived imperialism itself and metastasized from the colony to the metropole, where they endured as a form of what Ann Laura Stoler has called "imperial debris"—that is, the latent, yet stubborn traces, residues, or remnants of colonialism "that saturate the subsoil of people's lives and persist … over a [long] durée," well beyond the demise of empires themselves (5). As Mbomío Rubio's text illustrates, neither the end of imperialism nor the limited size of Spain's Black population in the 1960s and 1970s could prohibit the imagined polarized opposition between Black men and white women from "saturating the subsoil" of Spanish society, to use Stoler's phrasing.[9] This fact is made clear by the numerous instances in which Mbomío Rubio's white women protagonists are subjected to various forms of discipline, punishment, and even physical violence for daring to engage in romantic relationships with Black men. Paloma, the narrator and protagonist of Chapter 2, explains that after she lost her parents in a car accident, her brothers, who controlled the parents' estate, decided to deny her her inheritance due to her relationship with Cecilio, a Black man from Equatorial Guinea. Kika, the protagonist of Chapter 5, was prevented from leaving the family home for a whole year so that she could not keep seeing a Guinean man named José; yet, their relationship continued because Kika's little sister secretly passed letters between the lovers. Likewise, María, the narrator of Chapter 6, was also sequestered in her family's home in Oviedo for several months for being in a relationship with Javier, also a Black Guinean man. While some of her uncles threatened, "I'll kill her," her brother went beyond threats and actually beat her, thus causing a lifelong rift in the siblings' relationship (114).[10]

Confinement, disinheritance, and even physical violence: these are the consequences suffered by Spanish women whose relationship choices defied late Francoism's national narrative of racial whitening. Yet the fact that colonial anxieties about interracial relationships between Black men and white women took root in late Francoist Spain, whose population generally had extremely limited direct knowledge of colonial contexts, requires further explanation. I argue that the displacement of these anxieties from the colony to the metropole calls attention to the workings of what Alison Landsberg has termed "prosthetic memory," that is, a memory that travels beyond its original context through mass media and culture. The ability of memory to travel through mass media, which Rothberg identifies as a key component of knotted memories, "does not ... simply reinforce a particular group's identity by sharing memories. Instead, it opens up those memories and identities to persons from radically different backgrounds" (Landsberg 10–11). Although Landsberg emphasizes the transformative power of prosthetic memory to build collective solidarities and alliances, these alliances may sometimes be destructive. This is the case of media representations of Blackness in late Francoist Spain, which arguably created a kind of "alliance" between Spanish settlers and colonial administrators in the Guinean colony, North American white audiences such as those to which Hollywood catered, and ordinary Spaniards who may never have left Spain and had little direct contact with Black people, but who still stood to benefit from recognizing themselves as white. Specifically, the transference of prosthetic memories by mass media invited ordinary Spaniards to imagine themselves as both beneficiaries and defenders of the privileges of imperial and global whiteness—even after the end of the empire. These media images also contributed to the formation of a dulcified, palatable memory of imperialism that filled in the gaps of the regime's official silence on the subject.

Mbomío Rubio's text is rife with evidence of the traces of mass media's transmission of colonial anxieties, fears, and desires, especially in its depiction of white women's initial encounters with Black men. A prominent example surfaces in Chapter 3, which tells the story of the marriage of Neus and Alejandro from the perspective of Neus' unnamed mother. As this chapter begins, the narrator explains that her adult daughter Neus came home one day saying she had met "a chocolate man" and that she referred to him repeatedly by this moniker (55).[11] The mother also notes that, around that time, a man named Alejandro would frequently call the house asking for Neus, but the mother did not realize that Alejandro and the "chocolate man" were the same person because the caller spoke perfect Spanish (56). When the mother finally made the connection, she fainted and had to be slapped into consciousness by her husband (57). Although Neus and Alejandro's relationship lasted many years and produced a child, the initial framing of Alejandro as a "chocolate man" recalls widely circulated Spanish advertisements of the mid-twentieth century, such as the "Cola Cao" song or the Conguitos commercials, both of which linked colonial stereotypes of primitive Black Africans to the marketing and consumption of chocolate. As Silke Hackenesch has shown, these representations circulated transnationally and established conceptual connections between "plantation labor, brown-skinned peoples as well as the pleasure of consuming [chocolate]" (12). In Spain, these representations arguably served to encourage ordinary white Spaniards, including those of the less privileged classes who had no direct experience of colonialism, to imagine a link between Spain's status as a colonial power and their increasing power as consumers in the development era. The Conguitos commercials, such as one from the 1960s that depicts a white woman picking up tiny African men and dropping them into her mouth, could have enhanced a fantasy of Spain's racial and economic power by intertwining it with women's desires for empowerment in a patriarchal society. They could also have allowed viewers of any gender to fantasize about sexual encounters with Black men despite the strict taboos associated with interracial sex. In doing so, they also transmitted a prosthetic memory of colonialism in which the sweetness of chocolate served as a metaphor for the "sweetness" or innocence of European colonial endeavors in Africa, including Spain's.

Other examples of mass media's role in transmitting colonial anxieties and desires from colony to metropole emerge in Chapter 6, which is set in Oviedo and tells the story of María and Javier. The first instance occurs in a dialogue between María and her neighbors, Don Pablo and Doña Asunción, in which they discuss the scandalous rumor that a neighborhood woman is dating a Black man without realizing that María is the woman in question:

- They say there is a girl who works at the hospital who's going out with Black guy. What must her family think of her?"
- How embarrassing! Who could it be?
- Ha, ha, ha... a woman that no normal man would want, no white man. That's clear. Either that, or she's a tramp. (111)[12]

This dialogue reflects an underlying assumption that a white woman could only ever choose a Black man for two reasons: either out of desperation because she can't get anyone better, or because both partners share a perverse, uncontrolled sexuality. This second trait, of course, was imagined as innate to all Black men, but available to white women by choice. As I demonstrate in my forthcoming book, *Volatile Whiteness: Race, Cinema, and Europeanization in Spain*, this type of assumption about interracial relationships was commonplace in Spanish popular cinema of the 1960s and 1970s. Like colonial laws in Equatorial Guinea, domestic popular cinema in those years construed interracial sex as more permissible for Spanish men than for Spanish women. When *machos ibéricos* [Iberian macho men] chased Black women, it usually served as a metaphor that suggested Spanish men's spectacular virility could help the nation re-establish its lost geopolitical supremacy.[13] By contrast, as in colonial Guinea, the cinematic pairing of Black men and white women was often construed as rape.[14] In some cases, however, it figured as a union between a highly caricatured Black man and a morally compromised Spanish woman, such as a prostitute or a single mother—a formula that echoes the dialogue of María's neighbors.[15] Given the omnipresence of these media images, which circulated through dozens of films and reached millions of viewers in cinemas during late Francoism and the Transition, it is unsurprising that assumptions about Black men's hypersexuality and white women's fragile purity surface in various comments made in the narratives of *Las que se atrevieron*. These include not only the dialogue between María's neighbors, but also several other allusions to white women's vulnerability to Black men's cannibalism (62), promiscuity (114), or oversized genitalia (130). In these instances, a prosthetic memory of colonialism emerges from Spanish and global media's circulation of racial and gendered paranoias between colony and metropole. In peninsular Spain, prohibitions on interracial sex, especially between Black men and white women, were imagined as necessary to protect the nation's precarious whiteness during *desarrollismo*, given that a small but visible postcolonial diaspora punctured the regime's rhetoric of national "whitening" and presaged the nation's impending transformation into a multiethnic society.

Yet, importantly, *Las que se atrevieron* contains at least one allusion to mass media's influence that illustrates the ability of media not only to proliferate colonial anxieties and taboos about Black men's hypersexuality or hypermasculinity but also to revise or complicate such stereotypes. While María's neighbors view her relationship with Javier in a manner that reflects hegemonic tropes of Spanish popular cinema, María herself looks at Javier through a different cinematic lens—namely, that of Hollywood in the Civil Rights era. She explains that when she first laid eyes on Javier in 1968, she was struck by the thought that he was "a carbon copy of Sidney Poitier, the actor of *Guess Who's Coming to Dinner,* that movie about a white American woman who introduces her Black fiancé to her parents in an era in which relations between both races were unthinkable" (112).[16] By referencing this 1967 Hollywood film, María reveals that her first sighting of her husband was tinged with a lens of unreality, as though he had stepped out of a screen from a foreign film, and was filtered through the idealized aura of Poitier's performance as an urbane, refined, upper-class Black character. This allusion obviously draws on Poitier's avant-garde star persona, as he broke new ground in the Hollywood of his day by becoming a top box-office attraction as an African American lead actor. It also alludes to the status of *Guess Who's Coming to Dinner* as one of the best-remembered Civil Rights-era films to question deeply embedded taboos surrounding interracial relationships.

At the same time, even though María's perception of Javier as a "carbon copy of Sidney Poitier" (112) departs from dominant media stereotypes, it is also marked by a certain ambivalence in which the threatening, frightening, or destabilizing elements of Black masculinity are simultaneously underscored and disguised. For even though Poitier's films were groundbreaking in their portrayal of race relations, they also, as Charles Gentry has argued, transmitted a sanitized, contained image of Black masculinity that could "[appease] white desires and [displace] white alarm" by neutralizing Black men's presumed hypersexuality (2). Specifically, Gentry writes, Poitier's roles often "compromised his virility and masked his sex appeal" in order to make him more appealing to white audiences (189). This pattern is evident in *Guess Who's Coming to Dinner*, a film that juxtaposes Poitier's restrained, deferential demeanor with the coarse, abrasive, and often recalcitrant behavior of the film's other, less privileged Black characters.[17] As Andrea Levine has argued, the contrast between Poitier and other Black characters in *Guess Who's Coming to Dinner* suggests that the film is haunted by a "racial unconscious" that emphasizes "the danger of an undisciplined black masculinity" lurking behind the veil of Poitier's gentility (374). In this way, the comparison of Javier to Sidney Poitier bears a certain resemblance to Neus' view of her husband as a "chocolate man": in both cases, these white Spanish women initially view their future Black partners as titillating yet harmless, exotic yet safe, but still tethered to a larger, globally circulated "racial unconscious" that continued to objectify and vilify most Black men while construing some as exceptional, tame, or even appetizing.

Taken together, these various examples of mass media's influence on shaping ordinary Spaniards' perceptions of Blackness in Spain during the 1960s and 1970s expose the entrenched association of Black masculinity with foreignness and hypersexuality and of white womanhood with vulnerability to aggression, contamination and moral decline. Given the limited presence of Black people in Spain at the time, most white Spaniards likely absorbed their views about Black Africans from the media, which disseminated colonial anxieties about racial and gender purity to a metropolis where little real information about colonialism was available. Although the reference to Sidney Poitier is a notable outlier in this media universe, even this actor's star image exuded a palpable deference to the fears and desires of white audiences, and thus conveyed a certain ambivalence in which hegemonic stereotypes and assumptions about Black masculinity were outwardly challenged yet subtly reinforced. By highlighting how colonial racial anxieties traveled between colony and metropole, especially through mass media, Mbomío Rubio's text demonstrates how prosthetic memories of Black men as threats to the purity of white women and the larger Spanish nation supplanted the Franco regime's deliberate erasure of a more authentic colonial memory. This prosthetic memory was interwoven or knotted with Francoism's narrative of an upwardly mobile, "whiter" Spain that was shedding the "blackness" of the Black Legend and ascending into a fully European identity.

Crucially, however, *Las que se atrevieron* accomplishes more than *only* calling attention to the relationships between Francoist rhetoric, colonial ideologies, mass media discourses, and the proliferation of racial and gendered anxieties about conserving whiteness. For, as the text demonstrates, Spain's prosthetic colonial memories went beyond forming a destructive alliance between colonists and those who had never set foot in Africa but still stood to benefit from being recognized as white. Indeed, such memories also lead to the formation of politically constructive transracial and cross-gender alliances. Tellingly, the primary catalyst of these alliances is not the interracial relationships themselves, which, like all romantic relationships, are not guaranteed a happy ending but instead are marred by misfortunes like infidelity, illness, and unemployment. For instance, of the book's six relationship narratives, three culminate in separation or divorce despite having lasted for decades, and two end in the unexpected, premature death of the husband. Rather than romantic love, the main engine of transformation and alliance in this text is motherhood, since all six narratives pay ample attention to the relationships between white mothers and their biracial children. In particular, these narratives spotlight the ways in which mother/child relationships can forge visceral feelings of empathy and solidarity between white women and the larger Afro-Spanish community. Hence, *Las que se atrevieron* proposes the interracial mother/child bond as one way in which knotted memories can produce "new imaginations of relation across difference" (Rothberg 11).

One of the most interesting ways in which *Las que se atrevieron* transforms social apprehensions about the erosion of whiteness into a source of solidarity is by reframing anxieties about what happens to a white woman's womb when she has conceived Black children. These anxieties surface in Chapter 5, which narrates the relationship of Kika and José, and Chapter 6, which relates the story of María and Javier. Although María, as we recall, is physically beaten by her brother because of her relationship, her father's words may have been just as devastating as any physical blow. As news of her relationship spreads through Oviedo, her father tells her, "You're crazy! If you're not worried about yourself, think of your children, who will come out Black! Plus, Jesús the doctor told me that even if you marry a white man later, and have children with him, they'll still be born Black, because that can't be erased" (113).[18]

As his strident reaction suggests, María's father isn't only concerned that María's children will be Black; rather, he fears that their Blackness will somehow stain their mother's womb, which will continue to produce only Black children even if she ends up later in a relationship with someone who isn't Black. His logic mirrors an argument that Brigitte Fielder introduced in *Relative Races: Genealogies of Racial Kinship*. In this book, which focuses on the context of the nineteenth-century United States, Fielder argues that racial transference occurred not only vertically—that is, from parent to child—but also in "backward" and "horizontal" directions, such as from children to parents and between biologically unrelated persons (location 218). A compelling example of what she calls the "non-heteronormative trajectories of racial reproduction" concerns nineteenth-century American performances of Shakespeare's tragedy *Othello* (location 579). In many performances, Desdemona, the white female lead, would routinely end up smeared in black make-up from the actor who played Othello, who was usually a white man in blackface (location 708). This smearing of Blackness metaphorically epitomized the ways in which "white womanhood could be undone or resignified by intimate or sexual relations with Black men [and] how her race could be inherited through kinship with her husband or children" (location 719).

Despite the cultural and temporal distance between late Francoist Spain and the United States in the nineteenth century, María's father's fear that a Black child would transmit its Blackness not only to its mother but also to its as-of-yet unconceived half-siblings mirrors Fielder's argument about backwards and horizontal racial transfer. Yet, at the same time, the non-heteropatriarchal direction of racial transference also signals the potential of motherhood to engender powerful transracial bonds. This fact is especially evident in Chapter 5, which recounts the story of Kika and José as narrated by Kika's sister, who secretly delivers letters between the two while Kika is confined to home by her family. Although Kika and José's relationship outlasts that attempt to intercept it, José dies unexpectedly while Kika is six months pregnant with their only child, Laura. José's death is a shock to the whole family and creates a sense of loss that permanently marks Kika's life. Yet, as her sister notes, the passage of time does not erase Kika's feeling of connection to Equatorial Guinea. Her sister writes, "All in all, our relationship, and I say ours, with Guinea never disappeared. Laura was Guinea, she had it in her DNA, and I would say that Kika, having carried her in her womb for nine months, did too" (109).[19]

By suggesting that Kika, a white Spanish woman, bears the mark of Equatorial Guinea in her DNA because she conceived a child with a Guinean man, her sister shares an assumption with María's father seen in Chapter 6: namely, the idea that a white woman's body can be permanently marked or stained from having carried an interracial child. Yet, unlike María's father, who marshals the trope of the stained uterus to portray his daughter's relationship as a threat to the purity of whiteness, Kika's sister uses it to explain her sister's ongoing feelings of affinity with and belonging to the Guinean community. Even when Kika's sister narrates the story 42 years after José's death, Kika "still listens to music from Guinea, eats chicken with peanut sauce and still maintains friendships from that era … she feels Guinean, she is a white Guinean who has never been to Guinea, but who knows it as well as anyone" (109).[20] Although the description of Kika as a "white Guinean who has never been to Guinea" may come across as overly romantic and perhaps even as a colonizing gesture in its own right, it is helpful to remember that Kika's feeling of belonging to Guinean culture was born of the experience of having stood up to her family's racism, having unexpectedly lost a husband she loved, and having raised her interracial daughter as a single mother in 1970s Spain. These circumstances can help us understand her attachment to Guinean culture as a consequence of her need to seek feelings of shelter and comfort in the Guinean diaspora in a society like Spain of the 1970s, where a single-parent, interracial family would have been doubly marginalized. Kika's attachment to Guinea is also remarkable because it proliferates to other white Spaniards, including her sister, who not only passed letters between Kika and José as lovers, but was also the only member of Kika's family to attend their wedding (95–96). For instance, when Kika's sister states that, "Our relationship, *and I say ours*, with Guinea never disappeared," she calls attention to the idea that she, like her sister, has come to see the Guinean diaspora as a kind of family (109; my emphasis). In this way, Kika's womb is construed not only as a site of biological reproduction but also as the birthplace of an interracial kinship that extends beyond the nuclear family.

The capacity of the interracial mother/child bond to expand and develop into a broader solidarity becomes even more apparent at several other moments in the text. One such instance occurs at the beginning of Chapter 2, which tells the story of Paloma and her husband, Cecilio. As she begins her first-person narrative, Paloma, a middle-aged white woman with three interracial children, meditates on the experience of reading a newspaper article about the death of Ndombele Augustos Domingos, a Black Angolan teenager who became a victim of racial violence in Alcorcón in 2002. She writes:

> "So this is Ndombele?" I thought when I saw his pictures in the newspaper. Unlike the idea my brain had concocted, Ndombele was not a man-child. He was just a child: still underdeveloped, short, with

infantile features and a slight physique... He hadn't even turned twenty when a nightclub bouncer killed him in the Urtinsa zone of Alcorcón. He stabbed him and left his mother and father, Angolans from Fuenlabrada, without a son.

Until that moment, even though it had been impossible to steer clear of the news, I had tried to avoid it. Whenever anyone brought it up, I changed the subject, or I simply left. But then I saw the picture and it affected me just the way I knew it would. Inevitably, the image reminded me of [my son] José Antonio. I didn't want to be a Spanish mother from Leganés without a son, but I also couldn't stop him, a sixteen-year-old, from going out just like the others did. (31–32)[21]

In this excerpt, Paloma recounts a moment in which she had no choice but to recognize the disturbing yet moving resemblance between her own Black teenage son, José Antonio, and a Black youth who had been murdered due to racial hatred. She is surprised, she writes, by how youthful Ndombele's features are, noting that she expected him to appear more grown-up. Instead, when she looks at his photograph, she sees neither a hypermasculine figure nor any of the eroticized tropes common in film or advertising. Instead, triggered by his childlike appearance, she sees her own son, José Antonio, and grapples with the unavoidable fact that he is just as vulnerable to racist violence as Ndombele was.

Paloma's partial recognition of her own son in the face of Ndombele is significant because it engenders another layer of kinship, namely, Paloma's deep feeling of connection to Ndombele's parents. Despite the fact that they are Angolan and completely unknown to her, a striking parallelism marks the structure of the sentences in which she describes them and those in which she describes herself. When she refers to Ndombele's parents, she writes that the boy's killer "left his father and mother, Angolans from Fuenlabrada, without a son" (30). Referring to herself, she writes, "I didn't want to be a Spanish mother, from Leganés, without a son" (31). The near-exact grammatical mirroring of these two sentences calls attention to Paloma's recognition of herself in Ndombele's parents, with whom she shares the experience of being a parent to Black children in a Madrid suburb, Leganés, that neighbors theirs, Fuenlabrada. In this way, Paloma's bodily connection to her son leads her not only to see him in Ndombele but also to recognize herself in his parents despite never having met them, seen their faces, or heard their names. Her ability to feel a shared intimacy, closeness, and grief with absolute strangers accentuates the expansive quality of the mother/child interracial bond, which can generate empathy and solidarity across profoundly different embodied experiences of racial, national, and gendered identities.

Paloma's vicarious yet visceral experience of racism through her children stands out in the following excerpt, which describes what it feels like to be a white mother witnessing one's Black children suffer experiences of racism:

> We white mothers suffer racism almost as if it were in our own flesh, since those who suffer it are flesh of our flesh and blood of our blood. And I say almost, because we miss many things. We live in a state of semi-unconsciousness for being color-blind, because we only see beauty where others see difference and we feel love where others feel fear and … because if we walk down the street alone, no one whispers, nor are we stared at, nor do we elicit the same reaction as our offspring. I will never be able to put myself in my children's shoes, as much as I wish I could suffer in their place, I will never share their experiences. (49)[22]

Through this reflection, Paloma ruminates on the challenges and contradictions of bearing witness to racism, which she feels acutely "almost" as if it affected her own body, but which she nonetheless realizes she can never experience directly. Although, on one hand, Paloma's comments reiterate the idea that an interracial mother/child bond can create a bodily connection that transcends racial and national differences; at the same time, she recognizes the limits of her own empathy, given that she can never experience the same degree of social rejection and ostracism in her own skin as her children do. Yet even despite the limitations of empathy, Paloma's ability to "almost" feel her children's experiences as if they were her own signals a powerful destabilization of national and racial boundaries, such as the deeply engrained assumption that Blackness was or is foreign to Spanish national identity. Instead, she conveys the capacity of the interracial mother/child bond to invite a radical revision of the racial assumptions that have traditionally subtended Spanish national identity.

María, the protagonist of Chapter 6, also underscores the transformative potential of interracial motherhood. "Having Black children has made me change; my behavior is no longer the same," she writes (119).[23] Like Paloma, María, too, is deeply affected by bearing witness to her children's experience of racism. She recounts an incident in which her son Javi and his white friends were all arrested and jailed for participating in an antiracist demonstration that devolved into clashes with far-right sympathizers. The march was held to commemorate the 1992 murder of Dominican immigrant Lucrecia Pérez, an event that is widely recognized as Spain's first racial hate crime and a moment that "marked a before and after in terms of awareness of racism in Spain" (Repinecz, "Unearthing Spanish Racism" 176). María was particularly perturbed by the fact that her son was held in jail longer than any of his white friends and was only released after his father cajoled the police into freeing him. This incident, which poetically highlights how memories of past racial violence remain knotted with persistent racial inequities in the present, leads María to conclude, "As the white woman that I am, as a Spaniard, as a citizen who enjoys her rights and fulfills her obligations, I must recognize that Spain is a racist country, and it hurts to admit it because one doesn't like to say bad things about one's country" (119–20).[24]

Importantly, however, María's transformed outlook does not simply make her more protective of her children. On the contrary, it causes her to express outrage at racist acts and statements, including those aimed at total strangers, whether they occur at work, at home, or in public. Her searing anger toward racism becomes such an integral part of her that "Everyone tells [her she is] bad natured" (130).[25] She notes, for example, that when her second husband, a white man, reported to the police that his phone had been stolen by a Black man—a detail which María knew to be false—she responded in the following manner: "I grabbed my suitcase and left," thus ending their marriage (129).[26] She also recalls several other incidents that sparked her ire, including one at work when someone made a racist remark about Black men's genitalia and another in which she "began shouting like a lunatic" when she saw railway staff berate Black passengers who did not have tickets (130).[27] As with Paloma, these incidents demonstrate that María's role as a mother of Black children creates a deep, antiracist solidarity that expands beyond the biological connection into the realm of the broader community. In María's case, this solidarity is unusually potent because her empathy with strangers can entail a repudiation of traditional forms of kinship, which is suggested by her decision to end a marriage over racism. In this way, what others perceive as her "bad nature" is really a refusal to accept the status quo of white privilege and white racism in a society where both "saturate the subsoil" (Stoler 5). Instead, she reveals a deeply rooted commitment to channeling her rage into protest and resistance against racism whenever possible.

In sum, by underscoring the knotted relationship of Francoist national narratives and unsettled colonial memories, *Las que se atrevieron* accentuates not only the ways in which ideologies of racial and gendered segregation traveled between colony and metropole but also the way in which such ideologies are destabilized and refashioned by the generative potentiality of the interracial mother/child bond. On one hand, the text is replete with evidence that suggests that Spaniards of the late Franco era absorbed a wealth of domestic and global media that taught them to imagine themselves as the beneficiaries of colonial whiteness even as colonialism itself was on its deathbed. Yet, on the other hand, mediatized colonial discourses about Blackness could not impede the formation of powerful transracial and cross-gender alliances, especially those that emerged from the bond between white mothers and their Black children. Although the six stories contained in this text do not represent all experiences of motherhood, they nonetheless call attention to the ways in which individual bonds between a particular group of mothers and children created connections of kinship, solidarity, and empathy across chasms of diverse racialized and gendered embodied experiences. In this way, despite its myriad narratives of discrimination, suffering, and loss, *Las que se atrevieron* is a profoundly hopeful text, as it invites readers to meditate not only on the ways in which Spain's national identity has long been entangled with racism and misogyny but also on how memories of racism and misogyny are themselves interwoven with new opportunities for transformation.

Notes

1 All translations are mine unless otherwise noted.
2 Studies that examine Spain from a critical race studies framework have often tended to focus on what we might term the "era of immigration," which is usually framed as beginning in the 1980s or 1990s and continuing into the twenty-first century. Works that reflect this tendency include monograph studies published by Isolina Ballesteros, Silvia Bermúdez, Jeffrey K. Coleman, Daniela Flesler, N. Michelle Murray, Isabel Santaolalla, and Raquel Vega-Durán, as well as books-in-progress by Mary Kate Donovan and Catalina Iannone, among others. Critical race studies that focus on pre-immigration periods in Spain include monographs by Joshua Goode, Susan Martin-Márquez, Lisa Surwillo, and Eva Woods-Peiró, but these have paid scant attention to the 1960s and 1970s. Attention to race in that period has so far been limited to a handful of articles, including those by Rosalía Cornejo-Parriego and Martin Repinecz.
3 The term *desarrollismo* refers to the late Franco regime's widely used rhetoric of economic development and prosperity during the 1960s and 1970s, a period in which Spain's economy experienced rapid growth. The *desarrollismo* era marked a notable contrast with the regime's more overtly religious and imperialist rhetoric of the 1940s and early 1950s.
4 "un buen día, decidieron plantarle cara a su tiempo y a su entorno por amor."
5 "Hablaron en primera persona del plural cuando hacían referencia a los guineanos… y ya fueran separadas, viudas o solteras, transmitieron a sus hijos su dimensión identitaria negra o/ya africana."
6 "cambié sus nombres, alteré bastantes aspectos de su narración para que nadie sepa de quién hablo, incorporé anécdotas reales, de ellas y de otras y creé personajes basándome en las descripciones que me dieron en sus relatos."
7 All matters related to Equatorial Guinea and the Western Sahara were banned from Spanish media during the years 1971–1976 and 1972–1974, respectively. These laws were meant to hide aspects of each country's postcolonial aftermath that the Franco regime found embarrassing, such as Equatorial Guinea's descent into a bloody dictatorship led by Francisco Macías Nguema following independence in 1968. Similarly, foreign media such as cinema was also blocked or heavily censored in Spain if it portrayed anticolonial movements empathetically; such films were generally not available to be viewed in Spain until after the arrival of democracy. The effects of these strategies of repression

are still palpable today, as cultural memory of Spain's imperial endeavors in Africa remains very limited (Pardo Sanz 182; Muñoz Martínez 130).

8   Mass immigration to Spain accelerated dramatically in the late 1980s and throughout the 1990s. In earlier decades, immigration to Spain was vastly outpaced by emigration from Spain to Northern European countries. Immigration to Spain during the 1960s and 1970s was characterized by small waves of students and political refugees from countries such as Cuba, Argentina, and Equatorial Guinea, as well as well-to-do European retirees who were attracted to Spain's sunny climate and beaches (López de Lera 231–34).

9   Although a precise estimate of Spain's Black population during this period is not available, it is widely accepted that it remained extremely limited until the 1990s. Donato Ndongo Bidyogo describes Spain's Black community during the 1960s as consisting of geographically scattered, numerically small groups of Equatorial Guinean students, Cuban refugees, and African American soldiers stationed at American military bases. In 1978, Spain's Equatorial Guinean community was estimated to be about 6,000 (Fraguas).

10 "Yo la mato."

11 "un hombre de chocolate"

12 "'Dicen que hay una chica del hospital que sale con un negro. ¿Qué pensará su familia de ella?'
'¿Qué vergüenza! ¿Y quién será?'
'Ja, ja, ja… una a la que no quiera ninguno normal, vamos, ningún blanco. Eso está claro. O eso, o es una facilona.'"

13 Films that follow this tendency include *El alma se serena* (Dir. José Luis Saenz de Heredia, 1970), *Ligue Story* (Dir. Alfonso Paso, 1972), *Los bingueros* (Dir. Mariano Ozores, 1979), and *Los energéticos* (Dir. Mariano Ozores, 1979).

14 Films that portray Black men as raping or attempting to rape white women include *Cristo negro* (Dir. Ramón Torrado, 1963), *Encrucijada para una monja* (Dir. Julio Buchs, 1967), *Esa mujer* (Dir. Mario Camus, 1969), and *La noche de los brujos* (Dir. Armando de Ossorio, 1974).

15 Films that reflect this pattern include *Las que tienen que servir* (Dir. José María Forqué, 1967), *Cómo está el servicio* (Dir. Mariano Ozores, 1968), and *La Lola nos lleva al huerto* (Dir. Mariano Ozores, 1984).

16 "un calco de Sidney Poitier, el actor de *Adivina quién viene esta noche*, esa película de una mujer blanca estadounidense que va a presentar a su prometido negro a sus padres en una época en la que las relaciones entre ambas razas eran impensables."

17 The film's other Black characters include Tillie, the upper-class white family's socially conservative African American housekeeper, who repeatedly expresses outrage at the idea of interracial romantic relationships, as well as a young, working-class African American man who loses his temper when the white patriarch backs into his car.

18 "¡Tú estás loca! Si ya no es por ti, es por tus hijos, ¡que te van a salir negros! Además, Jesús el médico me ha dicho que aunque luego te cases con un blanco, y tengas hijos con él, van a seguir naciendo negros, porque eso no se quita."

19 "Con todo, nuestra relación, y digo nuestra, con Guinea nunca desapareció. Laura era Guinea, lo llevaba en su ADN y yo diría que Kika, después de nueve meses con ella en su interior, también."

20 "sigue oyendo música de Guinea, comiendo gallina con salsa de cacahuete y todavía mantiene amistades de esa época… ella se siente guineana, es una guineana blanca que nunca ha ido a Guinea, pero que la conoce como nadie."

21 "'¿Así que este es Ndombele?' pensé al ver sus fotos en el periódico. A diferencia de la idea que mi cerebro había urdido, Ndombele no era un niño hombre. Era un niño a secas: aún por hacer, bajito, con rasgos pueriles y complexión menuda… No había llegado a los veinte años cuando un portero de discoteca le asesinó en el polígono Urtinsa de Alcorcón. Le clavó un cuchillo y dejó a su madre y a su padre, angoleños de Fuenlabrada, sin hijo.

 Hasta ese momento, pese a que me había resultado imposible mantenerme ajena a la noticia, había intentado evitarla. Cuando alguien trataba el tema, cambiaba de asunto, o directamente, me iba. Pero entonces vi la foto y pasó lo que sabía que sucedería. Inevitablemente, la imagen me remitió a [mi hijo] José Antonio. Yo no quería ser una madre española, de Leganés, sin hijo, pero tampoco podía impedir que, a sus dieciséis años, saliera de igual modo que lo hacía el resto."
22 "Las madres blancas sufrimos el racismo casi como si fuera en nuestras carnes, ya que son carne de nuestra carne y sangre de nuestra sangre los que lo padecen. Y digo casi, puesto que nos perdemos muchas cosas. Vivimos en un estado de semi inconsciencia por ser ciegas a los colores, porque solo vemos belleza donde otros ven diferencia y sentimos amor done otros sienten miedo y … porque si vamos por la calle solas nadie murmura, ni nos miran, ni provocamos lo mismo que nuestros vástagos. Nunca podré ponerme en la piel de mis hijos, por más que quisiera padecer en su lugar, jamás tendré sus vivencias."
23 "Tener hijos negros me ha hecho cambiar. Mi forma de ser no es la misma."
24 "Como blanca que soy, como española, como ciudadana que disfruta de sus derechos y cumple con sus obligaciones, he de reconocer que España es un país racista, y me duele reconocerlo porque a una no le gusta decir nada malo de su tierra."
25 "Todo el mundo me dice que tengo mal carácter."
26 "Cogí la maleta y me fui."
27 "Me puse a gritarles como una energúmena."

Works Cited

Ballesteros, Isolina. *Immigration Cinema in the New Europe*. Intellect, 2015.
Bermúdez, Silvia. *Rocking the Boat: Migration and Race in Contemporary Spanish Music*. U of Toronto P, 2018.
Bhabha, Homi K. *The Location of Culture*. Routledge, 1994.
Coleman, Jeffrey K. *The Necropolitical Theater: Race and Immigration in the Contemporary Spanish Stage*. Northwestern UP, 2020.
Cómo está el servicio. Directed by Mariano Ozores. Filmayer, 1968.
Cornejo-Parriego, Rosalía. "*Black Is Beautiful*: Cuerpos negros en *Triunfo*." *Journal of Iberian and Latin American Studies*, vol. 3, no. 2, 2017, pp. 157–73.
Cristo negro. Directed by Ramón Torrado. Copercines, 1963.
El alma se serena. Directed by José Luis Saenz de Heredia. Chapalo Films, S.A., 1970.
Elena, Alberto. *La llamada de África: Estudios sobre el cine colonial español*. Edicions Bellaterra, 2010.
Encrucijada para una monja. Directed by Julio Buchs. Ízaro Films, 1967.
Esa mujer. Directed by Mario Camus. Proesa, 1969.

Fielder, Brigitte. *Relative Races: Genealogies of Interracial Kinship in Nineteenth-Century America*. eBook, Duke UP, 2020. Kindle.
Flesler, Daniela. *The Return of the Moor: Spanish Responses to Contemporary Moroccan Immigration*. Purdue UP, 2008.
Fraguas, Rafael. "Seis mil guineanos viven marginados en España." *El País*, 28 July 1978, https://elpais.com/diario/1978/07/29/ultima/270511201_850215.html.
Gentry, Charles. *The Othello Effect: The Performance of Black Masculinity in Mid-Century Cinema*. 2011. University of Michigan, PhD dissertation.
Goode, Joshua. *Impurity of Blood. Defining Race in Spain, 1870–1930*. Louisiana State UP, 2009.
Guess Who's Coming to Dinner. Directed by Stanley Kramer. Columbia Pictures, 1967.
Hackenesch, Silke. *Chocolate and Blackness: A Cultural History*. Campus Verlag, 2017.
Iannone, Catalina. *Contested Cities: Race, Culture and Urban Development in Madrid and Lisbon*. Vanderbilt UP, forthcoming.
La Lola nos lleva al huerto. Directed by Mariano Ozores. Ízaro Films, 1984.
La noche de los brujos. Directed by Armando de Ossorio. Hesperia Films, S.A., 1974.
Landsberg, Alison. *Prosthetic Memory: The Transformation of American Remembrance in the Age of Mass Culture*. Columbia UP, 2006.
Las que tienen que servir. Directed by José María Forqué. Ágata Films, 1967.
Levine, Andrea. "Sidney Poitier's Civil Rights: Rewriting the Mystique of White Womanhood in *Guess Who's Coming to Dinner* and *In the Heat of the Night*." *American Literature*, vol. 73, no. 2, 2001, pp. 365–86.
Ligue Story. Directed by Alfonso Paso. Arturo González Producciones Cinematográficas, 1972.
López de Lera, Diego. "La inmigración a España a fines del siglo XX: Los que vienen a trabajar y los que vienen a descansar." *REIS: Revista Española de Investigaciones Sociológicas*, no. 71, 1995, pp. 225–48.
Los bingueros. Directed by Mariano Ozores. Ízaro Films, 1979.
Los energéticos. Directed by Mariano Ozores. Bermúdez de Castro, 1979.
Martin-Márquez, Susan. *Disorientations: Spanish Colonialism in Africa and the Performance of Identity*. Yale UP, 2008.
Mbomío Rubio, Lucía Asué. *Hija del camino*. Grijalbo, 2020.
———. *Las que se atrevieron*. Sial, 2017.
Muñoz Martínez, Celeste. "África en nuestros archivos: La historia que aún no puede ser contada." *La necesidad de conocer África*, edited by José Luis Rodríguez Jiménez and María F. Sánchez Hernández. Dykinson, 2017, pp. 129–40.
Murray, N. Michelle. *Home Away from Home: Immigrant Narratives, Domesticity, and Coloniality in Contemporary Spanish Culture*. U of North Carolina P, 2018.
Ndongo Bidyogo, Donato. "Una nueva realidad: Los afro-españoles." *Asociación Gerard*, 11 Jan. 2011, http://gerardenlablog.blogspot.com/2011/11/una-nueva-realidad-los-afro-espanoles-i.html.
Nerín, Gustau. *Guinea Ecuatorial, historia en blanco y negro: Hombres blancos y mujeres negras en Guinea Ecuatorial (1843–1968)*. Ediciones Península, 1998.
Nora, Pierre. *Realms of Memory*, edited by Lawrence D. Kritzman. Columbia UP, 1996.

Pardo Sanz, Rosa. "La décolonisation de l'Afrique espagnole: Maroc, Sahara occidental et Guinée Équatoriale." *L'Europe face à son passé colonial*, edited by Olivier Dard and Daniel Lefeuvre. Riveneuve éditions, 2008, pp. 169–96.

Repinecz, Martin. "Spain Is (Not So) Different: Whitening Spain Through Late Francoist Comedy." *Transmodernity*, vol. 8, no. 2, 2018, pp. 91–109.

———. "Unearthing Spanish Racism, Then and Now: A Conversation with Tomás Calvo Buezas." *International Journal of Iberian Studies*, vol. 34, no. 2, 2021, pp. 171–77.

———. *Volatile Whiteness. Race, Cinema and Europeanization in Spain*. U of Toronto P, forthcoming.

Rothberg, Michael. "Introduction: Between Memory and Memory: From *Lieux de mémoire* to *Noeuds de mémoire*." *Yale French Studies*, no. 118–19, 2010, pp. 3–12.

Santaolalla, Isabel. *Los otros: Etnicidad y raza en el cine español contemporáneo*. Prensas Universitarias de Zaragoza, 2005.

Stoler, Ann Laura. *Imperial Debris: On Ruins and Ruination*. Duke UP, 2013.

Stucki, Andreas. *Violence and Gender in Africa's Iberian Colonies: Feminizing the Portuguese and Spanish Empire, 1950s–1970s*. Palgrave Macmillan, 2019.

Surwillo, Lisa. *Monsters by Trade: Slave Traffickers in Modern Spanish Literature and Culture*. Stanford UP, 2020.

Vega-Durán, Raquel. *Emigrant Dreams, Immigrant Borders: Migrants, Transnational Encounters, and Identity in Spain*. Bucknell UP, 2016.

Woods Peiró, Eva. *White Gypsies. Race and Stardom in Spanish Musicals*. U of Minnesota P, 2012.

7 Decolonizing the History of Afro-Spaniards
Afrofeminismo. 50 años de lucha y activismo de mujeres negras en España (1968–2018) by Abuy Nfubea

Dosinda García-Alvite

When examining the critical corpus analyzing the literary and artistic creations of Afro-Spaniards, it can be readily noted that the theoretical references used are generally Eurocentric. This is partly due to the hegemonic understanding that Afro-Hispanism has had only a recent and brief trajectory in Spain. In dialogue with and responding to this inaccurate perception, community organizer and cultural critic, Abuy Nfubea (Barcelona, 1953), has undertaken a historical review of less commonly recognized ways of being *Afro-español*. In *Afrofeminismo: 50 años de lucha y activismo de mujeres negras en España (1968–2018)* [Afrofeminism: 50 Years of Struggle and Activism by Black Women in Spain] (2021), he traces a genealogy of African women who have fought in Spain for the survival of their communities, mainly in the metropolitan areas of Madrid and Barcelona, through grassroots activism and continuous political involvement. His intent is evident in all elements of the book: from the opening dedication, in which he names the women who have had a direct influence on him, especially his mother, Dr. Basilisa Mangue, and her aunt, Doña Vicenta Avoro, to the prologue written by Cristina Fallarás, a noted Spanish feminist, through the epilogue penned by María Teresa Fernández de la Vega, the former vice-president in José Luis Rodriguez Zapatero's Socialist government in Spain (2004–2010) and current president of Fundación Mujeres de África. The format, with a cover that recalls the images of female Black Panthers like Angela Davis, who has visited Spain several times and met with Nfubea on several occasions, and more specifically, the dedication to "All of those women who seek points of reference on YouTube, even though they have them at home," unequivocally indicate his purpose of making visible the agency of Afro-Spanish women whose everyday engagement is confined to obscurity in public culture.[1] In response to the blatant lack of social value afforded to them, Nfubea argues that the women he honors are the invisible and unrecognized leaders of current *Afro-españoles*, which makes them noteworthy representatives of Womanist ideals.

DOI: 10.4324/9781003435051-8

Over the past twenty years, Spain has made some progress towards acknowledging the presence of its Afro-diasporic subjects. In popular culture, mainly through the influence of European and U.S. media, there is increasing familiarity with well-known Black artists, performers, athletes, and politicians, a recognition that feeds the slow process of being aware of home-grown Black figures. When asked about the Afro-Spanish community, many Spaniards can recall the names of athletes such as Ana Peleteiro and Serge Ibaka, politician Rita Bosaho, writers Donato Ndongo, Justo Bolekia, and Lucía Mbomío, performers Concha Buika, El Chojín, Frank T., Emilio Buale, and Goya prize-winning film director Santiago Zannou. Yet, this awareness is superficial and heavily influenced by Anglophone and Francophone references. For example, when discussing issues of race, most comments focus on injustices in the U.S., while in the case of Black literature, this recognition is tied primarily to translations from French- and English-speaking nations. Conversely, Nfubea's work undertakes a complete upending of the map of Black identities that dominate the Spanish imaginary. While the book title highlights its focus on women, the author introduces a philosophical background that combines Afro-centric, Pan-Africanist, and Maroonist credos rarely referenced elsewhere, whether in popular culture or academic criticism discussing Afro-Spanish identities. In dialogue with his analysis, this essay argues that, when confronted with the epistemic violence that erases the contributions of Afro-diasporic subjects to Spanish culture, Nfubea delineates a cartography of critical perspectives that help facilitate the mental and spiritual decolonization of Afro-Spaniards by establishing a triangular paradigm that connects the experiences of Black subjects in Spain with those of Black people in Africa and the Americas. This study examines how Nfubea presents the central tenets of his cultural identity model: Womanism, Afro-centric Pan-Africanism, and Maroonism, to expand the geographical map of connections generally recognized in Iberia, and, most importantly, the theoretical and philosophical underpinnings that can help root the identity of an Afro-diasporic subject in Spain.

Afrofeminism is structured as a series of interviews and minibiographies of women of African origin who have become the leaders of a wide variety of community organizations in Spain over the past 50 years. While about half of the interviewees were born in Equatorial Guinea, citizens born in Senegal, Ghana, Nigeria, Sudan, South Africa, Colombia, Cuba, and the United States complete the picture. The author's exhaustive approach in recording their activities, diverse backgrounds, and their work's repercussions at the micro- and macro sociopolitical levels provides an encyclopedic archive of their engagement in Spanish society. The compilation of biographies of over a hundred women creates an intricate mosaic that questions official Spanish history. The headings of the 45 chapters that make up the book serve as good indicators of the cartography Nfubea traces from the ground up, from a street-level point of view. For example, the first chapter is dedicated to "Maroon tradition."[2] Then, starting with what this critic considers the author's book's most novel contribution to Afro-Spanish studies, Chapter 5 states that "[women] invented Pan-Africanism." The following pages in the book analyze other topics through this specific lens, covering very important subjects for Afro-Spaniards. For example, as shown through their titles, Chapter 15 discusses "Raids and Institutional Racism," Chapter 18 explains how "Black Women Take on the Media," Chapter 32 focuses on "Neoslavery or Domestic Work," and Chapter 45 brings the book to a positive close, stating that "The Revolution Is Female and Has Never Been Televised."[3] The depth and breadth of the topics, some of which are dealt with repeatedly and from different perspectives, illustrate how Nfubea weaves stories of self and community into the chapters, a style that contrasts with existing and non-existent official records while situating the narrating subject not only as a compiler of stories but also as an agent of change, speaking from within the community.

The locus of enunciation fits with the author's private and public persona as he defines himself: "A Field Nigger journalist, political analyst, writer, Pan-African hip-hop speaker" whose activism has led him to become editor of Uhuru Afrika TV and a professor at the online Malcolm Garvey University.[4] This self-portrait holds similarities with that of Michael Eric Dyson, the U.S. "Hip-Hop Public Intellectual," whose collection of essays *Reflecting Black* exemplifies a "black criticism" that pays special attention to popular works and celebrates the successes of Black culture while also recognizing its failings. Their location of speech is centered on the Black subject in action, striving to bring intellectual references to popular culture in order to encourage political action, thereby recording history from the ground up. Nfubea's expression of "Field Nigger" forcefully anchors his positionality in the construction of his identity by highlighting the dichotomy between the "house and the field nigger." Malcolm X, who dwelled on this dichotomy as a parable to explain how Black people responded to the political and economic system that oppressed them, also referred to the two kinds of slaves. The "House Negro" worked in the master's house, sometimes supporting the oppressor's interests against those of the Black majority bending to the status quo. The "field Negros" were the opposite, working in the fields side-by-side with others like them, withstanding the hardships they suffered together. Field workers maintained a deep commitment to their freedom and that of their communities. By identifying himself as a "Field Nigger," Nfubea clearly states his locus of enunciation as that of an activist, a social and political critic, whose actions are directed towards improving the condition of his contemporaries. His use of the deeply offensive slur captures his awareness of the unequal position he is forced into by society and how, by confronting it, he reappropriates the insult in order to resignify it with a tone of pride. Furthermore, when he reiterates Malcolm X's provocative taxonomy of a racialized Black consciousness, Nfubea presents an ideological frame with which to analyze Afro-Spanishness that has seldom been encountered in Spain until now.[5] He frequently invokes Malcolm X, a towering, inspirational leader for countless African Americans, and extending his model one step further, Nfubea applies the pejorative term "tío Tom" [Uncle Tom] to denounce individuals who conceal their African heritage, cultures, and practices in an effort to be accepted into mainstream society (*Afrofeminismo* 69; 81–83; 88).[6] He recycles the metaphors of "House Negro" or "Uncle Tom" as anchoring points to advocate for justice and dismantle the social and intellectual structures oppressing Afro-Spaniards. His perspective reflects a view from the bottom up, a viewpoint that emanates from the grassroots, acknowledging and honoring overlooked voices of wisdom.

Recording Silenced History and Black-Centeredness Through Pan-Africanism

The dialogue between Nbufea, the chronicler, and the women he interviews offers a stunning meditation on how power operates in the making and recording of history. The disparity between these women's voices and the prevailing portrayal in Spanish media of individuals of African descent as newcomers who arrived in recent waves of immigration demonstrates Spaniards' failure to acknowledge the rich contributions of Afro-Spanish women to Spanish culture spanning over five decades. This contrast compels the reader to ponder how history is produced and recorded, drawing upon Michel-Rolph Trouillot's analysis discussed in *Silencing the Past*. His groundbreaking study delves into the life and legacy of Toussaint Louverture, the prominent leader of the Haitian Revolution (1791–1804). Despite being often described as the largest and most successful slave rebellion in the Western Hemisphere, the revolution has been conspicuously omitted from the collective global consciousness. Trouillot explains that we participate in history both as actors and narrators. For him, history means both "what happened" and "what is said to have happened." The former suggests the sociohistorical process, while the latter speaks to our knowledge and understanding of that process. Trouillot stresses that history is produced beyond academic circles. Scholarly discourse and university presses are not the only sites of production of historical narrative. Other figures, such as religious leaders, politicians, journalists, and activists like Nfubea, also contribute to the narrative and, more importantly, to history itself through the production of specific accounts. The convergence of the processes and conditions underlying their production helps us uncover the unequal exertions of power that enable certain narratives to emerge while silencing others (Trouillot 25).

In *Afrofeminism*, Nfubea's stated purpose is to challenge what he perceives to be a popular discourse among contemporary Spanish Afro-feminist bloggers who insist they do not have referents, which in turn leads to, in his opinion:

> the negation or systematic lack of knowledge of historical black processes in Spain in conjunction with an explicit desire to identify themselves as the true origin. As Malcolm X would say, "I am the only Black in this place," these expressions generate ignorance, negationism, Afro-pessimism, apocalyptic speeches and catharsis (*Afrofeminismo* 25).[7]

Although Nfubea's statement may raise concerns as he seemingly radicalizes his position by distancing himself from young Afro-Spanish leaders, what I find appealing is his approach to record-keeping and producing an alternative history of the community that counters hegemonic approaches. Furthermore, he demonstrates that the erasure of Black history in Spain has had lasting and profound effects on the nation at large and most especially within the Afro-diasporic community, which, unaware of its past, claims a lack of referents.

Nfubea's descriptions of the events he witnessed and the people he met draw to the surface new sources of information that invite discussion and contrast with official archives. For example, unlike the traditional image of the obedient colonized population and lack of resistance in Equatorial Guinea (Spain's former colony in West Central Africa), he argues instead that:

> since the colonization period, black women protested and demanded their rights through song, dance, theatre, out in the fields, in the kitchens, they wrote, they took up arms, they organized and they complained about gender-based injustices. In Equatorial Guinea, for example, we had María Jesús Ayecaba, very involved in politics alongside Acacio Mañe or Enrique Nvó, the fathers of independence. (*Afrofeminismo* 58)[8]

The ideological move of official historians is similar to those of the Haitian revolution, when plantation owners could not fully deny resistance but reiterated reassuring platitudes to public authorities, consequently trivializing all its manifestations. As Trouillot argues, "[r]esistance did not exist as a global phenomenon. Rather, each case of unmistakable defiance, each possible instance of resistance, was treated separately and drained of its political content," a process that ended up producing a discourse that claimed the contentment of the colonized, since acknowledging resistance meant recognizing the humanity and intelligence of the colonized subject (83). In Spain, a history of acquiescence by some public figures in the Black community and of "tolerant multiculturalism" by state policies has for years overshadowed radical histories and marginalized figures, often Black women, who have the potential to inform contemporary race struggles. The history of rebellion has been steadily eclipsed by the political and cultural emphasis on African immigration and acculturation that has arisen over the past twenty years in light of the growing numbers of subjects from Africa.

Refusing to settle for this state of affairs, Nfubea claims he wants to highlight the role Black women play in social, cultural, and economic organizations in Spain because they have contributed significantly to the contemporary struggle against racism and have transformed and radicalized Black subjectivities in political terms: "They founded Pan-Africanism, today they participate in the struggle for migrant rights and their granddaughters identify with the Black Lives Matter [movement]" (*Afrofeminismo* 43).[9] In his recording of fifty years of women's activism, Nfubea also introduces theoretical references that have directly and indirectly inspired change. Frequent mentions of Womanism, Afro-centrism, and, in particular, Pan-Africanism demand that readers explore these philosophies and their goals if they are not familiar with them.

Because Spain became a space of encounter for African and Afro-diasporic women, in examining the fifty-year period covered in the book, it is possible to deduce that activism reached its height in the 1990s, when these women adopted a horizontal rather than a vertical approach to their activism, linking their actions across the Iberian Peninsula in a broad network that was ideologically supported by Pan-Africanist ideals. It is precisely in the 1990s that a set of complex factors created a backdrop that gave rise to an awareness of the need to unite and to fight for visibility. In conjunction with the growth in the number of African migrants coming from a range of different countries, already established families and friends of African origin also saw their numbers increase through the birth of their own children, a second generation of Afro-Spaniards.[10] It was during this period that Spain became a full-fledged member of the European Union, turning its face towards the North and its back to Africa while implementing harsh "security measures" against migrants from the south. Historian Antumi Toasijé explains the phenomenon this way:

> With the Europeanization process in Spain, the contribution of Africans, the fact of the Africanity of Spain, and the importance of Black communities and elements to Spanish history have been definitively wiped out from the official discourse. This meant that now, old and

recent generations had to face growing racism in Spanish society, discrimination in jobs and housing, rising Neo-Nazi attitudes, and the ill treatment of the Spanish police and administration.

("The Africanity" 350)

Consequently, Toasijé opines, a significant number of young Afro-Spaniards developed combative attitudes and began to organize and fight against racism through associations and Pan-African groups similar to those found in the United States, the Caribbean, and Africa. These groups coalesced first in the rap and reggae scene, especially in 1992 after the release of Spike Lee's film *Malcolm X*, and by attending concerts by rap groups such as *Public Enemy* when they toured in Spain. Noteworthy examples were the *Colors Brotherhood* and the *Black Panthers of Spain* (known as Frente Organizado de Juventud Africana [FOJA] today), two groups created in the 1990s and led by Nfubea with the purpose of educating Black youth and defending Black people against rising Neo-Nazi groups and the police. Guided by the motto of Burkina Faso's Pan-Africanist Thomas Shankara that "[f]reedom can only be won through struggle," Nfubea shares a decolonial mindset that requires an Afro-centric positioning in order not to be erased by the dominant society (*Afrofeminismo* 121).[11] He is inspired by Black leaders from the US, founding members of the Pan-Africanist movement, and the decolonial school of thought in Latin America. He and other Afro-centric Spaniards do not want to remain undecided; they are going to fight (*Afrofeminismo* 121). In his stance, he aligns with the specific models of Afro-centrism created by Malcolm X and Marcus Garvey, who redefined the space Africa occupied in Black Americans' imaginary in their search for dignity.

Malcolm X's thought became a frequent and popular reference for Black people in the world since he challenged dominant paradigms both within and outside the establishment. After working for over twelve years with the Nation of Islam, an all-Black Muslim group led by Elijah Muhammad, Malcolm X became disenchanted and was eventually expelled from the organization in 1964. As a result, he started on a new path, founding the *Organization of Afro-American Unity* with the express purpose of working towards freedom and liberation for Black people and other oppressed groups. To better understand the suffering of peoples of African origin, he traveled twice to Africa and

> gave a number of speeches in the United States sharing a philosophy based on the unity of black people, the political and economic control of black communities by black people, the organization of both a national and an international struggle of black and oppressed people, and human rights for all people. (Harper 389)

For Malcolm X, Black unity and togetherness implied Black power: economic and political Black power to control Black communities and the ability to determine the destiny of Black people (397). Furthermore, he recommended that, before talking of integration, Black people first had to unite. To achieve this goal, the Black Panther Party started working at the grassroots level to unify and educate the Black community.

Nfubea's founding of the local Black Panthers, or *Panteras negras*, groups in Spain was motivated by these same goals, especially the denunciation of growing racism. In his view, beginning with the 1992 celebrations of Spain's colonization of the Americas, the country intensified a Eurocentric perspective that glorified its colonial past in Latin America, Equatorial Guinea, and Morocco and moved to legally punish migrants from those areas. A variety of Afro-centric youth groups emerged to respond to the institutional racism that erased and denied "negritud" [Blackness] as a political category of Hispanism, imposing assimilation or criminalization, and active denigration by the media (*Afrofeminismo* 113). Comparisons with the original Black Panther Party led to the legitimization of similar movements in Spain. Under pressure from government measures, they evolved into two factions: one, reformist and ready to dialogue, and a second one that promoted continued resistance, which in the US took the name of the Black Liberation Party. According to Akinyele Omowale Umoja, "Panther participation in the BLA [Black Liberation Army] represented a continuation of the radical legacy of the BPP and was a response to the counter-insurgency strategy to destroy the Party and the Black liberation movement" (132). Nfubea records the intense involvement in Spain of many groups adopting one or the other of these approaches:

> The brotherhoods that were more relevant because of their high degree of politicization and control of their area of influence were: *Radical Black Power, Madrid Vandals, Simplemente Hermanos, LPC-División Autónoma, MTR, NFG-Niggers Freedom Gangsters* (Madrid), *los Colours* (Fuenlabrada), *los BRA Black Revolutionary Artist* (Torrejón) *MAN, Beautiful People* y *West Side* (Barcelona), *Public Enemy Fan Club* (Alcalá), *BSP Black Skin Proud, Frente Afro* y *Borikua* (Zaragoza) y *Black Power* (Leganés). (*Afrofeminismo* 114)[12]

The sheer number of associations indicates that, even if unnoticed by the general public, there is lively activism among Afro-Spaniards. Working against common challenges in a context that undermines their presence, they seek to affirm their belonging in Spain, molding their action plans in line with successful movements abroad.

Decolonizing the History of Afro-Spaniards: Afrofeminismo 161

Many of Malcolm X's proposals echoed Pan-Africanism as US Black communities fought oppression, marginalization, exploitation, and racialization. The ideals of Pan-Africanism are deeply ingrained in Nfubea's thought, as his book's title indicates. Because of its long history, the movement has had multiple emphases, which Nfubea synthesizes, all of them keeping a strong focus on community affirmation and self-determination. According to Kwame Anthony Appiah, Pan-Africanism grew as a response to white racism so that, in its most straightforward version, it

> is the political project calling for the unification of all Africans into a single African state, to which those in the African diaspora can return. In its vaguer, more cultural, forms, Pan-Africanism has pursued literary and artistic projects that bring together people in Africa and her diaspora.

Following Victor Oguijiofor Okafor, Pan-Africanism was a movement aimed at the liberation of Africa and Africans from European political domination and economic exploitation. Pan-Africanists believe that for Africans to create and maintain Pan-African institutional linkages, the education they provide to diasporic and continental Africans must be infused with a global African consciousness, which requires them to follow the protocol of Africalogical inquiry.[13] Furthermore, Molefi Asante, the leading theorist of Afro-centrism, describes this as a universal African consciousness, or "the awareness of our collective history and future" (25). As he explains, the "Afrocentrist seeks to uncover and use codes, paradigms, symbols, motifs, myths, and circles of discussion that re-enforce the centrality of African ideals and values as a valid frame of reference for acquiring and examining data" (6). While Pan-Africanism and Afro-centrism have different historical and theoretical trajectories, both trains of thought put African ideals and values at the center in order to overcome their erasure in Euro/Western-centric cultures. Nfubea's frequent allusions to and quotes from Malcolm X, Molefi Asante, Cheikh Anta Diop, Kwame Nkrumah, Sekou-Touré, Patrice Lumumba, and especially from Marcus Garvey clearly spell out his philosophical alignment as an Afro-centrist and Pan-Africanist.[14]

The *Black Power* movement that attained visibility and effectiveness in the US found an inspirational figure in Jamaican-born Marcus Garvey, who created a counterhegemonic project through the organization he founded, the Universal Negro Improvement Association (UNIA). In the early twentieth century, Garvey proposed and sought to organize the Black Exodus of all Black people held in bondage in the Americas and their return to Africa, the motherland. Although his dream was never realized, it encouraged the mental and spiritual liberation of many who organized through his UNIA. Motivated by his vision, many Black subjects continue to fight for their "real emancipation." According to Garvey, freedom comes from intellectual liberation, since a Eurocentric Western education insidiously penetrates a subject's mindset: "It is a truth that he who controls the mind determines the production ... This is the mental slavery Bob Marley has been singing about" (qtd. in Kinni 153–57). This seems to be the principal driver in Nfubea's repetition of Garvey's credo, since most of his citations focus on the importance of intellectual decolonization. When recording the history of Pan-Africanism in Spain, he recalls Garvey's statement that "a people without history, or with a poorly represented history, is a people without identity, or, in the best of cases, with a distorted knowledge of itself" (*Afrofeminismo* 91).[15] This assertion underlines the need for affirmation of the African subject, who has been disconnected from their own historical roots and therefore cannot contribute their culture's distinctive idea of humankind to other societies. It also denounces how Western history has silenced that of colonized peoples to the point that Western scholars treat non-Western societies as fundamentally non-historical because there were no traditional libraries. In Spain, the absence in elementary and secondary school textbooks of the nation's long-standing ties to Africa, including the slave trade, continues to crush the spirit of Afro-Spaniards and to impede the recognition of their achievements. Toasijé criticizes this erasure, poignantly qualifying the process as one of "desafricanización" since it denies the existence of past ties and uses negative discourses toward African migrants, including the implementation of harsh surveillance measures in the Strait of Gibraltar, further distancing Africa and Spain ("La memoria").[16] It is, therefore, of the utmost importance that Afro-Spaniards establish support networks that sustain living under oppressive codes. In this sense, Nfubea's insistence on promoting a Pan-Africanist perspective allows Afro-diasporic and African subjects to expand connections beyond local realities by encouraging alliances and collaboration to seek justice and promote African values.

While Pan-Africanism has many benefits as it fulfills a unifying, pride-raising function in Spain, it is now evaluated with some reservations. Contemporary analysts have revised some of its original tenets in relation to how they were put into practice in certain global regions, proposing new approaches. According to Tunde Adeleke, Garvey's Pan-Africanism had strong cultural nationalist undertones, appealing to race and a glorious future for Black people in Africa, a vision that was "alluring to a black American populace entrapped in a vicious circle of poverty, violence, and despair" (105). As it is still necessary to affirm the African identity of many African and Afro-diasporic peoples, Adeleke argues that the definition of an "African identity" is problematic among Africans: "How can Pan-Africanism be revived in Africa where ethnocentrism and micro-nationalism have eroded the very foundation upon which Pan-Africanism could have thrived?" (124). Similarly, Ibrahim K. Sundiata, in agreement with Cameroonian Axelle Kabou, states that "Négritude (and by extension Afrocentric glorification of the African past) has only bolstered indigenous dictatorships in the name of 'a specious authenticity'" that is used by dictators to protect themselves against outside criticism (144). Furthermore, in keeping with the thinking of Universidad Complutense de Madrid Professor, Mbuyi Kabunda, traditional Pan-Africanism has become bland through its folkloric, broken, and culturalist approach that no longer responds to the collective pursuits of African peoples (44). In his opinion, a new type of Pan-Africanism is needed to achieve the liberation of African and African-descended peoples. Now the goal is to recover what he calls a maximalist Pan-Africanism as a political and intellectual project, in addition to turning it into the basis of an African political economy and of a true African renaissance, as opposed to traditional nationalisms. This alternative ideology and praxis would be called Neopanafricanism and would be based on an Afro-centrist development model. It should be based on a double strategy: first, the recovery of the internal dynamism of African peoples, and second, the pursuit of endogenous regional integration to solve political and economic problems and create a common front in national agreement (Kabunda 45). Thus, Neopanafricanism institutionalizes regional integration from the bottom up, including a range of people from cultural, commercial, financial, and technological transborder networks. Neopanafricanist intellectuals, attentive to the voice of the people, must confront the challenge and accept the historical mission of conceiving an autonomous and self-sufficient political project that achieves democratic legitimacy, that can be located at the center of the democratic project, and that delineates new references destined to favor the political, economic, and social development of the people (Kabunda 50–53).

Whether expounding on approaches to traditional Pan-Africanism or aspects of a renewed vision of it, what matters most in Nfubea's book is the impetus to define a vision that puts the African subject at the center. While the combination of influences from which to draw inspiration is highly personal, stressing the figures and philosophies of Malcolm X and Marcus Garvey (whose blended names are honored in the eponymous online classes Nfubea offers), what emerges is the effort to recognize needs and celebrate the achievements of the Afro-Spanish community, which is ready to engage in a dialogue with Spanish society on equal footing. Although the specifics of the development of Afro-Hispanic communities vary widely, there is a painful commonality with other peoples of African origin of having their histories silenced. Connecting with the wider perspective of Pan-Africanism, Nfubea portrays his book as an echo chamber from which the voices of African-centered subjects can be heard, be they Spanish—as most of them are—or leaders who have paved the way towards self-affirmation and dignity in the face of oppressive sociopolitical contexts.

Womanist "Cimarrona": Women Work Toward Decolonization

As previously noted, Nfubea's lengthy book captures important stories of Afro-Spanish women situated at the periphery of Spain's hegemonic culture who can become models for action. He argues that many cultural battles in the Hispanic world were led by Black women who influenced flamenco art, cultures of care, work, and political rights, including LGTBQ+ communities (*Afrofeminismo* 221). For example, Chapter 2, "There Is Nothing New Under the Spanish Sun," briefly reviews the contributions of five women that Nfubea deems to be foundational figures of contemporary Afro-Hispanic feminism: Elena de Céspedes, Teresa de Chikaba, María de la Luz, Salaria Kea, and Imelda Makole. While this selection illustrates his own perspective, it also serves to underscore that it is a false and deeply reactionary idea, promoted by a consumerist market, to believe there are no references for Black women in Spain (*Afrofeminismo* 57). With this background in mind, Nfubea traces a detailed map of Afro-Spanish women's activities, frequently buttressed by two additional global philosophical approaches: Womanism and Maroonism or "cimarronaje." While Pan-Africanism speaks to the geographical and emotional alliance of subjects of African origin across the world in the face of common challenges, be they political, economic, or historical, when talking about women, it is also necessary to present an Afro-centric view that conveys their experiences according to their gender identity. The process of erasure that undermines many aspects of Afro-Spanish women's identity is deeply problematic when external forces impose solutions, eroding the specificity of their experiences.

According to Nfubea, Pan-Africanist women carry out a "difficult and complex struggle against Eurocentric feminism," a process that has earned them the epithet of "right-wing Afro" because of their independent attitude towards hegemonic feminist groups' demands (*Afrofeminismo* 38). The issue is that, as Nfubea indicates, dominant feminist approaches tend to render Afro-Spanish women's experiences invisible. The reductive, simplistic perspectives of white middle-class feminists have the effect of "silencing a sea of different experiences" (38).[17] Widely accepted paradigms have not allowed space for Afro-Spanish women's voices to be heard or to

Decolonizing the History of Afro-Spaniards: Afrofeminismo 165

be understood as departing from the norm. As a result, the solutions proposed tend to be partial and ineffective, or what is worse, they are patronizing since they do not take into account the strengths of the Afro-Spanish community. Common understandings about women of African origin manage to generalize them by creating patterns of victimizer-victim, which result in robbing them of their agency. In response, many of the interviewees speak of Africana feminism, or Womanism, and the discourse of "cimarronaje" or maroon sensibilities, which is being redefined in Latin America among Afro and Native American communities as part of a strategy of mental and spiritual decolonization. Nfubea quotes Afro-Cuban activist Antoinette Torres Soler, who explained her reaction to simplistic approaches to multiculturalism by official representatives: "I am not a victim, so I don't need you to validate my existence ... I rather seek to exercise my rights as a citizen from the logic of the antiracist principles that govern the Black movement, such as the criticism of racism" (*Afrofeminismo* 451).[18] It is the statement of this blueprint of intellectual independence and the prototype of community alliances among African descendants in the Hispanic world that constitutes the distinctive contribution of Nfubea's book since it promotes a dialogue between Afro populations from Spain, Africa, and Latin America.

The resulting map of activism is one that highlights exactly that: the engagement of Afro-Spanish women and the resulting social transformation they facilitate. Women working inside and outside their homes began to create networks that would support their projects. Their militancy can be found at both ends of the political spectrum, from national Roman Catholic conservative groups like the "Sección Femenina," where many were educated during colonial times in Equatorial Guinea and Spain (*Afrofeminismo* 137–48), to associations founded during Spain's transition to democracy that adopted political agendas focused on providing visibility to African populations in Spain such as "Riebapua, Rombe, Asociación Cultural Bubi o el Círculo Cultural Afrohispano" (*Afrofeminismo* 150). Women from different geographical origins and social and economic backgrounds coalesced to support each other: economists, bankers, politicians, hairdressers, students, housewives, and small business owners (*Afrofeminismo* 221). Frequently, these organizations arose organically in response to immediate material needs in the context of lack of representation, social frictions in specific neighborhoods, seeking support for new businesses, educating children, and so on.

Recent campaigns have been closely related to migration policies and media treatment of African migrants that marginalize them and set back earlier advancements. In this regard, several groups argue that the integration policies promoted by successive Spanish governments constitute new forms of colonialism. According to Nfubea, African migrants do not arrive in Europe intending to become integrated. That would mean accepting and collaborating with the criminal system that produces deaths in *pateras* and continues to exploit and colonize Africa, provoking internal wars (*Afrofeminismo* 121).[19] The idea of integration is difficult to accept because it does not account for fundamental cultural differences that are impossible to translate. As Enrique Dussel points out, the idea of integration is a foundational myth. It replicates a "colonial" mode of thinking by imposing capitalism and social class as the main paths to community belonging, thereby limiting many other possible connections. For Black women in Spain, colonialism means exploitative work that relegates them to the bottom of the economic ladder, where they find themselves mostly at caregiving service jobs, and to ideological "slavery" that imposes social codes that marginalize physical and relational African modes (Nfubea *Afrofeminismo* 425–51).

The precision of the listings and descriptions that Nfubea shares with the reader is painstaking, revealing his admiration for the labor of those groups that run the risk of being forgotten amid the visibility of new formations and the silencing stratagems of official histories. His detailed naming and contextual situating should now become part of a new historical record. He repeatedly mentions Pan-Africanist women like Rufi Maaba, Martha Trujillo, Mbose Ndiaye, Bilangwe, and Maria Ndour (*Afrofeminismo* 38), as well as the founders of women's associations like Irene Yamba Jora, "The Queen of Moka" (207; 223), Maaba Nguema Rufi (222), and leaders of long-standing women's groups like *Riabapua*, *Rombhe*, *Viyil*, and *Bia Fang* (223), the *Asociación Afromujer de Andalucía*, established by Anastasia Obama (227), the *Asociación Mujeres entre Mundos*, founded by Nigerian Gloria Ekereuwem (238), and *E'Waiso Ipola*, whose name means "Walk woman" in Bubi, active since 1992 (222–23). The types of activism examined include the creation of radio programs like "La Voz de África," broadcasting since 1995, and the publication of newspapers and magazines that have engaged with sociopolitical issues locally, nationally, and internationally since their inception. A distinguished example among them is the journal *África Negra*, established by Isabel Cardoso in 1991, which turned into "not only a far-reaching medium for the configuration of Pan-Africanism in Spain, but also one of the first media outlets created or managed by Black women, since the magazine *Minerva* in 1885" (Nfubea, *Afrofeminismo* 234).[20] *África Negra* achieved such success that it soon grew into a publishing house for books and magazines in other languages. *Tam-Tam*, a magazine founded by Lucrecia Mba Ndong in Barcelona, drew a similar response, as later did *Wanáfrica*, a newspaper with a monthly circulation of 25,000. According to Nfubea, this trajectory in print media "was the instrument to combat forgetfulness in the project of erasure and cultural colonization carried out every single day so that the Black population became ignorant of its own history" (*Afrofeminismo* 243).[21] African women are not so much the keepers of history as they are the agents of it. Their continued engagement is proof that they do not need to be rescued, as some condescending policies contemplate. Instead, they actively seek answers from their own positions, which sometimes differ from hegemonic views. This is especially true when they call themselves Womanists, preferring that term to that of feminists.

Closely aligned with the Afro-centric tradition, Clenora Hudson-Weems proposes the most comprehensive articulation of Womanism in *Africana Womanism: Reclaiming Ourselves*.[22] She set out an agenda for Africana Womanists based on three principal tenets: agency, alliances, and attributes, which can be demonstrated through 18 characteristics, including self-naming, self-definition, adaptability, struggling with males against oppression, family-centeredness, recognition, and respect for elders. Self-naming, for example, is too critical for Black people to be left in the hands of the dominant group since it serves as the basis for collective action and individual identity. Additionally, while mainstream feminism seeks to dismantle traditional gender roles, Black women value some of their elements precisely because, forced by external circumstances to work outside of the home, they frequently assume unconventional gender roles. In the social sphere, "genuine sisterhood" and fighting "in concert with males" against Black oppression take priority over individual alliances to achieve goals. According to Hudson-Weems, gender oppression is a reality, however, "the salient phenomenon that plagues the Africana community is poverty, in which racism plays a major part" (*Africana Womanist* 68). Based on the prioritization of race, class, gender, and the importance of the politics of naming, it is clear that traditional feminism, which defined the category of "woman" very broadly, underserves the specific needs of Black women. Given the fact that in Spain feminism has a long trajectory but is not yet a widely popular movement, sustaining an Africana Womanism becomes a necessity (Nfubea, *Afrofeminismo* 105). Nfubea also favors the more nuanced approach presented by Kimberlé Crenshaw, who describes how race, class, gender, and other individual characteristics "intersect" with one another and overlap. With the main goal of eliminating racism, the focus is on eradicating discrimination and structural inequality. He underscores the efforts of *Afroféminas*, an online review that promotes a Womanist discourse by combating the dominant Eurocentrism that influences gender roles and feminism and adopts a patronizing and tokenizing attitude toward multicultural subjects (368). Pan-African Spanish Womanists are not interested in a pyramid of victimhood and inverting it to turn the tables on straight white men; their movement is about understanding the complexity of the experiences of Spanish citizens by opening Spanish society's eyes to the different and varied experiences of Afro-Spaniards.

A representative of Womanist thinking highlighted in the book is Winnie Madikizela Mandela, who commanded the attention of Nfubea's foremothers like Basilisa Mangue, Mbose Ndiaye, Pilar Obama, Remei, and Vicenta Avoro. Captivated by her charisma when they were young, they felt encouraged to start participating in several political arenas, even though they lacked political experience (Nfubea, *Afrofeminismo* 183). Winnie Madikizela was the well-recognized wife of the anti-Apartheid leader Nelson Mandela, who waited for her husband for over two decades while he was imprisoned by the South African government. During his incarceration, she had to endure "countless arrests, charges, courtroom dramas, interrogation and torture, imprisonments, detentions, restrictions, banning, banishment, and the continued absence of [her] husband" (Ndebele 60). As a result, the "Mother of the Nation," as she was labeled, involved herself in multiple political activities, organizing strikes and protests, to the point that she became a "larger than life" figure, acquiring many of the features of a mythological character (Van Zyl Smit 403). However, given some of her controversial decisions, readings of her legacy are not in agreement. Nfubea acknowledges these criticisms yet underscores Madikizela's ability to keep the struggle against Apartheid energized during Mandela's incarceration and her own 491-day confinement. For Nbufea and for Afro-Spanish Womanists, most important of all is that Madikizela became an example of sorority by blending theory and practice when defending women's place in education, politics, and art and by strategizing to support her people (*Afrofeminismo* 182).

In Nfubea's opinion, while the nineteenth-century suffragists supported the recognition of rights for Black people, in Spain and even in the most politically open times, such as in the wake of the arrival of democracy, white feminist organizations never opened a space to examine the country's intrinsic racism or to question white supremacy or pigmentocracy (*Afrofeminismo* 449). In search of spiritual support, Afro-Spanish women adopted what he calls a "cimarrona's modus operandi," which is that of a woman who runs toward freedom and disregards heteropatriarchal rules (45). In his words,

> Marronage is the essence of Pan-Africanism: there is no Pan-Africanism without marronage. It is different from other options in terms of its organization and lines of action, not so much in its theoretical or philosophical approach. Two of the most distinctive aspects of marronage are its critical view of formal and permanent organization, as well as its defense of direct action. (47)[23]

Decolonizing the History of Afro-Spaniards: Afrofeminismo 169

And the question is, why "cimarronaje" or "marronage"? Most critics indicate that its long tradition in Latin America is relevant to Afro-diasporic communities now. Marronage is germane to political self-representation for Afro-Latin American citizens. It is not a defensive, revisionist, or reactive use of memory; rather, it is a "(re)existential political project that reconstitutes the slave's subjectivity, transforming it into the opposite of slavery to the extent that one is the negation of the other" (León Castro 153).[24] In that line of thought, it is true that talk of marronage is frequently dismissed as something from the past, yet, according to Boaventura de Sousa Santos, rereading and reevaluating its meaning is a necessary act because slavery was not truly eliminated with its abolition. On the contrary, it is constantly revived through social conflicts and tensions that stem from the same ideologies that made slavery possible (58). At the same time, it is imperative to recognize that enslaved people sought freedom in a number of ways. Therefore, marronage now extends beyond resistance: it seeks to understand the range of strategies maroons used to form their "palenques," "quilombos," or "cumbes" in order to revive the creativity they displayed in constituting new subjectivities (León Castro 155). Still another way of being inspired by marronage_is to historically trace the cultural, political, and religious African elements maroons had in common and that allowed them to create a sense of belonging, so that they form the root of contemporary values and behaviors. In short, marronage is one of the most important notions underlying an emancipatory approach to being an Afro-diasporic subject. It represents a countercatastrophic mode of thinking as it challenges the domination of African racialized bodies and seeks to reconfigure intersubjective relations by excising the colonial logic that dehumanized human beings. It implies an undoing of colonial thought and a ubiquity to reconfigure a new praxis of being.

For Pan-Africanist Womanist citizens in Spain, marronage is a strategy of resistance, of historical reparation in which African women in the diaspora acquire a central position. It is part of a commemorative philosophy that validates, confirms, and sustains current programs and political goals for Afro-Spaniards. According to Jillian Hernández, the *cimarrona* approach is a practice of engagement that has several distinctive characteristics: (1) it privileges a Black Atlantic perspective; (2) it poses critical questions about Black embodiment in relation to racialized violence; (3) it centers Black women as knowledge producers and organizers; (4) it emphasizes narratives of liberation; and ultimately(5) it produces new narratives and identitarian representations invested in Black living and freedom (43). Nfubea's interviews include descriptions of Black women's everyday actions and track the development and affirmation of their beliefs and practices. They also demonstrate an appreciation for women's work and daily lives, since they are imbued with their values and worldviews,

170 *Dosinda García-Alvite*

sometimes not explicitly stated but truly transmitted through their actions. At the social level, they convey a relational perspective, always in dialogue with others, not from an individualist view. By telling the stories of his female elders and their colleagues and by recording their achievements, Nfubea establishes a productive relationship with his interviewees in their struggle for their rights. He reflects their alliances at the same time that he reinforces them by affirming them. This helps produce a stronger ability to resist attacks.

In conclusion, in *Afrofeminismo*, Abuy Nfubea restates and nurtures a historical African consciousness that has been erased from public view in Spain. Demonstrating an African-centered, Pan-African, Womanist, Maroonist perspective, he promotes a decolonial approach to being an Afro-Spaniard. As Catherine Walsh and Juan García Salazar wrote, giving credit to the philosophy and teachings of elders is a decolonial practice designed to recover, strengthen, reposition, and rebuild the existence of the Afro-diasporic subject as an ancestral right. Nfubea's stories construct a history of African Spain that communicates how he became aware of his oppression through the silencing of his foremothers' actions in the nation-state's version of its official history. The younger generations' lack of knowledge of their communities' past affects important aspects of their identity: gender, sexuality, ethnicity, race, class, and image. Thus, the book criticizes erasure at the level of politics, law, and social norms, and especially in the individual and communal spheres. By recording the multiple levels of these women's activities and goals, Nfubea promotes awareness in Afro-Spanish communities of their history and of how their struggle to have their rights respected can empower their circles of influence: family, collectives, community organizations, and nation.

Notes

1 "A todas las que hoy buscan referencias en YouTube, pero las tienen en su casa". Angela Davis is a noted African American educator, author, and political activist who was an active member of the Black Panther Party and the U.S. Communist Party in the 1970s. Because of her involvement and visibility, she became a symbol of the struggle for Black liberation, feminism, and anticapitalism.
2 Maroon communities, or free city-republics, like Palenque de San Basílio in Colombia, were created by runaway slaves in the Americas as early as the 1600s. Their rich civic culture and networks of solidarity and mutual aid to preserve their freedom have inspired contemporary movements for the visibility and empowerment of Afro-Hispanic communities throughout the world. For further information on Maroon traditions and philosophies, see Bernd Reiter.
3 The original Spanish titles of the chapters are: "Redadas o racismo institucional," "Las negras asaltan los medios," "Neoesclavitud o trabajo doméstico," and "La revolución es femenina y nunca ha sido televisada." Nfubea,

who defines himself as a hip-hop speaker engaged in popular culture activism, clearly alludes in the latter chapter to the 1971 poem and song by Gil Scott-Heron, "The Revolution Will Not Be Televised," based on the famous slogan of the 1960 U.S. Black Power movement, which in turn was a response to the spoken-word poem "When the Revolution Comes" by The Last Poets ("When the revolution comes some of us will probably catch it on TV"). The two pieces emphasize the passivity of some forms of revolution and how it is important to be physically involved.

4 This is his own description taken from his Twitter account. It is important to note that he is a second-generation Afro-Spaniard whose parents arrived from Equatorial Guinea in the 1960s. He spent his youth and most of his career in Barcelona. He is well-traveled, having worked in Latin America, especially Bolivia, as well as the United States and Europe.

5 Nfubea may be one of the top specialists on Malcolm X in Spain, since he reports publishing a book titled *Malcolm X y la generación hip-hop*, [Malcolm X and the Hip-Hop Generation], in addition to the numerous references to him in this volume (*Afrofeminismo* 62). A quick search of academic resources written about Malcolm X in Spain produces a limited number of articles, an exception being that of Antumi Toasijé who has also authored articles and book chapters on Malcolm X's influence on Spanish Pan-Africanists.

6 The famous protagonist of Harriet Beecher Stowe's novel (1852) is considered one of the most enduring fictional characters used to rally against the horrors of slavery yet, in the contemporary imagination, it has become synonymous with servility and self-hatred ("Why African-Americans"). The use of "Uncle Tom" as coterminous with "sell-out," like a slur or insult, has become distorted through partial representations of the novel in popular culture for mostly white audiences.

7 "La negación o desconocimiento sistemático del proceso histórico negro en España con una voluntad explícita de presentarse como la génesis. Como diría Malcolm X: 'I am the only Negro in this place', estas afirmaciones fomentan el desconocimiento, el negacionismo, el afropesimismo, los discursos apocalípticos y la catarsis" (25).

8 "Desde la colonización, las mujeres negras protestaban y reivindicaban sus derechos con canciones, danzas, teatro, en las fincas, en las cocinas, escribían, disparaban, se organizaban y se quejaban por las injusticias basadas en el género. En Guinea Ecuatorial, por ejemplo, teníamos a María Jesús Ayecaba, muy metida en política junto a Acacio Mañé o Enrique Nvó, padres de la independencia" (58).

9 "Ellas fundaron el panafricanismo, hoy participan en las luchas migratorias y sus nietas se identifican con el Black Lives Matter" (43).

10 In fact, Nfubea distinguishes among four generations of Afro-Spaniards, closely aligned with the political transformation of Equatorial Guinea as a former colony: first, those called "Black Spaniards" from the 1950–1960s; second, exiles from Francisco Macías Nguema's dictatorship in the 1970s; third, those who arrived in the 1980s escaping Teodoro Obiang Nguema Mbasogo's regime; and fourth, those who were born and raised in Spain, the majority of whom defend a combative attitude ("Orígenes remotos" 1004).

11 Two poignant cases Nfubea mentions frequently are those of "El negro de Banyoles" and Lucrecia Pérez. The first one arose when a dead Black man who had been mummified in the nineteenth century ended up exhibited at the Museum of Banyoles where he was considered one of its main tourist attractions.

In the early 1990s, a Spanish citizen born in Haiti, Doctor Alphonse Arcelín, whom Nfubea considers one of his mentors, launched a campaign to remove the display which became a rallying cause for Afro youth movements throughout Spain. The commercial use of a nameless African person in the museum was considered a primary example of dehumanization and institutional racism. In 1992, the xenophobic killing of Dominican migrant Lucrecia Pérez in Aravaca marked the most visible display of racist attitudes in Spain on the 500th anniversary of Christopher Columbus's arrival in the Americas.

12 "Las hermandades más relevantes por su alto grado de politización y control del territorio eran: Radical Black Power, Madrid Vandals, Simplemente Hermanos, LPC-Divisón Autónoma, MTR ..." (114).

13 Kini-Yen Kinni claims that Commander in Chief Toussaint Louverture was one of the initiators of Pan-Africanism as he proposed that an armed revolution was the path to follow against colonization, and so he led one and won against the French colonizers in Haiti (151; 154).

14 Asante has distinguished himself as the most outspoken Afro-centrist in US academia. His *Afrocentricy: The Theory of Social Change* (1980) became a reference book for placing African people's agency at the center of their history. Diop's book *African Origin of Civilization: Myth or Reality* presented ample research to show that Egyptian civilization had African origins, arguments that established a clear contrast with Western Egyptology, bringing up questions on how history is "made." Nkrumah, Sekou-Touré and Lumumba were the most visible anti-colonial leaders achieving independence and creating the first governments of Ghana, Guinea and Congo. Their philosophies and tactics were influential in the struggles for independence across Africa.

15 "Un pueblo sin historia, o con una historia mal representada, es un pueblo sin identidad o, en el mejor de los casos, con un sentido distorsionado de sí mismo" (91).

16 Toasijé summarizes the political measures taken in the 2000s to establish a physical and historical distance between Spain and Africa, explaining that "La desafricanización de España supone el borrado y la negación del legado africano en España, la persecución de los migrantes africanos y el establecimiento del dispositivo de vigilancia y control marítimo FRONTEX. El objetivo final es la plena aceptación de España como país europeo y la negación de su reconocida africanidad ... En el período de desafricanización las autoridades tienen un discurso especialmente hostil hacia los migrantes africanos negros y llevan a cabo o fomentan que terceros países lleven a cabo acciones de repatriación que contravienen los Derechos Humanos" ("La memoria" 289).

17 "un silenciamiento hacia un mar de experiencias diferentes."

18 "'No soy víctima, y no necesito que validéis mi existencia,' sino que a partir de las lógicas reivindicaciones antirracistas hegemónicas del movimiento negro, como es la crítica del racismo, busco el ejercicio de mi ciudadanía." Torres Soler is the founder and current director of *Afroféminas*.

19 *Pateras* are small rowing boats used to cross the Strait of Gibraltar or to reach the Canary Islands from Africa. These small boats frequently carry large numbers of people, which causes them to capsize or sink. Many migrants have drowned at sea trying to reach Europe this way.

20 "No solo en un medio transcendental para la configuración del panafricanismo en España, sino en uno de los primeros medios creados o dirigidos por mujeres negras, después de la revista *Minerva* de 1885." It appears Nfubea has a typo in the publication date but he rightly points at the silenced history

of an Afro-Cuban nationalist ideology, regularly represented in the feminist publication *Minerva, revista quincenal dedicada a la mujer de color*, published between 1888 and 1914 in Cuba, after the abolition of slavery in 1886.
21 "Fue el instrumento para combatir la desmemoria en un trabajo de borrado y colonización cultural que se llevó a cabo diariamente para que la población negra desconozca su propia historia."
22 There are multiple interpretations of Womanism as this philosophy has expanded its influence in recent decades. According to Hudson-Weems, "Africana Womanism as a theoretical concept and methodology defines a new paradigm, which offers an alternative to all forms of feminism. It is a terminology and a concept that consider both ethnicity (Africana) and gender (Womanism), which I coined and defined in the mid-1980s ... It was later established that the concept is neither an outgrowth nor an addendum to feminism ... Black feminism, African feminism, or Walker's Womanism that some Africana women have come to embrace ... critically addresses the dynamics of the conflict between the mainstream feminist and the Black feminist." Nfubea draws attention to this specific formulation by Hudson-Weems.
23 "El cimarronaje es la esencia del panafricanismo: no hay panafricanismo sin cimarronaje. Se diferencia de otras posturas en términos de organización y acción, y no tanto en términos teóricos o filosóficos. La crítica a la organización formal y permanente, junto a la defensa de la acción directa... serían los dos elementos más característicos del cimarronaje" (47).
24 "El cimarronaje va más allá de la Resistencia; es un proyecto político (re) existencial en tanto rehace la subjetividad del esclavizado, convirtiéndose en el antagónico de la esclavitud en la medida en que uno constituía la negación del otro."

Works Cited

Adeleke, Tunde. *The Case Against Afrocentrism*. U of Mississippi P, 2009.
Appiah, Kwame Anthony. "Pan-Africanism." *Africana: The Encyclopedia of the African and African American Experience*. 2nd ed., edited by Henry Louis Gates Jr. and Anthony Appiah. Oxford African American Studies Center, 1999, pp. 1484–86, https://doi.org/10.1093/acref/9780195301731.013.42855. Accessed 20 Oct. 2021.
Asante, Molefi. *Kemet, Afrocentricity and Knowledge*. Africa World Press, 1990.
Crenshaw, Kimberlé. "Demarginalizing the Intersection of Race and Sex: A Black Feminist Critique of Antidiscrimination Doctrine, Feminist Theory, and Antiracist Politics." *Feminism and Politics*, edited by Anne Philips. Oxford UP, 1998, pp. 314–43.
De Sousa Santos, Boaventura. *Descolonizar el saber, reinventar el poder*. Ediciones Trilce, 2010.
Diop, Cheik Anta. *The African Origin of Civilization: Myth or Reality*. Lawrence Hill, 1974.
Dussel, Enrique. *Philosophy of Liberation*. Translated by Aquilina Martinez and Christine Morkovsky. Orbis Books, 1985.
Dyson, Michael Eric. *Reflecting Black: African-American Cultural Criticism*. U of Minnesota P, 1993.

Harper, Frederick D. "The Influence of Malcolm X on Black Militancy." *Journal of Black Studies*, vol. 1, no. 4, 1971, pp. 387–402.
Hernández, Jillian. "Fugitive State: Toward a Cimarrona Approach for Florida Cultural Studies." *Departures in Critical Qualitative Research*, vol. 10, no. 2, 2021, pp. 41–49, https://doi.org/10.1525/dcqr.2021.10.2.41.
Hudson-Weems, Clenora. "Africana Womanism: A Historical, Global Perspective for Women of African Descent." *Call & Response: The Riverside Anthology of the African American Literary Tradition*, edited by Patricia Liggins Hall et al. Houghton Mifflin, 1998, pp. 1812–15.
———. *Africana Womanism. Reclaiming Ourselves*. Routledge, 2020.
———. *Africana Womanist Literary Theory*. Africa World Press, 2004.
Kabunda, Mbuyi. "Democracia, regionalismo y panafricanismo: las alternativas neoafricanistas." *Democracia y buen gobierno en el África Subsahariana*, vol. 21, 2007, pp. 33–66.
Kinni, Kini-Yen. *Pan-Africanism: Political Philosophy and Socio-Economic Anthropology for African Liberation and Governance*. Langaa RPCIG, 2015.
León Castro, Edizon. "Lectura crítica de la historia de los cimarrones de Esmeraldas (Ecuador) durante los siglos XVI–XVIII." *Historia y Espacio*, vol. 13, no. 48, 2017, pp. 149–78.
Ndebele, Njabulo. *The Cry of Winnie Mandela*. Ayebia Clarke Publishing, 2006.
Omowale Umoja, Akinyele. "Repression Breeds Resistance: The Black Liberation Army and the Radical Legacy of the Black Panther Party." *New Political Science*, vol. 21, no. 2, pp. 131–55.
Reiter, Bernd. "Palenque de San Basilio: Citizenship and Republican Traditions of a Maroon Village in Colombia." *Journal of Civil Society*, vol. 11, no. 4, pp. 333–47.
Sundiata, Ibrahim K. "The Diaspora and a Very Small Place in Africa." *Transition*, vol. 119, 2016, pp. 140–52.
Toasijé, Antumi. "La memoria y el reconocimiento de la comunidad africana y africano-descendiente negra en España: El papel de la vanguardia panafricanista." *Nómadas. Revista Crítica de Ciencias Sociales y Jurídicas*, vol. 28, no. 4, 2010, pp. 277–316.
———. "The Africanity of Spain: Identity and Problematization." *Journal of Black Studies*, vol. 39, no. 3, 2009, pp. 348–55.
Trouillot, Michel-Rolph. *Silencing the Past. Power and the Production of History*. Beacon Press, 1995.
Van Zyl Smit, Betine. "From Penelope to Winnie Mandela—Women Who Waited." *International Journal of the Classical Tradition*, vol. 15, no. 3, 2008, pp. 393–406, https://doi.org/10.1007/s12138-009-0047-0
Walsh, Catherine, and Juan García Salazar. "Memoria colectiva, escritura y Estado. Prácticas pedagógicas de existencia afroecuatoriana." *Cuadernos de Literatura*, vol. 19, no. 38, 2015, pp. 79–98, http:/dx.doi.org/10.11144/Javeriana.cl19-38.mcee. Accessed 12 Feb. 2022.
"Why African-Americans Loathe Uncle Tom." *Tell Me More*, NPR, 30 July 2008, https://www.npr.org/templates/story/story.php?storyId=93059468.
X, Malcolm. "Message to the Grass Roots." *Northern Negro Grass Roots Leadership Conference*, 10 Nov. 1963, King Solomon Baptist Church, Detroit, MI, http://www.csun.edu/~hcpas003/grassroots.html. Accessed 12 Oct. 2021.

8 Mapping Black Women Through Art and Social Media
The Case of Montserrat Anguiano

Stefania Licata

"Juntas somos una" (Exhibition e-Catalog *Dona, Mujer, Woman*)

In her public lectures in 1831, the African American teacher and abolitionist Maria W. Stewart encouraged Black women to "forge self-definition of self-reliance and independence" (Hill Collins 2), which she argued was fundamental to erasing the imagery of Black women as mammies, matriarchs, welfare mothers, and Jezebels, among other stereotypes (69).[1] Starting from Stewart's argument, this paper aims to show how Black identity is being built and redefined within Spanish culture through artistic representations. I will focus specifically on the production of Afro-Catalan artist Montserrat Anguiano. Born in Barcelona in 1982, she was adopted by a Spanish family. However, despite having spent all her life in Spain, she also reclaims her Equatorial Guinean roots. In a recent interview published in *Metal Magazine*, the artist affirms:

> My origin is African, from Equatorial Guinea, but I was born in Barcelona. A double identity. I did not belong either to my motherland or here. With time I understood that I belonged to both, I am both, and they represent me. Therefore, through painting I showed my two origins, my two houses." (Poll)[2]

She is, indeed, part of two cultural systems that complement each other and which she has captured—since she was 18 years old—through the visual arts and poetry to advocate for all underrepresented Black women. Anguiano is an interdisciplinary artist whose work includes paintings on canvas, murals, and body art, and she recently began writing poems related to the sensuality of the female body (Exhibition e-Catalog, *Dona, Mujer, Woman*). Her work has been displayed in Spain, New York, and Equatorial Guinea.[3] Moreover, she is an activist committed to raising awareness about Black history without geographical limitations.

DOI: 10.4324/9781003435051-9

Drawing on Black feminist and Memory Studies, as well as social media theories, I analyze two of Anguiano's recent art exhibitions, both of which are accessible online—*Dona, Mujer, Woman* (2022) and *Referent és nom de Dona* [Role Mode Is a Woman's Name] (2022)—to highlight how the artist promotes Black identity through her artistic representations, empowering other Black women beyond the borders of Spain.[4] The first exhibition, a collaboration with the Spanish artist Rubén Antón, focuses on revisiting Black women's history from the sixteenth century up to the present, with an emphasis on the past. *Referent és nom de Dona* in turn promotes a reframing of Black women's identity from a contemporary perspective, using living role models as inspiration for the future Black generation. Taken together, the two exhibitions provide a comprehensive overview of how Black women's identity can be separated from stereotypes and reconstructed in a new light through art. I argue that, in both exhibitions, Anguiano's focus on history and memory are tools used to denounce and reverse stigmatized images of Black women, aiming to deconstruct binary thinking about gender and race. Moreover, I show how Anguiano—who is very active on different social media platforms (personal website, *Facebook*, *YouTube*, and *Instagram*, among others)—builds a transnational and transcultural community through the Internet, creating a new arena for reflecting and connecting with other members of the African diaspora.

With her paintings, Anguiano connects herself to historical African American political activists, philosophers, and academics concerned with Black women's inequality and who fought—or continue to fight—for equal civil and social rights. As her personal website indicates, she is inspired primarily by three African American women: activist and entrepreneur Madam C. J. Walker (1867–1919), American-born French dancer and actress Josephine Baker (1906–1975), and activist and professor Angela Davis (1944–).[5] In Spain, Anguiano also collaborates with a number of activists belonging to the new generation of Afro-descendants, such as journalist and author Lucía Mbomío Rubio, activist and human rights advocate Isabelle Mamadou, musician Nêga Lucas, actress and author Asaari Bibang, and psychologist Yania Concepción Vicente. In their different fields, all these women denounce the denial of rights that Black women experience worldwide and the inequalities affecting women of different social and economic status.[6] In both the exhibitions I analyze, Anguiano establishes connections among the different elements of the society to which these women belong and seeks to create a new social image for Black women.

Reframing Black Women's Past

Scholars (Paul S. Landau, Deborah Kaspin, Ruth Mayer, and Matthew Fox-Amato, among others) have examined the specific iconography of African people that originated during slavery and the African colonial period. In the United States, for example, in the nineteenth-century antebellum period (1832–1860), photographs sought to hide and silence slave rebellions by representing them in living conditions that did not correspond to reality. In portraits of Black caretakers with white children, enslavers showed well-dressed slaves and "projected a comfortable, harmonious, and familial form of bondage, which purportedly treated its laborers as people, not commodities" (Fox-Amato 22). However, rather than express themselves with the pose they wanted, they were portrayed with an imposed one as their masters needed to maintain the hierarchy, and the negation of the slaves' identities invalidated their "personhood" (22–23).

By contrast, the images of colonized Black people in the context of African colonialism from the late nineteenth to the mid-twentieth centuries were mostly used to create categories that underlined the physical and mental difference with Western people. Indeed, "photography froze images of 'primitive people'" (Landau, "Empires" 144). This allowed the spread of colonizers' "scientific" studies meant to prove the superiority of whites over Black human beings. For example, Spain's *Instituto de Estudios Africanos* (IDEA), a political entity established in 1945 during Francoism, analyzed the inferiority of the Black inhabitants of Equatorial Guinea (back then *Guinea Española*, 1926–1968) compared to white Spaniards. This approach associated Equatorial Guineans with products exported to Spain from their homeland, such as cocoa. Brands like *Cola Cao* and *Conguitos*, among others, advertised their products with stereotypical images of Black individuals that included exaggerated facial features, noses and mouths in particular (Licata 31–32). As Landau argues, people use such images to "draw together previously inchoate social meanings from their *own* societies, and then ... to recognize people from *other* societies" ("Introduction" 2).[7] These visual representations have worked alongside dominant oppressive narratives to generate stereotypes about Black women. The "mammy" (caretaker) present in slavery photographs reflects one of the most prevalent stereotypes that circulated not only in nineteenth-century United States iconography but also in all the other nations involved in the slave trade and colonialist imperialism. *Dona, Mujer, Woman* aims to reverse these enslaved or colonial depictions of Black women to "decolonize the mind," following Kenyan author Ngũgĩ wa Thiongo's argument that African authors use their native languages to disaffirm colonial superiority. Anguiano's art has a similar goal, adopting the language of African art (specific colors, subjects, and meanings) to shift the perspective and create an awareness of Black women within Black feminist thought.

The *Dona, Mujer, Woman* exhibition was mounted in several cultural centers in Spain.[8] In a number of instances, the two artists, Anguiano and Antón, employ digital collage to combine virtual images of Afro-descendant women leaders with different kinds of flowers. The artists presented a series of collages made with images of more than 30 women of African descent and members of the LGBTQIA+ community (William Dorsey Swann, Marsha P. Johnson, and Cacao, among others) from different historical periods (ranging from the sixteenth century to the present) and geographical areas.[9] The exhibition emphasized feminism, anti-racism, and historical memory (Exhibition e-Catalog). In the final part of the e-Catalog, the central technique changes to the "pintura plástica sobre lienzo" (flat water-based paint on Canvas), which is Anguiano's specialty, and video art.[10] This collaborative project combined the two artists' expertise in Black women and LGBTQIA+ history; however, for the purpose of this essay, I will explore Anguiano's conversations about race and women.

The exhibition e-Catalog for *Dona, Mujer, Woman* opens with the following statement: "Three struggles come together in this pioneering exhibition for the first time in Barcelona, including relevant and dissident women throughout history. These are lives that we want to celebrate and remember in order for them not to be forgotten. Together we are one."[11] The fact that the title of the exhibit includes the word "woman" in Catalan, Spanish, and English expresses the unity of women who might be separated by their different native languages but who are nonetheless united in the same struggle for women's rights. This theme implies a link between Anguiano's dual identity and her artistic production because she is the only Black female artist featured in this exhibit. Moreover, several artworks portray African American women, demonstrating how Anguiano's identity as a Catalan-Spanish woman is also related to the African diaspora around the world. As nineteenth-century abolitionist and women's rights advocate Maria W. Stewart argued, retelling the struggles of relevant women and dissidents across time and being aware of their past is fundamental to creating self-reliance (Hill Collins 69). While Stewart wanted to convey the concept of self-reliance, to resist the white enslavers, here it acquires a more contemporary meaning: opposition to persistent racist stereotypes. But above all, "self-reliance," or the ability to depend on one's own skills, can also be understood not only as an individual's strength but also as a group's collaborative resilience. Therefore, in this context, it means developing a mutually supportive anti-racist community. The women displayed in the exhibition are self-reliant, confident, and dissident. Indeed, the Black women leaders included in this group are all non-conformists who dared to challenge unjust social systems. The history of Black people opposing systemic injustice was of vital importance; this commitment made Black women visible to a society that previously ignored them as human beings. The examples of enslaved women such as Sojourner Truth (1797–1883), an American born into slavery who escaped to freedom in 1826 and advocated for abolition, civil, and women's rights (Hill Collins 13), allow Black community members from different countries to get to know these iconic figures better.[12] Ultimately, the goal is to stimulate curiosity about these

Mapping Black Women: Montserrat Anguiano 179

female icons and offer alternative representations, giving them a place in collective memory rather than simply confining them to historical writing.

In *Dona, Mujer, Woman*, the juxtaposition of different photographs of African women and flowers in a collage builds a narrative that contrasts with racist iconography of Black women. This also extends to African women historically represented as slaves, such as Sara(h) Baartman (1789–1815), the "Hottentot Venus," who was exhibited in European salons as part of "ethnic" expositions and freak shows because of the shape of her body.[13] In his analysis of the perception of the female Hottentot, Sander L. Gilman underlines how

> her physiognomy, her skin color, the form of her genitalia label her as inherently different. In the 19th century, the Black female was widely perceived as possessing not only a "primitive" sexual appetite but also the external signs of this temperament–"primitive" genitalia. (213)

The photograph of Sara Baartman exhibited in 1810 in the Egyptian Hall in London's Piccadilly Street simultaneously caused a scandal and raised awareness regarding the abolition of slavery ("Sarah Baartman"). However, the distribution of this image, together with the narrative of difference compared to European women, has contributed to accentuating a racist philosophy nurtured until contemporary times.

The presence of Baartman (Figure 8.1) in *Dona, Mujer, Woman* is, therefore, very significant. The racialized imagery does not, however, represent Black women as victims of a dominant power. Instead, the juxtaposition with flowers (daisies, sunflowers, and peonies, among others) conveys the rebirth of these women's identities.[14] While the historic photographs maintain a link with racist depictions of Black women—in Baartman's case, the dehumanizing spotlight was on her steatopygia, or the large amounts of fat on the buttocks—(Gilman 219)—the flowers, on the contrary, add a different meaning, symbolizing loyalty, adoration, joy, purity, and new beginnings. In the poem after the collage, Anguiano describes Baartman as

> Categorical and eternal, exposed, sodomized deity,
> eyes that speak, which say
> that it is forbidden fertility, out of
> canons, goddess like an animal,
> firm woman, almost illegal femininity.
> (Exhibition e-Catalog)[15]

While Anguiano does not hide the violence that Baartman suffered, she focuses on her powerful femininity thanks to a generous physical shape that was "almost illegal" according to the strict canon of Western beauty.

180 *Stefania Licata*

Sara Baartman's physical features were used to degrade and dehumanize her, while this collage encourages women to reject the aesthetic standards imposed by society while also seeking to restore Baartman's stolen dignity.

The final part of the e-Catalog concentrates on the African continent itself. The digital collage *Afrika Floral en primarios* [Floral Afrika in primary colors] uses flowers in four different colors (red, yellow, blue, and white) to represent the shape of the continent (Figure 8.2).[16]

While according to the e-Catalog each flower symbolizes a different African State, they also represent the women spread all over the African continent, a topic of great importance in Anguiano's art. These women, although diverse, are also captured through three or four different kinds of flowers, highlighting similarities across geographical areas and projecting, consequently, the idea of a community of Black women regardless of their cultural backgrounds, geographical locations, or historical experiences. This juxtaposition of flowers of multiple kinds accentuates their commonalities without homogenizing and demonstrates the unity of a community of marginalized Black women from different regions of the world.

Figure 8.1 1789—Sara Baartman. Permission granted by the artist.

Mapping Black Women: Montserrat Anguiano 181

Furthermore, the choice of Africa, the departure point of origin of the diaspora, ultimately becomes the link that unites all these women with African roots. The Western imaginary of African people, in fact, causes the inequalities and racial injustices they face. The symbolism of this image also recalls the global movement of Pan-Africanism in terms of the sisterhood and solidarity that it engenders within and beyond Africa. The idea of unity and community across the African diaspora is, indeed, crucial in this exhibition. In addition, this representation of the African continent in Figure 8.2 reverses the persistent characterization of Africa as the Dark Continent, a term that came into circulation with nineteenth-century

Figure 8.2 Floral Afrika in primary colors—red (e-Catalog). Permission granted by the artist.

European explorers. Specifically, British explorer Henry M. Stanley's books *Through the Dark Continent* (1878) and *In Darkest Africa* (1890) were followed by other authors whose publications represented the vast continent in a similar way. This expression alluded to an unknown geographical area but also intensified ideas about Black people, rendering them as dark and "primitive," thereby justifying the colonizer's civilizing mission. *Dona, Mujer, Woman*, where each flower represents an African state or a woman, transmits, once again, an alternative positive view of the continent in contrast with its stereotypical darkness. The exhibition photo above depicts a colorful and lively continent, reframing Africa as a joyful place.

Notably, *Dona, Mujer, Woman* also breaks down gender and racial stereotypes with poems dedicated to the women in the collages, such as the one dedicated to Baartman. Anguiano's poems seek to empower these women by introducing them to a contemporary audience. For example, Anguiano begins her e-Catalog with a Black female leader, Ann Zingha (1583–1663),[17] the ruler of Ndongo and Matamba (old African kingdoms in present-day Angola), dedicating the following poem to her:

> The Queen of Matamba, the power
> and the redemption, the classic beauty
> and the endless strength. This is the unique
> and my favorite Queen. Blackness
> which fights for territorial unity and the peace
> of all its people. She is the first role model
> (Exhibition e-Catalog)[18]

The choice of the word "reina" [queen] to describe Ann Zingha is relevant here. In its most obvious meaning, *reina* refers to a woman born into a royal family. However, it also recalls the "Black queen," a popular concept in the African American community that refers to an admired and confident woman who is extremely skilled in what she does. This expression aims to empower a woman even more fully or to appreciate her by connecting her to ancient African queens, such as Zingha, who led their countries. It is also a way to refer to Africa's royal history that was erased by slavery and colonialism. Indeed, the strength and power these female leaders demonstrated by denouncing the inequalities that African women faced were transformative and led to social change.

Furthermore, Anguiano's poem emphasizes territorial unity and protecting people, since having a territory inhabited by a supportive community is fundamental to achieving equality. This relates to both the colonizer, who imposed new political borders, and the queen, who fought to maintain the original borders. Defending the political geography of a territory is also linked to the importance of having a group of people who encourage one another because they believe in its preservation. In addition, the poem alludes to the Ubuntu philosophy common to some African cultures, which expresses the interdependence of all members of a community—"I am because you are"—a life philosophy and mantra adopted by leaders like Nelson Mandela and Desmond Tutu. Including a poem for each woman also emphasizes how Anguiano honors the entire community of Black women, highlighting not its mere existence but, more importantly, its resilience. This is pivotal because without this resilience—embedded in each member—the inspiration for this exhibition, its paintings, and its poems would have been absent. The words of the poems are powerful and provide a counternarrative to dominant Western and colonial depictions of Africa, transforming the negative images into positive ones.

Anguiano feels a personal connection to the women seen in the exhibition. As a Black Spanish citizen, she was deeply inspired by their stories and their struggle against inequality. For example, in the poem dedicated to Sojourner Truth, which follows her image in a collage, the artist emphasizes once again how Black women have been fundamental not only in achieving their own freedom but also in inspiring the next generations:

Yearn for freedom, it's already yours
and your descendants, strength and
the authority of the word. Fighting for
your people, always.
(Exhibition e-Catalog)[19]

With this poem, Anguiano establishes a direct ideological ancestry with the African American activist. She recognizes the essential role that Truth played in the nineteenth century and continues to play in contemporary Black women's community. In addition, the artist emphasizes not just the importance of the words, such as the ones cited above, but also the charisma they convey.

These women helped Anguiano build, little by little, her double identity as a *Fang* from Micomeseng in Equatorial Guinea (Poll) born in Catalonia, as well as an artist, as her portraits demonstrate. Another example of this dual belonging is the exhibition's inclusion of successful Spanish Black women, such as Bisila África Bokoko, a multi-award-winning entrepreneur and global speaker working in the United States, and singer Concha Buika, famous for her fusion of jazz and flamenco. This connection is elucidated through the small poems, which aim to further validate each woman. For example, Anguiano dedicates the following words to Concha Buika:

> We are, more or less, the Afro-Spanish role model
> generation. We are healers for ourselves,
> empathy and strength. We represent both
> a people and a stigma. We destroy
> stereotypes with a raised fist.
> Give me your hand
> (Exhibition e-Catalog)[20]

The pronoun "we" indicates that Anguiano believes she and Buika belong to the same community of Afro-descendant women who were born in Spain and faced sociocultural discrimination. These women feel the responsibility of being role models for the next generation and for increasing diversity and inclusion in Spain. However, with this poem, Anguiano also highlights the collective work—"give me your hand"—that is needed by asking for help from other members. Moreover, as the artist is aware that Black women are stigmatized, she underscores the importance of being compassionate, resilient, and supporting each member of this community in order to reinforce their sisterhood.

Anguiano's identity as an Afro-Spaniard differentiates her from other people of African descent, yet, as previously mentioned, it is not homogeneity that is sought here but rather the understanding that despite these differences, she is nonetheless part of the community of Afro-women. Paul Gilroy's notion of a "Black Atlantic culture" underlines the creation of a hybrid cultural-political space due to the slave trade: it is not specifically African, American, Caribbean, or British (4). Here, Anguiano refers to all African descendants, not only those in the Americas, and engages with people from all over the world, given the importance of unity and connection. Nevertheless, such a diasporic connection also implies acknowledging that all African diasporas, however different, share the atrocious historical experience of slavery.[21]

The artist is looking for an unbiased space where she can express herself and be understood by people who share her roots. In the United States, extended families, churches, and organizations have been traditionally safe places for African American women to gather and reflect on the inequalities they experienced (Hill Collins 100). Even in different circumstances, Afro-descendant women in Spain still need a safe space to gather and reflect together. Anguiano has highlighted the importance of having a meeting place, even if only a virtual one, in both the local and international spheres. It is not a coincidence that she has an active presence on the Internet, using Instagram, among other social media, to engage in dialogue with her followers about the experiences of women of African descent and create, indeed, a sorority across borders. It is possible to state that the idea of the Black women's community in this exhibition is transnational and transcultural, for it extends far beyond Spain's national borders to reflect and embrace the diverse realities of Afro-descendants. Furthermore, this group of women is transhistorical due to the linkage of Black women from several historical periods. These three fundamental components—transnational, transcultural, and transhistorical—create the foundation for a shared past and a prospective future, namely a community that does not simply seek to be recognized but to make its presence visible and contribute to social justice.

Projecting a New Image of Black Women

In June 2020, launching an uncomfortable conversation within her online community about Black women's past, Anguiano posted an image of the advertisements related to the sale of two enslaved women that had appeared in the Spanish newspaper *Diario de la Marina* on February 3, 1856:

> A BLACK woman who recently gave birth is for sale. She has plenty of milk, is an excellent laundress and ironer, has basic cooking skills, is young, healthy, and without marks (defects), and is very humble.
> A BLACK woman is for sale because her owner does not need her. She is about 20 years old and from Congo; she has an 11-month-old baby that is healthy and without marks and is very loyal and humble. She had just one master and works regularly as a laundress, ironer, and cook. (@montserratanguiano)[22]

The condition of women slaves in the nineteenth century is central to this example, which demonstrates how descriptive and clear language was used in advertisements to persuade people to buy enslaved Black women. These advertisements reinforced the stereotype of Black mammies, Black women working in white households. The women described in these Spanish newspaper ads were healthy, humble, and good servants who could cook, clean, and iron. This description is certainly a Westernized view of Black women that prevailed in the United States and colonial territories. Indeed, these women played a similar role with the white Spanish families in Equatorial Guinea, as they could, among other tasks, raise children "with plenty of milk," as the description in the *Diario de la Marina* indicates.

Anguiano's choice of these advertisements also points to the importance of history and memory in her artistic production, as she offers new perspectives on Black women leaders of the past and the present. According to Pierre Nora, history and memory are oppositional terms: "History ... as the reconstruction, always problematic and incomplete ... and Memory ...

as a bond tying us to the eternal present" (8). For the artist, memory is central as she questions her Instagram followers about the nineteenth-century advertisements: "Do you have anything to say? I would like to know your opinion. Do you really think that this past is not still a ghost in the collective memory of Spanish society?" (@montserratanguiano).[23] Anguiano not only highlights Black history and its representation but also engages with the concept of memory, which for her means remembering the historical facts and the unequal conditions in which these women lived and then reflecting on their influence on contemporary Spanish society. This is a way to start a conversation within a community that shares history and lived experiences, and to attract and include new people in this virtual global community.

Recent scholarly work on memory and social media (Beer and Jacobsen; Bartoletti) argues that social media does not only begin communication but also creates different kinds of memories, such as individual and collective memory:

> Individual memory is linked to the construction of reality, of a sense of self (autobiographical memory), and of a connection to others, while collective memory is the memory of a concrete group that roots its identity also in its memories of a shared past to which the group ascribes significance, not only giving sense to the present and open to the future ... (qtd. in Bartoletti 85)

Anguiano is at once a facilitator who helps people remember the Black past and an educator who stimulates knowledge and remembering through social media. Her committed artistic work elicits both individual and collective memory. On the one hand, Anguiano attempts to reconstruct the incomplete history of Black women leaders from previous generations because she feels she shares a common history with Afro-descendants across the diaspora, and she proposes readings of that past that have been omitted or incorrectly recounted. On the other hand, living in Spain and being a member of the Afro-Spaniard community, she shares her own memory to reinforce her identity as part of her transnational and transcultural community. Through social media, she inevitably creates a collective memory that is essential in connecting the past with the future.

The exhibition *Referent és nom de Dona* works as a *trait d'union* with *Dona, Mujer, Woman* by continuing to build a transnational, transcultural community, centering, this time, on portraits and abstract paintings.[24] While history and memory remain pivotal, *Referent és nom de Dona* focuses on more contemporary Afro-women leaders (twentieth and twenty-first century) seeking to offer new perspectives to younger generations with role models chronologically closer to them.[25] This exhibition represents eighteen Afro-women icons, beginning with portraits of dancer and singer Josephine Baker (1906–1975) and ending with the American attorney and former first lady Michelle Obama (1964). The portraits include some of the female leaders already depicted in *Dona, Mujer, Woman*, and new ones, such as Rita Bosaho (1965), the Equatorial Guinean-Spanish member of Spain's political party *Podemos*, as well as Lupita Nyong'o (1983), the Kenyan-Mexican actress.

The emphasis on the twentieth and twenty-first centuries highlights the new generation of Afro-women and their commitment in contemporary times. These role models are creating a new history and influencing the future by advocating for the Black women's community. Roberta Bartoletti mentions the importance of supporting a collective memory that "not only giv[es] sense to the present" but also "open[s] to the future" and, in doing so, introduces new role models (86). The shift away from historical time between the first and second exhibitions demonstrates not only the importance of the past but also how the current generation of emerging artists and leaders could inspire future generations.

The title *Referent és nom de Dona* [Role Model Is a Woman's Name] is significant in Anguiano's words, "because the ROLE MODEL is a woman, it is very important to give them visibility. Without them, we are nobody. We don't exist. Her empowerment makes us strong and unique. Her voice recounts episodes of discrimination and anti-racist and feminist struggles" (Exhibition e-Catalog).[26] In line with a feminist approach, the artist does not mention Black male role models. All these female role models provide emotional guidance by inspiring her cultural and social values through their actions or writings. Indeed, they are central to her advocacy for freedom, equality, and community. In addition, they also act as role models for other Afro-women, motivating Anguiano to nurture this transnational and transcultural virtual community that supports each other online.

Moreover, in a society that still hypersexualizes Black women's bodies, the artist paints portraits of African women leaders that emphasize their intellect. The spotlight is not on the body, as in the case of Sara Baartman, or on the media that exoticizes the black body. Instead, the artist paints the human face and associates the women's features with their achievements. For example, when people look at the faces of Michelle Obama or Bisila África Bokoko, they do not think of their bodies but, instead, about their accomplishments.

One peculiar piece in *Referent és nom de Dona* is a triptych (Figure 8.3), a single canvas dedicated to three famous African American women who worked at NASA: Dorothy Vaughan (1910–2008), Katherine Johnson (1918–2020), and Mary Jackson (1921–2005). These "hidden" figures

Figure 8.3 Dones de la Nasa—Triptic [Nasa's women—Triptych]: from left to right, Dorothy Vaughan, Katherine Johnson, and Mary Jackson. Permission granted by the artist.

from the Post World War II Space Race, as the title of the film inspired by these women indicates, served as "human computers," according to the NASA website, since they could quickly perform complex mathematical calculations without the help of machines.[27] The inclusion of these resilient women who excelled in science, technology, engineering, and mathematics (STEM) fields that were predominantly white and male is in line with Anguiano's goal to make visible what has been ignored or not previously valued. The artist navigates different histories in a continuing journey, seeking to illustrate Black women's contributions. In this exhibit, she does not incorporate poems to explain the role models to the audience. Instead, the artist expects the viewer to undertake their own research to discover why these women are important in Black feminist history, creating an inherently active and activist community.

The triptych of Vaughan, Johnson, and Jackson recalls postage stamps and could be interpreted as an invitation to all governments to give more visibility to Black women and their role in the history of their respective countries by representing them on coins and stamps. While in the United States some Black women have already been featured in this way, this is not yet the case in Spain.

In *Referent és nom de Dona*, the background of each painting is filled with brushstrokes in different primary colors, while in the center, the artist outlines a stylized female role model in black. But Anguiano does not use color for the figure, as seen in the triptych. In fact, this space is intentionally left white. In an interview, Anguiano argues that:

> Representing and portraying my women in black and white as a Western symbol and sign and the background in full color, colors that represent

me, which are alive, strong, intense, unique. My imaginary used to understand Africa from those primary tones, and the reminiscence of the continent is clear.[28]

This is the way in which the artist articulates her double identity as a person of African descent and a woman born and raised in a Western country.

The brushstrokes of blue, red, yellow, black, and white that encircle the protagonists make these women bright and visible. In several interviews, Anguiano underlines that she chooses primary colors because of the strength they convey and because they are related to her origins in Equatorial Guinea—she was particularly struck by their prevalence in Equatorial Guinean houses when she traveled there in 2017 (Romaguera). Despite her Spanish family and living her whole life in Barcelona, she is extremely attached to her African roots. The sense of belonging to two or more cultural worlds is crucial here because the use of primary colors gives rise to different emotions within her. For example, in another exhibition in 2023, *Reinas, diosas y ancestras* [Queens, Goddesses, and Ancestors], the colors also have a key function. Anguiano mixes human portraits with abstract painting, devoting more space to the chromatic aspect and reducing the size of the portrait. This is also a way to demonstrate that her exhibitions are meant for everyone, regardless of skin color, and highlight the importance of emotions, regardless of race.

Anguiano's use of color in her paintings acts as a bridge to establish connections that go beyond verbal communication. Indeed, feelings are typically evoked without the need for words. For example, emotions can be communicated through laughter, or other facial expressions, or even through pictograms, such as the most recent use of emojis (Chmiel et al.). In Anguiano's case, it is her use of color that creates emotions by connecting specific shades with her roots. It is not a surprise, then, that her online group of followers is transnational, transcultural, and transhistorical since emotions tie the members together in an "emotional community," according to Barbara H. Rosenwein's definition: "groups in which people adhere to the same norms of emotional expression and value—or devalue—the same or related emotions" (2). A common past allows Black women to share similar values, which Anguiano believes is central to identity. With her art, I argue, Anguiano underlines that core values such as egalitarianism and freedom have been denied in Black history. Studies looking at groups united by emotional connections, such as those of Rosenwein and Victoria Camps, have mostly involved people who meet in local organizations, which is also the case for Anguiano with the Afro presence in Barcelona. However, her use of social media and the Internet extends these relationships beyond the local dimension. It is no coincidence that academic studies about e-communities are increasing and revealing how these communities are extremely important for social relations.[29] In this case, the artist finds a new way to establish connections with other Afro-descendant women worldwide based on sharing Africa as their point of reference.

In *Referent és nom de Dona*, the artist builds temporal and spatial continuity and uses social media as a space that helps to remember, forget, unite, and reflect. There is no doubt that social media is affecting our way of remembering and forgetting (Bartoletti 85–86), as we use it as a mnemotechnic device and as a form of archive (Jacobsen and Beer 1). For example, Facebook creates stories for its users based on the photos they upload. In this regard, I consider Anguiano's paintings to be memory devices that serve to reclaim the history of Black women, replace negative misconceptions with new perspectives, and build a stronger community. "Together we are one" is the slogan of the exhibition *Dona, Mujer, Woman*, emphasizing the importance of this sense of belonging.[30]

Regardless of the choice of technique and the selection of female leaders, both of Anguiano's exhibitions engage in a dialogue by focusing on the importance of the visibility of historical and contemporary Afro-descendant women who have been silenced, such as enslaved African women. Indeed, they do not have a strong presence in national and international history and are often anonymous to the local and global public. Anguiano creates a storyline that helps position African women leaders chronologically and that educates those who are foreign to Black feminist thought. Since her audience may not be familiar with the subjects selected for the exhibitions, either past or present, they create awareness of these women's stories and dismantle stereotypes about Black women. Even though the artist has not experienced female slavery personally, her history is linked to all the Black women who suffered. Her work contributes to the collective memory of the African diaspora. However, Anguiano further aims to link the past with present memories by involving the younger generations. This is a transhistorical perspective where history is a common ground that must be built upon. She contributes to ideologically reinforcing a community that shares a common historical trauma and is transnational, transcultural, and transhistorical. Emotions are a way to bring Black women from around the world together and advocate for equality. The portraits of African leaders and the use of color awaken the emotions of Anguiano's audience. Indeed, in both exhibitions, she creates an emotional historical map by guiding the viewer toward a different understanding of the past, present, and future to establish connections that lead to an awareness of what it means to be an Afro-woman, both as an individual and as part of a community. Furthermore, the use of the Internet is crucial for the artist because sharing her art creates awareness of the contemporary struggle for all Afro-descendants worldwide. This sharing with her community of followers becomes a tool of denunciation to reclaim equality and to gain visibility for every Afro-descendant. Certainly, this online community is a space of reflection that is free of oppression, reframes collective memories, and, in the process, fosters resistance to the established colonial imagery.

Notes

1 The term "Jezebel" means an "immoral woman who deceives people in order to get what she wants" (Cambridge Online Dictionary). It is a racist and sexist stereotype often applied to Black women.
2 All translations from Spanish into English are mine unless stated otherwise. "Mi origen es africano, de Guinea Ecuatorial, pero yo nací en Barcelona. Una doble identidad. No pertenecía ni a mi tierra madre ni a aquí. Con el tiempo entendí que era de las dos, ambas soy yo y me representan. Entonces con la pintura mostraba mis dos orígenes, mis dos casas."
3 For more information about her work, see <U>www.montserratanguiano.com/cv-montserrat-anguiano/.</U>
4 I use the e-Catalogs as my primary source of analysis.
5 Josephine Baker became a naturalized French citizen. In 2021 she became the first Black woman inducted into the Pantheon in Paris. For more information, see Gillett.
6 In *Dona, Mujer, Woman*, for example, she included African American women such as Harriet Tubman (1820–1913), a former escaped slave who helped other enslaved people escape through the Underground Railroad created in the eighteenth century by Black and white abolitionists and supported the struggle for women's rights; Madam C. J. Walker, who became a successful entrepreneur and advocate for women's economic independence, and Rosa Parks (1913–2005), who inspired the Montgomery Bus Boycott and was active in the Civil Rights Movement. The Montgomery Bus Boycott was a protest organized in 1955 by African Americans who protested against segregated bus seats. For more information, see the article "Montgomery Bus Boycott."
7 For more information on colonialist and stereotypical representations of Africa, see Paula Landau ("Empires") and Ruth Mayer. For the colonial imaginary in photographs and documentaries in the specific case of Equatorial Guinea, see Fernández-Fígares Romero de la Cruz and Nerín, among others.
8 *Centre Cívic Sarrià*, *Centre Cívic Convent De Sant Agustí*, and *Centre Cívic Can Basté* in Barcelona in 2022. That same year it was also mounted at the *Centre del Carme de Cultura Contemporànea* (CCCC) in Valencia, among other places. For more information about the exhibition, see https://www.montserratanguiano.com/cv-montserrat-anguiano/.
9 William Dorsey Swann (1858–1925) was an African American activist born in slavery; one of the first drag queens in the world, Swann was arrested for this same reason (see Marjorie). Marsha P. Johnson (1945–1992) was a transgender icon from the United States who became a famous drag queen in New York (see Rothberg). Cacao (1992) is a "joven disidente" (non-conformist young person) from Spain (Exhibition e-Catalog).
10 Given the length requirements for this essay, I am not including the paintings and video art featured in the last part of the e-Catalog.
11 "Tres luchas que confluyen por primera vez en esta exposición pionera en Barcelona, incluyendo mujeres relevantes y personas disidentes a lo largo de la

historia. Vidas que queremos celebrar y recordar para que no caigan en el olvido. Juntas somos una."
12 For further biographical information above these women, see www.womenshistory.org.
13 The original name is Saartjie known as "Sarah" or Sara Baartman. I adopt Sara in this essay to conform with the exhibition's e-Catalog.
14 Anguiano also featured Baartman in a more recent exhibition *Reinas, Diosas, Ancestras* (2023). In this case, Baartman's stylized figure in black and white is surrounded by brushstrokes of different colors, especially red.
15 "Rotunda y eterna, expuesta, deidad/ sodomizada, ojos que hablan, que / dicen que es fertilidad prohibida, fuera / de cánones, diosa como animal, / mujer firme, feminidad casi ilegal."
16 In the e-Catalog there are different versions of *Afrika Floral en primarios* with a background in red, yellow, and blue as well as a piece of video art.
17 Ann Zingha was the last queen in seventeenth-century pre-colonial Angola who fought to resist the Portuguese colonial invasion.
18 "La reina de Matamba, el poder / y la redención, la belleza clásica / y la fuerza infinita, la reina es única / y mi favorita. Negrura y lucha por / una unidad territorial y descanso de / su pueblo. Referente número 1."
19 "Anhela la libertad ya es tuya / y de tus descendientes Fortaleza y / autoridad de palabra. Luchando para los / tuyos, siempre."
20 "Somos la generación afro español de referentes, en mayor o menor medida. Somos curas para nosotras, empatía y fuerza. Representamos un pueblo y un estigma. Rompemos estereotipos con el puño levantado. Dame tu mano."
21 Here I refer to the important historical occurrence of being enslaved. Without assuming any homogeneity in the different slave deportations, I find important to understand the condition in which a human being ceases to be treated as one.
22 "UNA NEGRA se vende, recién parida, con abundante leche, excelente lavandera y planchadora, con principios de cocina, joven, sana y sin tachas (defectos) y muy humilde."
"UNA NEGRA se vende por no necesitarla su dueño, de nación conga, como de 20 años, con su cría de 11 meses, sana y sin tachas, muy fiel y humilde, no ha conocido más amo que el actual, es regular lavandera, planchadora y cocinera."
23 "¿Tenéis algo que decir? Me gustaría saber vuestra opinión. ¿De verdad pensáis que este pasado no sigue como un fantasma en la memoria colectiva de la sociedad española?"
24 *Referent és nom de Dona* was exhibited in different municipal facilities: in the Centre Cívic Drassanes in 2023, in Centre Cívic Sarrià, in the Centre Cívic Sant Martí and in the Espai Francesca Bonnemaison in 2022, and in Arxiu Tobella in 2021, among others.
25 Due to length requirements, I am not analyzing the abstract paintings in the e-Catalog.
26 "Perquè REFERENT, té nom de dona. És molt important donar-los visibilitat. Sense elles, no som. No existim. El seu enpoderament ens fa fortes i úniques. La seva veu relata escenes de discriminació, lluita antiracista i feminista."
27 *Hidden Figures* is a 2016 American movie directed by Theodore Melfi about these three African American scientists.
28 "Representando y retratando a mis mujeres en blanco y negro como símbolo y señal occidental y el fondo a full de color, colores que me representan, vivos, fuertes, intensos, únicos. Mi imaginario entendía a África desde esos tonos primarios, y es clara la reminiscencia al continente."

29 For more information on emotional community and social networks, see Chmiel et al. and Kanavos et al.
30 "Juntas somos una."

Works Cited

Anguiano, Montserrat. *Montserrat Anguiano*. 2023, www.montserratanguiano.com. Accessed 24 May 2023.

———. "Referent És Nom de Dona. Exhibition e-Catalog." *Monterrat Anguiano*, https://www.montserratanguiano.com/wp-content/uploads/2020/04/referentes-nom-de-dona-cataleg-dexposicio-ccsarria-cat.pdf. Accessed 24 May 2023.

———. "Reinas, diosas y ancestras. Exhibition e-Catalog." *Montserrat Anguiano.*

Anguiano, Montserrat, and Antón Rubén. "Dona, Mujer, Woman. Exhibition e-Catalog."

Bartoletti, Roberta. "Memory and Social Media: New Forms of Remembering and Forgetting." *Learning from Memory Body, Memory and Technology in a Globalizing World*, edited by Bianca Maria Pirani. Cambridge Scholars Publisher, 2011, pp. 82–111.

Camps, Victoria. *El gobierno de las emociones*. Herder Editorial, 2011.

Chmiel, Anna, et al. "Collective Emotions Online and Their Influence on Community Life." *PLoS ONE*, vol. 6, no. 7, 2011, p. e22207, https://doi.org/10.1371/journal.pone.0022207. Accessed 24 May 2023.

Fernández-Fígares Romero de la Cruz, María Dolores. *La colonización del imaginario: Imágenes de África*. Universidad de Granada, 2003.

Fox-Amato, Matthew. *Exposing Slavery: Photography, Human Bondage, and the Birth of Modern Visual Politics in America*. Oxford UP, 2019.

"From Hidden to Modern Figures." *NASA*, 12 June 2019, www.nasa.gov/modern-figures. Accessed 24 May 2023.

Gillett, Rachel Anne. "What Josephine Baker's Induction to the French Panthéon Reveals—And Obscures." *The Washington Post*, 2 Dec. 2021, www.washingtonpost.com/outlook/2021/12/03/what-josephine-bakers-induction-panthon-reveals-obscures/. Accessed 24 June 2023.

Gilman, Sander L. "Black Bodies, White Bodies: Toward an Iconography of Female Sexuality in Late Nineteenth-Century Art, Medicine and Literature." *Critical Inquiry*, vol. 12, no. 1, 1985, pp. 204–42.

Gilroy, Paul. *Black Atlantic: Modernity and Double Consciousness*. Harvard UP, 1993.

Hidden Figures. Directed by Theodore Melfi. 20th Century Studios, 2016.

Hill Collins, Patricia. *Black Feminist Thought: Knowledge, Consciousness, and the Politics of Empowerment*. Routledge, 2022.

Jacobsen, Benjamin, and David Beer. *Social Media and the Automatic Production of Memory: Classification, Ranking and the Sorting of the Past*. Bristol UP, 2021.

"Jezebel." *Cambridge Online Dictionary*. jezebel. Accessed 3 Oct. 2023, https://dictionary.cambridge.org/us/dictionary/english/jezebel

Kanavos, Andreas, et al. "Emotional Community Detection in Social Networks." *Computers & Electrical Engineering*, 4 Oct. 2017, www.sciencedirect.com/science/article/pii/S0045790617328975. Accessed 22 June 2023.

Landau, Paul S. "Empires of the Visual: Photography and Colonial Administration in Africa." *Images and Empires: Visuality in Colonial and Postcolonial Africa*, edited by Paul Landau and Deborah Kaspin. U of California P, 2002, pp. 141–71.

———. "Introduction. An Amazing Distance: Pictures and People in Africa." *Images and Empires: Visuality in Colonial and Postcolonial Africa*, edited by Paul Landau and Deborah Kaspin. U of California P, 2002, pp. 1–40.

Licata, Stefania. "Imaginario colonial y radionovela: El caso de *Se abren las nubes* y de la Guinea Española." *InVerbis, Lingue Letterature Culture*, vol. 21, no. 1, 2021, pp. 27–40.

Marjorie, Morgan. "From Slavery to Voguing: The House of Swann." *National Museums Liverpool*, www.liverpoolmuseums.org.uk/stories/slavery-voguing-house-of-swann. Accessed 22 June 2023.

Mayer, Ruth. *Artificial Africas: Colonial Images in the Times of Globalization*. U of New England P, 2002.

"Montgomery Bus Boycott—Facts, Significance & Rosa Parks." *History.com*, www.history.com/topics/black-history/montgomery-bus-boycott. Accessed 24 June 2023.

@montserratanguiano. "VENTA DE ESCLAVOS en la prensa española del s. XIX. Hace poco más de un siglo se vendían africanos en España y sus colonias ..." *Instagram*, 18 June 2020, https://www.instagram.com/p/CBkUb6qqI0s/.

Nerín, Gustau. "Imaginar África: Los estereotipos occidentales sobre África y los africanos." *Nuestro sur. La imagen de Guinea Ecuatorial y de los guineanos en las literaturas española y catalana*, edited by Antoni Castel and José Carlos Sendín Gutierrez. Los libros de la Catarata, 2010, pp. 107–28.

Nora, Pierre. "Between Memory and History: Les Lieux de Mémoire." *Representations*, vol. 26, 1989, pp. 7–24, https://doi.org/10.2307/2928520. Accessed 24 May 2023.

Poll, Helena. "Montserrat Anguiano. Artivismo como modus operandi." *Metal Magazine*, www.metalmagazine.eu/es/post/interview/montserrat-anguiano. Accessed 22 June 2023.

Romaguera, Àlex. "Montserrat Anguiano: 'A través del arte podemos descolonizar nuestras mentes.'" *Público*, 6 June 2022, www.publico.es/culturas/entrevista-montserrat-anguiano-arte-descolonizar-mentes.html. Accessed 24 May 2023.

Rosenwein, Barbara H. *Emotional Communities in the Early Middle Ages*. Cornell UP, 2007.

Rothberg, Emma. "Marsha P. Johnson." *National Women's History Museum*, www.womenshistory.org/education-resources/biographies/marsha-p-johnson. Accessed 24 June 2023.

"Sarah Baartman (1789–1815)." *Royal Collection Trust*, www.rct.uk/collection/661166/sarah-baartman-1789-1815. Accessed 26 June 2023.

Stanley, Henry Morton. *In Darkest Africa*. Charles Scribner's Sons, 1890.

———. *Through the Dark Continent*. Grädener, 1878.

Thiong'o, Ngũgĩ wa. *Decolonising the Mind: The Politics of Language in African Literature*. East African Educational Publishers, 1994.

9 From Below and from Within
Urban Peripheries in Lucía Mbomío's *Barrionalismos*

Rosalía Cornejo-Parriego

"Have you found your place?" "Alcorcón!" That was Lucía Mbomío's categorical response to a student's question in the fall of 2020, when the writer graciously accepted to virtually visit my seminar "Global and Local: The Latest Narratives from Spain." We had read her novel *Hija del camino* (2019), following Sara, the protagonist, on her extensive travels, always attempting to find her place in the world. Like the writer, Sara is the daughter of a Spanish woman and a man from Equatorial Guinea whose life experiences alternate between the United Kingdom, France, Portugal, Equatorial Guinea, and the *barrio* of Alcorcón in Madrid.[1] My student's question was, therefore, extremely pertinent. Facing, like other minorities, constant suspicion about whether she is *truly* a Spaniard due to her skin color, which makes her a foreigner in her own country, when Lucía Asué Mbomío Rubio claims a *barrio* in Madrid as her own space of belonging, she is unequivocally affirming her identity as a Spanish woman while simultaneously signaling the urgency of redefining national and European identity.[2] At the same time, her reply suggests the need to replace the language of nationality with that of locality, as the writer Taiye Selasi proposed in a 2014 TED Talk significantly titled "Don't Ask Me Where I Am From, Ask Me Where I Am a Local." Underlying this issue, both Selasi and Mbomío's words reflect the paradoxical conjunction of the global and the local when talking about belonging, or, to put it differently, how the local can be profoundly global and diasporic. This is evident in Mbomío's *Barrionalismos*, a column focusing on Alcorcón—with brief references to other Madrid barrios (e.g. Fuenlabrada, Móstoles)—that appeared in Spain's leading national newspaper *El País* from 2018 to 2020.

Barrionalismos, as this essay will demonstrate, shares many features and parallels with other journalistic and creative texts by Mbomío: the preservation of collective memory, the urgency of self-representation, the blend of global and local, and the focus on diasporic communities. Furthermore, her defense of—both material and symbolic—peripheries always leads to a fundamental question: How do we represent the margins? In a series of articles, Mbomío confronts the traditional hegemonic gaze—external and from above—on the *barrio*, depicting instead urban peripheries as heterogeneous spaces where *vecinos* remember, exercise their agency, and defy stereotypes. Moreover, she explores how, in the context of the global health crisis (COVID-19), *barrios* face additional discursive challenges.

There is no doubt that, as a reporter, author, and activist, Mbomío has become an outspoken voice for racialized Spaniards. Through her novel *Hija del camino*, her collection of stories *Las que se atrevieron* (2017), and numerous contributions to the press and to digital communities created around sites like *Conciencia Afro*, *Afroféminas*, *Negrxs*, *Ctxt*, and *Pikara Magazine*, to name a few, she has reflected on border identities, migration, the legacies of colonialism, and Spain's Afro-amnesia.[3] That is, she has addressed global issues pertaining to what she calls the "nación de la afro-descendencia" [nation of Afro-descendance], a nation without borders, which she fiercely claims as her own (*Hija* 191). Furthermore, she has tirelessly advocated in favor of constructing a non-colonialist archive and library and promoted diversity and ethical reporting in the media to counter stereotypical or dehumanizing representations of Black Spaniards as well as of minorities in general. She has stressed the importance of role models and the need to revise school curricula to include Spain's colonial history in Africa. Her numerous interviews not only of writers and artists but also of ordinary people from all sectors of society illustrate her efforts to promote the visibility of Afro-descendants (Angone 2). At the same time, she has unequivocally expressed the exhaustion that this constant pedagogical effort entails ("Por qué necesitamos"). Echoing Reni Eddo-Lodges's *Why I'm No Longer Talking to White People about Race*, Mbomío writes in her article "Pedagogía estéril" [Fruitless Pedagogy] about the debilitating effects of having to constantly explain racism and even Black existence to non-racialized people. Considering the limited results of this *pedagogía*, not to mention the frustrations involved, she calls on her fellow Afro-descendants to shift the focus in order to avoid wasting any more valuable time. In "Narrarse a sí misma" [Narrating Oneself], she invites them to start looking inward and turn toward the hidden stories and the already existing rich Spanish "circuit of Black cultural production."[4] Highlighting self-representation as an empowering tool, Mbomío is, in fact, agreeing with Stuart Hall's assertion: "I do not think the margins could speak up without first grounding themselves somewhere" ("The Local" 36).

Considering this global Afro-diasporic dimension of her writing and her activism, her focus in *Barrionalismos* might surprise her readers. Indeed, the shift away from international settings to one that is as local as it can get seems, at first, quite radical. As Mbomío herself acknowledges, her numerous writings on race confirm what Amin Maalouf explains in *In the Name of Identity: Violence and the Need to Belong*, namely that people tend to relate most strongly to the element of their identity that they feel is under attack.⁵ Nevertheless, the author of *Hija del camino* is fully aware of her multiple belongings; *Barrionalismos* reflects her decision to tackle another dimension of herself without ignoring her Blackness. Her purpose is, therefore, to talk about a space of belonging—the *barrio*—from her perspective as a Spaniard of dual ancestry: "I am speaking here about *barrios*, because I decided not to confine myself within my skin but to speak from it. And that is what I am going to do" ("No es").

Rituals, Memory, and Resistance

"Barrionalismo" has become a concept used in popular culture—we might recall the hip-hop duo Los Chikos del Maíz and their song "Barrionalistas" (2019) as well as the subject of scholarly inquiry. In line with Selasi's confrontation of nationality and locality, Luis de la Cruz Salanova defines *barrionalismo* in relation to Benedict Anderson's notion of nationalism. While the latter is the expression of an imagined community, *barrionalismo* denotes, for de la Cruz, the expression of a real one that is anchored in an individual's daily life and interactions on a local scale (26). Stoyanka Eneva underlines the potential of this notion, which "represents the neighborhood from the perspective of the lived experience, the common characteristics of its inhabitants and the possibilities of collective organisation" (221). However, Eneva insists on the importance of connecting Racial and Urban Studies to properly understand the complexity of contemporary "racial urbanities" (214). Although acknowledging the neighborhood as a "territory of possibilities to build identity, belonging and anti-racist political demands," she cautions against its idealization because, despite their feelings of attachment and mutual support, migrants and racialized Spaniards can still be marginalized (221–22).⁶ Interestingly, Eneva points to Mbomío and Chenta Tsai's columns as examples of racialized perspectives on urban spaces, calling them "new voices in the research of racialization and territorial roots" (221).⁷

Mbomío, herself a product of both national and international migration, clearly considers her *barrio* to be a space of belonging:

> For many children of migrants (Segovia and Niefang-Equatorial Guinea, in my case), the *barrio* is the only space of recognition, the place in which we do feel and, importantly, they feel we are one of their own, the place we call home, where we have a name, face and history. ("Volver")⁸

Nevertheless, she does not view it as a utopian space—"not everything is beautiful ...We know its limits," she admits ("Volver")—but as one that has faced and continues to face significant challenges, primarily due to class and racial discrimination.⁹ For Selasi, locality entails three basic components, which she calls the three Rs: rituals, relationships, and restrictions. She elaborates on the third one in the following manner:

> We're local where we carry out our rituals and relationships, but how we experience our locality depends in part on our restrictions. By restrictions, I mean, where are you able to live? What passport do you hold? Are you restricted by, say, racism, from feeling fully at home where you live?

In her column in *El País*, Mbomío incorporates all three elements because, as she proudly proclaims in her *pregón* during Alcorcón's 2019 festivities, *Barrionalismos* is at once a declaration of love and an exercise of justice.[10]

Displaying a great sense of humor, many of Mbomío's pieces adhere to the traditional *costumbrista* genre.[11] She presents social types, trades ("Horas muertas"; "Pues ya hemos votado"; "El ciclo"), small businesses ("Ya no están"), and typical cultural products that range from dances ("La jota") to pastries ("Las empanadillas"). She describes customs and rituals ("De pipas"; "Las peñas"; "A pie"; "El rey"; "Parques"), which not only call to mind the traditional *artículos de costumbres* but also Selasi's first element of locality.[12] She confronts past and present in pieces such as "Ah, cómo hemos cambiado" [How Much We Have Changed], where she proudly reminisces about Alcorcón's *Cabalgatas de Reyes*, which, unlike in most Spanish locations, never featured King Balthasar in blackface, still an important subject of contention in the country.[13] She writes about resilience in the face of death and loss and the role of female solidarity and care. In a tribute to older women who have lost their life partners, she describes how in their new phase of life they turn to their *vecinas*, who, while having been there all along, now provide additional support and "change their name to friends" ("Juntas").[14]

In addition, Mbomío acknowledges other peripheries within the *barrio*, or the existence of peripheries within the periphery. Such is the case of a couple who migrated from Extremadura to Alcorcón, where they tried to maintain the culture of their marginalized and impoverished region, while also fighting for the interests of their new home. For Mbomío, the 40th anniversary of the *Agrupación Extremeña de Alcorcón* is a reason to celebrate ("Primer apellido"). Furthermore, she remembers the effects of Spain's twentieth-century history on its citizens, particularly on members of the LGBTQ+ community, as Alberto's story in "No desandar el camino" [No Retracing of Steps] illustrates. The protagonist, a victim of Franco's regime and the *Ley de Vagos y Maleantes* [Law on Vagrants and Criminals], which was amended in 1954 to add the criminalization of homosexuality, spent the dictatorship in and out of prison due to his sexual orientation. Mbomío ends her article with a categorical statement—"Not one step back"—recognizing the hard-fought battles and the painful road traveled in search of equality and dignity.[15]

Many of the *Barrionalismos* pieces are based on interviews that allow Mbomío to name her neighbors, explain their backgrounds, and provide details about their lives.[16] She often includes photographs of her interviewees. Putting names and faces to the community's challenges and successes constitutes an effective tool to reach a broader audience and have a greater impact. It becomes evident that for *Barrionalismos* to truly become a repository of intergenerational collective memory, *costumbrismo* is insufficient: the writer must move beyond the *costumbrista* practice of depicting types to embrace the individuality of her subjects and focus on the relationships that define the *barrio*, and, for Selasi, locality. In the author's words, "You love your *barrio* (village, locality) with your gut and your heart, not because of its beauty but because it is where your memories, your childhood friends and your neighbors, who are family, reside" ("Volver").[17]

Moreover, statements such as the one that concludes the article "No desandar el camino" warn against historical amnesia and corroborate that Mbomío envisions her section not merely as a space for the nostalgic remembrance of an idealized *barrio* but rather as an instrument for advocacy and activism. Her articles depict Alcorcón's "micro-spaces of resistance" (Eneva 222), while simultaneously becoming ones themselves. According to the writer, *barrionalismo* is "to denounce when there is an injustice and to support people around you, as if they were your own. In a way, they are" ("Maldita carta").[18] She demands, therefore, urgent action in response to the proliferation of gambling houses, since, as current research confirms, gambling has become a silent epidemic, particularly in low-income neighborhoods ("Mercerías 1—Casa de apuestas 0").[19] In "El juego también es una droga" [Gambling Is Also a Drug], Mbomío condemns gambling advertisements on television and the opening of new premises near schools. Recalling the wave of drug abuse that ravaged some *barrios* during her youth, she exposes the severity of the problem and its devastating effects, which are spurring local initiatives to combat this addiction ("El juego"). She looks at other systemic problems, such as gender-based violence and the community's efforts to memorialize the victims ("Un banco") as well as the lack of accessible spaces for those with limited mobility ("Sin anclas"; "El barrio"; "Maldita carta"). After listening to local residents, she shares with readers their struggles and, using a specific example, her neighbor César's understanding of disability as the result of an Othering process: "it's not that people in wheelchairs are disabled, rather society disables them" ("Cerrando").[20] For Mbomío, César's perspective applies just as well to the representation of other marginal or peripheral groups—including the *barrios*—and explains her own preference for the term *periferizar* [peripherize], a neologism that she believes better defines the discursive construction of urban (or any) margins ("Pregón").

Prejudices and Pride: The Urgency of Self-representation

Graphically comparing it to being "outed," Mbomío describes her own discovery of the *barrio* as a space of Otherness populated with "picturesque" inhabitants who are part of an "us versus them" dichotomy constructed through a series of fixed images (Hall, "The Spectacle" 257–59):

> Leaving the periphery helped me become aware of how we were perceived outside. All of a sudden, Alcorcón was no longer "here" but "there" and, even, "beyond." It was as if they had outed me from the closet of the neighborhoodness, where I was feeling great, and attached a lot of labels to me. ("Cuando salí")[21]

Indeed, she learns that *periferizar* implies associating *barrios*, among other qualifiers, with ridicule and bad taste—demonstrating the connection between the judgment of taste and social origin analyzed in Pierre Bourdieu's *Distinction*—as well as criminal activity and disease. Her eloquent summary—"*Choni* customs, murders, fights, plagues of galeruca or rats, fires, various misfortunes and, of course, diseases" ("Miedo")—captures Alcorcón's limited and stereotyped presence in the news media.[22] It is, in fact, mainly circumscribed, she adds, to instances such as the 2014 Ebola case, which ignited a wave of collective psychosis and led to the controversial sacrifice of the dog Excalibur to avoid potential transmission (Silió, Barroso, and Lillo; Minder and Belluck), and, at the time of *Barrionalismos*'s publication, the global COVID-19 pandemic ("Miedo"). Diseases determine, thus, to a great extent, the alarmist or suspicious visibility of *barrios* in the media, as we shall further explore in the next section.

In his study of the discursive construction of Madrid's urban spaces since the early nineteenth century, de la Cruz Salanova considers sensationalist and ethnographic journalism as partially responsible for the pejorative image of the *barrios* and their working-class or lower-middle-class *vecinos*. This image, he adds, has been imposed "from above, halfway between moral recrimination ... and exotic fascination" (71).[23] Mbomío unequivocally rejects this earlier approach and firmly defends the voice of the insider, proposing to "talk not only about the *barrio*, but fundamentally from the *barrio*" ("¡Hasta la próxima!").[24] Indeed, *Barrionalismos* is written from within and from below, and the plural of the title already underscores its purpose of affirming the diversity that challenges the stereotypes about the urban margins ("No somos"). In this vein, Mbomío applauds the community-generated reporting of "alcorconófilos" ("Las Musas"; "El 'Alcorconófilo'") and initiatives such as those of "Carabancheleando," a group that combines activism and research about the peripheries and encourages residents to be creators of their own narratives ("Somos jóvenes").[25] In addition, following in the footsteps of other marginalized groups, she proudly reclaims precisely those characteristics that outsiders have used to stigmatize them and which the *vecinos* themselves have often internalized ("¡¿Vives?!"; "Croissants").[26] Consequently, for Mbomío, the ridiculed language—the *barrionalero*, a product of the *barrio*'s impressive "fábricas de neologismos" [neologism factories]—and the scorned aesthetics and fashion choices constitute an expression of creativity and signs of identity ("Yo me entiendo"; "Ni choni").[27] Moreover, she confronts the "exotic fascination" that might have originated with a certain type of journalism but that has been reinforced more recently through tourism and commodification. Like Chikos del Maíz, who in their song "Barrionalistas" forcefully decry the tourists and the condescending gazes that turn neighborhoods into a circus in "No somos una moda" [We Are Not a Trend] Mbomío questions the fleeting appropriation of clothing styles and the *fashionable* co-optation of the *barrios* as video settings. This commodification ignores, nevertheless, institutional neglect and, once these *barrios* are no longer in vogue, will condemn them again to oblivion and prejudice: "when the trend is over, you will no longer be fashionable ... they [specific locations] will no longer be cool and will return to invisibility or, worse, will be designated as vulgar."[28]

The dominant depiction of the outskirts also leads the author to a general reflection on the ethics of representing marginalized people in the media, a topic she has frequently tackled in different venues. She warns of the dangers of converting people's lives and customs into folklore and confusing "reportajes de denuncia" [social justice journalism] with abject exercises of *pornomiseria* [poverty porn] that do not explore the reasons for social exclusion and precariousness ("Sin miedo"). In Mbomío's words, in this type of reporting, "we splurge on the what without the why, contributing to the fattening and polishing of stereotypes" ("Sin miedo").[29] She invites reporters, including herself, to exercise self-criticism, to ponder how to responsibly convey these stories, and to listen to people's accounts of their own experiences ("Sin miedo"). Moreover, if journalists contributed to the creation of the negative and stereotypical perception of the *barrios*, as de la Cruz Salanova contends, the urgency of creating a new type of journalism that generates alternative narratives, helps resignify urban spaces, and defies the dangerous "single story"—to recall Nigerian author Chimamanda Ngozi Adichie—becomes evident.[30]

"Little Roman Salutes": Writing the *Barrio* in COVID-19 Times

As previously mentioned, diseases determine to a great extent the visibility and profile of the *barrios* in the media. This connection between urban spaces and clinical discourse is not new, as Michel Foucault argues in *L'archéologie du savoir* (68–74). Moreover, the creation of a sociomedical topography is also significantly coupled with the community's morality (Cruz Salanova 67). In the case of early nineteenth-century Madrid, de la Cruz Salanova refers to the design of maps where the city's infection sites were directly correlated to the moral standing of its residents. The same can be said about the official discourse on Spain's postwar *extrarradios* [outskirts], which Carmen Martín Gaite poignantly examines in *Usos amorosos de la posguerra española*. Their abject poverty did not merit any kind of compassion or institutional intervention. On the contrary, the outskirts were demonized as clinically, morally, and politically infectious foci (93–96).[31]

Considering the recurrent clinical view of the *barrios* and their association with disease, it is particularly noteworthy that Mbomío writes part of *Barrionalismos* exactly at the height of the COVID-19 pandemic. In addition to chronicling daily life under very unusual circumstances (e.g., meetings in the park with her parents ["Odio"]), she uses her texts to support small businesses ("A cubierto") and report on solidarity initiatives that set aside ideological differences to unite neighbors during the most critical moments ("La gente bonita"; "Arrimar"). However, she is equally aware of the looming threats, particularly the exacerbation of the far-right discourse and fascist revival that the global health crisis sparked, manifested in the case of Spain by the reappearance of Francoist flags and gestures: "a climate of discord, with pre-constitutional flags, insults or 'little Roman salutes'" ("Esto no").[32] This is far from being a simple coincidence.

The traditional clinical discourse about the *barrios*, which was primarily class-driven, has been reinforced by the arrival of migrants from the Global South or less wealthy Eastern European nations who find a new home on the outskirts. Indeed, the pathologizing (and criminalization) of migrants constitutes a constant tenet of xenophobic propaganda worldwide. The depiction of migrants as carriers of diseases and contaminating bodies has prevailed throughout history, as Susan Sontag reminds us (150). Establishing an undisputable link "between imagining disease and imagining foreignness" (136), Sontag states in her ground-breaking *AIDS and Its Metaphors* that "The fact that illness is associated with the poor—who are, from the perspective of the privileged, aliens in one's midst—reinforces the association of illness with the foreign: with an exotic, often primitive place" (139). In this vein, AIDS was perceived as "another infestation from the so-called Third World" (139–40) and blamed on "despised and feared minorities" (142). While several decades separate the AIDS epidemic that devastated communities in the 1980s and 1990s from the COVID-19 pandemic, the parallelism is evident. As numerous reports have shown, as the virus spread, so did racism ("El COVID-19") or, to paraphrase the editors of *COVID-19 and Racism*, a collision of two pandemics took place, namely, COVID-19 and racism (Lander et al. 2). A rhetoric of blaming and shaming certain racial and ethnic groups (2) as well as disenfranchised communities spread globally, and Spain was no exception (D. Domínguez).[33]

When Mbomío refers to the "little Roman salutes," it is not hard to guess that she has in mind Spain's far-right party, Vox, and a number of populist politicians who have not only exhibited a Francoist nostalgia but also shamelessly manipulated information to heighten social anxiety by demonizing immigrants.[34] It should not come as a surprise then that the pandemic provided them with invaluable material for xenophobic propaganda, because, as Sontag observes, "Authoritarian political ideologies have a vested interest in promoting fear, a sense of the imminence of takeover by aliens—and real diseases are useful material..." (149–50). In "Los del Sur" [The Southerners] Mbomío exposes the hypocritical accusations levelled at immigrants (not tourists) for their alleged responsibility for the transmission of COVID-19:

> Let's not forget that the narrative of some political parties involves considering migrant people responsible for the transmission of COVID-19, for stealing jobs and, interestingly, at the same time, for not working, but still receiving financial assistance. Those same voices have celebrated the arrival of tourists as if they were immune to a virus that has clearly shown that it doesn't care about flags and borders.[35]

Further depicting the political climate, Mbomío mentions Isabel Díaz Ayuso, the president of the *Comunidad de Madrid* and a member of the right-wing *Partido Popular*, who blamed the spread of COVID-19 "on the way of life of our immigration in Madrid and the population density" ("Los del Sur").[36] For Mbomío, Díaz Ayuso is opportunistically pointing fingers while failing to explain the reasons for the higher COVID-19 rates in less privileged urban areas, such as jobs that do not allow remote work and require public transportation for the daily commute.[37] Pinning the responsibility on racialized communities—broadly and incorrectly labeled as immigrants, since this disregards the existence of Spanish citizens of color—only serves to bolster the existing discrimination towards people and places (Mbomío, "Los del Sur"). Sontag's assertion that "diseases acquire meanings ... and inflict stigma" (183) is painfully clear in Díaz

Ayuso's words: highlighting the "different way of life" conveys the subliminal message that "our immigration" is not really *us* and these outsiders are contaminating the *general population*, meaning *us*. Furthermore, in line with Sontag's explanation, emphasizing the blame attached to migrants and not to tourists—graphically expressed through the "champagne for tourists/barricades for migrants" opposition ("Menudo verano")—Mbomío demonstrates the intersection of foreignness and poverty, or the combination of racism and aporophobia.

The title *Los del Sur* proves, then, very apt. Located south of the center (Madrid), Alcorcón and other *barrios* have become the destination for individuals from Spain's impoverished southern (and central) regions and, more recently, newcomers from the Global South.[38] Nevertheless, the material reality of the South cannot escape its metaphorical and symbolic value in hegemonic discourse. Mbomío lucidly concludes that the racialized blaming that spread during the global health crisis has been deliberately fostered to unnecessarily remind geographical and metaphorical Southerners of their (marginal) place within the nation, or as Selasi would put it, their restrictions. To which Mbomío can only sarcastically add, "As if we didn't know" ("Los del Sur").[39]

As I was writing this essay, Spain's general elections of July 23, 2023, had recently been held, and the danger of a governing national coalition between the right-wing *Partido Popular* (PP) and the far-right Vox had seemingly been averted. Vox suffered a major defeat, losing nineteen seats and, consequently, much political agency and leverage at the national level. However, it remains troubling that on election day, at Vox's headquarters, while awaiting the results, supporters listened to recorded speeches by leader Santiago Abascal that included statements such as the following: "Yes to the traditional *barrios*, no to multicultural ghettos! Yes to the civilization of the cross and no to Islamic violence!" (I. Domínguez).[40] These xenophobic, Islamophobic, and racist outbursts that explicitly target racial and cultural diversity prove that Abascal ignores, or chooses to ignore, that the *barrios* have always been a destination for migrants and are, therefore, inherently fluid and heterogeneous. Defined by class, these urban spaces contrast sharply with those that occupy both the literal and, above all, the symbolic center of Madrid, and which might be the "barrios de siempre" [all-time *barrios*] to which Abascal is referring. Indeed, Madrid's Barrio de Salamanca, for example, home to the *Milla de oro* [Golden Mile], with the highest concentration of luxury retailers and where some of Spain's largest fortunes converge, offers an unmistakable contrast with the outskirts. Unlike the collective hybridity and openness of the peripheries, the social and economic inbreeding of this wealthy district perpetuates the homogeneous identity of hegemonic groups.[41] Furthermore, Abascal's perception of these "multicultural ghettos" recalls the spatial segregation in European cities that Fatima El-Tayeb analyzes in connection with French *banlieues*. Referring to the "borders running through urban centers" that create segregated spaces, she declares: "Containing superfluous populations, they became foreign territory, an enclave of the non-West, finally invading Europe itself" (662).

Mbomío's writings clearly contradict Abascal's essentialist understanding of the *barrios* as static entities and as violent hubs that threaten "the civilization of the cross." Reflecting on the diverse regional origins of her high school classmates in the late 1980s, evident, among other things, in their range of accents and culinary traditions, the narrator of *Hija del camino* notes: "The rings encircling the big cities have always been enclaves of arrival and places where a fluid identity, which adapts and is very open, is created. Now it is also Latina, Romanian, Ukrainian, Nigerian or Equatorial Guinean."[42] *Barrionalismos* captures this hybridity and diasporic nature by including *vecinos* who might not have been born in Spain but who affirm their belonging to the *barrio*, and whose lives negate stereotypes applied to the outskirts and migrants. A good example is Congolese athlete Nayanesh Ayman Parikh Bumba, who stayed and decided to give back to the community by opening a gym, offering women free self-defense lessons—a tribute to his mother, a victim of domestic violence—and allowing high school students to join if they were performing well academically ("La lealtad"). Another example is Ethiopian Yeshi Beyene Hagos, who opened her beauty salon decades ago in Fuenlabrada, catering to a racially diverse clientele, yet has maintained her roots and established AYME, an NGO, to support women in childbirth in her native country ("Fuentiopía"). While the stories of Nayanesh and Yeshi are meant to dispel prejudices, ironically, the existence and persistence of stereotypes can sometimes lead to unexpected consequences. In "Escuela y barrio," Mbomío introduces the Cervantes school, habitually branded as "a ghetto school" due to its ethnic diversity and which, owing precisely to this reputation, benefits from low enrolment, an exceptional student-teacher ratio, and excellent programs that have resulted in students' happiness and success. The author ends her article firmly defending the liberation from confining labels: "Labels, both on people and on clothes, it's best to remove them because they are annoying and almost never of any use" ("Escuela").[43]

Finally, in her extensive journeying through Alcorcón, Mbomío finds the perfect symbol for her *barrio* in a unique gathering place—a barbershop:

> Latin music and rap blast in the barbershop and the television shows the corresponding videoclips while five professionals work non-stop. They are from Italy, Ecuador, Colombia, Dominican Republic and Madrid, each from a corner of the planet and perhaps it's due to the melody that one hears, but watching them work resembles a choreography. All of them know their next step and they execute it masterfully. That is why the place is full of clients and people who are waiting, all skin colors,

all ages, all creeds and all places. Yesterday's Alcorcón was built with bodies that came from the South and center of the Peninsula, now it is fortified with those that arrive from the South of the South, the East and also the other side of the Atlantic. This is Alcorcón. ("Barrio")[44]

Depicted in an article graphically titled "Barrio con flow," this barbershop represents an inclusive and intercultural space that welcomes multiple diasporas and personal stories. What clearly stands out for the author is the perfectly executed choreography that epitomizes her *barrio* as a harmonious, *flowing*, and open territory of local belonging.[45] Undoubtedly, this choreography represents a challenge to the discourse of fear and anxiety regarding urban peripheries, migrants, and racialized Spaniards.

In the opening statements of this essay, we underscored the parallelisms between *Barrionalismos* and Mbomío's other journalistic and creative texts, such as her emphasis on collective memory and self-representation and her focus on marginalized and diasporic communities. We also began by referring to Sara, the protagonist of *Hija del camino*, and her search for a place of her own, which proves quite an elusive objective, as her multiple unfulfilling destinations suggest. In this regard, critics have noted that the novel expresses the futility of trying to fit into a society that has previously defined you (Angone 4) and that it conceptualizes diasporic identity as deterritorialized (Cucarella Ramón 26). In our study of *Barrionalismos*, the similarities are evident, but equally apparent is a significant difference between *Hija del camino* and the pieces in *El País*. Indeed, while the narrative can accurately be read as a story of "non-belonging" and deterritorialization, *Barrionalismos*, on the contrary, constitutes a chronicle of belonging and an unequivocal affirmation of locality and territorial roots. For Mbomío, her chronicle is above all—and with a great sense of humor—a tribute to Alcorcón, her "pequeña 'matria'" [little motherland] ("Hasta la próxima").[46] She speaks as a racialized insider firmly grounded in a very precise local identity that does not deny her diasporic belonging. She claims the history, the spaces, the rituals, and the people of the *barrio* as her own and advocates for them. Moreover, the diverse personal accounts in *Barrionalismos* illustrate her profound desire to provide alternative narratives and perspectives from within in order to neutralize the dominant stereotypical and one-dimensional discourse about the *barrios*. In her crusade to resignify urban peripheries, Mbomío uses a leading national newspaper as a platform to create a counterdiscourse that exposes some of the mechanisms and strategies traditionally adopted to *periferizar*, and which are dangerously being recycled and revitalized in Spain today. In times of a global health crisis and political involution, the need for this counterdiscourse is more urgent than ever.

Notes

1 Translating *barrio* into English is difficult. It should not be translated as suburbs. Although often situated in the outskirts, its social composition and dynamics are very different from a North American suburb, and "ser de barrio" (being from the barrio) is generally associated with lower income and specific characteristics, as we shall see. I will, therefore, maintain the Spanish word in most cases. I am also aware that *barrio* and geographical periphery are not exactly the same (Cruz Salanova 16). Examples are Chueca and Lavapiés, *barrios* in Madrid that are not located on the outskirts, but that are home to low-income populations and more recently immigrants. Gentrification is another (global) phenomenon that these *barrios* are experiencing. I will also often use *vecinos* instead of neighbors to better convey its connotations in the context of the *barrios*.

2 This is not an exclusive Spanish phenomenon. As Fatima El-Tayeb explains, "the majority of people of color currently living in Europe are officially and unofficially defined as being part of a 'migrant population,' even when they were born there" (660).

3 For Dorothy Odartey-Wellington, the digital world is becoming ever more important for Afro-Hispanic diasporas (3). See also Borst and Gallo González.

4 "circuito de producción cultural negro." All translations are mine.

5 This is very evident in the novel *Hija del camino*. As the narrator explains, while in Spain she has to primarily defend her racial identity, while in Equatorial Guinea, it is her female identity (304).

6 This is evident in *Barrionalismos*, where Mbomío recalls episodes such as the assassination in 2002 of Ndombele Augusto Domínguez in Alcorcón ("No es una entelequia"), confirming that their *barrio* is not always safe for immigrants and racialized Spaniards.

7 Chenta Tsai's column "Otres" also appeared in *El País* (2018–2020) and illustrates "the intersection between racialisation and sexual dissidence in Madrid" (Eneva 222).

8 "Para muchos hijos de migrantes (Segovia y Niefang—Guinea Ecuatorial, en mi caso), el barrio es el único espacio de reconocimiento, el sitio en el que sí nos sentimos e, importante, nos sienten como propios, al que denominamos casa, en el que tenemos nombre, rostro e historia."

9 "no todo es hermoso. … Sabemos dónde están sus límites."

10 I am grateful to the author for a private exchange (WhatsApp and Instagram) on July 5, 2023 in which, among other things, she expressed how much it meant to her to have been selected as one of the *pregoneros* [opening speakers] for the 2019 Alcorcón festivities. Her *pregón* [opening speech] included many of the ideas captured in her column, in addition to a shoutout to all the people she had interviewed.

11 For an illustration of her humorous writings, see for example: "Eres más de barrio que…" or "Solo nos queda reírnos." She also mentions two humorous and satirical Twitter accounts @Hardcorcon and @alcorcontoday ("Eres más"). The latter one follows in the footsteps of *El Mundo Today*. In "Ratas" she refers to @Hardcorcon as their own "tuitstar."

12 *Costumbrismo* is a genre generally associated with the nineteenth-century literature and press and, in the case of Spain, with authors such as Mesonero Romanos and Estébanez Calderón and their picturesque depictions of social types and customs in Madrid and Andalucía. However, as Mey-Yen Moriuchi

explains in her *Mexican Costumbrismo*, it is a far-reaching genre with transnational appeal as her analysis of *casta* paintings demonstrates.
13 On January 5 Spain celebrates the arrival of the Three Wise Men or Three Magi bearing gifts with big parades (*Cabalgata de Reyes*) all over the country. The names of the Magi, popular among Spanish children, are Melchior, Gaspar, and Balthasar, the latter being the only Black king of the three.
14 "pasan a llamarse amigas."
15 "Ni un paso atrás."
16 As *Alcorcón Today* humorously put it: "no eres de barrio si no te ha entrevistado Lucía Mbomío" [you're not from a *barrio* unless Lucía Mbomío has interviewed you] (qtd. in Mbomío, "Eres").
17 "Al barrio (al pueblo, a la localidad) se le quiere de estómago y de corazón, no por su belleza sino porque en él residen los recuerdos, las amigas de infancia y los vecinos que son familia."
18 "denunciar cuando hay una injusticia y apoyar a la gente de tu entorno, como si fuera de los tuyos. En cierto modo, lo son."
19 The hip-hop duo Chikos de Maíz tackles the problem of this "new heroin" in their song "Barrionalistas," proposing a radical solution: "Vamos a pegarle fuego a la casa de apuestas / ... Aunque ya no veas yonquis en las esquinas / están en las casas de apuestas, la nueva heroína" [Let's burn down the gambling house ... Even if there are no longer junkies on the street corners / they are in the gambling houses, the new heroin]. Mbomío also alludes to gambling in her *pregón*.
20 "que no es que las personas que van en silla de ruedas sean discapacitadas sino que la sociedad las discapacita."
21 "Salir de la periferia me sirvió para tomar conciencia de la manera en la que nos percibían fuera de ella. De repente, Alcorcón dejó de ser 'aquí' para ser 'allí' e, incluso, 'el más allá'. Fue como si me sacaran del armario del barrierío, donde yo estaba la mar de bien, y me calzaran un montón de etiquetas."
22 "Costumbrismo choni, asesinatos, peleas, plagas de galeruca o de ratas, incendios, desgracias varias y, por supuesto, enfermedades." *Choni* refers to an urban female subculture whose fashion sense includes heavy makeup, flashy jewelry, tight clothing, and particular mannerisms and speech. The derogatory perception is obvious in the definition of the term in the Dictionary of the Spanish Royal Academy: "chabacano, vulgar" [tacky, vulgar]. The film *Yo soy la Juani* (Bigas Luna, 2006) features a *choni* as the protagonist. For a vindication of *chonismo*, see Mbomío's "Ni choni ni chono," which is accompanied by a photograph from Bigas Lunas's film.
23 "desde arriba, a medio camino entre la recriminación moral ... y la fascinación exótica." Ironically, the same journalists who walked without encountering any problems in those neighborhoods would later describe them as terribly dangerous (Cruz Salanova 68).
24 "hablar no solo sobre el barrio, sino, fundamentalmente, hacerlo desde el barrio."
25 "Carabanchealeando" is a neologism based on Carabanchel, another *barrio* in Madrid, that could be loosely translated as "doing Carabanchel" or "Carabancheling." See Bravo and Delgado's reviews of *Diccionario de las periferias. Métodos y saberes autónomos desde los barrios* sponsored by "Carabancheleando." Carabanchel is well-known for being the neighborhood of the famous working-class child protagonist of Elvira Lindo's very successful Manolito Gafotas novels, for which she won the National Children's and Young People's Literature Award.

26 In the context of colonization, Mbomío also addresses the pernicious effects of internalizing stereotypes in *Hija del camino* in a conversation between the narrator and her paternal uncle (303).
27 See also "Eres más de barrio que..." where she collects a series of humorous negative sayings about *alcorconeros* resignifying and vindicating them with pride.
28 "cuando se acabe la moda volverás a dejar de estar de moda ... dejarán de ser *cool* y retornarán a la invisibilidad o, peor, a ser señalados por vulgares." One example is the recent revival of "lo quinqui," as seen in Daniel Monzón's film *Las leyes de la frontera* (2021) based on Javier Cercas's homonymous 2012 novel. "Lo quinqui" is associated with marginalized youth (unemployed, delinquents, drug addicts) from the outskirts during Spain's transition to democracy. For more information, see Llopis. In her last article in *El País*, "Unos ojos tristes," Almudena Grandes is very critical of this trend that forgets the 1970s misery that produced this phenomenon.
29 "en los que derrochamos qué sin porqué, contribuyendo a engordar y dar lustre a estereotipos."
30 In her famous TED Talk, Adichie fundamentally discusses the recurrent unidimensional negative representation of Africa. She does extend, however, her argument to any social group whose complexity and multidimensionality are erased in representation and public perception.
31 While conditions in most *barrios* have significantly improved, there are notable exceptions such as the Cañada Real, a southern shantytown in Madrid and one of the poorest *barrios* in Europe.
32 "un clima de discordia, con banderas preconstitucionales, insultos o 'saluditos romanos.'"
33 Chinese people have been a key target of racist attacks during the pandemic. This has led to creative initiatives by Spaniards of Chinese descent. See Ahijado's "No soy un virus."
34 The MENAS (Menores Extranjeros No Acompañados), unaccompanied and undocumented migrant minors, have been a frequent and manipulated target in this context. See, for example, "Vox carga contra los menores migrantes con datos manipulados en sus carteles de campaña." Mbomío speaks against the criminalization of these minors in "La bilis verde" [The Green Bile] where she explicitly notes the rise of Vox in the periphery and questions the media's responsibility in providing it with a platform.
35 "No olvidemos que la narrativa por parte de determinados partidos políticos consiste en convertir a las personas que migran, en responsables de la transmisión de covid19, de quitar los puestos de trabajo y, curioso, al tiempo, de no trabajar pero sí recibir ayudas. Esas mismas voces han celebrado la llegada de turistas, como si estos fueran inmunes a un virus que a estas alturas ya ha dejado bien claro que le traen al pairo las banderas y las fronteras." Likewise, in "Menudo verano" [What a Summer] she compares celebrating the arrival of tourists with champagne while constructing barricades against migrants during the pandemic.
36 "por el modo de vida que tiene nuestra inmigración en Madrid y por la densidad de población."
37 See also Grasso, Zafra, and Ferrero's report, which attributes the higher incidence of the pandemic in low-income areas to the socioeconomic reasons that Mbomío notes, adding the housing situation (smaller homes that make distancing and isolating almost impossible).

38   In terms of internal migration, it is crucial to remember the *éxodo rural* [rural exodus] which refers to the rural migrations to the cities that started in Spain in the 1950s and that have resulted in what is known as the "España vaciada" [emptied Spain] or rural depopulation.
39   "Como si no lo supiéramos."
40   "¡Sí a los barrios de siempre, no a los guetos multiculturales! ¡Sí a la civilización de la cruz y no a la violencia islamista!" We might also recall the speech of television presenter Ana Rosa Quintana who, upon receiving the Medal of the City of Madrid, declared "Me he criado en Usera, en un barrio obrero y trabajador, antes de que fuera Chinatown" [I was raised in Usera, a working-class *barrio*, before it became Chinatown].
41   Neither should we forget that the Barrio de Salamanca was built with the fortune that Juan Manuel Manzanedo (1803–1882) made from the slave trade. Cuban plantations and slavery financed to a great extent Spain's "modernity" (the banking system, the railroad, etc.) and played an essential role in the construction of today's socioeconomic and racial privilege. See Cañas and Sota.
42   "Los cinturones de las grandes urbes siempre han sido lugares de llegada y en ellos se crea una identidad que fluye, se adapta y es muy abierta. Ahora también es latina, rumana, ucraniana, nigeriana o guineo-ecuatoriana." Juan Goytisolo very graphically depicts these urban transformations in his novel *Paisajes después de la batalla* (1999). He employs the metaphor of a cake with many layers to illustrate the different migrant waves in the protagonist's Parisian *barrio*.
43   "Las etiquetas, tanto en las personas como en la ropa, es mejor cortarlas porque molestan y casi nunca sirven para nada."
44   "La música latina y el rap suenan con brío en la barbería y en la televisión se suceden los correspondientes videoclips, mientras, cinco profesionales trabajan sin pausa. Son de Italia, Ecuador, Colombia, República Dominicana y de Madrid, cada uno de un punto del planeta y quizá sea por la melodía que se escucha, pero verles trabajar parece una coreografía. Todos conocen el paso que les toca y lo ejecutan con genialidad. Esa es la razón por la cual el local está lleno de clientes y de gente que espera, de todas las teces, todas las edades, todos los credos y todos los sitios. El Alcorcón de ayer se construyó con los cuerpos que vinieron del sur y del centro de la Península, ahora se fortalece con los que llegan del sur del sur y del este y del otro lado del Atlántico. Alcorcón es esto." Barbershops have played important community roles in marginal communities, i.e. the African American community, as different studies and films have shown ("The Community Roles").
45   Concha Buika, the Spanish singer of Equatorial Guinean descent, also claims her belonging to the *barrio*, where multiple cultures converge. This allows her to create a flexible identity for herself and musical spaces of local, national, and global belonging (García Alvite 235).
46   In her last *barrionalista* article, she bids farewell paying tribute to Alcorcón, promising to continue working from the margins and hoping to see again the readers who do not suffer "centritis" ("Hasta la próxima").

Works Cited

Adichie, Chimamanda Ngozi. "The Danger of a Single Story." *TED Talk*, July 2009, https://www.ted.com/talks/chimamanda_ngozi_adichie_the_danger_of_a_single_story.

Ahijado, Manuel. "'No soy un virus': Los jóvenes de origen chino se rebelan contra el racismo en España." *El País*, 10 May 2020, https://elpais.com/elpais/2020/05/06/icon/1588776253_396715.html. Accessed 4 Sep. 2023.

Angone, Odome. "Ser o estar: Las 'negras realidades' de la afrodescendencia española en *Las que se atrevieron* e *Hija del camino* de Lucía Asué Mbomío Rubio." *Hispanismes*, vol. 5, 2022, pp. 1–11.

Borst, Julia, and Danae Gallo González. "Narrative Constructions of Online Imagined Afro-Diasporic Communities in Spain and Portugal." *Open Cultural Studies*, vol. 3, no. 1, 2019, pp. 286–307.

Bourdieu, Pierre. *Distinction. A Social Critique of the Judgement of Taste*. Translated by Richard Nice, Harvard UP, 1984.

Bravo, Eduardo. "Carabancheleando crea un diccionario para impulsar el habla de los barrios." *Yorokobu*, 3 Apr. 2018, https://www.yorokobu.es/carabancheleando/. Accessed 4 Sept. 2023.

Cañas, Jesús A., and Idoia Sota. "De Medina Sidonia a Goytisolo: Las casas y las fortunas que se levantaron en España con el dinero de la esclavitud." *El País*, 13 Nov. 2020, https://elpais.com/icon-design/arquitectura/2020-11-13/casas-dinero-esclavos-espana-medina-sidonia-goytisolo.html. Accessed 3 Mar. 2023.

Cruz Salanova, Luis de la. *Barrrionalismo*. Editorial Decordel, 2018.

Cucarella Ramon, Vicent. "Diáspora y auto representación en la literatura afroespañola: *Hija del camino*, de Lucía Asué Mbomío." *Anales de la literatura española*, no. 37, 2022, pp. 11–31.

Delgado, Manuel. "'Barrionalismo.' El barrio como fuente de identidad individual y colectiva." *El País*, 24 Jan. 2018, https://elpais.com/elpais/2018/01/14/seres_urbanos/1515932437_091211. Accessed 5 Sept. 2023.

Domínguez, Dani. "Racismo y xenofobia durante la pandemia en España." *La marea*, 12 June 2020, https://www.lamarea.com/2020/06/12/racismo-y-xenofobia-durante-la-pandemia-en-espana/. Accessed 8 Oct. 2023.

Domínguez, Iñigo. "Vox quería creer que todavía quedaba mucha noche." *El País*, 24 July 2023, https://elpais.com/espana/elecciones-generales/2023-07-23/vox-queria-creer-que-todavia-quedaba-mucha-noche.html. Accessed 24 July 2023.

"El COVID-19 aumenta la xenofobia y el racismo contra los asiáticos en todo el mundo." *Human Rights Watch*, 12 May 2020, https://www.hrw.org/es/news/2020/05/12/el-covid-19-aumenta-la-xenofobia-y-el-racismo-contra-los-asiaticos-en-todo-el-mundo. Accessed 15 Oct. 2023.

El-Tayeb, Fatima. "'The Birth of a European Public': Migration, Postnationality, and Race in the Uniting of Europe." *American Quarterly*, vol. 60, no. 3, 2008, pp. 649–70.

Eneva, Stoyanka. "Between Hope and Despair: How Racism and Anti-Racism Produce Madrid." *European Cities. Modernity, Race and Colonialism*, edited by Noa K. Ha and Giovanni Picker. Manchester UP, 2002, pp. 213–34.

Foucault, Michel. *L'archéologie du savoir*. Gallimard, 1969.

García Alvite, Dosinda. "La música de Concha Buika en el mercado cultural global: Alianzas locales y transnacionales." *Trans-afrohispanismos. Puentes culturales críticos entre África, Latinoamérica y España*, edited by Dorothy Odartey-Wellington, Brill/Rodopi, 2018, pp. 221–39.

Goytisolo, Juan. *Paisajes después de la batalla*. Ediciones del Norte, 1982.

Grandes, Almudena. "Unos ojos tristes." *El País*, 27 Nov. 2021, https://elpais.com/eps/2021-11-28/unos-ojos-tristes.html. Accessed 20 July 2023.

Grasso, Daniele, Mariano Zafra, and Berta Ferrero. "Covid de ricos, covid de pobres: Las restricciones de la segunda ola exponen las desigualdades de Madrid." *El País*, 17 Sept. 2020, https://elpais.com/espana/madrid/2020-09-16/covid-de-ricos-covid-de-pobres-las-restricciones-de-la-segunda-ola-exponen-las-desigualdades-de-madrid.html. Accessed 15 Oct. 2023.

Hall, Stuart. "The Local and the Global: Globalization and Ethnicity." *Culture, Globalization, and the World-System. Contemporary Conditions for the Representation of Identity*, edited by Anthony D. King. U of Minnesota P, 1997, pp. 19–39.

———. "The Spectacle of the 'Other.'" *Representation: Cultural Representations and Signifying Practices*, edited by Stuart Hall. Sage Publications, 1997, pp. 223–79.

Lander, Vini, et al., editors. *COVID-19 and Racism: Counter-Stories of Colliding Pandemics*. Policy Press, 2023.

Llopis, Enric. "La cultura quinqui, 'borrón' de la Transición." *El viejo topo*, no. 337, Feb. 2016, https://www.elviejotopo.com/articulo/la-cultura-quinqui-borron-de-la-transicion/. Accessed 15 Sept. 2023.

Los Chikos del Maíz. "Barrionalistas." *Barrionalistas*, Richie la Nuit, 2019. *Spotify*, https://open.spotify.com/track/4hmt365nYmExwaR5nqzPKQ?

Maalouf, Amin. *In the Name of Identity. Violence and the Need to Belong*. Translated by Barbara Bray. Penguin Books, 2003.

Martín Gaite, Carmen. *Usos amorosos de la postguerra española*. Anagrama, 1987.

Mbomío Rubio, Lucía Asué. "A cubierto." *El País*, 6 Apr. 2020, https://elpais.com/espana/madrid/2020-04-05/a-cubierto.html. Accessed 20 July 2023.

———. "A pie." *El País*, 23 Feb. 2020, https://elpais.com/ccaa/2020/02/20/madrid/1582201522_064370.html. Accessed 20 July 2023.

———. "Ah, cómo hemos cambiado." *El País*, 6 Jan. 2020, https://elpais.com/ccaa/2019/12/30/madrid/1577705284_482923.html. Accessed 20 July 2023.

———. "Arrimar el hombro." *El País*, 18 May 2020, https://elpais.com/espana/madrid/2020-05-17/arrimar-el-hombro.html. Accessed 20 July 2023.

———. "Barrio con flow." *El País*, 15 July 2019, https://elpais.com/ccaa/2019/07/09/madrid/1562666870_097546.html. Accessed 25 July 2023.

———. "Cerrando." *El País*, 27 July 2020, https://elpais.com/espana/madrid/2020-07-26/cerrando.html. Accessed 25 July 2023.

———. "Croissants sin desgracias." *El País*, 1 Nov. 2020, https://elpais.com/espana/madrid/2020-11-01/croissants-sin-desgracias.html. Accessed 20 July 2023.

———. "Cuando salí del barrio." *El País*, 16 Feb. 2020, https://elpais.com/ccaa/2020/02/14/madrid/1581695674_590574.html. Accessed 25 July 2023.

———. "De pipas, chuches y otras historias." *El País*, 30 Nov. 2020, https://elpais.com/espana/madrid/2020-11-29/de-pipas-chuches-y-otras-historias.html0. Accessed 25 July 2023.

———. "El 'Alcorconófilo'." *El País*, 11 Feb. 2019, https://elpais.com/ccaa/2019/02/08/madrid/1549630052_339029.html. Accessed 25 July 2023.

———. "El barrio, para todas." *El País*, 17 June 2019, https://elpais.com/ccaa/2019/07/09/madrid/1562666870_097546.html. Accessed 25 July 2023.
———. "El ciclo de la vida en el barrio." *El País*, 10 Dec. 2018, https://elpais.com/ccaa/2018/12/07/madrid/1544197157_620389.html. Accessed 25 July 2023.
———. "El juego también es una droga." *El País*, 2 Mar. 2020, https://elpais.com/espana/madrid/2020-03-01/el-juego-tambien-es-una-droga.html. Accessed 25 July 2023.
———. "El rey del barrio." *El País*, 1 June 2020, https://elpais.com/espana/madrid/2020-05-31/el-rey-del-barrio.html. Accessed 25 July 2023.
———. "Eres más de barrio que..." *El País*, 21 Oct. 2019, https://elpais.com/ccaa/2019/10/18/madrid/1571417375_133405.html. Accessed 25 July 2023.
———. "Escuela y barrio." *El País*, 7 Jan. 2019, https://elpais.com/ccaa/2019/01/04/madrid/1546596566_514120.html. Accessed 25 July 2023.
———. "Esto no ha terminado, no fue una broma." *El País*, 25 May 2020, https://elpais.com/espana/madrid/2020-05-24/esto-no-ha-terminado-no-fue-una-broma.html. Accessed 25 July 2023.
———. "Fuentiopía." *El País*, 12 Nov. 2018, https://elpais.com/ccaa/2018/11/08/madrid/1541696871_001728.html. Accessed 25 July 2023.
———. "Hasta la próxima." *El País*, 7 Dec. 2020, https://elpais.com/espana/madrid/2020-12-06/hasta-la-proxima.html. Accessed 25 July 2023.
———. *Hija del camino*. Grijalbo, 2019.
———. "Horas muertas." *El País*, 22 July 2019, https://elpais.com/ccaa/2019/07/17/madrid/1563349188_992202.html. Accessed 25 July 2023.
———. "Juntas." *El País*, 2 Feb. 2020, https://elpais.com/ccaa/2020/01/31/madrid/1580487670_444936.html. Accessed 25 July 2023.
———. "La bilis verde." *El País*, 18 Nov. 2019, https://elpais.com/ccaa/2019/11/15/madrid/1573821033_353167. Accessed 25 July 2023.
———. "La gente bonita, las cosas bonitas." *El País*, 30 Mar. 2020, https://elpais.com/espana/madrid/2020-03-29/la-gente-bonita-las-cosas-bonitas.html. Accessed 25 July 2023.
———. "La jota de Alcorcón." *El País*, 19 Dec. 2019, https://elpais.com/ccaa/2019/12/12/madrid/1576174774_180577.html. Accessed 10 Aug. 2023.
———. "La lealtad de los astros." *El País*, 21 Jan. 2019, https://elpais.com/ccaa/2019/01/16/madrid/1547651435_948524.html. Accessed 25 July 2023.
———. "Las empanadillas de Móstoles existen." *El País*, 24 Sept. 2018, https://elpais.com/ccaa/2018/09/21/madrid/1537541443_828466.html. Accessed 25 July 2023.
———. "Las Musas." *El País*, 18 Feb. 2019, https://elpais.com/ccaa/2019/02/15/madrid/1550222124_276298.html. Accessed 25 July 2023.
———. "Las peñas urbanas." *El País*, 27 Jan. 2020, https://elpais.com/ccaa/2020/01/24/madrid/1579878610_867246.html. Accessed 25 July 2023
———. "Los del Sur." *El País*, 28 Sept. 2020, https://elpais.com/espana/madrid/2020-09-27/los-del-sur.html. Accessed 25 July 2023,
———. "Maldita carta." *El País*, 19 Apr. 2019, https://elpais.com/ccaa/2019/04/18/madrid/1555617975_214655.html. Accessed 25 July 2023.

———. "Menudo verano." *El País*, 14 Sept. 2020, https://elpais.com/espana/madrid/2020-09-13/menudo-verano.html. Accessed 25 July 2023.

———. "Mercerías 1-Casa de apuestas 0." *El País*, 5 Nov. 2018, https://elpais.com/ccaa/2018/10/30/madrid/1540887689_239576.html. Accessed 25 July 2023.

———. "Miedo a toser." *El País*, 9 Mar. 2020, https://elpais.com/espana/madrid/2020-03-08/miedo-a-toser.html. Accessed 25 July 2023.

———. "Narrarse a sí misma." *Pikara*, 29 Apr. 2020, https://www.pikaramagazine.com/2020/04/contarse-asi-misma/. Accessed 15 Jan. 2023.

———. "Ni choni ni chono." *El País*, 19 Nov. 2018, https://elpais.com/ccaa/2018/11/16/madrid/1542362837_685272.html. Accessed 25 July 2023.

———. "No desandar el camino." *El País*, 14 Oct. 2019, https://elpais.com/ccaa/2019/10/11/madrid/1570814023_536975.html. Accessed 25 July 2023.

———. "No es una entelequia." *El País*, 25 Mar. 2019, https://elpais.com/ccaa/2019/03/22/madrid/1553254962_962310.html. Accessed 25 July 2023.

———. "No somos una moda." *El País*, 9 Nov. 2020, https://elpais.com/espana/madrid/2020-11-08/no-somos-una-moda.html. Accessed 25 July 2023.

———. "Odio la nueva normalidad." *El País*, 26 Oct. 2020, https://elpais.com/espana/madrid/2020-10-25/odio-la-nueva-normalidad.html. Accessed 25 July 2023.

———. "Parques que eran playas." *El País*, 7 Sept. 2018, https://elpais.com/ccaa/2018/09/16/madrid/1537095562_932170.html. Accessed 25 July 2023.

———. "Pedagogía estéril." *Pikara*, 17 Oct. 2019, https://www.eldiario.es/pikara/pedagogia-esteril_132_1328023.html. Accessed 8 Apr. 2023.

———. "Por qué necesitamos periodistas racializados en los medios." *Pikara*, 5 Sept. 2018, https://www.eldiario.es/pikara/resulta-necesario-periodistas-racializades_132_1950413.html. Accessed 28 Sept. 2023.

———. "Pregón de Fiestas Alcorcón 2019." *YouTube*, uploaded by Ayto. Alcorcón, 5 Sept. 2019, https://www.youtube.com/watch?v=BNY_MuTZK2I.

———. "Primer apellido: Alcorcón." *El País*, 20 July 2020, https://elpais.com/espana/madrid/2020-07-19/primer-apellido-alcorcon.html. Accessed 25 July 2023.

———. "Pues ya hemos votado (o no)." *El País*, 28 Apr. 2019, https://elpais.com/ccaa/2019/04/24/madrid/1556127821_360002.html. Accessed 25 July 2023.

———. "Ratas." *El País*, 19 Jan. 2020, https://elpais.com/ccaa/2020/01/19/madrid/1579460571_456469.html. Accessed 25 July 2023.

———. "Sin anclas." *El País*, 2 Dec. 2019, https://elpais.com/ccaa/2019/11/06/madrid/1573050360_056943.html. Accessed 25 July 2023.

———. "Sin miedo." *El País*, 4 Feb. 2019, https://elpais.com/ccaa/2019/02/01/madrid/1549032449_686762.html. Accessed 25 July 2023.

———. "Solo nos queda reírnos." *El País*, 4 Mar. 2019, https://elpais.com/ccaa/2019/02/28/madrid/1551357824_619641.html. Accessed 25 July 2023.

———. "Somos jóvenes." *El País*, 15 Apr. 2019, https://elpais.com/ccaa/2019/04/10/madrid/1554893902_515468.html. Accessed 25 July 2023.

———. "Un banco morado." *El País*, 25 Nov. 2019, https://elpais.com/ccaa/2019/11/22/madrid/1574419414_979810.html. Accessed 25 July 2023.

———. "¡¿Vives en Alcorcón?!" *El País*, 8 Oct. 2018, https://elpais.com/ccaa/2018/10/04/madrid/1538647166_159936.html. Accessed 25 July 2023.

———. "Volver al telefonillo." *El País*, 10 Sept. 2018, https://elpais.com/ccaa/2018/09/09/madrid/1536527913_267225.html. Accessed 25 July 2023.

———. "Ya no están." *El País*, 9 Feb. 2020, https://elpais.com/ccaa/2020/02/07/madrid/1581079020_876704.html. Accessed 25 July 2023.

———. "Yo me entiendo." *El País*, 26 Nov. 2018, https://elpais.com/ccaa/2018/11/25/madrid/1543163964_261007.html. Accessed 25 July 2023.

Minder, Raphael, and Pam Belluck. "Spain, Amid Protests, Destroys Dog of Ebola-Infected Nurse." *The New York Times*, 8 Oct. 2014, https://www.nytimes.com/2014/10/09/science/ebola-dog-excalibur-nurse-spain.html. Accessed 23 Sept. 2023.

Moriuchi, Mey-Yen. *Mexican Costumbrismo: Race, Society, and Identity in Nineteenth-Century Art*. Penn State UP, 2018.

Odartey-Wellington, Dorothy. "Trans-afrohispanismos." *Trans-afrohispanismos. Puentes culturales críticos entre África, Latinoamérica y España*, edited by Dorothy Odartey-Wellington. Brill/Rodopi, 2018, pp. 1–19.

Selasi, Taiye. "Don't Ask Me Where I Am from, Ask Me Where I Am a Local." *TED Talk*, Oct. 2014, https://www.ted.com/talks/taiye_selasi_don_t_ask_where_i_m_from_ask_where_i_m_a_local.

Silió, Elisa, F. Javier Barroso, and María Lillo. "La inquietud se desata en Alcorcón por la enfermera contagiada de ébola." *El País*, 8 Oct. 2014, https://elpais.com/ccaa/2014/10/07/madrid/1412715030_810427.html. Accessed 23 Sept. 2023.

Sontag, Susan. *Illness as Metaphor and AIDS and Its Metaphors*. Anchor Books/Doubleday, 1989.

"The Community Roles of the Barber Shop and Beauty Salon." *National Museum of African American History & Culture*, https://nmaahc.si.edu/explore/stories/community-roles-barber-shop-and-beauty-salon#:~:text=Since%20the%20turn%20of%20the,of%20importance%20in%20the%20community.

"Vox carga contra los menores migrantes con datos manipulados en sus carteles de campaña." *Eldiario.es*, 20 Apr. 2021, https://www.eldiario.es/madrid/vox-coloca-publicidad-electoral-estacion-sol_1_7840154.html. Accessed 23 Sept. 2023.

Yo soy la Juani. Dir. Bigas Lunas, 2006.

10 An Inconclusive Conclusion
Autoethnography as a Model for Epistemic Decolonization

Ana León-Távora

Throughout this volume, we have explored a number of instances illustrating the pervasiveness of a colonialist mindset that has historically framed the reception of Blackness in Spain. Such a mentality has resulted in the misrepresentation and/or deficient representation, misappropriation, and lack of visibility of Black people, and in the spread of an Afro-amnesia that has significantly distorted the history of the country and shaped a view of African Black people as the Other. In contrast with this colonial gaze, however, we have also read about voices of resistance that defy past appropriations and reclaim their own identities. These Black authors, artists, and activists represent a new *activismo afro* that challenges Spain's white-centered notions of national identity. By dismantling the preponderance of Eurocentric knowledge, their discourses prioritize the peripheries, personal accounts, and artistic expressions of self-representation, carving out a space for Afro-Spaniards and the African Diaspora and building a complete, inclusive history that honors the indelible connection between Africa and Spain while also drawing a map of international Pan-African ties.

We cannot end this volume without devoting a chapter to the pivotal role that autoethnography plays in the decolonization of Eurocentric epistemology and the development of Spanish antiracist activism. Indeed, in recent years, the Spanish book market has witnessed the emergence of many first-person testimonies written by Afro-descendant authors. Among the most recent ones are Desirée Bela-Lobedde's *Ser mujer negra en España* [Being a Black Woman in Spain] (2018) and Moha Gerehou's *¿Qué hace un negro como tú en un sitio como este?* [What Is a Black Dude Like You Doing in a Place Like This?] (2021), Asaari Bibang's *Y a pesar de todo, aquí estoy* [And Here I am, in Spite of Everything] (2021), Adriana Boho's *Ponte en mi piel. Guía para combatir el racismo cotidiano* [Put Yourself in My Skin. A Guide to Combating Everyday Racism] (2022), and Afropoderossa's (Silvia Ayang, although she prefers to be addressed familiarly as "Perla") *España no es solo blanca* [Spain Isn't Only White] (2023). While Chapter 5 discusses autobiographical texts by

DOI: 10.4324/9781003435051-11

Afrodescendant women in Spain which extend beyond the biographical to a collective level, the works analyzed here, rather than autobiographies, would better fit into the genre of autoethnography. In them, their authors go beyond a mere historical narrative of main events in their lives to weave instead a concentric narrative pattern that extends from the most individual circumstances to local and international events, connecting personal anecdotes with wider social themes to share their viewpoint as Black people in Spain, and also including pedagogical practice and strategies of resistance to racialized readers.

This chapter examines the autoethnographic genre, read as an example of a "situated point of view" (Haraway), by discussing selected excerpts from the works mentioned earlier while alternating with personal testimonies from other Black public figures in the Spanish media and the cultural sphere. Reading Michel Foucault's argument of the indissoluble relationship between power and knowledge as a colonial form of control through the imposition of a Eurocentric epistemic system that displaces and/or eradicates other cultural forms of knowledge(s), our essay will provide a brief account of the Western white-centering of a single form of knowledge, seemingly universal and neutral, proposing instead first-person subjective accounts as models of "epistemic disobedience" (Mignolo; Ramirez). More specifically, a close examination of selected excerpts from the autoethnographies of Bela-Lobedde, Gerehou, Bibang, Boho, and Afropoderossa will reveal this genre to be a strategy of resistance that helps the authors question notions of Spanish identity and provide alternative epistemologies, ultimately calling for a shared antiracist activism.

Autoethnographies as Alternative Epistemologies

Autoethnography, a research method used mainly in the social sciences, combines autobiography (personal experiences narrated through storytelling devices) and ethnography (writing about culture and cultural experiences); hence, autoethnography relies on personal experiences to reflect on cultural beliefs and practices "in order to identify and interrogate the intersections between the self and social life" (Adams et al. 1). While the term "autoethnography" was first introduced by anthropologist Karl G. Heider in the 1970s, followed by Walter Goldschmidt's description of the genre as "self-ethnography" (Adams et al. 1), it emerged in the 1990s as a reaction to the methods found in the social sciences, which were dominated by white/Western voices, becoming a powerful tool to disrupt Eurocentric norms of research and representation by re-centering the researchers as participants in their own local and historical contexts (Chawla and Atay 4). This new narrative form provides researchers with an opportunity to engage in a process of self-examination while also analyzing significant events in their lives "through an understanding of one's social-historical and community context" (Camangian et al. 58).

Autoethnography, thus, is a hybrid genre, often simply mislabeled as autobiography, or as "testimony" (although it includes testimonial sections), or more vaguely, as "nonfiction" narrative. In the hybridity of the genre, however, resides its beauty, as it could be said that its format precisely embodies the histories it accounts for, which deviate from the "purity" of the white-centered uniformity of the neutral perspective, advocating diverse perspectives instead. It may be possible to relate the origins of this form of discourse to the personal narratives of enslaved Black people, which, to Norman Ajari, represented "the first printed manifestation of the vindication of Afrodescendants in modern times" (97), and that could be taken as a reference point for current narratives of social transformation. Ajari contends that these personal accounts, which combine autobiographical details with philosophical elucidations and emotional expressions, present a deviation from the imposed premises of the Eurocentric epistemology of "zero-point" (Castro-Gómez), already discussed in this volume's Introduction, and, rather than aiming at an impossibly objective positionality, they carry embodied reflections and their authors' personal experiences, as well as their geohistorical situations (Ajari 95).

Interestingly, two essential purposes of all autoethnographies are to help fill in the gaps in existing research by nuancing cultural aspects, on the one hand, and, on the other, to articulate cultural knowledge from an insider's perspective instead of allowing others to tell stories they do not own. Notably, autoethnography can become a powerful tool of agency for marginalized, oppressed, and disenfranchised voices to reclaim their own experiences, since "[a] person who has directly experienced institutional oppressions and/or cultural problems, such as racism, loss, or illness, can talk about these issues in ways different from others who have limited experiences about these topics" (Adams et al. 3). Hence, we can agree that autoethnography acts as a model of counternarrative that serves to dismantle cultural appropriations and misrepresentations, or in other cases, to center voices that have been relegated to the peripheries because their histories do not conform to the single one of the hegemonic majority, with their knowledge(s) being dismissed as mere subjectivities. Likewise, they arise as tools for the attainment of intellectual decolonization that authors such as Marcus Garvey and Abuy Nfubea proclaim, as previously discussed in Chapter 7.

Indeed, counterstories have been critical in combating deficit narratives of people of color. In Critical Race Theory Studies, as Patrick Roz Camangian et al. explain, the use of counternarratives has multiple advantages: first, by serving as models, they enable disenfranchised minority groups to build community among those that have been relegated to the margins of

Autoethnography as a Model for Epistemic Decolonization 219

society; they also challenge misrepresentations and stereotypes created by centered perspectives; they create opportunities for marginalized people, demonstrating that they are not alone; and finally, they teach others that by combining personal experiences with current events, they can build a richer world (58). In their counterstories to stereotyped Spanish narratives and misrepresentations of Blackness, all the authors examined here open the door for other Afro-Spaniards and Afro-descendants to make their voices heard and provide their testimonies by reflecting on experiences that are common to many Black people in Spain. In so doing, these new narratives also offer advice and information that can assist Black readers in responding appropriately to situations of discrimination, or that can even help them recognize that they are the target of microaggressions and other forms of racism. Certainly, many times the person of color develops a cognitive dissonance response to mask the painful realization of being oppressed, a form of oblivion that at some point is abruptly destroyed by what Bibang brands "el despertar negro" [the Black awakening], or:

> when you stop looking for excuses and apologies for all the racist situations in which you find yourself entangled throughout your life; when you realize how many racist jokes and jests you laughed at your whole life to avoid feeling excluded; all the comments you let slip past; all the times you felt special for being called exotic.... ("Madurez").[1]

Notably, in a recent interview, Afropoderossa states "I didn't know I was Black until I arrived in Spain" (@afropoderossa and @ehuniverso), a statement that inevitably recalls W.E.B. Du Bois' concept of the double consciousness of the Black person.[2] While Afropoderossa evidently knew that her skin color was darker than that of most Spaniards, she explains that what she did not know was that it was a catalyst for alterity and discrimination. Although all the authors cited here offer guidelines for racialized people, in the case of Boho's book, the recommendations are deliberately grouped into easily recognizable sections, which seems logical since its title explicitly states that the book is meant as a guide to combat racism. Therefore, some of the chapters carry titles such as "Practical Advice on How to Act in Situations of Microaggression" or "Tips for Antiracist Activism on Social Media."[3] In all these stories, the authors' past lack of awareness of situations of social injustice is immediately followed by the recounting of a lived experience where they are confronted with a racist situation, which compels them to seek answers and become informed. In an act of altruism, they decide to share this knowledge to help their readers identify symptoms of social oppression, even if that same oppression emanates from the person of color's internalized bias, as the following anecdote about linguistic prejudice in Gerehou's book illustrates.

In his autoethnography, ¿Qué hace un negro como tú en un sitio como este?, Gerehou confesses to having felt a sense of inadequacy with respect to African languages as he was preparing his *curriculum vitae* for his first job applications. In the section where he listed the languages he could speak, he declares having intentionally omitted the African language Soninke, which he speaks fluently, to include French instead, even though he has not mastered that language and can hardly maintain a conversation with a native French speaker. He did not mention the African language because, he admits, "I considered it would not open any doors for me, an idea that I had internalized" (64).[4]

One of the most important realms where colonization has thrived historically, in effect, is the imposition of the colonizer's language over and above the native languages of the colonized. This act of epistemological subjugation dominates the hierarchy of languages taught in Western academic institutions, which has the stated objective of providing a more "global" education. As Mignolo explains, there has traditionally been a domain of what he calls the "six imperial modern European languages": Italian, Spanish, and Portuguese, which spread from the Renaissance until the Enlightenment, and German, English, and French, from the Enlightenment onwards ("Epistemic Disobedience" 164). These six languages, Mignolo notes, are based on a Greek and Latin foundation, which excludes those that do not share a common root, such as Arabic, Urdu, or Nahuatl. Languages have been effective tools in the construction of a Eurocentric epistemology that extends from the imperialist nations in Europe to the colonized territories in the Americas, Asia, and Africa (Mignolo, "Epistemic Disobedience" 164), while delivering the message that the colonizer's world order is the only right one and far superior to the colonized "innocent" cognitive systems. Linguistic subordination, as with other acts of assimilation, gives rise to a sense of inadequacy on the part of the colonized person who succumbs to internalized oppression, deeming the colonized language an impoverished, deficient one, and assimilating instead to the linguistic realm of the colonizer, either by learning the new language or, if already raised within that linguistic tradition and being fluent in it, detaching from the linguistic legacy of the colonized culture.

Speaking the colonizing language, however, is not a guarantee of being "integrated" within the culture of the oppressor or of being perceived as part of the hegemonic majority, as Frantz Fanon argues in his analysis of the linguistic assimilation of "the Antillean man": "There is nothing more exasperating than to hear, 'How long have you lived in France? You speak very good French.' There is nothing more sensational than a black man speaking correctly [a European language], for he is appropriating the white world" (19). If, as Fanon continues, to speak a language equates to appropriating its world and culture (21), the sense of "appropriation" receives a different interpretation based on who the appropriator is: if speaking of Western colonization practices, "appropriation" must be read as synonymous with the colonizer's ownership; if, on the other hand, the colonized persons are the ones trying to own the colonizing language, they immediately become imposters, and the act of appropriation is seen as an act of imitation, of mimicry that creates a difference that renders the Other as almost identical but not quite (Bhabha 126), and even as a threat.

In a similar manner, Spanish actor, comedian, and activist Lamine Thior illustrates the perpetual foreignization of racialized people in Spain based solely on their having a different skin color from the hegemonic majority. Thior, born in Senegal but having been raised and lived in Spain since he was only two, self-identifies as "Afro-Andalusian" because he is from Algeciras, a town in the Andalusian province of Cadiz. As such, he naturally speaks with an Andalusian accent. Although his personal testimony does not come in written form, unlike the other examples cited in this essay, Thior usually creates sketches and monologues for stand-up comedy in which he makes jokes that convey a sharp social critique of racist situations suffered daily in his personal life. One of his first-person anecdotes relates how one day, at his uncle's restaurant, he was introduced to a couple from Chiclana (another town in Cadiz). The couple initiates a conversation about their Cadiz commonality, to which Thior replies in his natural accent, which propels the couple to exclaim in awe, "Ah! But he speaks like us!"[5] Thior then wraps up by adopting a false accent, like pidgin English, of what a Black African person "should" sound like in the non-Black Spanish imaginary, verbalizing what he would have liked to reply to the couple while making his thoughts clear to anyone sharing that same racist mentality. The anecdote immediately brings to mind Fanon's imitation of a Black man's broken English when trying to give directions, while admitting, evidently full of sarcasm, that a lot of Black people speak in pidgin: "Yes, sonny boy, you go corridor, you go straight, go one car, go two car, go three car, you there" (18). Like Thior, in her chapter titled "Una negra que habla catalán," [A Black Woman Who Speaks Catalan], Boho recounts the many times people who spoke with her by telephone before meeting her in person are taken aback that she can speak Catalan once they discover she is Black. In all these examples, language, as a tool of epistemic power, demonstrates that it shocks white people to encounter a Black person with a similar, or even higher, intellectual level, simply because, as Fanon argues and Thior's and Boho's personal experiences corroborate, "the European has a set idea of the black man" (18).

But Gerehou's narration does not end with the author's confession of his own linguistic bias. In fact, he connects his personal anecdote to a similar experience related by his good friend Sani Ladan, who speaks nine languages fluently, according to Gerehou. Ladan, a writer, social educator, and activist who fights against current border policies and the effects of colonialism in Africa, decries in his social media account how, during a job interview, his potential employers told him that the African languages he had listed in his CV, Hausa and Fula, were not competitive ones because "they are only spoken by African tribes" (Gerehou 65). Furthermore, the versatile nature of the autoethnography genre provides Gerehou with the opportunity to extend his experience to wider connections, drawing a line that goes from his personal account to his friend's story, and finally, to a report on international data that serves, on the one hand, to challenge the misinformed Eurocentric prejudices about African languages and, on the other, to correct the author's own internalized bias:

> The reality is that Hausa is the second most spoken language in Africa, employed in countries like Nigeria, Cameroon, Ghana, Burkina Faso, or Togo, while Fula is the official language of territories like Mauritania, Senegal, or Mali. But we will never hear anyone deride Italian, even though it is spoken by fewer people than Hausa and is only the official language of Italy and Vatican City. (65)[6]

After this reflection, Gerehou recognizes his own prejudices and agrees with Ladan that keeping the African languages in their CVs is an act of resistance as well as a sign of identity (65). The validation of a language as belonging to the category of "global," it appears, does not depend on the number of its speakers but on the socioeconomic systems of power that control what knowledge (in this case, *what* language and the knowledge of what language) really matters.

Beyond the linguistic domain, the self-serving ego of Western epistemology is such that it questions the intellectual capabilities of the person of color, as is the case with the discouraging unsolicited advice that Boho received after expressing her desire to pursue a degree in Administration and Finance: "Are you sure you can pass this course? There are easier options for people like you" ("Una negra que habla").[7] Like Gerehou, Boho offers up her individual experience to let the reader know that this is not a rare incident but a very common misconception held about the intelligence of people of color. Lastly, Boho warns of the lack of inclusivity in the admissions practices of many institutions of higher learning, including prestigious ones such as Cambridge and Oxford universities, which were both recently accused of having a discriminatory admissions system that did not allow for diversity among the student population.[8] As seen in the examples above, the use of autoethnography guides the authors through a reflection on painful memories in the act of learning from their experiences, what Ajari calls the empowerment of "anamnesis" in putting knowledge into practice (90). After this self-discovery, the authors' narratives undertake a displacement of the geopolitical center through alternative viewpoints that in turn examine social events. This relocation emphasizes the close relationship between the individual and the social, making it clear that the authors' personal encounters signal a deeper problem within Spain's social structure.

The Power of Non-knowledge: Epistemic Ignorance

When reflecting on the perception of Blackness in Spain and on Spain's African legacy—and conversely, on Spain's imprint on Africa—we must tackle the power of non-knowledge, or ignorance. Not of ignorance understood as an innocent deficit in knowledge, but rather as a selective choice of knowledge and of non-knowledge, knowing and not-knowing, what scholars Robert N. Proctor and Londa Schiebinger have called "agnotology," a concept that Proctor defines as "the history of ignorance making, the lost and forgotten" ("Preface" viii). Proctor explains that one manifestation is passive agnotology, described as a selective choice of what to know and what to ignore, for example, by choosing to not know any information that is not relevant or useful to us ("Agnotology" 6). This lack of intellectual curiosity is exhibited in Spain's colorblindness and inability to acknowledge and accept its own racism.

"Spain is not racist" is a popular maxim that most non-racialized Spaniards often articulate with pride. In *España no es solo blanca*, Afropoderossa dedicates a whole chapter to answering the question "¿Es España racista?" [Is Spain Racist?] (Chapter 6). Although the answer to Afropoderossa's question is a resounding *yes*, the author recognizes that Spain does not want to admit it. The problem resides in an ignorance of what constitutes racism and a willingness to remain ignorant about it; in other words, a reluctance to know. Such ignorance is rooted in the privilege of not needing to know—since whiteness does not need to justify its racial identity—and in a colorblind mindset that refuses to recognize the signs of structural racism (Mills, "White Ignorance" 246) because, as Afropoderossa points out, white persons "no lo viven" [don't experience it] (Chapter 6). To this cognitive passivity, Afropoderossa adds the many linguistic expressions and historical traditions that Spaniards have learned and repeat without realizing they are just perpetuating the old racist mentality that created them, like the use of blackface on many Spanish holidays and at celebrations.

This act of humiliating appropriation, already discussed in previous chapters of this volume, is fiercely defended by many non-racialized Spaniards as a harmless tradition, and in fact, any reservations about it are often met with outright hostility, as a group of women "dressed up" in blackface during carnival season reacted when Afropoderossa called out their racist decision, exclaiming: "So now it appears that we murder Black people because we paint our faces black, right?"[9] Limiting racism to the murder of people of color denotes a profound non-knowledge of what actually constitutes racism, which is unequivocally due to passive agnotology, or a lack of needing to learn. Anti-Black racism, Ajari underlines, does not simply translate into the massive extermination of Black people, in the same way that any form of racism is not limited to committing genocide (129). On the contrary, the insidiousness of racism manifests itself in daily remembrances of the "indignity" of minoritized groups that are situated at the peripheries and whose existence becomes a "cotidianidad mutilada" [mutilated everyday life] (Ajari 129). For people of color, this alterity manifests itself whenever they feel fearful of carrying out normal activities that white people would find innocuous.

While few things are more routine and ingrained in the Spanish cultural landscape than the game of soccer, soccer matches have nevertheless become a breeding ground for blatant displays of racism, with some fans hurling racist insults at soccer players of color (almost always Black players). As mentioned in Chapter 2, it seems incredible that even as this book is being completed, yet another case of racism was reported at a game between Valencia and Real Madrid in May 2023, when Valencia fans chanted a racist slur against Vinicius Jr., who plays for Real Madrid. The Afro-Brazilian player complained that this was not the first racist attack to which he had been subjected in Spain and that the Spanish league "now belongs to racists" (Azzoni). According to professor David Moscoso Sánchez, the behavior does not originate in the sport itself but in an ideology fed by the extreme right wing, which incites hatred "against foreigners, immigrants, or those with a different skin color" (Rosas). During a conversation in the podcast *No hay negros en el Tibet* [There Are No Black People in Tibet] hosted by Bibang, Thior, and musician Frank T, former soccer player Alberto Edjogo Owono explains that most of these soccer fans refuse to be catalogued as "racist," arguing that they only utter racial slurs to provoke the players and undermine their performance ("Cuando tratan de justificar"). Owono clarifies that, on the contrary, their attitude is not something spontaneous that could be switched off once the game is over; rather, it demonstrates an internal bias that they feel free to verbalize since they expect to be shielded by the clamor in the stadium and the anonymity the crowd provides: "one does not become a racist intolerant right after entering the stadium."[10] Owono adds that this disgraceful type of language is also inflicted on racialized children who play sports, not just adults, forcing them to develop tough skin in response to racist slurs.

Another common experience of Black people in Spain that is generally dismissed by non-racialized Spaniards is the constant "racial profiling" by the police, discussed in Chapter 4 of this volume, and so widely faced by people of color that it seems like a cruel "rite of passage" required to prove their "Spanishness." Not surprisingly, it has merited a mention in all the autoethnographies analyzed in this essay, as well as in poetry and media appearances. For example, Bela-Lobedde shares a detailed account of a terrifying and humiliating encounter that she endured in her teenage years. In the episode "Los Papeles" [The Documents], she recalls being stopped by the *Guardia Civil*, who asked her to show her "DNI" or ID when she was only thirteen.[11] Later, as an adult, she denounces the injustice of the situation once she possesses the knowledge needed to call the incident by its rightful name: "[N]ow, as an adult, I know that what happened to me … is called 'detention for racial profiling.' They are racist detentions. It is institutionalized racism" (56).[12]

Racial profiling also makes an appearance in Gerehou's book. The author explains how, after spending an afternoon playing basketball with a friend of Colombian descent—dark-skinned, like the author—on their way home, both young men were stopped by two police officers and asked to show their IDs. When the young men asked why, one of the officers simply answered, "Do I bother you when you are doing your job? I am doing my job" (Gerehou 162), a display of entitlement that was followed by a totally unrelated question as to whether the two young men were carrying any drugs; after their negative answer, the officers left.[13] Afro-Colombian-Spanish poet, politician, and activist Yeison F. García López also captures a childhood memory of racial profiling in his poem "Control aleatorio" [Random Check], in which a group of Black children, including himself, were playing on the street when they were accosted by three white men emerging from a car to ask them why they were running. The kids, only thirteen at the time—like Bela-Lobedde when she was exposed to racial profiling—give an innocent answer, which is followed by a short, sharp exchange between the white men and the Black kids that closes the poem: "Do you have drugs? / No" (14–15).[14] The poem's last lines echo Gerehou's account and leave a bitter aftertaste that inevitably invites the reader to reflect on the iniquity of the situation. As Thior declared in a recent interview, as a Black person, you cannot "be in a moment of hurry and exercise your right to be in a hurry" without being stopped by a police patrol questioning your reasons for running.[15] Unfortunately, the popular belief in Spain is that the Spanish police is not as racist as their counterparts in the United States, a comparison that Thior rejects, clarifying that racism is not a competition and thanking the Spanish police with a sarcastic remark: "Ah, thank you for not shooting me eight times, sir, truly."[16] In addition, Gerehou debunks the popular Spanish belief, apparent throughout Thior's interview as well, that police prejudice against Black people—and in fact, people of color in general—only occurs in the United States.

Drawing on his own experience, Gerehou provides examples of other targets of racial profiling in Spain as well as information about several studies aiming to determine what demographic groups the police is most likely to stalk. In one study, conducted over two consecutive months in 2015 at the Granada central bus station by the association *Pro Derechos Humanos* [Pro-Human Rights] of Andalusia, the results demonstrated an inconvenient truth: the Spanish police mostly stopped people with dark skin, with African Black people being the most often accosted, followed by Roma, Maghrebi, and Latin Americans (Gerehou 166). Aside from the generalized criminalization determined purely by darker skin color, Bela-Lobedde complains about the unsympathetic responses from some of her white friends who do not understand her point of view when she shares the incident with the police and who try to minimize its importance, comparing being targeted for your skin color to being targeted by any random feature, like hair color: "I feel they do not understand the difference between them being stopped because 'they may look trashy' or because they may be doing something weird, and me being stopped for being Black. It's not the same. It isn't" (57).[17]

Furthermore, there exists still another form of non-knowledge. According to Proctor, next to the passive ignorance for lack of interest is the agnotology that results from a strategic ploy or active construct, for example, when "certain people don't want you to know certain things" or manipulate information to "help maintain (your) ignorance" ("Agnotology" 8). The absence in the Spanish education system of a Black Spanish history that acknowledges the nation's active role in the transatlantic trade of African Black persons, the reluctance to recognize and honor Africa's irrefutable influence in what is now considered to be a collective set of traits that constitute "Spanish culture," and the lack of recognition given to prominent Afro-Spanish historical figures, are clear examples of the latter type of agnotology, embraced by institutions in order to deflect any responsibility for past events; indeed, as Charles W. Mills argues, by getting rid of a line of causality the collective amnesia or "a convenient amnesia about the past and its legacy in the present" allows for a blaming of discriminated groups as agents of their own marginalization ("White Ignorance" 246).[18] Racism is a structural and systemic problem fed by the media, institutions, and public organizations sometimes concealing information, sometimes distorting it. In fact, it is almost impossible to build an antiracist society when most of its institutions and the news media refuse to take responsibility for racist incidents by hiding them under a different name, or by denying their existence altogether. If, as Eduardo Mendieta posits, "epistemic privilege" is an artifact that is sustained by political economies of power and violence (253), conversely, "epistemic oppression" happens when specific knowledge is concealed, what Mendieta, citing Miranda Fricker, calls "hermeneutical injustice," perpetrated against epistemic resources "that are excluded, disauthorized, derogated, and marginalized from informing and guiding our world-forming interpretative practices" (261).

Looking back at previous examples through the lens of this active form of agnotology, then, one cannot help but notice the intentional deletion by the media and the government of the "race" equation from many of Spain's social issues, or the minimization of the impact of these events. For example, when Amnesty International decided to investigate the many reports of racial profiling they received from Spanish NGOs and other organizations, the investigation led them to conclude that "[t]here is a marked absence of official data on the frequency and motives of identity checks, and the ethnicity of the individuals subjected to them," and also to encounter "the Spanish authorities' refusal to acknowledge the facts when faced with these findings" ("Spain: Stop Racism" 6). Likewise, even though racist attacks are on the rise in Spanish schools, there are no protocols to handle episodes of this nature, which tend to be dismissed or their seriousness minimized, Bibang argues, in order to preserve the school's reputation ("La escuela"). Boho, on the other hand, shares instances that happened to her and to her siblings and for which the schools did not assume any responsibility ("Una negra que habla"). Although Boho refers to international news reports about racism in schools to broaden her example, there are innumerable reports made about Spanish schools, albeit without bearing the label of racism. In an article published in 2019, for example, Sara Plaza Casares studies the case of Camila Ferreyra, a Black girl who was subjected to constant harassment by her classmates, who called her "negra de mierda" [shitty n*****]. Due to the negligence of the institution in responding to the racism, her mother, Petra Ferreyra, decided to take the case to court, contending that, during the whole process, "the word racism [was] taboo."

The privileged hegemony is unlikely to be receptive to alternative epistemologies, Mills explains, firstly, because hegemonic ideologies support their version of what is happening and reject other viewpoints; and secondly, because alternative versions, especially when it comes to racism, do not proffer a complementary view but instead a contradictory one (*Blackness Visible* 29). This clearly shows in the defense mechanism to which white people resort whenever there is a conversation about racism, as authors Reni Eddo-Lodge and Robin DiAngelo examine in their respective works *Why I'm No Longer Talking to White People About Race* (2017) and *White Fragility. Why It's So Hard for White People to Talk About Racism* (2018). Conversations about racism are uncomfortable for the hegemonic majority because, as Bela-Lobedde states, they elicit an uneasiness that white people have never felt before, since being privileged as part of the hegemonic group equates to never being questioned (58).

This discomfort is not comparable to the trauma these experiences cause among racialized people. In fact, according to Amnesty International, constant identity checks in places with a large immigrant and ethnically diverse population create a false association between being ethnically different and criminality and produce feelings of "fear," "humiliation," and lack of belonging among those targeted ("Spain: Stop Racism" 11). Moreover, children who are Othered at school because of the color of their skin show serious Post-Traumatic Stress Disorder symptoms, like Camila Ferreyra, who suffered from "lack of confidence, insecurity, inability to relate to her peers, and depression" (Plaza Casares).[19] In Bibang's words, "the hatred of racism dies if it is not spread" ("La escuela"), but first, its existence must be acknowledged.[20] Thus, it is crucial to avoid increasing and perpetuating racist traditions, jokes, laws, and institutional practices, continues Bibang, who ends by condemning the insensitivity of some people: "that's why it hurts to witness good people who remain silent to racism, as if it were as irrelevant as Brussel sprouts" ("La escuela").[21] Bibang, who humorously confessed at the beginning of the chapter that she hated the vegetable but, unlike racist people, did not need to display that feeling in her daily life, employs humor to point out that the issue at hand goes much deeper than a mere conversation: it is not enough "to talk the talk"; in fact, it is vital to pierce the superficial layers of conversations about racism to generate an empathic response because the situations these Black authors relate are not isolated or occasional. They are instead experiences that affect a whole social group's identity development and trigger emotional trauma, as do the silence and insensitivity of white people when faced with these manifestations of social inequity.

Empathy, Humor, and Antiracist Education

In an online workshop that UNAF, or the *Unión de Asociaciones Familiares* [Union of Family Associations], hosted on June 15, 2023, Paola Hurtado, a psychologist specializing in counseling for racial trauma and migratory mourning, explained that the former is a lasting condition: because racism does not end, persons exposed to it will likely endure the same situations repeatedly throughout their lives.[22] Although other people of color in Spain also suffer from it, Hurtado decries that "the darker a person is, the stronger the social rejection" ("UNAF visibiliza").[23] One of the solutions to combating racial trauma, says Hurtado, consists in reinforcing the person's identity. But the caveat is that in Spain, "racialized people do not possess the space to define [themselves], because the Spanish state is usually white in its majority and [for a racialized person] to develop [their] identity, it is necessary to have a background that serves as a reference point" ("UNAF visibiliza").[24] Creating a support system where people of color can share their experiences is very helpful. However, since it is a structural problem, as Hurtado goes on to note, racism must be fought through collective activism and policy changes that incorporate antiracist education in institutions while promoting initiatives where people of color feel empowered and where their emotional responses can be addressed.

Indeed, in *'Racism Is Not Intellectual': Interracial Friendships, Multicultural Literature, and Decolonizing Epistemologies*, Paola Moya cites a verse from a poem by Chicana author Lorna Dee Cervantes to defend the epistemological value of emotions in people who have been the target of racism. Cervantes' poem contests the opinion of a young white man who dismisses the existence of racial disparities and the emotional baggage they entail, declaring, "Racism is not intellectual / I cannot reason these scars away" (qtd. in Moya 169). Claims about racism made by people of color are usually discredited for being too emotional and, therefore, at odds with the Western idea of rationality (Moya 173). On the contrary, as Moya argues, it is by observing the meanings and origins of emotions that we can begin to perceive the social structures that affect our lives, both positively and negatively: "Emotions, therefore, are mediated by the shared ideologies through which individuals construct their social identities. As such, emotions necessarily refer outward—beyond individuals—to historically and culturally specific social relations and economic arrangements" (172).

The personal recollections in the narratives studied here are not devoid of emotions either; Bela-Lobedde, for example, repeatedly highlights in those sections of her book that correspond to her childhood memories how the jokes that non-Black children made about the color of her skin or the realization that none of her friends had ever experienced an encounter with the police made her feel alienated and ashamed.[25] After discussing several examples of institutionalized racism, Boho concedes that the feeling of impotence and sadness in that type of situation "is indescribable."[26] Gerehou, on the other hand, describes the combination of pain, impotence, and rage that overcame him after he was denied access to a club while his friends were admitted because, as the bouncer said to him, "We don't allow Blacks or Moors in here" (119),[27] a habitual practice in many Spanish venues where the underlying racism is more frequently hidden under the commonplace "derecho de admisión" [right of admission], and which, not coincidentally, provides the title for García López's poetic anthology. The sharing of emotions, far from detracting from the value of autoethnography, contributes to humanizing these stories and appeals to the reader's empathy, while making clear that no matter how much one learns about racism, *knowing* intellectually is not the same as *knowing* from experience:

"There is an unwritten rule about racism in Spain and that is that we Black people do not know about racism, we suffer racism" (Bibang, "Madurez").

Not all the emotions present in these personal histories are negative, though. In fact, humor abounds in many of them, as is evident in some of the examples above. Because we started this collection of essays with a chapter in which anti-Black humor became a weapon to perpetuate white supremacy, we want to end on a humorous note, but this time with jokes that Black people make as a form of resistance. According to Jonathan P. Rossing, humor can become emancipatory, helping to point out gaps in "equality, justice, and freedom, and the realities of discrimination, social injustice, and oppression" (615). For example, Gerehou includes in his book the introduction to his TED talk, where he mentions his main hobbies and traits: "I like rap music, playing basketball, I love to dance, and no, I do not have a big penis" (134).[28] In this opening statement, which the audience greets with laughter, Gerehou demystifies the false expectations related to the physical endowment of Black men, a product of the colonialist hypersexualization of Black bodies. In a similar tone, Thior surprises one of the guests on his podcast, voice actor Rafael Arkebi, by posing racist questions during their interview. After Arkebi explained that he had arrived in Spain from Equatorial Guinea when he was sixteen, Thior stated that Arkebi was, then, a "new" Black person and that he was surprised he could speak Spanish so perfectly after such a brief period in the country. While the joke caught everyone off guard, creating an uncomfortable moment of confusion among both Arkebi and Thior's colleagues, the actor immediately reacted by playing along with the joke (@negroseneltibet, "Cuando Lamine te resume"). This type of humor also appears frequently in Bibang's comedy, where she uses irony to expose racist beliefs, like the concept of meritocracy or the recent cultural misappropriating practice known as "Blackfishing."[29] Finally, it is worth mentioning Bela-Lobedde's hilarious "Negrito" episode in her chapter "De anuncios y canciones" [On Commercials and Songs], where she exposes the absurdity of stereotyping Black skin as chocolate in the launch of the popular Spanish ice cream "Negrito" [Little Black Man] (38–39). In a hysterical description of the stupidity of the advertising images and the mocking chants of children singing the "Negrito" jingle to her, which were met by the author's vindicating response the year the company launched the white chocolate version "Blanquito" [Little White Man], Bela-Lobedde invites her non-Black readers to reverse history and witness past experiences that are part of a shared collective Spanish memory, this time from the viewpoint of a Black person.

The counternarratives presented here contain significant amounts of knowledge (emotional, supportive, and educational) that alter and complete what we have always known with what we should know, alerting us to what we cannot fail to know. Indeed, the epistemic value of these autoethnographies multiplies; firstly, they are packed with recommendations and directions that can serve as strategic guidelines for a Black audience to navigate microaggressions and different types of racism in their daily lives by pointing out institutional services where they can report injustices, as well as by including tips on how to act when they are the targets of racist abuse. The support and comfort in letting Black readers know that they are not alone add a healing element to the intrinsic value of autoethnography, while the emotional side of the testimonies humanizes their experiences and appeals to white readers' sense of empathy. Moreover, by turning anti-Black racist jokes around, the authors and artists analyzed here use humor as a pedagogical tool to subvert hegemonic racism (Rossing 499) and to urge white readers to reimagine history from the viewpoint of a Black person, an inversion of perspective that, as Mills argues, is one of the characteristic features of alternative epistemologies (*Blackness Visible* 28). At the same time, the autoethnographies strive to overcome Spain's tenacious Afro-amnesia by recovering the names of prominent Black Spanish figures, questioning white-centered concepts of nationhood, and establishing historical and cultural connections with Africa and the African Diaspora.

The radical effect of these first-person counternarratives is to truly decolonize Eurocentric epistemology by defying the Western discourse, "redrawing the map," and centering other knowledges that help to "give a more veridical picture of the dynamics of the social system" (Mills, *Blackness Visible* 28), since no epistemology can pretend to be universal and objective while at the same time ignoring other views and perspectives; it is precisely by including partial perspectives "that the possibility of sustained, rational, objective inquiry rests" (Haraway 584). Decolonizing acts, Mignolo affirms, must pursue common interests and not individual ones (*The Politics* 33); therefore, at the end of these narratives, the authors extend an invitation to their readers to join them in their antiracist activism. For this reason, our conclusion must be an inconclusive one. This does not end here, as we hope that these voices are amplified and multiplied, obliterating the biased accounts that they sold us as the "objective truth" and building a new tapestry of Spain with all the knowledges that constitute its rich and diverse history. To close this chapter and, with it, this volume, we will adopt Gerehou's proclamation at the conclusion of his book as our statement of intent: "Each story we share must be another brick in the wall that, on the one hand, isolates us from racism, and on the other, builds the walls of the home that we imagine ... Being antiracist starts from oneself, but it must necessarily continue in a collective manner" (249).[30]

Notes

1 "cuando dejas de buscar excusas y disculpas para todas las situaciones racistas en las que te ves envuelta al cabo del día; cuando caes en todos los chistes y gracietas racistas que has reído a lo largo de tu vida para no sentirte excluída; en todos los comentarios que dejas pasar, en todas las veces que te has creído especial al ser exotizada."
2 "Yo no supe que era negra hasta que llegué a España."
3 "Consejos prácticos de actuación en casos de microrracismos" and "Tips para hacer activismo antirracista en las redes sociales."
4 "consideraba que no me abriría ninguna puerta, una idea que tenía bastante interiorizada."
5 "¡Ah! ¡Pero que habla como nosotros!"
6 "La realidad es que el hausa es la segunda lengua más hablada en África y se utiliza en países como Nigeria, Camerún, Ghana, Burkina Faso o Togo, mientras que el fular es lengua oficial en territorios como Mauritania, Senegal o Mali. Pero nunca oiremos a nadie despreciar el italiano, pese a que lo hablen menos personas que el hausa y solo sea lengua oficial en Italia y Ciudad del Vaticano."
7 "¿Estás segura que podrías sacarte este curso? Hay opciones más fáciles para la gente como tú." This skepticism also extends to other racialized groups like Roma people in Spain. Many Roma students complain that educators have no expectations and give up on them due to stigmatization (Alcutén).
8 Boho refers to a public accusation of "social apartheid" made to both British universities in 2017 by the former British education minister David Lammy after data revealed that in 2015, nearly one in three Oxford colleges and six Cambridge ones failed to admit any Black British A-students (Adams and Bengtsson).
9 "Ahora resulta que, como tenemos las caras pintadas, matamos a negros, ¿no?"
10 "Uno no se vuelve racista intolerante cuando pasa el torno del estadio."
11 The *Guardia Civil* or Civil Guard is one of the two police institutions in Spain, the other one being the *Policía Nacional*. While the latter acts within the city limits, the former controls rural areas, roads, and highways. "DNI" stands for *Documento Nacional de Identidad* [National Identity Document].
12 "[A]hora, de mayor, sé que lo que me pasó … se denomina 'detención por perfil étnico.' Son detenciones racistas. Es racismo institucional."
13 "¿Te molesto yo cuando estás haciendo tu trabajo? Estoy haciendo mi trabajo."
14 "-¿Tenéis drogas? / -No." Although García López was born in Colombia, he moved to Spain when he was nine. Therefore, the situation described in the poem most likely occurred in Spain.
15 "en el momento en el que tienes prisa, y ejerces tu derecho a tener prisa."
16 "Ay, gracias por no pegarme ocho tiros, caballero, de verdad."
17 "siento que no entienden la diferencia entre el hecho de que a ellos les paren 'porque llevan pintas' o porque están haciendo algo raro y a mí por ser negra. No es lo mismo. No lo es."
18 Mills uses the Jim Crow laws in the United States as an example: erasing them from books on US history could lead to losing a holistic perspective and to justifying current poverty levels among Black Americans because of their alleged unwillingness to work ("White Ignorance" 242).
19 "falta de confianza, inseguridad, incapacidad para relacionarse con sus iguales y depresión."

20 "el odio del racismo si no se esparce muere."
21 "y por eso duele tanto el silencio de las personas de bien que callan ante el racismo como si fuera algo tan irrelevante como las coles de Bruselas."
22 UNAF consists of twenty-three different associations from all over Spain which provide education on different social issues, such as racism and gender violence; they offer support to different collectives such as persons with disabilities, Roma women, divorced and separated women, and single-parent or immigrant families, and they also undertake different initiatives and collaborative project to promote social transformation.
23 "cuanto más oscura sea una persona, más rechazo social existe."
24 "Las personas racializadas no tenemos el espacio para definirnos porque el entorno del estado español suele ser mayoritariamente blanco y para formar la identidad es importante tener un entorno en el que referenciarte."
25 For a deeper analysis of the role of shame in Bela-Lobedde's autoethnography, see Ana León-Távora.
26 "es indescriptible."
27 "Aquí no pueden entrar ni negros ni moros."
28 "me gusta la música rap, jugar al baloncesto, me encanta bailar y no, no tengo el pene grande."
29 "Blackfishing" is a trend among non-Black celebrities and influencers who appear in the media and at public events with a dark complexion in an attempt to emulate successful Black artists. Online, this can be done using editing software, and in both cases makeup is often used to change the skin tone and features.
30 "Cada historia que compartimos tiene que ser un ladrillo más en una pared que, por un lado, nos aísle del racismo, y por otro, construya las paredes del hogar que nos imaginamos ... Ser antirracista empieza por uno mismo, pero debe seguir necesariamente por lo colectivo."

Works Cited

Adams, Richard, and Helena Bengtsson. "Oxford Accused of 'Social Apartheid' as Colleges Admit No Black Students." *The Guardian*, 19 Oct. 2017, https://www.theguardian.com/education/2017/oct/19/oxford-accused-of-social-apartheid-as-colleges-admit-no-black-students.

Adams, Tony E., et al. "Autoethnography." *The International Encyclopedia of Communication Research Methods*, edited by Jörg Matthes, Christine S. Davis, and Robert F. Potter, John Wiley & Sons, Inc., 2017, pp. 1–11, https://onlinelibrary.wiley.com/doi/pdf/10.1002/9781118901731.iecrm0011#:~:text=A%20brief%20history%20of%20autoethnography. Accessed 2 Sept. 2023.

Afropoderossa. *España no es solo blanca*. eBook, Molino, 2023.

@afropoderossa and @ehuniverso. "La historia de Perla." *Instagram*, 12 July 2023, https://www.instagram.com/reel/CumnOp9smvg/?igshid=MzRlODBiNWFlZA==. Accessed 23 Sept. 2023.

Ajari, Norman. *Dignidad o muerte. Ética y política de la raza*. Translated by Cristina Lizarbe Ruiz, Editorial Txalaparta, 2021.

Alcutén, Jacobo. "Los gitanos alzan la voz contra el fracaso y la discriminación en el colegio: 'Mi mejor amiga no me invitó a su cumpleaños por mi raza.'" *20 Minutos*, 6 Sept. 2023, https://www.20minutos.es/noticia/5169753/0/

gitanos-alzan-voz-contra-fracaso-discriminacion-colegio-mejor-amiga-no-invito-cumpleanos-ser-gitana/.

Azzoni, Tales. "Vinicius Junior Says Spanish League 'Now Belongs to Racists' After Enduring More Abuse." *AP News*, 21 May 2023, https://apnews.com/article/vinicius-junior-racism-real-madrid-valencia-spanish-league-6eea3f8129dabcbefa76545c39d58fe8.

Bela-Lobedde, Desirée. *Ser mujer negra en España*. Plan B, 2018.

Bhabha, Homi. "Of Mimicry and Man: The Ambivalence of Colonial Discourse." *Discipleship: A Special Issue on Psychoanalysis*, vol. 28, Spring 1984, pp. 125–33.

Bibang, Asaari. *Y a pesar de todo, aquí estoy*. eBook, Bruguera, 2021.

Boho, Adriana. *Ponte en mi piel. Guía para combatir el racismo cotidiano*. eBook, Libros Cúpula, 2022.

Camangian, Patrick Roz, et al. "Upsetting the (Schooling) Set Up: Autoethnography as Critical Race Methodology." *International Journal of Qualitative Studies in Education*, vol. 36, no. 1, 2023, pp. 57–71.

Castro-Gómez, Santiago. *Zero-Point Hubris: Science, Race, and Enlightenment in Eighteenth-Century Latin America (Reinventing Critical Theory)*. eBook, Rowman & Littlefield Publishers, 2021.

Chawla, Devika, and Ahmet Atay. "Introduction: Decolonizing Autoethnography." *Cultural Studies ↔ Critical Methodologies*, vol. 18, no. 1, 2018, pp. 3–8.

DiAngelo, Robin. *White Fragility. Why It's So Hard for White People to Talk About Racism*. Beacon P, 2018.

Du Bois, W.E.B. *The Souls of Black Folk*. Gramercy Books, 1994.

Eddo-Lodge, Reni. *Why I'm No Longer Talking to White People About Race*. Bloomsbury Publishing, 2019.

Fanon, Frantz. *Black Skin, White Masks*. Translated by Richard Philcox, Grove P, 2008.

Foucault, Michel. *Power/Knowledge. Selected Interviews & Other Writings. 1972–1977*. Edited by Colin Gordon, translated by Colin Gordon et al. Vintage Books, 1980.

García López, Yeison F. "Control aleatorio." *Derecho de Admisión*. Laimprenta, 2021, p. 50.

Gerehou, Moha. *¿Qué hace un negro como tú en un sitio como este?* Península, 2021.

Haraway, Donna. "Situated Knowledges: The Science Question in Feminism and the Privilege of Partial Perspectives." *Feminist Studies*, vol. 14, no. 3, 1988, pp. 575–99.

León-Távora, Ana. "Afectos y activismo estético en *Ser mujer negra en España*, de Desirée Bela-Lobedde." *El reflejo de Medusa: Representaciones mediáticas de las mujeres contemporáneas*, edited by Esther Alarcón Arana, Advook Editorial, 2023, pp. 203–17.

Mendieta, Eduardo. "The Ethics of (Not)-Knowing: Take Care of Ethics and Knowledge Will Come of Its Own Accord." *Decolonizing Epistemologies: Latino/a Theology and Philosophy*, edited by Ada María Isasi-Díaz and Eduardo Mendieta. Fordham UP, 2011, pp. 247–64.

Mignolo, Walter D. "Epistemic Disobedience, Independent Thought, and Decolonial Freedom." *Theory, Culture & Society*, vol. 26, no. 7–8, 2009, pp. 159–81.

Mignolo, Walter D. *The Politics of Decolonial Investigation*. Duke UP, 2021.

Mills, Charles W. *Blackness Visible: Essays on Philosophy and Race*. Cornell UP, 1998.
———. "White Ignorance." *Agnotology. The Making and Unmaking of Ignorance*, edited by Robert N. Proctor and Londa Schiebinger. Stanford UP, 2008, pp. 210–30.
Moya, Paula M. L. "'Racism Is Not Intellectual': Interracial Friendship, Multicultural Literature, and Decolonizing Epistemologies." *Decolonizing Epistemologies: Latino/a Theology and Philosophy*, edited by Ada María Isasi-Díaz and Eduardo Mendieta. Fordham UP, 2011, pp. 169–90.
@negroseneltibet. "Cuando Lamine te resume en un minuto todo lo que no hay que decir." *Instagram*, 18 Sept. 2023, https://www.instagram.com/reel/CxWAySNq9OK/?utm_source=ig_web_copy_link&igshid=MzRlODBiNWFlZA==. Accessed 23 Sept. 2023.
———. "Cuando tratan de justificar los insultos r*cistas en el fútbol." *Instagram*, 22 May 2023, https://www.instagram.com/reel/CsjXVz2h97d/?igshid=MzRlODBiNWFlZA==. Accessed 23 Sept. 2023.
Plaza Casares, Sara. "Racismo en la escuela: Asignatura pendiente." *Elsaltodiario.com*, 8 Sept. 2019, https://www.elsaltodiario.com/educacion/racismo-escuela-asignatura-pendiente. Accessed 20 Sept. 2023.
Proctor, Robert N. "Agnotology: A Missing Term to Describe the Cultural Production of Ignorance (and Its Study)." *Agnotology. The Making and Unmaking of Ignorance*, edited by Robert N. Proctor and Londa Schiebinger, Stanford UP, 2008, pp. 1–20.
———. Preface. *Agnotology. The Making and Unmaking of Ignorance*, edited by Robert N. Proctor and Londa Schiebinger, Stanford UP, 2008, p. vii.
Ramirez, Carla. "Epistemic Disobedience and Grief in Academia." *Education Sciences*, vol. 11, no. 447, 2021, pp. 1–15.
Rosas, Paula. "Vinícius | Cuánto racismo hay realmente en España: El intenso debate que generaron los insultos al futbolista brasileño." *BBC News Mundo*, 26 May 2023, https://www.bbc.com/mundo/noticias-internacional-65703703. Accessed 23 Sept. 2023.
Rossing, Jonathan P. "Emancipatory Racial Humor as Critical Public Pedagogy: Subverting Hegemonic Racism." *Communication, Culture & Critique*, vol. 9, no. 4, pp. 614–32.
"Spain: Stop Racism, Not People. Racial Profiling and Immigration Control in Spain." *Amnesty International*, https://www.amnesty.org/en/documents/eur41/011/2011/en/. Accessed 20 Sept. 2023.
Thior, Lamine. "La reacción que tiene la gente cuando escucha hablar a Lamine Thior: 'Ah, pero que hablas como nosotros.'" Interview by Thais Villas. *El intermedio*, 1 Dec. 2022, https://www.lasexta.com/programas/el-intermedio/reaccion-que-tiene-gente-cuando-escucha-hablar-lamine-thior-pero-que-hablas-como-nosotros_20221201638925380779b000016c6304.html. Accessed 15 Sept. 2023.
"UNAF visibiliza el trauma racial y cómo abordarlo." *Unión de Asociaciones Familiares* (UNAF), https://unaf.org/unaf-visibiliza-el-trauma-racial-y-como-abordarlo/. Accessed 2 Sept. 2023.

Index

Note: Page numbers followed by "n" denote endnotes

Abascal, Santiago 31, 36, 42, 204–05; see also Vox
abolition 47n24, 62, 169, 173n20, 178–79; abolitionist 94, 175, 178, 191n6
activism 4, 9, 11, 13, 16, 51, 81, 89, 95, 98–99, 103n6, 108, 112, 117, 118, 121, 129n37, 130n56, 154–55, 158, 160, 165–66, 171n3, 196, 199, 201, 216–17, 229, 231, 234
Adam, Tania 7; "España negra" 7; *Radio Africa Magazine* 7, 12
África negra 12
aesthetics 7, 45, 201
African American history 11, 215; African American community 11, 182, 210n44
African migration 116
Africanisms 32
Afrodescendance 112, 114, 115, 117, 119, 122; Afrodescendant 111, 112–13, 115, 116–17, 119, 120–27, 127–28n6; *afrodescendiente* 18, 104n12, 108–09, 112, 129n22, 130n46, 131, 189n9; Afro-Andalusian 221; Afro-Catalan 14, 175; Afro-French 2; *Afro-madrileño* 7; Afrospanish 111, 116–17, 120, 125, 126, 128n15
Afrocolectiva 103n6, 106
Afroféminas 7, 9, 12, 47n3, 85, 88–93, 96, 97–102, 103n3, 103n6, 103n7, 103n10, 111, 128n15, 167, 172n18, 196
Afromayores 17n11

Afropea 2; Afropean 2, 11–12, 14; Afropean(ness) 111; Afroeurope 111; see also Pitts
Afropessimism 8, 15, 51–52, 59, 61–62, 65, 66n1
Afropoderossa 15, 216, 217
Afropolitan 58
Afro-Spanishness (or Afrospanishness) 3–5, 13, 15, 112, 116–17, 120, 124–26, 128, 128n15, 156; *afroespañolidad* 111; Spanishness 9, 13, 92, 120, 225; non-Spanishness 54
agency 5, 12–15, 47n22, 63, 113, 123, 127, 154, 165–67, 172n14, 196, 204, 218
agnotology 223–24, 226, 227, 235
Ajari, Norman 16n6, 17, 218, 224; *cotidianidad mutilada* 224
Akam, Paulo 91, 100
Albert Sopale, Silvia 48n30, 112
Alcorcón 17, 19, 144–45, 150n21, 195, 198–201, 204–06, 207n6, 207n10, 207n11, 208n16, 208n21, 209n27, 210n44, 210n46; *alcornófilo* 201
American Reconstruction 40
Amin, Idi 56
amnesia 2, 3, 199, 226; Afro-amnesia 4, 9, 15, 88–89, 196, 216, 231
anamnesis 222
Anguiano, Montserrat 14, 175–80, 182–86, 188–90; 192n14; *Dona, Mujer, Women* 14, 176; *Referent és nom de Dona* 176, 186–90, 192n24

animalization 26
Annobón 8, 52, 57–58, 62–65, 67n17, 68–71
anthropology 24–25, 54, 174
anthropophagy 29, 46n19; cannibalism 29–30, 32, 140; cannibalistic 29, 32, 35, 44, 47n19
anti-racism 9, 72–73, 78, 81, 100, 103n6, 178; antiracist 9, 89–90, 102, 104n8, 107, 119, 121, 146–47, 165, 173, 192, 216–17, 219, 226, 228, 229, 231
Antón, Rubén 176
aporophobia 204
Appiah, Kwame Anthony 16n2, 161
appropriation 6, 201, 216, 218, 220–21, 223; misappropriation 40, 47n22, 216, 217; re-appropriation 123
Aravaca 53–55, 74, 172n11
Archer-Straw, Petrine 22, 25, 28, 31, 35, 45, 47n24
Arkebi, Rafael 230
Arroyo Pizarro, Yolanda 102, 106n39
Art Deco 40
Asante, Molefi 161, 172n14
assimilation 160, 220
autobiography 4, 128n9, 135, 217, 218; autobiographical 10, 111–12, 114, 116, 127, 128n9, 186, 216, 218
autoethnography 15, 18, 216–18, 220, 222, 229, 231, 233n25
avant-garde 7, 21, 22–23, 25, 34, 40, 45, 48, 140
Ayim, May 2, 17

Baartman, Sarah 179, 180, 182, 187, 192n13, 192n14
Baker, Josephine 36, 37, 49, 176, 187, 191
barbershop 205, 206, 210
barrio 15, 128n15, 195–200, 202, 205, 206, 207n1, 207n6, 207n8, 207n16, 208n17, 208n24, 210n42; Barrio de Salamanca 204, 210n41; *barrionalero* 201; *Barrionalismos* 14, 15, 195–98; *barrionalista* 199, 200, 205–06, 207n6; *banlieues* 8, 205; *see also* neighborhood
Battle of Annual 25
Bayangue 119

Bela-Lobedde, Desirée 12, 15, 92, 129n37, 130n56, 216–17, 225–27, 230, 233n25; *Ser mujer negra en España* 12, 17, 103n5, 108, 216
bell hooks 94, 97, 98
belonging 2, 3, 8, 10, 12, 14–15, 44, 75, 78, 89, 90–92, 97, 100, 112–14, 117–20, 121, 124, 144, 160, 166, 169, 176, 183, 190, 195, 197, 205–06, 228
Bermúdez, Rubén H. 7, 12, 101, 111
Bermúdez, Silvia 4, 85n8, 148n2
bias 99, 122; internal 224; internalized 219, 222; institutional 98; linguistic 221; white 97
Bibang, Asaari 15, 48n30, 176, 216–17, 219, 224, 227–28, 230
Black Americans 11, 159, 233n18
Black Archive (s) 6, 7, 12, 13
Black Atlantic 106n40, 193; culture 184; perspective 169
Black bodies 8, 26, 27, 31, 35, 40, 45, 230
Black Europe 2, 17n14, 20; Black Central Europe 12
Black Iberian Studies 7
Black Legend 136, 142
Black Lives Matter 4, 10, 158, 171n9
Black masculinity 61, 141
Black Panthers 153, 159–60; Black Panther Party 160, 170n1; *Panteras Negras* 160
Black Power 10, 160–61, 171n3, 172n12
Black women 10, 14, 47n20, 89, 94–98, 101, 104n10, 122, 124, 126, 137, 140, 153, 157–58, 164, 166–67, 169, 175–80, 183–86, 188–90
Blackface 21, 33, 38–42, 44, 48n30, 77, 143, 198, 223
Blackfishing 230, 233n29
Blackness 1–4, 8, 10, 12–13, 15, 17n12, 26, 42, 45n4, 54–55, 57, 60–62, 64–65, 77, 80–81, 112, 115–17, 119–20, 122–24, 127n1, 128n19, 136, 138, 141–43, 146, 147, 160, 182, 197, 216, 219, 223, 227, 231; anti-Blackness 54–55, 72, 73
Blumenbach, Johann Friedrich 26, 46n10

Index 239

Boampong, Johanna 114
Boho, Adriana 216–17, 221–22, 227, 229, 232n8
Bokassa, Jean-Bédel 56
Bokoko, Bisila África 183, 187
Bolekia, Justo 154
Borst, Julia 3, 16n3, 113, 129n37, 207n3
Bosaho Gori, Rita 117, 124, 128n11, 154, 187
Bourdieu, Pierre 200
Buale, Emilio 154
Buen Humor magazine 7, 21–24, 28–32, 35–36, 39, 42–44
Buika, Concha 154, 183–84, 210n45

Cabral, Amílcar 56, 66n8
Cachita 4
Cakewalk 34, 47n26
Camps, Victoria 189
Carabanchel 208n25, *Carabancheleando* 201, 208n25; *see also* barrio
Casillas, Iker 60, 61; *see also* Zamora Loboch
Castizo, Reyes 34
Castro-Gómez, Santiago 6; zero-point hubris 5, 17, 218
Caucasian 24, 26, 46n10
Céspedes, Elena de 164
Charleston 34–35, 42, 48n32; *charlestón* 47n27, 47n28
Chikaba, Teresa de 164
Chikos del Maíz, "Barrionalistas" 197, 201, 208n19; *see also* barrios; gambling
chocolate man 138–39, 141; chocolate skin 31, 34–35, 47n27, 230
choni 200–01, 208n21, 214; chonismo 208n22; *Yo soy la Juani* 208n22
citizen 2, 4, 12, 52, 74–75, 88, 97, 99, 123, 147, 154, 165, 168, 191, 199, 203; Afro-Latin American citizens 169; Black citizen 12, 63, 183; citizenship 2–3, 14, 52, 60, 64, 66n3, 78, 119; non-citizen 8, 60–61; Pan-Africanist Womanist citizens 169
Cola Cao 139, 177
Coleman, Jeffrey K. 4, 76, 148n2

collective memory 14, 116, 179, 186–87, 190, 195, 206
colonialism 6, 10, 28, 52, 54–56, 61–65, 103n4, 134, 137, 139–41, 147, 166, 177, 182, 196, 222; anxieties 138–41, 147; colonial discourse 8, 13, 57, 62–63, 136; gazes 4; history 2, 12, 54, 58, 196; iconography 14, 24; neocolonialism 8, 57, 61
coloniality 5, 8, 12, 20, 57, 61; *see also* power
colonization 5, 51, 157, 160, 167, 172n13, 209n26, 220–21; decolonization 6, 7, 15, 57, 136, 154, 162, 164–65, 216, 218
colorblindness 3–4, 15, 223; colorblind 223
commodification 201
Concepción Vicente, Yania 176
Conciencia Afro 7, 88–89, 196
Conguitos 139, 177
Coop. Periferia Cimarronas 88
Cornejo-Parriego, Rosalía 4, 37, 128n15, 148n2
Cortés Damian, Lydia 121, 124, 128n11, 130n56
cosmopolitan 22, 24, 42
costumbrista genre 198–99; *artículos de costumbres* 198
counterdiscourse 206; *see also* narratives
COVID-19 83, 100, 200, 202, 203
Crenshaw, Kimberlé 94, 98, 167
Critical Race Theory Studies (CRT) 3, 87, 148n2, 218
Crosland, Alan 40; *The Jazz Singer* 40
Cruz Salanova, Luis de la 197, 200–02, 207n1, 208n23

Dark Continent 14, 181, 182
darky iconography 39, 40; *Darktown Comics* 40
Davis, Angela 153, 170n1, 176
decoloniality 6; decolonial 4–5, 9, 13, 65, 90, 159, 170; decolonization 6–7, 15, 57, 136, 154, 162, 164–65, 216, 218
desarrollismo 13, 134, 140, 148n3
deterritorialization 206; deterritorialized 135, 206

diaspora 12–14, 19, 47, 55, 61, 112, 140, 169, 174, 181, 186; African 111, 131, 133, 161, 176, 178, 181, 190, 216, 231; Afrodiasporic knowledge(s) 116, 124, 127, 128n9; Afro-diasporic subject(s) 10–11, 115, 121, 154; Afro-diasporic 4, 10–13, 17, 126, 154, 157–58, 162, 169–70, 196; Black 3–4, 10–12; Black European 14
Díaz Ayuso, Isabel 139, 203
dictatorship 12, 24, 47n20, 52, 58, 134, 148n7, 171n10, 198
didacticism 89, 98
Dieng, Omar 11–12
disability 72, 199
discrimination 84, 89, 93, 96–98, 100, 117, 119, 120, 124, 148, 159, 167, 184, 187, 197
disease 35, 42, 56, 200, 202–03; *see also* COVID-19
Domingos, Ndombele Augustus 144–45, 207n6
Dominican Republic 53, 55, 205
Du Bois, W. E. B., double consciousness 88, 219
Dussel, Enrique 16, 166
Dyson, Michael Eric 155

Edjogo Owono, Alberto 224
Ekoka Hernandis, Deborah 10, 112, 115–27
El Chojín 72, 73, 77–81, 83–84, 86, 103, 107, 154
El Duende de Madrid 22
El negro que tenía el alma blanca (film) 7, 22, 40
El-Tayeb, Fatima 2–3, 10, 14, 204, 207n2
emotions 115–16, 124, 189–90, 229, 230
empathy 102, 134, 142, 145–48, 184, 228–29, 231
empower 89, 98, 114–15, 126, 170, 182
Eneva, Stoyanka 197, 199, 207n7
enslaved 1, 32, 56, 60–61, 63, 169, 177–78, 185, 190, 191n6, 192n21, 218; enslavers 61, 177–78

epistemology 15, 24, 64, 216, 218, 220, 222, 231; epistemological 9, 72, 229; epistemic 217, 221, 223, 226–27, 231
equality stamps 9, 72, 73, 75–84, 84n1, 85n10, 85n16, 85n18, 85n20, 86, 86n23, 86n24, 87
Equatorial Guinea 4, 8, 12–13, 20, 46n19, 52–55, 57–59, 64, 66n3, 68, 70, 102n1, 127n2, 135, 137, 140, 143, 148n7, 149n8, 154, 157, 160, 165, 171n4, 176, 177, 183, 185, 189, 191n7, 195, 207n5
Essed, Philomena 74
Essonti Luque, Agnes 111, 119, 121–22, 126, 128n11, 129n26, 129n37
EstadoEspañolNoTanBlanco (#) 89–90
ethnographic journalism 200
ethnographic museums 25
ethnology 24
Eurocentrism 9, 89–90, 94, 167; Eurocentric 15, 32, 88, 100, 102, 115–16, 129n37, 153, 160, 162, 216–18, 220, 222, 231
Europeanization 136, 158
exile 20, 52–53, 55, 57, 59, 62, 69–70

Fanon, Frantz 6, 26, 42, 44, 220–22; negrophobia 45n4; phobogenesis 46n17; sociogenesis 42; white gaze 120
Federación SOS Racismo 72–74, 81, 93; *see also* equality stamps
feminism 3, 95, 99, 103n6, 167, 170n1, 178, 234; Black 17, 98, 117; digital 99; Eurocentric 164; hegemonic 97, 99, 102, 167; intersectional 95; white, mainstream 9, 94–95
feminist strike *Huelga Feminista* 95; 8M Feminist Strike 98; Strike Manifesto 96; *see also Afroféminas*
flamenco 164, 183
Floyd, George 9–10, 72, 84n1, 93
foreignness 3, 54, 141, 202, 204; foreignization 96–97, 101, 221
Foucault, Michel 5, 202, 217
Foxtrot 34
Fra-Molinero, Baltasar 4, 8, 26–27, 46n14, 47n20, 92

Index 241

Franco, Francisco 52–53, 74, 136, 142, 147, 148n3, 148n7; Francoism 13, 135–36, 140, 177
Frank, T. 154, 224
Freud, Sigmund 22
Friedan, Betty 94

Gallo González, Danae 3, 207
gambling 199, 208n19; *see also* Chikos del Maíz
García López, Ricardo (K-Hito) 21
García López, Yeison F. 7, 17n5, 225; *Madrid Negro* 7
Garvey, Marcus 159, 161–63, 218
gaze 15, 24, 29, 33, 45, 95, 120, 196, 216
Gellner, Ernest 91
gender-based injustices 157; violence 199
genealogy 13–14, 90, 125, 154
Gérard, Mathieu 24, 46
Gerehou, Moha 7, 15, 18, 47n30, 84n2, 89, 90, 103n5, 111, 128, 217, 220–22, 225–26, 229–30
Global South 76, 77, 94, 202, 204
Gómez de la Serna, Ramón 21, 22, 23, 24, 40, 45
Goode, Joshua 24'25, 136, 148n2
Goytisolo, Juan 210n42
Gurumbé 4
Gutiérrez magazine 21–24, 27, 29, 35, 37–38, 41, 44, 46n9

Haitian Revolution 156–57
Hall, Stuart 7–8, 12
Haraway, Donna 5, 231; situated point of view 217
Harlem Renaissance 10
Hartman, Saidiya 55, 60–61
hegemony 16, 113, 227
Hispanidad 55
home 10, 18, 20, 52, 67, 94, 112, 119–21, 137, 197–98, 202, 207n1, 231; Afro home 124; African home 2, 13; homeland 12, 52, 112, 127
human exhibitions 46n13; live exhibits 25
humor 5, 7–8, 15–16, 22–24, 26, 29, 42, 44–45, 45n5, 120, 129n20, 198, 206, 228, 230–31; *humorismo* 21, 23, 45; Humor Studies 23
hybridity 135, 218, 204–05; experiences 6; identities 10
hypersexuality 140–41; hypersexualization 230

Ibaka, Serge 154
identity 142, 146, 148, 154, 162–64, 170, 184, 186, 195–97, 204–06, 216–17, 223, 228; Black identity 175–76; dual/double identity 178, 183, 189
ignorance 15, 90–91, 157; active 226; passive 223
immigration 3–4, 55, 74, 76, 136, 142n2, 149n8, 156, 158, 203–04; *see also* migrants
imperialism 24, 68, 90, 102, 137–38, 177; imperial debris 137
inequalities 176, 181–82, 184; inequities 147; inequity 228
Insúa, Alberto *El negro que tenía el alma blanca* 22, 40–41, 44
integration 8, 160, 163, 165
interracial 117, 134, 136–42, 144–47, 149n17
intersectionality 96–97, 100, 102, 105n27
invisibility 1, 8, 124, 201; invisibilization 88, 91, 96, 101, 113, 118; *see also* visibility

Jackson, Mary 187, 188
Jardiel Poncela, Enrique 32, 47n22
jazz 21, 33, 34, 35, 36, 39, 40, 42, 50, 183; jazz band 34, 36, 39, 47n27; *Jazzbandismo* 40; *Le Danseur de Jazz* 40; *The Jazz Singer* 40
Jezebels 175
Jim Crow 33, 232n18
Johnson, Katherine 187–88
Jones, Nicholas R. 47n22

knots of memory (*noeuds de mémoire*) 13, 134–35
knowledge 1, 3, 9–10, 16n5, 58, 102, 112, 114–15, 119–22, 125–26, 138, 156, 162, 169, 186, 218–19, 222, 225–26, 230; Afrodiasporic

242 Index

124, 126–27, 127n6; archives of 112, 114; antiracist 90; collective 114; colonial 90; Eurocentric 217; marginalized 10, 112; power and knowledge 5, 8, 15, 217; silenced/hidden 128n6, 226

Ladan, Sani 221–22
Landsberg, Alison 138
language of joy 10, 112, 123
Lavapiés 16n3, 58–59
Le Rire 42
León-Távora, Ana 88, 233n25
Ley de Vagos y Maleantes 198
LGBTQ+ community 198
liberation 11, 56, 62, 121, 159, 161–63, 169; Black liberation 170n1; Black Liberation Party 160
Lindo, Elvira 208n25
Little Black Sambo 40
lo quinqui 229n28
locality 14, 195, 197–99, 206
Lombardi-Diop, Cristina 2, 16n4
López Rubio, Francisco 35
López Rubio, José 35
Lucas, Nêga 176
Lumumba, Patrice 161, 172n14

Maalouf, Amin 196
Macías Nguema, Francisco 12, 52, 56, 58, 66n2, 66n3, 148n7, 171n10
Madre, cómprame un negro 34, 47n27
Malcolm X 155–57, 159, 160–61, 163, 171n5, 171n7; Spike Lee's *Malcolm X* 159
Mamadou, Isabelle 103n2, 176
Mami, el negro está rabioso 77
mammies 175, 185
Mandela, Nelson 168, 183
Mandela, Winnie Madikizela 168
margins 44, 90, 95, 113, 120, 195–96, 201, 210n46, 218
Mariannes Noires 2
maroonism 13, 154, 164; marronage 168–69; *cimarronaje* 164–65, 169, 173n23, 173n24
Martín Gaite, Carmen 202
Mayo, Remei Sipi 123–24, 128n11, 168
Mbembe, Achille 62; necropolitics 7, 22, 44, 62; necropolitical 7, 45, 76

Mbomío Rubio, Lucía Asué 6, 7, 11, 154, 198–200, 202–04; *Hija del camino* 6, 13, 103n5, 134, 195–97, 207n5, 209n26; *Las que se atrevieron* 13, 134–36, 140, 142, 147–48
Memín Pinguín 75, 84n6
memory 8, 52, 54, 57, 65, 138, 169, 176, 186, 190, 197, 225; anticolonial 59; autobiographical 186; collective 14–15, 116, 149, 179, 186–87, 195, 206, 230; colonial 13, 134, 142; historical 64, 178, 185–86; prosthetic 138–40, 142; Memory Studies 176
MENAS 209n34
meritocracy 230
Mesa, Ondo 120, 124–25, 128n11
mestizaje 54
Metamba Miago 10, 12, 111, 113–19, 121, 123–25, 127, 128n6, 128n8, 128n9, 128n11
metropole 137–40, 142, 147
Metropolitan Museum of Art (the Met) 1
microaggressions 103n5, 112, 117, 219, 231
Mignolo, Walter 5–6, 16n5, 217, 220, 231
migrants 3, 75, 112, 119, 160, 197, 202, 204–06, 209n35; African 158, 162, 165; *pateras* 172n19; see also immigration
misogyny 13, 148
misrepresentation 22, 45, 217–19
missionaries 63–64
Modern Figures 193
modernity 5, 7, 16n6, 21, 24, 33–34, 45, 64, 92, 103n4, 113, 210n4; *modernidad* 47
Morreall, John 23
Murray, N. Michelle 4, 103n4, 148n2
Murillo, Bartolomé Esteban 1
Mwasi 12, 16n10

narratives 2, 4, 7–8, 10, 13–15, 40, 112–14, 116, 135–36, 140, 142, 147–48, 157, 169, 177, 195, 201, 206, 218–19, 222, 229, 231; counternarratives 3, 6, 13, 15, 218, 230–31

nationhood 13, 15, 90, 102, 231
Nazi Germany 25, 136
Ndongo Bidyogo, Donato 53, 66, 149, 154
Negra Flor 92
Negrito ice cream 230
Négritude 10, 163
Negro de Banyoles 48n30, 171n11
negrophilia 7, 22, 34, 40, 44–45; *négrophilie* 22; negrophiliac 47n24
negrophobia 34, 44, 45n4; negrophobic 22, 33
Negrxs Magazine 7, 111, 196
neighborhood 14, 119, 139, 165–97, 199, 201; *see also* barrio
Neo-Nazi groups 74, 159
Nfubea, Abuy 13, 14, 95, 153–56, 158–61, 163–64, 166–68, 170, 170–71n3, 171n5, 171n10, 171–72n11, 172n20, 173n23, 218; *Malcolm X y la generación hip-hop* 171n5
Ngozi Adichie, Chimamanda 88, 103n3, 201, 209n30
NGXMGZ 88
No hay negros en el Tibet (#) 224; @negroseneltibet 230, 235
Nora, Pierre 185; sites of memory, *lieux de mémoire* 135
notas oficiosas 24
Nyong'o, Lupita 187
Nzambi, Angela 122–24, 128n11

Obama, Michelle 187
Okafor, Victor Oguijiofor 161
online communities 4, 88
oppression 95, 96, 98, 116, 118, 161, 167, 170, 191, 219–20, 226, 230
Organization of Afro-American Unity 159
Ortega Arjonilla, Esther (Mayoko) 95, 109, 128n11, 128n19
Ortega y Gasset, José 22, 45, 46n7
Otele, Olivette 47n21
Othello 143

Pan-Africanism 11, 16n3, 156, 158, 161–64, 166, 168, 172n13, 181; Neopanafricanism 163
Pareja, Juan de 1, 4, 7
Peleteiro, Ana 154

Pérez Matos, Lucrecia 53–54, 74, 84, 101, 106n37, 146, 171–72n11
periferizar 200, 206
Pickaninny child 40
Pitts, Johny 2, 7, 16n3, 17n12; Afropeans 2; *The Afropean* 12; *see also* Afropea
Podemos (political party) 187
Poitier, Sidney 140–41, 149n16; *Guess Who's Coming to Dinner* 140–41, 151
political involution 206
pornomiseria 201
postcolonial nations 8
power 67n12, 100, 106, 138–56, 157, 182, 222; colonial 6, 66n3, 139; coloniality of 61; empowerment 1, 7, 13, 14, 15, 89, 95, 98, 103n3, 111, 119–20, 123, 139, 170n2, 182, 187, 193, 222; imperial, imperialistic 25, 44, 46n13; *see also* knowledge
prejudices 200, 205, 222
primitive 16n6, 25, 32, 35, 44, 137, 177, 179, 182, 202
Primo de Rivera, Miguel 24, 47n20
privilege 82, 95, 104n8, 127n1, 128n6, 147
Pro Derechos Humanos 226

Quijano, Aníbal 61

R. de la Flor, José Luis 22–23, 45n2, 46n7
race 3–4, 11, 13, 16n4, 26, 40, 44, 55, 61, 72, 74–77, 80, 92, 94–95, 98, 135, 137, 139, 141, 143, 154, 158, 162, 167, 170, 176, 178, 189, 196–97, 227–28; critical 3, 148, 219; 92–93, 137, 140–42, 144, 218; racelessness 3–4, 9
racial profiling 84n2, 93, 109, 224–27, 235
racialized 9–10, 14, 54, 57, 60, 73–74, 76, 81–83, 88, 90, 92–93, 96–97, 99, 101, 103n4, 112, 115, 124, 136, 148, 156, 169, 179, 196, 197, 204, 206, 217, 219, 221, 225, 228, 232n7;14; women 9, 89, 94–97, 99, 100, 115, 118, 127

racism 3, 8, 9, 10, 12–13, 15, 24, 52, 54, 67n14, 72–84, 90, 92, 95–97, 112–14, 116–17, 123, 136, 144, 146–48, 155, 159–61, 165, 167–68, 196, 198, 203–04, 218–19, 223–24, 227–31, 233n22; anti-Black 5, 7, 9, 11, 21, 55, 89, 103n5, 117; anti-racism 72, 100, 103n6, 178; everyday 5, 74, 84n2, 216; hegemonic 231; institutionalized 160, 172n11, 225, 229; internalized 45n4; structural 97, 104n8, 124, 223; systemic 91, 94, 102, 226
Rankovic, Bita 123–24, 128n11
rap 159, 205, 210n44, 230, 233n28
Repinecz, Martin 55, 61, 136, 148n2
Reyes Magos 48n30
Roaring Twenties 22
Rothberg, Michael 135

Salami, Minna 10, 115–17, 120, 122–23, 126, 127n6, 133
Sampedro Vizcaya, Benita 52, 63
Sánchez Arteaga, Juanma 24–25, 47n19, 49
Scaramella, Evelyn 40
Schomburg, Arthur A. 1, 2, 3; Schomburg Center for Research in Black Culture 16n1
Sección femenina 165
Second Republic 8, 62, 64
Selasi, Taiye 14, 195, 197, 199, 204
self-representation 4, 5, 169, 196, 200, 206
Sevilla Negra 7
Shankara, Thomas 159
slave trade 8, 52, 54, 57, 61, 102n1, 162, 177, 184, 210n41
slavery 1, 4, 7, 24, 47n24, 52–56, 58, 60–62, 66, 76, 101, 162, 166, 169, 171n6, 173, 176–78, 182, 184, 190, 191n9
social media 74, 80–81, 83, 85n7, 90, 175–76, 184, 186, 190, 219, 222
Sontag, Susan 202–03
Sorority 168, 184
steatopygia 179
stereotypes 2, 8, 15, 16, 136, 139, 140–41, 175–78, 182, 190, 196, 200–01, 205, 209n26, 219

Stewart, Maria W. 175, 178
Stoler, Anna Laura 137, 147
storytelling 9–10, 89, 98, 100–02
Strachey, James 22
Sundiata, Ibrahim K. 66n2, 163

testimony 1, 4, 17n14, 218, 221
The Other Generation of 1927 21
Thior, Lamine 48n30, 221, 225, 230
Third Space 135
Toasijé, Antumi 4, 9, 89, 91, 102n13, 112–13, 123, 131, 158–59, 162, 171n5, 172n16
Torres Soler, Antoinette 88, 93–94, 97–98, 165, 172n18; *Viviendo en modo Afroféminas* 89, 103n3
transatlantic trade 226
transcultural 12, 176, 185, 187, 189–90
transhistorical 8, 12, 54, 185, 189–90
transition 13, 92, 134–36, 140, 165, 209n28
translocality 10, 14
transnationality 14, 53, 56–57, 60; transnational 4, 8, 10, 51–58, 62, 64–65, 72, 185–87, 189, 190, 208n12
transracial 13, 134, 142, 143, 147
trauma 45n4, 190, 52, 228
Truth, Sojourner 94, 178, 183
Tsai, Chenta 197, 207n7
Tu cara me suena 48n30
Turner, Nat 56
Tutu, Desmond 183

Ubuntu philosophy 183
Ugarte, Michael, *emiexile* 4, 12, 55
Uncle Tom 156, 171n6
United Minds 112
urban peripheries 4, 14, 15, 195–96, 206

Valdés, Pedro (Peter Wald, Peter Wal) 42, 44, 49
Vázquez Montalbán, Manuel 58
vecinos 196, 200–01, 205, 207n1, 208n17
Vega-Durán, Raquel 4, 148n2
Velázquez, Diego 1, 7
Verkami, platform 116, 127
Villahermosa Borao, Pedro Antonio (Sileno) 21

Vinicius, Jr. 59, 60, 67n14, 224
virtual global community 14, 186
visibility 11, 89–90, 98, 126, 158, 161, 165–66, 170n2, 187–91, 196, 200, 202, 217
Vox 203–04, 209n34; *see also* Abascal

Wa Thiongo, Ngũgĩ 177
Walker, Madame C.J. 176, 191n6
Wanáfrica 167
white supremacy 8, 10, 54, 62, 92, 102, 104n8, 112, 126, 168, 230
whiteness 8, 10, 13, 26, 44, 54, 62, 73, 76–78, 81, 91, 112–13, 115–16, 120, 127, 135–36, 138–40, 142, 144, 147, 223
whitening 4, 13, 91, 102, 134, 136, 138, 140
whitewashed 6, 29
Wilderson III, Frank B. 52, 59, 62

Womanism 13, 154, 158, 164–65, 167, 173n22
Woodard, Vincent 32
Woods Peiró, Eva 24, 33
World War I 33
World War II 136, 188
Worth, Thomas 40

xenophobic killing 172n11; propaganda 202–03

Zamora Loboch, Francisco 8, 55–56, 60, 70, 74. *El Caimán de Kaduna* 57, 60–62; *Conspiración en el green* 8, 52, 57–59; *Cómo ser negro y no morir en Aravaca* 8, 52–53, 65; *La república fantástica de Annobón* 8, 52, 57, 62, 64
Zannou, Santiago 111, 154; *La puerta de no retorno* 12
Zingha, Ann 182, 192n17

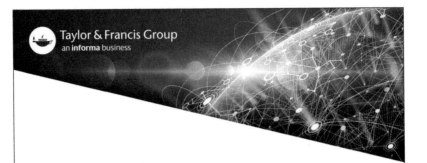